Tolley's Guide
Tax Simplificat

by

Alec Ure
Consultant
Alec Ure & Associates

Members of the LexisNexis Group worldwide

United Kingdom	LexisNexis Butterworths, a Division of Reed Elsevier (UK) Ltd, Halsbury House, 35 Chancery Lane, London, WC2A 1EL, and RSH, 1–3 Baxter's Place, Leith Walk Edinburgh EH1 3AF
Argentina	LexisNexis Argentina, BUENOS AIRES
Australia	LexisNexis Butterworths, CHATSWOOD, New South Wales
Austria	LexisNexis Verlag ARD Orac GmbH & Co KG, VIENNA
Canada	LexisNexis Butterworths, MARKHAM, Ontario
Chile	LexisNexis Chile Ltda, SANTIAGO DE CHILE
Czech Republic	Nakladatelství Orac sro, PRAGUE
France	LexisNexis SA, PARIS
Germany	LexisNexis Deutschland GmbH, FRANKFURT and MUNSTER
Hong Kong	LexisNexis Butterworths, HONG KONG
Hungary	HVG-Orac, BUDAPEST
India	LexisNexis Butterworths, NEW DELHI
Italy	Giuffrè Editore, MILAN
Malaysia	Malayan Law Journal Sdn Bhd, KUALA LUMPUR
New Zealand	LexisNexis Butterworths, WELLINGTON
Poland	Wydawnictwo Prawnicze LexisNexis, WARSAW
Singapore	LexisNexis Butterworths, SINGAPORE
South Africa	LexisNexis Butterworths, DURBAN
Switzerland	Stämpfli Verlag AG, BERNE
USA	LexisNexis, DAYTON, Ohio

© Reed Elsevier (UK) Ltd 2006
Published by LexisNexis Butterworths

A CIP Catalogue record for this book is available from the British Library.

ISBN 10: 0 7545 2947 9
ISBN 13: 9780754529477

Typeset by Letterpart Ltd, Reigate, Surrey
Printed and bound in Great Britain by William Clowes Limited, Beccles, Suffolk
Visit LexisNexis Butterworths at www.lexisnexis.co.uk

Foreword

Alec Ure has kindly asked me to write the foreword to this, his latest book. With technical experience gained over many years inside the former Pension Schemes Office and outside as a senior consultant in the pensions industry, and as an author on the complicated subject of pensions in the UK, there is no one better qualified in my view to write on this subject.

The taxation of pension schemes in the UK will change completely and for the better in its much simplified form from 6 April 2006, so the publication of this book is indeed timely. But it is more than that. This book is not just aimed at the pensions industry, which has been gearing up over the last three years for the new pensions regime in order to grapple with the new legislation, but it will also be an invaluable tool for the accountancy and legal professions, financial advisers and officers of companies who are responsible for pension schemes. They will all need in future from time to time to dip into its contents in order to answer queries or give advice.

The playing field on which UK pension schemes will operate is being hugely simplified, but much of the legislation is nonetheless far from straightforward and Alec, in his usual forthright style in this book, cuts through the verbiage to present the detail in a succinct manner that everybody can understand. There is clear and detailed coverage of all aspects of the new pensions regime, with numerous practical examples and even some generic advice on pensions planning. Even the restrictions announced in the pre-Budget Report of 5 December 2005 and the tax treatment of unapproved schemes after 5 April 2006 are included.

This is not just a reference book for the bookshelf, but one that will I suspect be used every day for some time to come until we are all familiar with the new regime. I am sure this book will be warmly received by many and I know that, despite my many years in pensions and consultancy, I will be thumbing through it as a source of reference on a regular basis. I recommend it to all pensions practitioners and to all those who advise pension schemes, their sponsors and their members.

John Hayward
Consultant
January 2006

Preface

I am pleased to present the first edition of *Tolley's Guide to Pensions Tax Simplification*. There is no doubt that the changes which came into effect on 6 April 2006 ('A-Day') are going to have a significant effect on tax-efficient pension provision in the United Kingdom for a long time to come. Everyone who is involved in pension schemes, whether they be professional persons including actuaries, lawyers, accountants and fund managers, or consultants, members and their trustees, will need to be fully aware of the impact of the major tax changes that have taken place this year.

The genesis of the new simplified tax system was the government's establishment of an Inland Revenue (now HMRC) and HM Treasury Simplification Team with a remit to effectively replace the existing complex rules which applied before A-Day with a single tax regime. For new pension provision after A-Day the report by the Simplification Team largely achieved its objective, and its recommendations gave rise to the *Finance Act 2004*. The report was dated 10 December 2003 and it was the most defining moment in tax planning for pensions for over 50 years.

The great majority of individuals who currently enjoy private pension schemes in the UK will potentially be better off, and employers and their schemes will need to consider how best to take advantage of the new opportunities which have become available. Members are not limited in their permitted levels of benefit provision to the extent that they have been in the past, and the removal of virtually all of the pre-existing benefit limits should be of benefit to most. The government's hope is that this will encourage greater pension provision in the future. There is no doubt that defined benefit schemes will continue to be more closely regulated than money purchase schemes, largely due to the new DWP practice and other social security legislation. Nevertheless, there are important tax considerations to be addressed under the new rules. The new annual allowance limits and lifetime allowance limits are generous, and the freeing up of investment activity and the opening up of pension schemes to all are significant tax-planning incentives.

There has also been a major relaxation in the transfer rules, including transfers to overseas schemes. The changes in the European Union are largely reflected in the new tax laws and practice, and give membership and tax relief rights to migrants. There is true simplicity in the air, although there are inevitably certain rules to be followed which are accompanied by potential penalties and charges for non-compliance.

As with all major changes in legislation, consideration must be given to protecting the interests of those persons who have rights and expectations under prevailing rules. The accrued rights of such persons are largely protected by way of transitional protection provisions under the new regime. This is an area in which some legislation is still developing, but the main principles have been laid down and legislation has been put into place both by primary statutes and by regulations and orders. When one considers the complexity of the old tax rules it is inevitable that transitional protection in itself is highly complex in nature. Therefore, it will come as no surprise to the reader that **Chapter 6** of this book, which deals which such protection, contains substantial detail. As is the case with some of the more detailed aspects of the new tax regime, specific working examples have been inserted in **Chapter 6** in order to assist the reader in understanding how the rules work in practice.

Throughout the book the new single tax regime has been explained in a comprehensive fashion, and guidance has been given on the practical application of the new rules and the tax implications of relevant actions and decision-making. I hope the book will assist readers in recognising and understanding the new opportunities which these changes make available.

Finally, given the certainty that people will be working longer in the future, the new flexibility to drawdown pensions and lump sums while remaining in employment should indeed be a major attraction to many individuals.

My very warmest thanks for the support which I have received from my ex-colleagues in the public and private sector. Also, to my current associates and, of course, John Hayward, who wrote the foreword to this book and **Chapter 7**. I would also like to acknowledge that essential source of reference, the *Registered Pension Schemes Manual*, and the sterling IT and secretarial support provided by Cyberbis, my long-suffering associate.

Alec Ure
Consultant, Alec Ure & Associates
1 March 2006

Contents

Contents

List of abbreviations

ASP	=	Alternatively secured pension
AVC(s)	=	Additional voluntary contribution(s)
AVR	=	Actuarial valuation report
CGT	=	Capital Gains Tax
DTA	=	Double taxation agreement
DWP	=	Department for Work and Pensions
ECJ	=	The European Courts of Justice
EFRBS	=	Employer-financed retirement benefits scheme
ESC	=	Extra Statutory Concession by HMRC
EU	=	European Union (formerly European Community)
FA	=	Finance Act
FICO	=	Financial Intermediaries Claims Office, now based in Bootle in its role as part of IR SPSS
FSA	=	Financial Services Authority – the single regulator from 28 October 1997
FSAVC	=	Free-standing additional voluntary contributions
FSMA 2000	=	Financial Services And Markets Act 2000, previously the Financial Services Act 1986
FURBS	=	Funded Unapproved Retirement Benefit Scheme
GAD	=	Government Actuary's Department
GMP	=	Guaranteed Minimum Pension as described in the Pension Schemes Act 1993
GN	=	Actuarial Guidance Note
HMRC	=	Her Majesty's Revenue & Customs (previously known as the Inland Revenue)
ICTA 1988	=	Income and Corporation Taxes Act 1988
IHTA 1984	=	Inheritance Tax Act 1984
IORPs	=	Institutions for Occupational Retirement Provision
IR SPSS	=	Inland Revenue Savings, Pensions, Share Schemes; including the former PSO (Pension Schemes Office)
ITEPA 2003	=	Income Tax (Earnings and Pensions) Act 2003
LLP	=	Limited liability partnership
MFR	=	Minimum funding requirement
NAPF	=	National Association of Pension Funds

OEIC	=	Open-ended investment company
PA 1995	=	Pensions Act 1995
PN(s)	=	Practice Notes issued by IR SPSS The most version was PN(2001) but PN(1979) was still extant pre A–Day for some schemes.
PPF	=	Pension Protection Fund
PSA 1993	=	Pensions Schemes Act 1993
RAC	=	Retirement annuity contract
RAS	=	Relief at source
RPI	=	The Government's Index of Retail Prices
RPSM	=	Registered Pension Schemes Manual, published by HMRC on its website
SI	=	Statutory Instrument
SIPPs	=	Self-invested personal pension schemes
SSASs	=	Small self-administered schemes
S2P	=	The State Second Pension, which replaced SERPS as a second-tier state pension from 6 April 2002 for the future
TCGA 1992	=	Taxation of Chargeable Gains Act 1992
TMA 1970	=	Taxes Management Act 1970
UK	=	United Kingdom
UURBS	=	Unapproved Unfunded Retirement Benefit Scheme
VAT	=	Value Added Tax
VATA 1994	=	Value Added Tax Act 1994

Glossary

The *Registered Pension Schemes Manual* contains the following glossary of terms. Some additional definitions have been added for ease of interpretation below the Manual's list.

Active member	An individual who has benefits currently accruing for or in respect of that person under one or more arrangements in the pension scheme.
Active membership period	The active membership period

- begins with the date on which benefits first began to accrue to or in respect of the individual under the *registered pension scheme* or, if later, 6 April 2006, and
- ends immediately before the benefit crystallisation event or, if earlier, the date on which benefits cease to accrue under the scheme.

Alternatively secured pension	Payment of income withdrawals direct from a money purchase arrangement to the member of the arrangement (who is aged 75 or over) and that meet the conditions laid down in *paragraphs 12* and *13* of *Schedule 28* to the *Finance Act 2004*.
Alternatively secured pension fund	Funds (whether sums or assets) held under a money purchase arrangement that have been 'designated' to provide a scheme member (who is aged 75 or over) with an alternatively secured pension, as identified in *paragraph 11* of *Schedule 28* to the *Finance Act 2004*. Once sums or assets have been 'designated' as part of an 'alternatively secured pension fund' any capital growth or income generated from such sums or assets are equally treated as being part of the 'alternatively secured pension fund'. Similarly, where assets are purchased at a later date from such funds, or 'sums' generated by the sale of assets held in such funds, those replacement assets or sums also fall as part of the 'alternatively secured pension fund' (as do any future growth or income generated by those assets or sums).

Annual allowance

The annual allowance is such amount, not being less than the amount for the immediately preceding tax year, as is specified by order made by the Treasury.

Annual allowance charge

A charge at the rate of 40% in respect of the amount by which the *total pension input amount* for a tax year in the case of an individual who is a member of one or more *registered pension schemes* exceeds the amount of the *annual allowance* for the tax year.

Annuity protection lump sum death benefit

A lump sum benefit paid following the death of a scheme member who died before age 75 and was in receipt of a either a *lifetime annuity* or *scheme pension* under a *money purchase arrangement*, and which does not exceed the limits imposed through *paragraph 16 Schedule 29 Finance Act 2004.*

Appropriate date

The earlier of

- a nominated date falling in the tax year immediately after that in which the last pension input period ended, and
- the anniversary of the date on which the period ended.

Arm's length bargain

A normal commercial transaction between two or more persons.

Arrangement

A contractual or trust-based arrangement made by or on behalf of a member of a pension scheme under that scheme. A member may have more than one arrangement under a scheme.

Authorised employer payment

Authorised employer payments are

- public service scheme payments,
- authorised surplus payments,
- compensation payments,
- authorised employer loans,
- scheme administration employer payments, and
- any other payment prescribed by Regulations.

Authorised member payment

Authorised member payments are

- pensions that comply with the pension rules in *section 165 Finance Act (FA) 2004* or the pension death benefit rules in *section 167 FA 2004,*

- lump sum payments to comply with the lump sum rule in *section 166 FA 2004* or lump sum death benefit rule in *section 168 FA 2004,*

- recognised transfers that comply with *section 169 FA 2004,*

- scheme administration member payments,

- payments in accordance with a pension share in order or provision, and

- any other payment prescribed by Regulations.

Authorised open-ended investment company
A body incorporated by virtue of regulations under *section 262* of the *Financial Services and Markets Act 2000* in respect of which an authorisation order is in force under any provision made in such regulations by virtue of *subsection (2)(l)* of that section.

Bank
One of the following

- a person within *section 840A(1)(b)* of the *Income and Corporation Taxes Act 1988 (ICTA)* (persons other than building societies etc. permitted to accept deposits), or

- a body corporate which is a subsidiary or holding company of a person falling within *section 840A(1)(b)* of *ICTA* or is a subsidiary of the holding company of such a person (subsidiary and holding company having the meanings in *section 736* of the *Companies* [sic]

Basis amount
The basis amount is the base calculation for determining the maximum level of *unsecured pension* or *alternatively secured pension* (and the *dependant* equivalents) payable from a *money purchase arrangement*. The basis amount represents the annual amount of lifetime annuity (or 'relevant annuity') income the *unsecured pension fund* or *alternatively secured funds* (etc) could purchase at the initial calculation and review points.

BCE
Benefit crystallisation event

Benefit crystallisation event
Is a defined event or occurrence that triggers a test of the benefits 'crystallising' at that point against the individual's available *lifetime allowance.* There are eight such events.

Block transfer

The transfer in a single transaction of all the sums and assets held for the purposes of (or representing accrued rights under) the *arrangements* under the *pension scheme* from which the transfer is made, which relate to the member in question and at least one other member of that pension scheme, where before the transfer either the member was not a member of the pension scheme to which the transfer is made, or he has been a member of that pension scheme for no longer than such period as is prescribed by regulations (not laid yet). (Note Paragraph 4C of the Technical Note which appeared on the Inland Revenue website on 16 February 2005 explained that a transfer will still be a block transfer if at the time of the transfer, the member had not been a member of the receiving scheme for more than one year).

Building society

This means a building society within the *Building Societies Act 1986*.

Cash balance arrangement

A type of *money purchase arrangement*. An *arrangement* is a cash balance arrangement where the *member* will be provided with *money purchase benefits*, but where the amount that will be available to provide those benefits is not calculated purely by reference to payments made under the arrangement by or on behalf of the member. This means that in a cash balance arrangement, the capital amount available to provide benefits (the member's 'pot') will not derive wholly from any actual contributions (or credits or transfers) made year on year.

For example, the scheme may promise that on retirement, a specified amount will be made available to provide the member with benefits for each year of pensionable service. The specified amount might be an absolute amount, e.g. £5,000 per year of service, or might be a percentage of the member's salary for each relevant year of service. Optionally, the scheme might also guarantee a rate of investment return on the specified amount. The member knows what will go into the promised pot each year (regardless of any contributions actually made) and so can ascertain the amount that accrues in that promised pot each year. It is possible that in a cash balance arrangement the promised pot builds up entirely notionally year by year, being funded only at the end. So, during the build-up phase, the amount in any actual fund held in respect of the member (whether more or less than the amount in the promised pot) is irrelevant. And when benefits ultimately become due, the amount in the promised pot is funded and it is that amount that is used to provide benefits.

In a cash balance arrangement, some of the investment and mortality risk is transferred to the scheme (or, if there is one, the employer); the fact that all or part of the pot is guaranteed or promised means that the promised amount must be made available to provide benefits irrespective of the level of actual funds held.

Chargeable amount

The amount that crystallises for *lifetime allowance* at a *benefit crystallisation event* that is not covered by an individual's available lifetime allowance at that time, plus any 'scheme-funded tax payment'. The chargeable amount is the amount on which the *lifetime allowance charge* arises.

Charity lump sum death benefit

A lump sum benefit paid from a *money purchase arrangement* to a charity (as defined in *section 506 Income and Corporation Taxes Act 1988*) following the death of a scheme member (or a *dependant* of such a member) who is aged 75 or over which meets the conditions of *paragraph 18, Schedule 29* to the *Finance Act 2004*. Such a lump sum cannot be paid where there is still a surviving *dependant* of the member.

Deferred member	An individual who has rights under a pension scheme and who is neither an active member, nor a pensioner member.
Defined benefits	Benefits provided under a *pension scheme* that are calculated by reference to earnings or service of the member or any other factor other than by reference to an amount available under the scheme for the provision of benefits to or in respect of that member (so which are not *money purchase* benefits).
Defined benefits arrangement	An *arrangement* other than a *money purchase arrangement* that provides only *defined benefits*. 'Defined benefits' are calculated by reference to the earnings or the service of the *member*, or by any other means except by reference to an available amount for the provision of benefits to or in respect of the member, (thus making the definitions of money purchase and defined benefit arrangements mutually exclusive). A defined benefit arrangement is, typically, a 'final salary' scheme, that is, one where the level of benefits paid is calculated by reference to the member's final salary and length of service with the employer. Contributions are often made to such an arrangement, and so there may be a pension fund or pot, but the benefits that may be paid are not calculated by reference to that fund or pot.
Defined benefits lump sum death benefit	A lump sum benefit paid from a *defined benefits arrangement* following the death of the scheme member before the age of 75 (and within two years of that date of death), and as defined in *paragraph 13, Schedule 29* to the *Finance Act 2004*.
Dependant	A person who was married to the member at the date of the member's death is a dependant of the member.

A child of the member is a dependant of the member if the child has

- not reached the age of 23, or

- has reached age 23 and, in the opinion of the *scheme administrator*, was at the date of the member's death dependent on the member because of physical or mental impairment.

A person who was not married to the member at the date of the member's death and is not a child of the member is a dependant of the member if, in the opinion of the *scheme administrator*, at the date of the member's death the person was financially dependant.

Dependants' alternatively secured pension

Payment of income withdrawals direct from a *money purchase arrangement* to a *dependant* of a scheme member who is aged 75 or over, that meets the conditions laid down in *paragraphs 26 and 27 of Schedule 28* to the *Finance Act 2004*.

Dependants' alternatively secured pension fund

Funds (whether sums or assets) held under a *money purchase arrangement* that have been 'designated' after the death of a scheme member to provide a particular *dependant* of that member (who is aged 75 or over) with a *dependants' alternatively secured pension*, as identified in *paragraph 25 of Schedule 28* to the *Finance Act 2004*. Once sums or assets have been 'designated' as part of a 'dependants' alternatively secured pension fund', any capital growth or income generated from such sums or assets are equally treated as being part of the 'dependants' alternatively secured pension fund'. Similarly, where assets are purchased at a later date from such funds, or 'sums' generated by the sale of assets held in such funds, those replacement assets or sums also fall as part of the 'dependants' alternatively secured pension fund' (as do any future growth or income generated by those assets or sums).

Dependants' annuity

An annuity paid by an *insurance company* to a *dependant* of a scheme member following the death of that member that meets the conditions laid down in *paragraph 17, Schedule 28* to the *Finance Act 2004*.

Dependants' scheme pension

A pension paid to a *dependant* of a member of a *registered pension scheme* following the death of that member, the entitlement to which is an absolute entitlement under the scheme and that meets the conditions laid down in *paragraph 16, Schedule 28* to the *Finance Act 2004*.

Dependants' short–term annuity

An annuity contract purchased from a *dependants' unsecured pension fund* held under a *money purchase arrangement* that provides that *dependant* with an income for a term of no more than five years (not reaching to or beyond their 75th birthday), and which meets the conditions imposed through *paragraph 20, Schedule 28* to the *Finance Act 2004*. This definition covers replacement assets purchased after the initial 'designation' from such funds, or any capital growth from or income generated by assets held in the fund (whether held at the time of 'designation' or where replacement assets).

Dependants' unsecured pension

Payments of income withdrawals direct from *a money purchase arrangement*, or income paid from a *dependants' short-term annuity* contract purchased from such an *arrangement*, to a *dependant* (who is aged under 75) of the scheme member who established the *arrangement* and that meets the conditions laid down in *paragraph 20* and *23* to *24* of *Schedule 28* to the *Finance Act 2004*.

Dependants' unsecured pension fund

Funds (whether sums or assets) held under a money purchase arrangement that have been 'designated' after the death of a scheme member to provide a particular dependant of that member (who is aged under 75) with a dependants' unsecured pension, as identified in *paragraph 22* of *Schedule 28* to the *Finance Act 2004*. Once sums or assets have been 'designated' as part of a 'dependants' unsecured pension fund', any capital growth or income generated from such sums or assets are equally treated as being part of the 'dependants' unsecured pension fund'. Similarly, where assets are purchased at a later date from such funds, or 'sums' generated by the sale of assets held in such funds, those replacement assets or sums also fall as part of the 'dependants' unsecured pension fund' (as do any future growth or income generated by those assets or sums).

Employer-financed retirement benefits scheme	This means a scheme for the provision of benefits consisting of or including relevant benefits to or in respect of employees or former employees of an employer. However, neither a registered pension scheme nor a *section 615(3)* scheme is an employer-financed retirement benefits scheme.

EU member state

Any of the following:

Austria, Belgium, Czech Republic, Cyprus, Denmark, Estonia, Finland, France, Germany, Greece, Hungary, Ireland, Italy, Latvia, Lithuania, Luxembourg, Malta, Netherlands, Poland, Portugal, Slovakia, Slovenia, Spain, Sweden, United Kingdom.

European Economic Area (EEA) investment portfolio manager

This means an institution which:

- is an EEA firm of the kind mentioned in *paragraph 5(a)*, *(b)* or *(c)* of *Schedule 3* to the *Financial Services and Markets Act 2000* (certain credit and financial institutions), or

- qualifies for authorisation under *paragraph 12(1)* or *12(2)* of that *Schedule*, or

- has permission under the *Financial Services and Markets Act 2000* to manage portfolios of investments.

Ex-spouse

An individual to whom *pension credit* rights have been or are to be allocated following a *pension sharing order*, agreement or equivalent provision.

Former approved superannuation fund

Any fund which immediately before 6 April 2006 was an approved superannuation fund for the purposes of *section 608 Income and Corporation Taxes Act 1970*, that:

- has not been approved for the purposes of *Chapter 1 Part 14 Income and Corporation Taxes Act 1988* since 5 April 1980, and

- has not received any contributions since 5 April 1980.

FSAVCS

A *registered pension scheme* that was originally approved by the Board before 6 April 2006 as a retirement benefits scheme by virtue of *section 591(2)(h) Income and Corporation Taxes Act 1988*, established by a pension provider or the trustees of an approved centralised scheme for non-associated employers to which the employer does not contribute and which provides benefits additional to those provided by a scheme to which the employer does contribute.

GAD

The Government Actuary's Department.

GAD tables

The Government Actuary's Department Tables on a single life basis.

GMPs

Stands for guaranteed minimum pensions and has the same meaning as in the *Pension Schemes Act 1993*.

Hybrid arrangement

An *arrangement* where only one type of benefit will ultimately be provided, but the type of benefit that will be provided is not known in advance because it will depend on certain given circumstances at the point benefits are drawn.

For example, a hybrid arrangement may provide the member with *other money purchase benefits* based on a pot derived from the contributions that have accrued over time, but subject to a *defined benefit* minimum or underpin. If the benefits provided by the money purchase pot at the point benefits are drawn fall below a certain defined level, for example 1/60ths of final remuneration for every year worked, that higher defined benefit will be provided. So the benefits will be either other money purchase benefits, or defined benefits.

When benefits are drawn, if the benefits actually provided are other money purchase or *cash balance benefits* then the arrangement will become a *money purchase arrangement*. And if the benefits provided are defined benefits then the arrangement will become a *defined benefits arrangement*.

Insurance company Either:

- a person who has permission under *Part 4* of the *Financial Services and Markets Act 2000* to effect or carry out contracts of long-term insurance, or

- a European Economic Area (EEA) firm of the kind mentioned in *paragraph 5(d)* of *Schedule 3* to the *Financial Services and Markets Act 2000* (certain direct insurance undertakings) which has permission under *paragraph 15* of that *Schedule* (as a result of qualifying

Lifetime allowance The lifetime allowance is an overall ceiling on the amount of tax privileged pension savings that any one individual can draw. The exact figure will be whatever the 'standard lifetime allowance' for the tax year concerned is or a multiple of this figure where certain circumstances apply.

Lifetime allowance charge A charge to income tax that arises on any chargeable amount generated at a 'benefit crystallisation event'. The rate of charge is either 25% or 55%, depending on whether the 'event' giving rise to the charge was the payment of a lump sum or not. The scheme administrator and member are jointly liable to the charge, except where the chargeable amount arises following the death of the member. Here, the recipient of the payment giving rise to the charge is solely liable.

Lifetime allowance excess lump sum A lump sum benefit paid to a member of a *registered pension scheme* (who is aged under 75) because they have used up their available *lifetime allowance*, and which meets the conditions of *paragraph 11* of *Schedule 29* to the *Finance Act 2004*.

Lifetime annuity An annuity contract purchased under a *money purchase arrangement* from an *insurance company* of the member's choosing that provides the member with an income for life, and which meets the conditions imposed through *paragraph 3, Schedule 28* to the *Finance Act 2004*.

Market value	The market value of an asset held for the purposes of a pension scheme is to be determined in accordance with *section 272* of the *Taxation of Chargeable Gains Act 1992* and *section 278(2)* to *(4)* *Finance Act 2004* (where dealing with a right or interest in respect of money lent directly or indirectly to certain parties).
Member	An individual who is either an active member, a pensioner member, a deferred member or a pension credit member of a pension scheme.
Money purchase benefits	Benefits provided under a pension scheme, the rate or amount of which is calculated by reference to an amount available for the provision of benefits to or in respect of the member (whether the amount so available is calculated by reference to payments made under the scheme by the member or any other person or employer on behalf of the member, or any other factor).
Money purchase arrangement	An arrangement is a money purchase arrangement if, at that time, all the benefits that may be provided to or in respect of the member under the arrangement are cash balance or other money purchase benefits.
Nominated date	This means:

- in the case of a *money purchase arrangement* other than a *cash balance arrangement*, such date as the individual or *scheme administrator* nominates, or

- in the case of any other arrangement, such date as the *scheme administrator* nominates.

Occupational pension scheme	A pension scheme established by an employer or employers and having (or capable of having) effect so as to provide benefits to or in respect of any or all of the employees of that employer or employers, or any other employer (whether or not it also has effect so as to provide benefits to or in respect of other persons, or is capable of having such effect).
Other money purchase arrangement	A *money purchase arrangement* other than a *cash balance arrangement*.

An *arrangement* is an other money purchase arrangement where the member will be provided with *money purchase benefits*, and the amount that will be available to provide those benefits is calculated purely by reference to payments made under the arrangement by or on behalf of the *member*. This means that in an other money purchase arrangement the capital amount available to provide benefits (the member's 'pot') will derive wholly from actual contributions (or credits or transfers) made year on year.

The *scheme administrator* or trustees may use the payments made under the arrangement to make investments of any kind on behalf of the member (for example, cash on deposit, shares, other investment assets, a life assurance policy on the member's death). As long as the pot ultimately used to provide benefits is wholly derived from the original payments, the arrangement is an other money purchase arrangement. The subsequent investment income and any capital gains are derived from payments made under the arrangement, and they themselves become part of the member's pot.

It is a feature of other money purchase arrangements that the member bears all the investment and mortality risk. The scheme simply pays out whatever benefits the amount in the pot, including the proceeds of all the investments that have been made using the payments into the scheme, will support.

Overseas arrangement active membership period

This is the period beginning with the date on which the benefits first began to accrue to, or in respect of, the individual under the recognised overseas scheme arrangement or, if later, 6 April 2006 and ending immediately before the recognised overseas scheme transfer. If benefits ceased to accrue under the recognised overseas scheme arrangement before the transfer then it is this date on which the overseas arrangement active membership period is treated as ending.

Overseas pension scheme	A *pension scheme* is an overseas pension scheme if it is not a *registered pension scheme* but it is established in a country or territory outside the UK and satisfies the requirements in the [Pension Schemes (Categories of Country and Requirements for Overseas Pension Schemes and Recognised Overseas Pension Schemes) Regulations 2006 (SI 2006/206)].
Pension commencement lump sum	A lump sum benefit paid to a member of a registered pension scheme (who is aged under 75) in connection with an arising entitlement to a pension benefit (other than a short-term annuity contract), and which meets the conditions detailed in *paragraphs 1* to *3* of *Schedule 29* to the *Finance Act 2004*.
Pension credit	Pension sharing on divorce was introduced in 1999 under the pension sharing provisions in the *Welfare Reform and Pensions Act 1999* (*WRPA*) and *Schedule 10* of the *Finance Act 1999*. This introduced the 'pension credit' and 'pension debit'. The 'pension debit' is the amount by which the original member's pension is reduced and the 'pension credit' the corresponding amount by which the ex-spouse's pension rights are increased. *Section 29 WRPA* determines the value of the pension credit to be transferred to the ex-spouse.
Pension credit member	An individual who has rights in a pension scheme which are directly or indirectly attributable to pension credits.
Pension debit	Pension sharing on divorce was introduced in 1999 under the pension sharing provisions in the *Welfare Reform and Pensions Act 1999* (*WRPA*) and *Schedule 10* of the *Finance Act 1999*. This introduced the 'pension credit' and 'pension debit'. The 'pension debit' is the amount by which the original member's pension is reduced and the 'pension credit' the corresponding amount by which the ex-spouse's pension rights are increased.
Pension input amount	The amounts as arrived in accordance with *sections 230* to *237* of *Finance Act 2004*.

Pension input period	This means:

- the period beginning with the *relevant commencement date* and ending with the earlier of a *nominated date* and the anniversary of the *relevant commencement date*, and

- each subsequent period beginning immediately after the end of a period which is a *pension input period* (under either this or the earlier paragraph) and ending with the *appropriate date*.

Pension protection lump sum death benefit

A lump sum benefit paid following the death of a scheme member of a *registered pension scheme*, who died before age 75 and was in receipt of a *scheme pension* under a *defined benefits arrangement* and which does not exceed the limits imposed through *paragraph 14* of *Schedule 29* to the *Finance Act 2004*.

Pension scheme

A pension scheme is a scheme or other arrangements which is comprised in one or more instruments or agreements, having or capable of having effect so as to provide benefits to or in respect of persons on retirement, on death, on having reached a particular age, on the onset of serious ill-health or incapacity or in similar circumstances.

Pension sharing order

An order or provision made following the divorce of two individuals as listed in *section 28(1)* of the *Welfare Reform and Pensions Act 1999* (or the *Welfare Reform and Pensions (Northern Ireland) Order 1999 (SI 1999/3147)*).

Pension year

The period the maximum *unsecured pension* and *alternatively secured pension* limits apply to (and the *dependant* equivalents). In the legislation these are referred to as 'unsecured pension years' and 'alternatively secured pension years'. These periods run in consecutive 12-month periods from the point initial entitlement to such pensions actual arise under a *money purchase arrangement*. These periods are set at the point that initial entitlement arise, and cannot be changed from that point onwards (although the pension year the member or *dependant* dies or reaches age 75 will be deemed to end immediately before such an occurrence – these truncated 12-month periods are treated as a whole 12-month period for limit purposes).

Pensioner member	A member of a pension scheme who is entitled to the payment of benefits from the scheme *and* who is not an active member.
Personal pension scheme	A pension scheme previously approved by the Board of Inland Revenue under *section 631 Income and Corporation Taxes Act 1988*.
Personal representatives	In relation to a person who has died, this means (in the UK) persons responsible for administering the estate of the deceased. In a country or territory outside the UK, it means the persons having functions under its law equivalent to those administering the estate of the deceased.
Prescribed occupation	Any of the following occupations:
	Athlete, Badminton Player, Boxer, Cricketer, Cyclist, Dancer, Diver (Saturation, Deep Sea and Free Swimming), Footballer, Golfer, Ice Hockey Player, Jockey – Flat Racing, Jockey – National Hunt, Member of the Reserve Forces, Model, Motor Cycle Rider (Motocross or Road Racing), Motor Racing Driver, Rugby League player, Rugby Union Player, Skier (Downhill), Snooker or Billiards Player, Speedway Rider, Squash Player, Table Tennis Player, Tennis Player (including Real Tennis), Trapeze Artiste, Wrestler.
Property investment LLP	A Limited Liability Partnership whose business consists wholly or mainly in the making of investments in land and the principal part of whose income is derived from that business.
Protected rights	As defined in *regulation 3* of the *Personal and Occupational Pension Schemes (Protected Rights) Regulations 1996*, but should be read as including safeguarded rights, wherever appropriate.
Public service pension scheme	A pension scheme:

- established by or under any enactment,

- approved by a relevant governmental or Parliamentary person or body, or

- specified as being a public service pension scheme by a Treasury order.

Qualifying overseas pension scheme	An overseas pension scheme is a qualifying overseas pension scheme if it satisfies certain HMRC requirements. The scheme manager must notify HMRC that the scheme is an overseas pension scheme and provide evidence to HMRC where required. The scheme manager must also sign an undertaking to inform HMRC if the scheme ceases to be an overseas pension scheme and comply with any prescribed benefit crystallisation information requirements imposed on the scheme manager by HMRC. The overseas pension scheme must not be excluded by HMRC from being a qualifying overseas pension scheme.
Qualifying recognised overseas pension scheme	A *recognised overseas pension scheme* is a qualifying recognised overseas pension scheme if it satisfies certain HMRC requirements. The scheme manager must notify HMRC that the scheme is a recognised overseas pension scheme and provide evidence to HMRC where required. The scheme manager must also sign an undertaking to inform HMRC if the scheme ceases to be a recognised overseas pension scheme and comply with any prescribed information requirements imposed on the scheme manager by HMRC. The recognised overseas pension scheme must not be excluded by HMRC from being a qualifying recognised overseas pension scheme.
Recognised European Economic Area (EEA) collective investment scheme	This means a collective investment scheme (within the meaning given by *section 235* of the *Financial Services and Markets Act 2000*) which is recognised by virtue of *section 264* of that Act (schemes constituted in other EEA states).
Recognised overseas pension scheme	A recognised overseas pension scheme is an overseas pension scheme which is established in a country or territory listed in the [Pension Schemes (Categories of Country and Requirements for Overseas Pension Schemes and Recognised Overseas Pension Schemes) Regulations 2006 (SI 2006/206)]. An overseas pension scheme may also be a recognised overseas pension scheme if it is of a description prescribed in those regulations, or if it satisfies any requirements in those regulations.

Recognised transfer

A transfer representing a member's accrued rights under *a registered pension scheme* to another *registered pension scheme* (or, in certain circumstances, to an *insurance company*) or a *qualifying recognised overseas pension scheme*.

Refund of excess contributions lump sum

A lump sum benefit paid to a member of a *registered pension scheme* because they have contributed more to the scheme than they are entitled to tax relief on, and which meets the conditions of *paragraph 6, Schedule 29* to the *Finance Act 2004*.

Registered pension scheme

A *pension scheme* is a registered pension scheme at any time when, either through having applied for registration and been registered by the Inland Revenue, or through acquiring registered status by virtue of being an approved pension scheme on 5 April 2006, it is registered under *Chapter 2* of *Part 4* of the *Finance Act 2004*.

Relevant administrator

For a *retirement benefits scheme*, former approved superannuation fund or relevant statutory scheme as defined in *section 611A Income and Corporation Taxes Act 1988 (ICTA)*, or a pension scheme treated by HMRC as a relevant statutory scheme, this is the person(s) who is/are the administrator of the pension scheme under *section 611A of ICTA*.

For a deferred annuity contract where the benefits are provided under one of the types of scheme above, or a retirement annuity, this is the trustee(s) of the pension scheme, or the insurance company which is a party to the contract in which the pension scheme is comprised.

For a Parliamentary pension scheme or fund, this is the trustees of the scheme or fund.

For a *personal pension scheme*, this is the person who is referred to in *section 638(1)* of the Income and *Corporation Taxes Act 1988*.

Relevant commencement date

This means:

(a) in the case of a *cash balance arrangement* or a *defined benefits arrangement* or a *hybrid arrangement*, the only benefits under which may be cash balance benefits or defined benefits, the date on which rights under the arrangement begin to accrue to or in respect of the individual, or

	(b) in the case of a *money purchase arrangement* other than a cash balance arrangement, the first date on which a contribution within *section 233(1)* of *Finance Act 2004* is made, or
	(c) in the case of a *hybrid arrangement* not within paragraph (*a*), whichever is the earlier of the date mentioned in that paragraph and the date mentioned in paragraph (*b*).
Relevant consolidated contribution	A contribution made by way of discharge of any liability incurred by the employer before 6 April 2006 to pay any pension or lump sum to or in respect of the individual.
Relevant overseas individual	An individual who either does not qualify for UK relief on contributions paid to a *registered pension scheme* because they are not a 'relevant UK individual' as defined in *section 178 Finance Act 2004*, or an individual who is not employed by a UK resident employer and only qualifies for UK relief on pension contributions because they were resident in the UK both during 5 years immediately before the tax year under consideration and when they became a member of the *registered pension scheme*.
Relevant UK earnings	This means:

- employment income,
- income which is chargeable under Schedule D and is immediately derived from the carrying on or exercise of a trade, profession or vocation (whether individually or as a partner acting personally in a partnership), and
- income to which *section 529* of *Income and Corporation Taxes Act 1988* (*ICTA*) (patent income of an individual in respect of inventions) applies.

Relevant UK earnings are to be treated as not being chargeable to income tax if, in accordance with arrangements having effect by virtue of *section 788* of *ICTA* (double taxation agreements), they are not taxable in the United Kingdom

Relevant UK individual	An individual is a relevant UK individual for a tax year if:

- the individual has relevant United Kingdom (UK) earnings chargeable to income tax for that year,

- the individual is resident in the UK at some time during that year,

- the individual was resident in the UK both at some time during the five tax years immediately before that year and when the individual became a member of the pension scheme, or

- the individual, or the individual's spouse, has for the tax year general earnings from overseas Crown employment subject to UK tax.

Relievable pension contribution

A contribution paid to a *registered pension scheme* by or on behalf of a member of that scheme, unless one or more of the following exceptions applies. A payment is not a relievable contribution if:

- the member was aged 75 or over when the contribution was made, or

- the contribution is paid by the member's employer, or

- the payment is an age related rebate or a minimum contribution paid by HMRC to a contracted-out pension scheme under *section 42A(3)* or *section 43* of the *Pension Schemes Act 1993* or the corresponding Northern Ireland legislation.

Retirement annuity contract

A retirement annuity contract or trust scheme previously approved by the Board under *Chapter 3* of *Part 14* of *Income and Corporation Taxes Act 1988*.

Retirement benefit scheme

A retirement benefit scheme is any of the following:

- a scheme which was approved under *Chapter 1* of *Part 14* of *Income and Corporation Taxes Act (ICTA) 1988*;

- a relevant statutory scheme (as defined in *s 611A ICTA 1988*);

- a scheme treated as a relevant statutory scheme; or

- an old code scheme approved under *s 208 ICTA 1970* that has not received contributions since 5 April 1980.

RPI	Stands for the Retail Price Index, which is the index of retail prices compiled by the Office for National Statistics. Where that index is not published for a relevant month any substitute index or index figures published by the Office for National Statistics may be used. (See *section 279 Finance Act 2004*.)
Scheme administration member payment	Payments made by a *registered pension scheme* to a member, or in respect of a member, for the purposes of administration or management of the scheme.
Scheme administrator	The person(s) appointed in accordance with the *pension scheme* rules to be responsible for the discharge of the functions conferred or imposed on the scheme administrator of the pension scheme by and under *Part 4* of *Finance Act 2004*. This person must be resident in an *EU member state* or in Norway, Liechtenstein or Iceland (EEA states which are not EU states). The person must have made the declarations to HMRC required by *section 270(3) Finance Act 2004*.

Scheme chargeable payment

Scheme chargeable payments are:

- any unauthorised payment by the pension scheme other than a payment that is exempted by section 241(2) Finance Act 2004 from being a scheme chargeable payment (see list below), and
- a payment that the pension scheme is treated as having made and classed as a scheme chargeable payment by *section 183* or *184 Finance Act 2004* because of unauthorised borrowing.

The following unauthorised payments are not scheme chargeable payments.

1. The payment is treated as having been made by *section 173 Finance Act 2004* and the asset used to provide the benefit is not a wasting asset as defined in *section 44 Taxation of Capital Gains Act 1992*.

2. The payment is a compensation payment as defined by *section 178 Finance Act 2004*.

3. The payment is made to comply with a court order or an order by a person or body with the power to order the making of the payment.

4. The payment is made on the grounds that a court or any such person or body is likely to order (or would be were it asked to do so) the making of the payment.

5. The payment is of a description prescribed by regulations made by HMRC.

Scheme pension
A pension entitlement provided to a member of a *registered pension scheme*, the entitlement to which is an absolute entitlement to a lifetime pension under the scheme that cannot be reduced year on year (except in narrowly defined circumstances) and meets the conditions laid down in *paragraph 2* of *Schedule 28* to *Finance Act 2004*.

Section 9(2B) Rights
Rights derived through *section 9(2B)* of the *Pension Schemes Act 1993*.

Secured pension
Either a *lifetime annuity* or *scheme pension*.

Short service refund lump sum
A lump sum benefit paid to a member of an *occupational pension scheme* because they have stopped accruing benefits under the scheme and have less than two years of pensionable service under the scheme, and which meets the conditions of *paragraph 5, Schedule 29* to the *Finance Act 2004*.

Short-term annuity
An annuity contract purchased from a member's *unsecured pension fund* held under a *money purchase arrangement* that provides that member with an *unsecured pension* income for a term of no more than five years (not reaching to or beyond their 75th birthday), and which meets the conditions imposed through *paragraph 6, Schedule 28* to the *Finance Act 2004*.

Sponsoring employer
In relation to an occupational pension scheme means the employer, or any of the employers, to or in respect of any or all of whose employees the pension scheme has, or is capable of having, effect as to provide benefits.

Standard lifetime allowance
The overall ceiling on the amount of tax-privileged savings that any one individual can accumulate over the course of their lifetime without taking any special factors into account that may increase or decrease the tax-privileged ceiling. For the year 2006–07, this amount is £1,500,000. The standard lifetime allowance for following tax years will be specified by an annual order made by the Treasury, and will never be less than the amount for the immediately preceding tax year.

Total pension input amount	The aggregation of the *pension input amounts* in respect of each arrangement relating to an individual under a registered pension scheme of which the individual is a member.
Transfer lump sum death benefit	A lump sum benefit paid from a *money purchase arrangement* for the benefit of another member of the same pension scheme following the death of a scheme member (or a *dependant* of such a member), who is aged 75 or over, which meets the conditions of *paragraph 19, Schedule 29* to the *Finance Act 2004*. Such a lump sum cannot be paid where there is still a surviving *dependant* of the member.
Trivial commutation lump sum	A lump sum benefit paid to a member of a *registered pension scheme* (who is aged under 75) because their pension entitlements (under both that scheme and other such schemes) are deemed trivial, and which meets the conditions of *paragraphs 7* to *9* of *Schedule 29* to the *Finance Act 2004*.
Trivial commutation lump sum death benefit	A lump sum benefit paid to a *dependant* of a scheme member of a *registered pension scheme* (who died before age 75) because that *dependant's* entitlement under that scheme is deemed trivial, and which meets the conditions of *paragraph 20* of *Schedule 29* to the *Finance Act 2004*.
Unauthorised employer payment	An unauthorised employer payment is: ● a payment by a registered pension scheme that is an occupational pension scheme to or in respect of a sponsoring employer which is not an authorised employer payment, or ● anything which is specifically prescribed as being an unauthorised payment in respect of the member.
Unauthorised member payment	An unauthorised member payment is: ● a payment by a registered pension scheme to or in respect of a member of that pension scheme that is not an authorised member payment, or ● anything which is specifically prescribed as being an unauthorised payment in respect of the member.

Unauthorised payments charge	Tax due under *section 208 Finance Act 2004* on either *unauthorised member payments* or *unauthorised employer payments*. The rate of tax is 40% of the unauthorised payment.
Unauthorised payments surcharge	Tax due under *section 209 Finance Act* that is paid in addition to the *unauthorised payments charge*. The tax will be due where total unauthorised payments go over a set limit in a set period of time of no more than 12 months. The rate of tax is 15% of the unauthorised payments.
Uncrystallised funds	Funds held in respect of the member under a *money purchase arrangement* that have not as yet been used to provide that member with a benefit under the scheme (so have not crystallised), as defined in *paragraph 8(3) of Schedule 28* to the *Finance Act 2004*. These are defined differently for *cash balance arrangements*. Here it is what funds there would be if the member decided to draw benefits on a particular date not the funds actually held in the cash balance arrangement at that time.
Uncrystallised funds lump sum death benefit	A lump sum benefit paid from a *money purchase arrangement* following the death of the scheme member before the age of 75 (and within two years of that date of death) from any *uncrystallised funds* the member held in that *arrangement* at the point of death, and as defined in *paragraph 15, Schedule 29* to the *Finance Act 2004*.
Unit trust scheme manager	This means one of the following:

    (*a*)   a person who has permission under *Part 4* of the *Financial Services and Markets Act 2000* to manage unit trust schemes authorised under *section 243* of that Act, or

    (*b*)   a firm which has permission under *paragraph 4* of *Schedule 4* to the *Financial Services and Markets Act 2000* (as a result of qualifying for authorisation under paragraph of that *Schedule*; Treaty firms) to manage unit trust schemes authorised under that section.

Unsecured pension	Payment of income withdrawals direct from a *money purchase arrangement,* or income paid from a *short-term annuity* contract purchased from such an *arrangement,* to the member of the *arrangement* (who is aged under 75) and that meet the conditions laid down in *paragraph 6* and *8* to *10* of *Schedule 28* to the *Finance Act 2004.*
Unsecured pension fund	Funds (whether sums or assets) held under *a money purchase arrangement* that have been 'designated' to provide a scheme member (who is aged under 75) with an *unsecured pension,* as identified in *paragraph 8* of *Schedule 28* to the *Finance Act 2004.* Once sums or assets have been 'designated' as part of an 'unsecured pension fund' any capital growth or income generated from such sums or assets are equally treated as being part of the 'unsecured pension fund'. Similarly where assets are purchased at a later date from such funds, or 'sums' generated by the sale of assets held in such funds, those replacement assets or sums also fall as part of the 'unsecured pension fund' (as do any future growth or income generated by those assets or sums).
Unsecured pension fund lump sum death benefit	A lump sum benefit paid from a *money purchase arrangement* following the death of the scheme member before the age of 75 from any *unsecured pension fund* the member held in that *arrangement* at the point of death, and as defined in *paragraph 17, Schedule 29* to the *Finance Act 2004.*
Valuation assumptions	The valuation assumptions in relation to a person, benefits and a date are assumptions:

(*a*) if the person has not reached such age (if any) as must have been reached to avoid any reduction in the benefits on account of age, that the person reached that age on the date, and

(*b*) that the person's right to receive the benefits had not been occasioned by physical or mental impairment.

Winding-up lump sum	A lump sum benefit paid to a member of an occupational pension scheme because the scheme is being wound-up and their accrued benefits under the scheme are deemed 'trivial', and which meets the conditions of *paragraph 10, Schedule 29* to the *Finance Act 2004.*

Winding-up lump sum death benefit	A lump sum benefit paid to a *dependant* of a member of an *occupational pension scheme* because the scheme is being wound-up and their accrued benefits under the scheme are deemed 'trivial' , and which meets the conditions of *paragraph 21, Schedule 29* to the *Finance Act 2004*.

Additional definitions

Other useful definitions, which are used in this book, are given below.

Continued rights	The status which is conferred on an individual for pension purposes by virtue of the *Occupational Pension Schemes (Transitional Provisions) Regulations 1988 (SI 1988/1436)* (as amended) or the *Retirement Benefits Schemes (Continuation of Rights of Members of Approved Schemes) Regulations 1990 (SI 1990/2101)* (as amended) in order that such a person may benefit from the pre-*Finance (No 2) Act 1987* or the pre-*Finance Act 1989* (as appropriate) tax regime.
Earnings cap	The pre A-Day permitted maximum on earnings as previously described in *s 590C(2)* and, for personal pension schemes, *s 640A*, of the *Income and Corporation Taxes Act 1988*.
Her Majesty's Revenue & Customs	Previously known as the Inland Revenue.
Pension Protection Fund	The fund which was set up by the *Pensions Act 2004* to compensate members of certain schemes which are in deficit.
Pensioneer trustee	An individual or person who has had such status conferred on him or her by IR SPSS for the purpose of conducting business in connection with small self-administered schemes.

Pensions Ombudsman   Deals with disputes about pension entitlement and maladministration, and extended powers under the *Pensions Act 2004*.

Pensions Regulator   The body appointed to regulate pension schemes by the *Pensions Act 2004*.

Pensions Update   The successor to PSO Memoranda and Updates, and available in electronic form on the HMRC website.

Chapter 1
The new tax regime, and post A-Day considerations

Introduction

Background to simplification 1.1

There have been many reviews of the complex tax regimes that have applied to exempt approved pension schemes in the UK over the past 15 years. Several of these have involved consultative processes with pension industry representatives. Three particular areas of complexity were identified at an early stage. These were:

- the different benefit regimes (that is, mainly, pre-1987 continued rights, pre-1989 continued rights and post-1 June 1989 rights);

- the complexities arising from retained benefit checks; and

- the rules that applied to tax-free lump sums on commutation of pension.

HM Revenue and Customs (HMRC) had never considered a 'trade off' between the removal of the exemption for tax-free lump sums from occupational pension schemes in exchange for the acceptance of a general simplification of HMRC limits to be acceptable or workable. Nevertheless, the drive toward tax simplification became relentless, and it was accompanied by wider reviews of pension provision and regulation. It was also recognised that transitional provisions might be required to achieve true simplification, and this has been carried through under the new tax regime.

The main events which led to the current changes, some involving matters which are covered under both the *Finance Act 2004* and the *Pensions Act 2004*, were:

- an NAPF report in 1998, together with DSS (now DWP) proposals;

- the Myners Report, dated 16 May 2000, which reviewed institutional investment and called for the removal of the barriers to investment growth, recommended greater familiarity with investment issues, independent custody and shareholder activism;

- the Sandler Review, dated 9 July 2001, which supported a simplification of products and advice and significant reductions in costs and overheads;

- the Pickering Report, dated 11 July 2002, which supported pensions simplification and easier methods for employers, commercial providers and citizens to accumulate retirement benefits; and

- the Inland Revenue Pensions Simplification Team/HM Treasury Report *Simplifying the Taxation of Pensions: The Government's Proposals*, dated 10 December 2003. The document offered a single set of new tax rules after 'A-Day'. A-Day was designated as 6 April 2006 in the Budget 2004. The simplification report replaced the first report, which was published on 17 December 2002, and had been opened to consultation.

The run up to A-Day presented trustees, scheme administrators, employers and employees with some important decision-making. Any actions taken by such persons in this period will need to be considered when applying the new regime. To assist such persons during this period, guidance was provided by various authorities and was published on their applicable websites. The main sources were:

- HMRC Pensions Tax Simplification Newsletters.

- HMRC workshops – a series of 'Preparing for A-Day' workshops (website: http://www.hmrc.gov.uk).

- The 'Better Regulation Stakeholder Group' and the 'Trustee panel' of the DWP (website: http://www.dwp.gov.uk).

- The Pensions Ombudsman – provision to members of more detailed information about their rights and benefits (website: http://www.pensionsombudsman.gov.uk).

- The Pensions Regulator – briefing for trustees, five-point action plan for use by employers and trustees (website: http://www.thepensionsregulator.gov.uk).

The Finance Act 2004 and the Finance Act 2005   1.2

The new pensions tax simplification regime came into effect on 6 April 2006 ('A–Day'). The main legislation, which contains the rules that apply as from A-Day, is contained in the *Finance Act 2004*, as revised by the *Finance Act 2005* and regulations and orders (see **2.4** below for the relevant references). The regulations and orders are listed in **APPENDIX 1** at the end of this book.

True tax simplification – but transitional rules apply

The changes are significant and they bring in real simplification in the field of taxation of pensions schemes and the rules which will apply to them for the future. The changes have been accompanied by protection of many of the existing rights of members, some for a transitional period only. These transitional provisions are important, but the rules are complex. They are described in **CHAPTER 6** in some detail, together with worked examples to help the reader understand the objectives of the legislation in this area.

Summary of the new tax rules   **1.3**

The discretionary powers of HMRC have been effectively removed from A-Day. Future reliance is placed on compliance by schemes, trustees, advisers, administrators, fund managers (and other persons connected with pension provision) with the relevant primary legislation, regulations, orders, published practice and prescribed conditions which apply to regulated arrangements. As penalties and sanctions may be incurred in the event of non-compliance, it is important that everyone who is involved in pension provision is fully aware of their duties under the new regime.

The Finance Act 2004 classifies tax-advantaged pension schemes as *registered schemes*. The main features of the new regime, which are dealt with in detail in this book, are:

- as from A-Day approved schemes are treated as 'registered' unless they opt out of the new tax regime (see **8.5** below);

- new schemes must apply for registration if it is required (see **8.5** below);

- there is a new tax-free pension fund *lifetime allowance* for pension funds (see **3.8** and **3.9** below);

- there is a new annual tax-allowable *annual allowance* (input limit) into pension funds (see **3.2–3.4** below);

- there are tax charges on amounts in excess of the above allowances (see **3.5** and **3.11** below);

- lump sums are normally limited to 25% of the lifetime allowance (see **2.19** below);

- there is no limit on pension provision (see **2.16** below);

- the self-assessment procedure is used to manage the allowances (see **8.16** and **8.17** below);

- there are new reporting procedures (see **CHAPTER 8**);

- there are higher levels of tax-relievable contributions (see **4.9** and **4.12** below);

- investment income and capital gains are largely exempt from tax (see **5.4** below);

- there is a 35% tax charge on some death benefit lump sums (see **2.33** and **7.8** below);

- membership may be open to virtually all, including non-UK residents (see **4.2** below);

- funded non-registered (including previously unapproved) schemes are classified as *employer-financed retirement benefits schemes* (EFRBS), and they now enjoy no tax privileges (see **CHAPTER 10** below);

- pensions and lump sums which are payable out of benefits accrued under EFRBS will not be tax free (see **CHAPTER 10** below);

- transitional protections for benefit entitlements which were in place as at A-Day are available under either *primary protection* or *enhanced protection,* at the member's choice (see **CHAPTER 6** below);

- there are provisions to drawdown pensions while in service, and different methods of drawing and/or securing benefits are available (eg secured, alternatively secured and unsecured pensions), encouraging flexible retirement provision (see **2.50–2.60** below);

- most investment restrictions (such as residential property) are removed (but there are special rules for small schemes) – see **CHAPTER 5** below;

- transfers may be made freely between registered schemes (see **9.2** below);

- there are significant relaxations for overseas members (eg migrants who come to the UK will be given tax relief on their contributions in place of corresponding relief provisions) – see **9.16–9.18** below;

- subject to certain conditions, UK registered schemes will be able to transfer a member's fund to an overseas scheme if the overseas scheme is regulated as a pension fund in its country of establishment and undertakes to comply with information reporting requirements (see **9.2** below).

Additionally:

- registered schemes may be either occupational (employer-sponsored), personal or stakeholder pension schemes;

- registered schemes are entitled to tax relief on both employers' and employees' contributions;

- pension benefits are taxed as earned income under the *Income Tax (Earnings and Pensions) Act 2003*, while lump sums (subject to an upper limit) are tax free;

- pension benefits from employer-sponsored occupational schemes can be provided on either a defined benefit, a defined contribution or a hybrid basis;

- registered personal pension schemes operate on a defined contribution basis and stakeholder pension schemes also operate in this way;

- multiple-employer schemes are permitted, whether or not the employers are connected, and members may be concurrent members of any number of schemes.

Administration   1.4

The new pensions tax regime has presented an opportunity to bring in sweeping changes to scheme administration for the future of pension schemes. This has proven to be a significant challenge to most consultants and scheme providers in view of the nature of the changes, which have moved tax-efficient pension provision away from a benefit limits regime to a funding limits regime, and removed most of the existing benefits-testing structures which were previously in place.

However, scheme administration has always been problematic in view of the amount of work that had to be undertaken in order to meet the stringent requirements of the pre A-Day tax regimes. The design of systems which could cope with the complexity of the old rules was not only costly and time-consuming, but often meant dealing with nearly insurmountable problems. There are new systems under development to deal with the new simplified regime, and some are already on the market. The first decision for trustees and employers has been whether to find an appropriate external provider from the pension consultancy market, or to rely on the use of in-house administration systems. The appropriate choice is largely dependent on the size of the scheme and the complexity of its structure.

On the positive side, the ongoing administrative problems will be a short transitional stage for many providers, trustees and managers. The long-term effect of the legislation is intended to simplify scheme administration and reduce the high pension costs which are often incurred in scheme management. Familiarity with the new regime through use should ensure that the new systems will adapt into more streamlined products in the future, and the discipline of collecting information for record-keeping is largely front-ended. The self-assessment system will carry forward the required information under the new procedures and it will be automatically updated on each *benefit crystallisation event* (see **3.15** below).

In future, trustees must become increasingly involved in administrative procedures, and it is likely that professional trustees will become more common on pension scheme trustee boards.

Systems   1.5

A number of independent financial advisers and third party administrators have been developing and investing in software planning systems to assist them in scheme administration under the new regime. These systems take into account the member's need for fund values, benefit calculations and the storage of personal information relating to employment and benefits. This information is required in order to ensure that the new self-assessment and reporting requirements are being met.

Many schemes are using an in-house paper system, adapted for the new tax regime, while more sophisticated or cost-efficient systems are being developed for the market. Scheme advisers have been busy assisting trustees and managers in drawing up timetables and project plans. These have been necessary in order to ensure seamless ongoing administration for existing schemes as from A-Day.

In order that the new administrative procedures and forms may operate effectively, it is imperative that full member and scheme information is obtained and efficient record-keeping is in place. Dedicated software systems and calculators can assist with the tax-efficient planning of remuneration policy and investment decisions and the collation of member information.

Investment tracking   1.6

Trustees and administrators will need to ensure that fund values are tracked against the lifetime allowance, and they will need to obtain appropriate investment advice as a means of identifying potential charges on future excess funds. If a member considers at a future date that he or she has suffered loss by being caught by the lifetime allowance charge (see **3.11** below), that person may endeavour to seek redress against passive trustees, administrators and fund managers.

Training   1.7

No matter how good a new administrative system may be, it will of course only be fully effective if the persons who operate it have been fully trained in its use. It is therefore important that trustees ensure that the scheme administrators, including themselves, are familiar with the new procedures at an early date. This will call for internal training, unless of course an external provider of the administrative system is able to offer such a service. It is clear that trustees and administrators will need to consult with their professional advisers concerning any major changes to administrative procedures.

Scheme considerations   1.8

Balanced consideration must be given to any changes which could be made to schemes in future, and much of this will depend on the nature of the workforce who are in membership of the pension schemes, and the employer's ability to sustain existing levels of pension provision. Taking advantage of increased flexibility in benefit provision should not incur disproportionate cost by bringing in expensive and unwieldy administrative systems, and careful forethought is needed.

An important consideration which will impact on scheme benefits, particularly the amount of available tax-free lump sums, is the actuarial factors which are written into, or used by, the scheme. The scheme actuary must be consulted on this matter, if this has not already been done, and the trustees and employer should give due consideration to his or her findings.

Trustees will also need to be aware of the following official statements:

- The government published a discussion paper on inheritance tax on 21 July 2005. Following the publication of that paper, HMRC announced in August 2005 that it will close a loophole that would have enabled individuals to put assets such as property into their pensions as a way of avoiding inheritance tax. Details of how inheritance tax would be charged, and whether it would be in addition to the 35% tax charge on death that will be levied on income drawdown pensions, are awaited.

- HMRC stated in August 2005 that: 'It will not condone attempts to avoid new rules that limit pension savings to a maximum of 1.5 million pounds'. The concern was that the pension entitlement of some members of company schemes were being artificially inflated by altering the terms of the scheme so that those persons appeared to be entitled to a far larger pension than they actually were, even though there are no funds to support the benefit. It was conjectured that this action was taken in an attempt to apply for special protection and effectively avoid tax on future pension savings. HMRC stated that this is unacceptable tax avoidance and will be dealt with appropriately. Accordingly, any applications for enhanced or primary protection must be carefully scrutinised before they are put to HMRC.

- The government stated in August 2005 that it had concern that investment in residential property in self-invested personal pension schemes (SIPPs) could result in individuals losing out on their pension benefits. This is contrary to the purpose of encouraging pension saving by the granting of tax reliefs, and HMRC has stated that such investments are only 'a realistic proposition for those with the largest pension pots'.

- A Technical Note was issued by the government on 5 December 2005 in which it expressed concern about the potential use of certain schemes for tax-avoidance purposes. The government's main target was SIPPs, which it felt may take advantage of the relaxation in the investment rules in order to buy second homes. The note stated that SIPPs (which it describes as 'self-directed' schemes) 'will be prohibited from obtaining tax advantages when investing in residential property and certain other assets such as fine wines' from A-Day. It also stated that, from A-Day, there will be changes to the disclosure of tax avoidance scheme regime. Further measures to tackle inheritance tax avoidance schemes and the exploitation of offshore companies and trusts have effect from 5 December 2005. For more detail see **5.18** below.

Documentation

Earnings cap   1.9

The earnings cap was of major significance to benefit provision for high earners under pre A-Day rules. If the cap has been, or will be, removed from the rules of existing schemes, the effect on member's benefits must be carefully considered. A defined benefits arrangement could incur significant additional pension costs if the cap is removed, although this could be offset by the savings in cost to the employer of all, or part of, any existing unapproved pension provision which is discontinued.

Any amendments of scheme rules which have an effective date of A-Day or later should not be submitted to HMRC SPSS. However, any changes which had effect before that date should have been submitted under existing procedures (Pensions Update 156).

General review, and seeking legal advice   1.10

Paragraph **2.61** below describes the extension of the time limit for updating scheme documentation to reflect the new tax regime. Despite this relaxation, there are many good reasons to review current wording before the ultimate deadline, apart from the removal of the earnings cap and most benefit limits which are described above. The impact of the overriding nature of the legislation can have an unexpected effect on existing schemes, and employers and trustees should seek legal advice on this matter.

Review of employee benefit provision   1.11

Many employers have already considered whether to restructure their existing employee pay and benefit provisions. The trustees and scheme advisers must be fully aware of any changes which have been made, or are about to be made, which will affect future pension provision for members. Scheme and member documents will need to be updated to reflect the latest position. A list of some of the considerations which are likely to have been taken into account is given below:

- raising pensionable pay for high net-worth members before A-Day;

- considering whether there should be a limit on the maximum level of benefits post A-Day, including a retention of the earnings cap;

- deciding whether the new limited price indexation cap of 2.5% pa for future service should be adopted for appropriate schemes;

- deciding whether to restructure death-in-service benefits or replace them with lump sum benefits post A-Day;

- considering a cessation of pension accrual provision for any members post A-Day;

- considering a replacement for any existing top-up schemes;

- deciding how to deal with flexible retirement post A-Day;

- reviewing any unfunded promises, and designing new ones;

- considering cash as an alternative to pension for high earners;

- considering offering flexible pay packages;

- considering offering share options;

- considering possible offshore trust provision.

If any of the above have been undertaken, the trustees and legal advisers will require sight of the supporting documents.

The provision of cash allowances is already proving to be popular, and there is a significant interest in providing new unfunded benefit promises. Employers will have to have taken into account any existing agreements with workers and trades unions, and the need to comply with any established consultative procedures which are in place.

The effect of enhanced protection or primary protection   1.12

The decision of whether to register for enhanced protection or for primary protection (see **CHAPTER 6**) is a critical one. In the case of a high net-worth member with a pension fund entitlement of £1.5m or greater, it is difficult to see how additional contributions after A-Day could be of benefit if primary protection is chosen. The member's future accrual in the scheme will be subject to the lifetime allowance charge, and there will also be charges on the occasion of a benefit crystallisation event on the member's own allowance as at A-Day to the extent that it exceeds the proportionate increase in the standard lifetime allowance.

There can be no doubt that sound financial and tax advice will be required. At present, for high net-worth members, it seems that enhanced protection will be more beneficial than primary protection, if the member has ceased contributions from A-Day.

Registration for enhanced protection or primary protection   1.13

A decision on whether to register for enhanced protection or primary protection did not have to be made before A-Day (see **6.10**), but contributions had to cease at A-Day if the option to elect for enhanced protection was to continue. It is important to remember that it is not possible to seek enhanced protection once primary protection has been chosen, or where benefit accrual has continued after A-Day.

Member considerations

General   1.14

The new tax simplification rules are potentially of benefit to the majority of members of UK approved pension schemes. From A-Day, members have much greater flexibility in choosing the times at which their benefits may be taken, if their scheme rules permit. Most of the pre A-Day benefit limits have been removed, meaning that higher benefits can be provided, and there is scope for more efficient tax planning on benefit withdrawal. However, high earners will still need to consider alternative provision if the lifetime allowance is exceeded. Such high earners may seek unfunded promises, cash, share options, offshore trusts etc.

The following headings consider the range of possible member choices.

Additional contributions   1.15

There is scope for most members to pay higher contributions into their schemes. The tax advantages of a registered scheme are considerable, and the government's hope is that this will encourage more people to save for their retirement. The ability to drawdown benefits while still in employment is a further inducement to save for pension provision through registered schemes.

A review of existing additional voluntary contributions arrangements (AVCs) will be required, and it is likely that the employer and trustees will have already undertaken this task. The government's view is that the new tax rules effectively render AVC provision unnecessary.

Investment considerations 1.16

CHAPTER 5 describes the wide investment opportunities which are available from A-Day, and the special constraints which apply to small schemes with member control ('self-directed' schemes). Members may wish to familiarise themselves with the new opportunities, and should approach the trustees for guidance and assistance if they wish to do so.

It is important for members to bear in mind that the trustees have the ultimate say in investment decisions. They will consider the best interests of the member, the fund liquidity and the suitability of the investments, among other things. For example, there has been a great deal of publicity concerning property in recent years, as property did not suffer badly from the stock market decline. However, property is rarely a sound investment on which to rely for full pension entitlement, and balanced portfolios are not only likely to be in the member's interest but are increasingly becoming a requirement of law (see **5.32** and **5.33** below).

Lump sums 1.17

The introduction of the new unsecured pensions rules from A-Day may be attractive to members who wish to extract their maximum tax-free cash sums, leaving the balance of their entitlements in an unsecured pension. It is important that members seek proper advice when drawing lump sums in this manner, and much will depend on their need to retain a level of pension which will meet their future retirement expectations. Benefit provision under the new regime is described in **CHAPTER 2**, and the transitional protection considerations are explained in **CHAPTER 6**.

Timing of benefit payments 1.18

Members will need to be made aware of the following new rules, which should be considered in relation to other benefits, if they are to be able to make meaningful decisions:

- the introduction of income withdrawal while in service up to 120% of a flat-rate annuity;

- the introduction of alternatively secured income payments, and term-certain annuities;

11

- the incoming minimum early retirement age of 55 to members;

- the impact of the cessation of certification of tax-free cash limits;

- the cessation of the previous surplus requirements;

- children's pensions which come into payment after A-Day must normally cease at age 23;

- if members in drawdown maximised their lifetime allowance at A-Day, tax will be incurred on the amount by which the growth in their fund exceeds the relevant lifetime allowance at the time of annuity purchase (for such persons, it may be beneficial to purchase an annuity in order to avoid the extra charge).

Communications

Involved persons   1.19

The sweeping extent of the pensions tax simplification changes means that effective communication between all the relevant parties is of critical importance. There are already a wide range of people involved in pension schemes apart from the membership itself. These include: the scheme administrators; professional advisers; consultants; service providers; pay-rolling and human resource departments; trustees and employers.

Records   1.20

It is the responsibility of the employers, trustees and scheme administrators to ensure that employees and members are provided with essential information. This means that it is necessary to update records of all the information that trustees and administrators hold in order to ensure that employees and members are properly informed, and to obtain further information. This information must be safely stored, and similar information must be obtained from new members. It is therefore recommended that comprehensive questionnaires are issued to such persons in order to assist in the communication process.

The approach of A-Day gave rise to a large number of external seminars to which employees and members could be sent with regard to the provision, storage and dissemination of information, according to their individual circumstances, and some of these are still available for ongoing education. Additionally, many employers and the trustees of their schemes have formulated in-house briefing meetings concerning the requirements of legislation and the new changes.

The current value of existing pension rights must be retained, together with full details of all other (aggregate) member benefits. Members and scheme advisers will have important decisions to make, and self-assessment forms to complete. Schemes may require assistance with estimating fund values, and there are industry standards available (for example, from the Society of Pension Consultants).

The following is a summary of the main subjects for consideration:

- ensuring ongoing ready access to information on fund values in excess of, or close to, the lifetime allowance;

- identifying the percentage of the lifetime allowance that is taken up by each member's benefit crystallisation event;

- insertion of annual updates on the lifetime allowance in the members' benefits statements;

- regular reviews of investments.

Policyholders   1.21

An area which should not be overlooked concerns a large number of pension policyholders in the UK. It is likely that many of these policyholders will have no central means of communication concerning the A-Day changes. Pension policy providers are responsible for informing their policyholders of these changes, including the opening up of investment opportunities post A-Day.

Member information   1.22

Scheme documentation, including member announcements and booklets, must be up to date and maintained properly in order to reflect ongoing changes. In addition to providing members with details of the changes and the decisions that have been made, members will also need to be given full details of their scheme benefits and any other benefits to which they are entitled.

Normal retirement age   1.23

In addition to reporting any review of the scheme normal retirement age in the light of the relaxations in the timing and amount of pension payments and the alternatives of secured and unsecured pensions, it is also important to take into consideration the impending changes concerning age discrimination.

The *Age Diversity at Work* code of practice requires compliance with the EU Directive on Equal Treatment in Employment and Occupation (2000/78/EC) by the year 2006. The draft Employment Equality (Age) Regulations 2006 are under consultation, and are due to come into force on 1 October 2006. Any required changes to existing employment contracts may well impact on the normal retirement age which is stipulated in an existing pension scheme. The present proposals are for a default retirement age of 65. Employees will be able to request their employers to permit them to work beyond their compulsory retirement ages and employers will be required to consider their employees' requests.

HMRC Registered Pension Schemes Manual   1.24

HMRC has published a pensions manual on its website, entitled the *Registered Pension Schemes Manual* (RPSM). The RPSM gives guidance for trustees, employers and members on the protection of members' rights from tax charges through transitional protection and under the rules of the new tax regime. It is an essential point of reference, and it extends to a large number of volumes. A comprehensive list of the contents of the manual is given in **APPENDIX 2** at the end of this book.

Press and industry coverage   1.25

Not surprisingly, the major changes to the tax legislation, combined with other recent changes in pensions law, have given rise to significant media coverage. The following are examples of informed comment by the pensions media:

- The ongoing cost of maintaining defined benefits schemes in view of their complexity and regulation has been, and remains, a common subject of discussion. A survey in late 2005, by Aon Consulting, revealed that 88% of UK companies were concerned about the financial cost of such schemes, although 32% of finance directors questioned felt that too much time was being spent on scheme management. Much of the complexity arises not from the new tax regime but from the changes brought about by the *Pensions Act 2004* and those which remain under the *Pensions Act 1995*. It is hoped that the concerns about scheme management costs will begin to fall away, as described in **1.4** above.

- The trade magazines and publications which relate to the pensions industry made much of the lack of preparedness of the industry for the post A-Day changes. As recently as the end of 2005 there were concerns that half of the senior employees and executives who are in UK pension schemes would not be ready, and similar findings were made in relation to many trustees, administrators and UK companies. The surveys which led to these conclusions came from highly reputable professional firms and advisory bodies and heralded increased activity in the review of pension provision for high earners.

- A survey in November 2005 by Deloitte's found that most companies had not finalised any post A-Day planning for their high net-worth employees. Of the small number that had done so, 73% said that cash was the most popular alternative, followed by the new EFRBS and unfunded promises. There was also some relatively minor interest in employee benefit trusts and family benefit trusts. It is somewhat surprising that EFRBS featured so highly in view of the removal of tax privileges for future accrual by such non-tax advantaged schemes.

- A later survey by Deloitte's found that arrangements had only been finalised by 12% of companies whose high-earning executives would be adversely affected by the new pensions tax regime. 'Organisations are waiting to learn what their competitors are doing in respect of pension provision before they make a final decision about what changes to offer their own executives,' commented Bill Cohen, partner at Deloitte, 'However, time is running out and companies need to urgently agree their post A-Day policies with executives.'

Conclusion   1.26

Encouragingly, no doubt partly as a result of such coverage, there are positive signs that employers, pensions schemes, trustees, administrators and advisers became more proactive in their relevant fields in preparation for the new regime. The tax simplification changes are far-reaching. There are many new rules to be learned, and this book endeavours to assist scheme advisers, consultants, professionals, trustees, employers and members to understand how the changes work and how they affect them in their respective fields.

Chapter 2
Benefits

Introduction

The new tax regime offers considerable flexibility in the choice of style of benefit provision and the dates at which benefits may be drawn. Pre A-Day approved schemes will already have had established structures of benefits and/or contributions in place, based within the previous regulatory framework for HMRC limits. Such schemes may have revised their existing rules to accommodate the new regime before A-Day. For example, many will have removed the benefit limits rules (although some will have retained the earnings cap), restructured death benefits and introduced flexible payment dates, in addition to assimilating any existing unapproved provision to the extent that it is possible to do so within the new tax exemption limits. Reviews of trustees' discretionary powers have also been undertaken by many schemes (dependent upon individual scheme wording) as the effect of the overriding legislation can be wider than expected.

Schemes which have not revised their documentation will need to consider how the new legislation will affect the operation of their scheme. There may need to be a fundamental change to scheme design if benefits and/or contributions are to change for future accrual.

The main effect of the new regime is that the imposition of limits on benefits, with the exception of lump sums and some minor exceptions, has disappeared with effect from A-Day. In place of the old HMRC benefits regime there are new allowances on the maximum amount which may be paid into a scheme in any one year ('annual allowance') and the maximum amount of fund over a member's lifetime ('lifetime allowance') which can benefit from full tax reliefs. These new allowance limits are described in detail in **CHAPTER 3**.

The following important changes to permitted benefit provision are described in this chapter:

- the removal of the existing tax regimes (except for transitional protections);

- new general benefit rules for pensions, including annuities and income withdrawal, as applied to defined benefit schemes and money purchase schemes;

- new general death benefit rules for defined benefit schemes and money purchase schemes;

- new alternatively secured pension provisions;

- rules for the purchase of a lifetime annuity contract;

- the compulsory offer of an open market option to members of an occupational money purchase pension schemes before they purchase annuities;

- tax-free lump sum limits, which are normally restricted to 25% of the capital value of the pension;

- taxation of pensions payable (normally under PAYE);

- a new early retirement abatement percentage of 2.5% pa, which is applied to the lifetime allowance;

- continuation of ill-health and incapacity pensions;

- continuation of serious ill-health commutation;

- new taxation levels applicable to a refund of member contributions;

- new trivial commutation rules;

- new secured, alternatively secured and unsecured pension provisions.

Legal advice   2.2

It is important that pension schemes seek legal advice in order to determine the effect of the new tax regime on their extant rules, as the new regime does not override existing trust provisions in most circumstances. If the legal advisers have changed since the trust deed and rules were executed, or the scheme has been amended by resolutions or other instruments without the involvement of the current lawyers, it is imperative that the trustees ensure that the current provisions of the scheme are referred to those advisers, together with any supporting documentation.

Removal of existing tax regimes   2.3

The objective of the tax simplification exercise was to remove the existing tax regimes entirely, together with the complex rules which applied to different types of UK pension provision within those regimes (see **1.1**). For the majority of scheme members this has largely been achieved. The continuation of the existing provisions will, in future, only be relevant to pre A-Day protections concerning benefits and assets (see **CHAPTER 6**). These transitional protections will, in time, fall away. There are now real opportunities to simplify pension scheme design significantly, if desired.

Tax reliefs under the new tax regime are dependent on the single concept of 'registered' pension schemes. The benefit limits have largely been replaced by a cap on the tax-free level of input to schemes and the ultimate fund value (see **CHAPTER 3**).

The enabling tax legislation   2.4

The *Finance Act 2004* received royal assent on 22 July 2004 and has subsequently been revised by the *Finance Act 2005*. *Sections 149–284* and *Schedules 28–36* concern pension schemes. The *Finance (No.2) Act 2005* restored some of the provisions of the original Finance Bill, together with adding some new provisions.

General benefit rules   2.5

The *Finance Act 2004*, and draft regulations and subsequent legislative changes, contain detailed explanations of the new tax rules. The new tax-advantaged input and fund limits which are described in **CHAPTER 3** replace the previous benefits and contributions limits.

General benefit rules for pensions   2.6

The *Finance Act 2004* introduced new general benefit rules under which a pension has the meaning of an annuity or income withdrawal. The general benefit rules for pensions are that pensions must:

- commence before age 75;

- not normally commence before age 55 from the year 2010;

- normally be paid for life;

- be paid in at least annual instalments;

- be non-assignable, except where otherwise permitted by HMRC;

- not normally be guaranteed for more than ten years;

- not offer a capital guarantee of more than value protection (pension protection lump sum death benefit) up to age 75;

- normally be taxed as income under the *Income Tax (Earnings and Pensions) Act 2003*, formally PAYE.

General death benefit rules 2.7

The Act also introduced new general death benefit rules. A pension death benefit is deemed to be a pension payable on the death of a member, other than a ten-year guaranteed pension. The general death benefit rules are:

- children's pensions must normally cease at age 23 unless dependency continues by reason of disability (transitional arrangements will protect children's pensions in payment at A-Day, and pensions from arrangements of a person who had retired by A-Day where there was in place a facility to continue pensions in cases of continuing education);

- adult dependants' pensions must normally be paid for life;

- in circumstances where neither of the above situations apply, a person may be deemed by the administrator to be a dependant if the administrator considers that, at the date of the member's death, he or she was:
    - financially dependent on the member;
    - mutually dependent; or
    - dependent because of physical or mental impairment;

- an individual's own right pensions do not normally need to be restricted to the member's pension level, but they must not be value-protected or guaranteed; and

- non-assignment and non-surrender rules apply, except where pensions-sharing is in point.

Pensions 2.8

There are few restrictions on pensions under tax simplification. The rules which do apply are described below.

When may benefits become payable? 2.9

The *Finance Act 2004* draws certain distinctions between defined benefits arrangements and money purchase arrangements:

Defined benefits arrangements

Under pension rule 3 in *s 165* of the *Finance Act 2004*, a defined benefits arrangement must pay a 'scheme pension'. This means that the general benefit rules apply to the payment date (see **2.5** above). A defined benefits arrangement does not enjoy the wider flexibility of alternative benefit provision which is available for money purchase arrangements (see **2.50** below).

Money purchase arrangements

A money purchase arrangement may pay a scheme pension, provided that the member has been offered an open-market option. Alternatively, a scheme or arrangement may:

- secure a lifetime annuity with an insurance company (see **2.56** below) of the member's choice; or

- pay an unsecured pension by way of income withdrawal and/or a short-term annuity up to age 75 maximum; or

- pay an alternatively secured pension from age 75.

The *Registered Pension Schemes Manual* contains an example of decision-making on drawing benefits by a member of a money purchase arrangement.

Compulsory annuity purchase requirement – removal   2.10

An initial requirement of *Sch 28, para 2(1), Finance Act 2004*, was that schemes with fewer than 50 members must secure annuities for members with an insurance company. This requirement was removed by *Sch 10, Finance Act 2005*. HMRC is intending to seek to protect small pensions through funding regulations, changes to the unauthorised payments rules and the Pension Protection Fund.

Deferred annuity contract/section 32 policy   2.11

If an entitlement under a retirement benefit scheme:

- was secured before A-Day through the purchase of a deferred annuity contract (a 'section 32 contract') with an insurance company; and

- benefits had not come into payment under that contract by that date;

the contract automatically became a registered pension scheme on A-Day (see **CHAPTER 8**).

This also applies to such contracts secured under a relevant statutory scheme as defined by *s 611A, Income and Corporation Taxes Act 1988 (ICTA 1988)* (known as a public service pension scheme from A-Day) and certain old code funds approved under the *Income and Corporation Taxes Act 1970* before 6 April 1980.

If benefits had come into payment before A-Day that contract will only become a registered pension scheme if an application to register the contract is made to HMRC, and it meets the conditions for registration.

If a registered pension scheme purchases a deferred annuity contract on or after A-Day, that contract is treated as having become a registered pension scheme at the point of purchase.

Equivalent pension benefits and state scheme premiums   2.12

Equivalent pension benefits and state scheme premiums will be taxed in the same manner as trivial pensions (see **2.47** below).

Lifetime annuity   2.13

A lifetime annuity contract may only be purchased from a money purchase arrangement and on the following occasions:

- before age 75, from either uncrystallised funds or an unsecured pension fund; or

- after age 75, from an alternatively secured pension fund.

The contract must generally:

- be purchased from an insurance company that the member had the opportunity to select;

- be payable for the member's life;

- be paid at least once a year, either in advance or in arrears;

- only allow the amount paid each year to either stay level, increase or go down in circumstances prescribed by HMRC regulations;

- not allow the payment, either directly or indirectly, of a capital sum triggered by the member's death (apart from annuity protection); and

- not be capable of assignment or surrender (except to give effect to a pension sharing order). If the annuity is guaranteed to be paid for a set period the annuity may be assigned during that period either by the terms of the member's will, or by their personal representatives in the distributing the member's estate, to allow:

–   a testamentary disposition or the rights of those entitled on an intestacy; or

–   an appropriation of the annuity to a legacy or a share or interest in an estate.

The contract must provide benefits that are authorised under the tax rules; any other payment made by the contract will be taxed as an unauthorised payment.

What is an annuity? 2.14

There is no formal definition of an annuity in the *Finance Act 2004*. The *Registered Pension Schemes Manual* states that:

'there is case law (both tax and other) defining what an "annuity" is. The tax rules set out only the form of benefits that may be paid out in respect of funds held in a registered pension scheme and do not determine whether or not a particular contract represents an "annuity". This is for the scheme administrator or insurance company to ascertain, seeking legal opinion where necessary'.

Lifetime pension requirement 2.15

It remains an underlying principle of pensions tax law that a pension in payment should normally continue for the duration of a beneficiary's lifetime. There are seven exceptions to this rule:

(*a*)   where there is a pension sharing order;

(*b*)   bridging pensions which reduce a pension by an amount which is limited to the amount of the state pension;

(*c*)   the member recovers from ill-health;

(*d*)   the reduction in the rate of scheme pension payable is being applied to all scheme pensions being paid under the scheme to or in respect of its members;

(*e*)   the rate of scheme pension payable is being reduced due to forfeiture of entitlement, in a manner consistent with circumstances prescribed by regulations laid by HMRC;

(*f*)   the pension is being reduced in consequence of a court order; and

(*g*)   a pension payable under a public service pension scheme is reduced due to abatement.

Limit on pension level 2.16

The *Finance Act 2004* offers great flexibility in the type of benefits which may be paid and the timing of their payment. There are no limits on the level of pension which may be paid, and consequently there is no need to conduct a limits check. The main procedure to be followed on the payment of a pension concerns the test against the lifetime allowance (see **CHAPTER 3**).

Open market option – requirement for money purchase schemes 2.17

Money purchase occupational schemes must offer an open market option to a member before they purchase an annuity. There will be no minimum level of income under the two types of income withdrawal.

Regulatory sources 2.18

The following sources are relevant to pensions under the *Finance Act 2004*:

- *s 165*: the detailed pension rules.
- *Sch 28 (Pt 1)*: defines ill-health and describes: scheme pension; unsecured pension; alternatively secured pension and the payment of scheme pensions; and drawdown while in service (where the rules of the scheme permit).

Lump sums

Normal maximum level which may be paid 2.19

The normal limit which applies to tax-free lump sums is 25% of the capital value of the pension which comes into payment. A payment must be deemed to be a pension commencement lump sum if it is to be paid tax free.

Payment of lump sum 2.20

Lump sums must come into payment:

- by age 75, or at an earlier crystallisation date; and
- before the member's lifetime allowance has been fully used up.

24

Additionally, a lump sum which is paid on behalf a member who has become entitled to a pension must be paid within three months of that entitlement arising.

The *Registered Pension Schemes (Meaning of Pension Commencement Lump Sum) Regulations 2006 (SI 2006/135)* disapply the three-month deadline (from the date of entitlement) and the age 75 requirement so that a scheme administrator can pay a further pension commencement lump sum to a member in a situation where the administrator has deducted too much lifetime allowance charge, remitted it to HMRC and had the overpayment back from HMRC. There is, however, a three-month deadline, from the date of receipt of the overpayment from the Revenue, for the administrator to pay the lump sum to the member.

There are seven types of authorised lump sums which can be paid, subject to the scheme rules:

- a pension commencement lump sum;

- a serious ill-health lump sum;

- a refund of excess contributions lump sum;

- a trivial commutation lump sum;

- a lifetime allowance excess lump sum;

- a short service refund lump sum; and

- a winding-up lump sum.

As the method of calculating the lump sum can be fairly complex in certain cases, some examples are given below.

Example 1 – the effect of drawing benefits in stages

[**A** = the scheme member]

*In 2006/07, when **A** is 58*

A has pension rights under a scheme of £500,000.

A decides to take a cash lump sum of £50,000 and continue working.

He/she must draw an unsecured pension from £150,000 of the fund (£200,000 less 25% (£50,000) = £150,000), leaving £300,000 (£500,000 less £200,000) in the fund not subject to payment of the unsecured pension.

In 2009/10

The fund has grown to £360,000.

A decides to take a further lump sum of £40,000 and continue working part-time.

He/she must now draw a further unsecured pension from £120,000 of the fund (£160,000 less 25% (£40,000) = £120,000) leaving £200,000 (£360,000 less £160,000) in the fund not subject to payment of the unsecured pensions.

In 2014/15

The fund has grown to £260,000.

A finally retires and decides to take the remainder of his/her benefits from the fund.

A decides to take a further cash lump sum of £65,000 (25% of £260,000) and with the balance of £195,000 plus the funds supporting his/her unsecured pensions purchases a lifetime annuity.

Example 2 – the effect of pension credits on lump sum payments

A formula is given under *para 2, Sch 29, Finance Act 2004*, for the purpose of calculating maximum lump sums where a pensions credit is payable on divorce. Where all the member's rights under the arrangement under which the member becomes entitled to the relevant pension are attributable to a *disqualifying pension credit*, there is no permitted maximum lump sum. A disqualifying pension credit concerns circumstances when, at the time at which the member becomes entitled to the pension credit, the person subject to the corresponding pension debit has an actual (rather than a prospective) right to payment of a pension under the relevant arrangement. Where this is not the case, the permitted maximum lump sum is the lower of:

- the available portion of the member's lump sum allowance; and

- the applicable amount, calculated in accordance with *para 3, Sch 29* (see Example 3 below).

The available portion is:

$$\frac{CSLA - AAC}{4}$$

where:

CSLA is the current standard lifetime allowance; and

AAC is the aggregate of the amounts crystallised by each benefit crystallisation event which has occurred in relation to the member before the member becomes entitled to the lump sum, as adjusted under *sub-paragraph* (7) (and if no such benefit crystallisation event has occurred, is nil). *Sub-paragraph* (7) states that the adjustment of an amount crystallised by a previous benefit crystallisation event referred to in the definition of **AAC** is the multiplication of the amount by:

$$\frac{CSLA}{PSLA}$$

where:

CSLA is the current standard lifetime allowance; and

PSLA is the standard lifetime allowance at the time of the previous benefit crystallisation event.

If the amount given under the available portion is negative, no portion of the member's lump sum allowance is available.

Example 3 – the effect of income withdrawal on lump sum payments

A formula is given under *para 3, Sch 29, Finance Act 2004*, for the purpose of calculating maximum lump sums where income withdrawal is in point. The applicable amount is one-third of the aggregate of:

(*a*)   the amount of the sums designated as available for the payment of unsecured pension on that occasion; and

(*b*)   the market value of the assets so designated.

Any of the sums and assets so designated which represent rights attributable to a disqualifying pension credit are to be disregarded.

Where the member becomes entitled to a lifetime annuity, the applicable amount is one-third of the annuity purchase price, which is the aggregate of:

(*a*)   the amount of such of the sums held for the purposes of the pension scheme; and

(*b*)   the market value of such of the assets held for the purposes of the pension scheme;

as are applied in (or in connection with) the purchase of the lifetime annuity and any related dependants' annuity (as defined in *sub-paragraph (4A)* of *Schedule 29*), but any of the sums and assets applied in (or in connection with) the purchase of the annuity which:

(*a*)   have been designated as available for the payment of unsecured income; or

(*b*)   represent rights which are attributable to a disqualifying pension credit;

are to be disregarded. There is to be deducted from that aggregate:

(*a*)   if the sums or assets applied in (or in connection with) the purchase of the annuity or any related dependants' annuity consist of or include sums or assets representing the whole or part of the member's unsecured pension fund, the aggregate of the amount of those sums and the market value of those assets; and

(*b*)   in any case, so much (if any) of the sums or assets applied in (or in connection with) the purchase of the annuity or any related dependants' annuity as represents rights which are attributable to a disqualifying pension credit.

The formula where the member becomes entitled to a scheme pension determines the applicable amount, which is:

$$\frac{LS + AC}{4}$$

LS is the amount of the lump sum; and

AC is the amount crystallised by reason of the member becoming entitled to the pension (disregarding *para 3* of *Sch 32*, which prevents overlap on certain benefit crystallisation events under *s 216*).

There is to be deducted from the aggregate of the amount of the lump sum and the amount crystallised:

(*a*)   if the scheme pension is funded (in whole or in part) by the application of sums or assets representing the whole or part of the member's unsecured pension fund, the aggregate of the amount of those sums and the market value of those assets; and

(*b*)   in any case, so much (if any) of the aggregate of the lump sum and the amount crystallised as represents rights which are attributable to a disqualifying pension credit.

Permitted maximum and the applicable amount

The terms 'permitted maximum' and the 'applicable amount' in *Sch 29* to the *Finance Act 2004* mean as follows:

(*a*) the permitted maximum is calculated using a divider of 25% of the standard lifetime allowance (see **3.8** below) after deducting any crystallised benefits; and

(*b*) the applicable amount is one-third of the market value of the assets underlying the member's unsecured fund on income withdrawal, or one-third of the annuity purchase price if the lump sum is linked to the lifetime allowance.

A payment will not be treated as a pension commencement lump sum if it exceeds the lower of these amounts.

It is not always the case that 25% of the available lifetime allowance may be commuted. This is particularly the case for defined benefits arrangements which do not use the commutation factor of 20:1 which is described in **3.9** below. The government has stated that any anomalies between defined benefits arrangements and money purchase arrangements will be included in the Finance Bill 2006.

AVCs 2.21

Lump sums under AVC arrangements need not be restricted to the level stated in the arrangement. The maximum amount payable may be based on the scheme level. If no benefits were taken from the arrangement prior to A-Day, a tax-free pension commencement lump sum may be taken when benefits are taken after A-Day, subject to the terms of the arrangement.

Exceptions from the maximum level of lump sum 2.22

There are transitional arrangements which permit the 25% ceiling to be exceeded. These are described in detail in **CHAPTER 6**. In brief, the following concessions apply:

● lump sums which exceed £375,000 at A-Day on registration for primary protection or enhanced protection can be protected;

● uncrystallised rights that are greater than 25% of uncrystallised rights prior to A-Day for members who are not registered for primary protection or enhanced protection, or whose lump sum rights at A-Day are valued at less than £375,000, may be protected.

If protection of accrued rights in excess of 25% is achieved, schemes must recalculate the protected sum if there has been a transfer of rights (for example, from an AVC arrangement) which related to the original calculation.

Excessive lump sums   2.23

Excessive lump sums may be repaid, and will be taxed at 55% under *s 204, Finance Act 2004.*

HMRC clarification   2.24

HMRC has clarified the treatment of protected lump sums recently, and has drawn up draft orders to remedy some of the anomalies. Its notes are described in **CHAPTER 6** and fall under the following headings on the HMRC website:

- Protection of rights to more than 25% lump sum and early pension age where the scheme is wound up.

- Protection of rights to more than 25% lump sum and early pension age where the scheme is restructured in the period between 10 December 2003 and 5 April 2006.

- Protection of large lump sums under enhanced protection.

- Lump sums held over until after A-Day.

- Lump sum death benefit/pre-commencement pensions.

Lump sum certificates   2.25

Any existing lump sum certificates can be ignored once post A-Day valuations for transitional protection have taken place, but where a personal pension scheme received a transfer from an occupational pension scheme the lump sum must not exceed that shown on the certificate.

Lump sums taken before A-Day   2.26

The following restrictions apply on post A-Day payments:

- any lump sum which has been taken prior to A-Day will be taken into consideration for the purpose of the 25% test in respect of any further lump sum taken after A-Day;

- any person who has taken a lump sum prior to A-Day, but deferred his or her pension until after A-Day, will not be permitted to take a further tax-free lump sum in relation to that employment.

Tax calculation – multiple arrangements   2.27

Where a number of small arrangements within a scheme are commuted, the tax calculation should take proper account of any pensions being commuted which are not already in payment.

Regulatory sources   2.28

The following sources are relevant to lump sums under the *Finance Act 2004*:

- *s 166* and *Sch 29, Pt 1*: the normal tax-free level for lump sums;

- *s 166(1)(a)*: no lump sum may be paid other than a pension commencement lump sum;

- *Sch 29* and *Sch 36, Pt 3, paras 24–30*: protection for lump sums which exceed £375,000 at A-Day;

- *Sch 36, paras 31–34*: protection for uncrystallised rights in excess of 25% of uncrystallised rights prior to A-Day for members who are not registered for primary protection or enhanced protection, or whose lump sum rights at A-Day are valued at less than £375,000;

- *Sch 29 (Pt 1)*: descriptions of: pension commencement lump sum; serious ill-health lump sum; short service refund lump sum; refund of excess contributions; trivial commutation; and trivial wind-up lump sum.

Death benefits   2.29

The normal requirement is that death benefits must become payable on the death of a member before age 75. Direct or indirect capital payments after age 75 will not be permitted. Unvested pensions that are not yet in payment may be paid to dependants either in pension form or, if a member has not yet reached age 75, by way of a lump sum. However, death benefit limits are more complex than those which apply to other benefits, and they are described below in some detail.

Main rules   2.30

The main rules which apply are:

(*a*) on the death of a member before age 75 with vested or partly vested funds, the tax treatment will depend on whether or not income has been secured (see **2.50** below);

(b)   where income has been secured, a ten-year guarantee may apply from the date of vesting (no guarantee is permitted if income had not been secured before the end of that period);

(c)   where income is unsecured, dependants' pensions may be taken in a similar form until age 75 at which age they will be subject to the secured pension rules, or undrawn funds can be repaid and lump sum payments will be taxed at 35%;

(d)   dependants' pensions may be taken as unsecured income until age 75, at which time they shall become subject to the secured rules (as an alternative, undrawn funds may be repaid as a lump sum and taxed at 35%) – dependants may defer payment of their pensions until a guarantee period ends, but if value protection is in point, lump sums must be paid before age 75;

(e)   lump sum death benefits may be paid to any person, except for trivial commutation and winding-up lump sum death benefits which have to be paid to dependants (*s 168*, and *Sch 29, Pt 2, Finance Act 2004*);

(f)   the definition of dependant may be extended to cover a person who was married to the member when the pension commenced but was divorced before the member's death;

(g)   lump sum death benefits may be paid tax free to charities on the death of a member or dependant on or after age 75 who has an alternatively secured pension fund and no dependants;

(h)   limits are imposed on the amount of dependants' benefits to prevent avoidance of the lifetime allowance (see **CHAPTER 3**) when it is valued incorporating an element for the dependant's pension and for the calculation of the maximum tax-free cash sum;

(i)   on the death of a member after age 75, the aggregate of dependants' benefits must not exceed the member's pension at the date of death and future pension increases are restricted in order to avoid getting around the initial limit;

(j)   dependants' pensions no longer need to be paid for life, cessation of marriage or dependency, and a spouse may include an ex-spouse to whom the member was married when the benefit came into payment.

Guaranteed lump sums   2.31

There had long been a controversy over whether or not guarantee payments made in lump sum form should be tax free under the previous pensions taxation rules. From A-Day, a five-year guarantee may continue for a money purchase arrangement, but it was not originally intended that the payment should be tax free. For a defined benefits arrangement, the payment is tax free if the sum is within the lifetime allowance by virtue of *Ch 5, ss 216* and *217* and *Sch 32, para 16, Finance Act 2004*. In the light of ongoing controversy, the government has stated that 'clearly, it is only right that transitional protection be extended to people who have a five-year guarantee arrangement already in place to allow a tax-free lump sum to be paid if death occurs within five years of retirement'.

The continuation of a five-year guarantee which may be paid before or after age 75 in respect of persons with pensions in payment prior to A-Day is covered by *Sch 36, Pt 3, para 36, Finance Act 2004*.

There is also a value protection alternative to both of the above, as for personal pensions which are otherwise unchanged by this as the guarantee is not commutable.

Notifying the legal personal representative   2.32

Where lump sums are not paid directly to the legal personal representatives, that person must be notified of the payment and of the amount of the lifetime allowance used up. Where the member's lifetime allowance has been exceeded, a charge of 55% on the excess falls on the beneficiary. There will be no additional charge on any pension payments which are made.

Tax charges and exemptions

Charges   2.33

Pensions payable on death are taxed under PAYE at the recipient's marginal tax rate.

Certain lump sums attract tax charges (see **7.8** below). *Section 206, Finance Act 2004*, imposes a 35% tax charge on the administrator on:

- a pension protection lump sum death benefit (this is described as 'value protection', and it applies to a pension derived from a defined benefit origin);

- an annuity protection lump sum death benefit (meaning value protection on an annuity derived from a money purchase origin); and

- an unsecured pension fund lump sum death benefit (meaning a return of fund under income drawdown by a member or a dependant of a money purchase scheme).

If the rules permit, the tax may be recovered from the payment. There will be special rules to provide for the lump sum to be paid to the deceased member's nominee, subject to the 35% charge on the administrator in order that payments made by insurance companies are covered.

Exemptions

No tax charge arises on a defined benefit lump sum death benefit if:

- the member had not reached age 75 at date of death;
- the benefit is paid in respect of a defined benefits arrangement;
- the benefit is paid before the end of two years from date of death; and
- the benefit is not a pension protection lump sum death benefit, a trivial commutation lump sum death benefit, or a winding-up lump sum death benefit.

No tax charge arises on a money purchase uncrystallised funds lump sum death benefit if it does not exceed the amount of the uncrystallised funds.

Regulatory sources   2.34

The following sources are relevant to death benefits under the *Finance Act 2004*:

- *s 167*: the general death benefit rules;
- *Sch 29 (Pt 2)*: descriptions of: defined benefit lump sum death benefits; money purchase uncrystallised lump sum death benefits; annuity protection lump sum death benefits; unsecured lump sum death benefits; charity lump sum death benefits; transfer lump sum death benefits; trivial commutation lump sum death benefits and trivial wind-up lump sum death benefits.

Divorce   2.35

Where pension-splitting orders were in place as at A-Day, the value of the lifetime allowance may be ignored for the purpose of the lifetime allowance for both parties. For orders which are made after A-Day, pension credits will count against the recipient's lifetime allowance but pension debits will not count against the donor's lifetime allowance, nor towards the annual allowance. Pre A-Day rights of benefits will be protected and an additional lifetime allowance will be made available.

Where a pension credit is received that relates to a pension that is already in payment , and the credit relates to both crystallised and uncrystallised rights, only the crystallised element is taken into account.

Schedule 36, Pt 2, para 18, Finance Act 2004, explains the method of calculation for the lifetime allowance enhancement factor in respect of pre A-Day pension credits.

DWP and contracting-out aspects 2.36

The HMRC *Registered Pension Schemes Manual* (RPSM09100520) draws attention to the fact that:

'Whilst HMRC tax rules will not differentiate specifically between the various types of pension schemes, DWP legislation will still make that distinction. DWP legislation still identifies with and differentiates between both occupational pension schemes and personal pension schemes (which, for DWP purposes, can in some circumstances cover RACs and *FSAVCS*), and imposes different restrictions and requirements on the respective scheme types.'

'This distinction is perhaps most apparent in the context of benefit provision where the respective schemes are used to contract-out of the state second pension (or the State Earnings Related Pension Scheme as it was prior to 6 April 2002). With *occupational pension schemes* providing *defined benefits* there are still certain rules relating to the payment of *GMPs* and *section 9(2B) rights.* And with *money purchase* occupational pension schemes and *personal pension schemes* there are still certain rules governing the payment of *protected rights.*'

It is necessary to extinguish all rights in order to qualify for a short service refund lump sum (see **2.44** below). This is a relevant consideration where there are protected rights (see *Registered Pension Schemes Manual* RPSM09104720).

Early retirement 2.37

Early retirement is still available under the new tax regime. This is subject to the following:

● where benefits are taken before 'normal minimum pension age', an abatement percentage of 2.5% p a is applied to the lifetime allowance;

● the abatement applies to persons who have a protected right to take a pension before age 50 (55 from 2010);

● the member's protected pension age is the age from which he or she had an actual or prospective right to receive payment of benefits as at A-Day (the right may be protected on making a block transfer into a scheme);

- subject to certain exceptions for some statutory schemes, any age lower than 55 must be in place throughout the period commencing on the publication date of the tax simplification paper (10 December 2003);

- the *Finance Act 2004* does not have effect so as to give a member a protected pension age of more than 50 at any time before 6 April 2010.

Regulatory sources   2.38

The following sources are relevant to early payment of pensions under the *Finance Act 2004*:

- *Sch 36, Pt 2, para 19, Finance Act 2004*: describes the annual 2.5% abatement for early retirers before normal minimum pension age;

- *Sch 36, Pt 3, Finance Act 2004*: covers the transitional provisions for rights to a low pension age and the transitional provisions for early retirement pension;

- the *Registered Pension Schemes (Prescribed Schemes and Occupations) Regulations 2005 (SI 2005/3451)*: a list of the prescribed occupations under which benefits may be taken before normal minimum retirement age. The member must have had that right or prospective right on 5 April 2006 and the rules of the scheme must have included such provision on 10 December 2003.

Funeral benefits   2.39

Any existing one-off tax-free payments to cover funeral benefits may continue, provided that the right would have been offered if the member had joined the scheme on 10 December 2003 and if the member retired before A-Day. There is no provision under the new tax rules to permit the payment of funeral benefits for members who are aged 75 or over at date of death.

Ill-health and incapacity   2.40

Ill-health and incapacity pensions are still available under the new tax regime (*Sch 28, paras 1* and *2, Finance Act 2004*). The rules are:

- the member must have left the employment to which the pension relates (either now or at a previous date);

- the administrator must obtain proper medical evidence that the member is incapable of continuing in his or her current occupation.

It is intended that, if the scheme rules permit, a scheme may temporarily suspend a pension if the member recovers sufficiently to return to his or her original job.

Ill-health insurance contracts, which were approved for personal pension schemes before 6 April 2001, or for retirement annuities, will not be regarded as unauthorised payments under the new regime (*Sch 36, para 37, Finance Act 2004*).

Serious ill-health   2.41

Serious ill-health commutation is permitted for registered schemes out of uncrystallised benefits. The administrator must obtain written medical evidence that the member's life expectancy is less than one year and must notify HMRC. There will be no tax liability on the payment if the lifetime allowance is not exceeded.

Late retirement   2.42

The existing facility for pre-1989 members to take pension or lump sum at or after normal retirement age, and to defer the balance, ceases at A-Day. Benefits may only be drawn under the new rules, and lump sums must be paid within three months of the date of payment of the pension.

Payments, and attaining age 75   2.43

The meaning of the term 'payments', as concerns payments from registered schemes to, or in connection with, a member or employer, is contained in *Ch 3, s 161, Finance Act 2004*. The term is used extensively in the Act, in connection with receipt of benefits, transfers and chargeable events in general. The main meaning includes:

- a transfer of assets or money's worth;

- a payment or benefit in respect of scheme assets;

- payments made to persons connected with the member or the sponsoring employer;

- payments made to persons who are not a member or a sponsoring employer;

- any increase in the value of an asset held by, or reduction in the liability of, a person connected with a member or sponsoring employer (or who was connected with a member at the date of the member's death) – this will be treated as an increase or reduction for the benefit of the member or sponsoring employer.

The term 'connected' has the meaning within *s 839, Income and Corporation Taxes Act 1988.*

Once a member reaches the age of 75 a pension may only be provided for the life of that member, either through the purchase or provision of a secured pension or, if benefits are from a money purchase arrangement, as an alternatively secured pension.

Refunds of contributions and compensation payments to employers 2.44

A member with less than two years' qualifying service may take a refund of member contributions. Such refunds will be permitted on leaving pensioned employment, or on winding up the scheme, and will be taxed at 20% on the first £10,800 and at 40% on any excess (*Ch 5, s 205, Finance Act 2004*).

Compensation payments will be permitted to authorised employers in respect of a criminal, fraudulent or negligent act or omission by a scheme member (*Ch 3, s 178, Finance Act 2004*).

Retained benefits 2.45

The retained benefit check for testing HMRC limits is removed if member's earnings (that is, P60 plus P11d) are less than £50,000 in the tax year which preceded A–Day.

Scheme administration member payments 2.46

Payments may be made to or in respect of a member for the purposes of the administration or management of the scheme. They must take the form of authorised member payments, which are general administration costs of running the scheme, whether or not paid to the member. For example:

● the payment of wages, salaries, fees etc to persons involved in the administration of the scheme (the administrator, lawyers, advisers etc); and

● payments relating to the purchase of scheme assets (property purchase costs etc).

Payments made must be reasonable, and paid at a rate commensurate with an arm's-length rate. Details may be laid down in regulations. Any excessive rate will be taxed as an unauthorised member payment.

Trivial commutation   2.47

Although trivial commutation will still be permitted, it will no longer be at the trustees' discretion. The member must show that his or her total pension is not in excess of the new limit described below, and must commute any benefits themselves. The rules are:

- there must be no other trivial commutation paid;

- all rights must be extinguished;

- tax is charged on 75% of the commuted value;

- in cases of low aggregate value pensions, 100% may be commuted between age 60 and 75 in a twelve-month period (*Sch 29, para 7, Finance Act 2004*) – the applicable limit is 1% of the standard lifetime allowance disregarding any non-trivial tax-free lump sums already taken, or to be taken, and the payment will count towards the lifetime allowance.

Dependants' pensions   2.48

It is possible to commute dependants' pensions but these will count towards the lifetime allowance of the member. Where contracted-out rights are involved, it will only be possible to commute on grounds of triviality or subject to legislative requirements. If dependants' benefits are commuted before a member's benefit has vested, they will be tax free. If a lump sum is paid after vesting, tax will be charged at 35%.

Winding up   2.49

Trivial commutation will be permitted on a scheme wind-up where the employer ceases all contributions to registered schemes and scheme benefits do not exceed 1% of the standard lifetime allowance. This option does not affect a member's right to voluntarily commute or a member's lifetime allowance.

Secured and unsecured pensions, income withdrawal

Meaning of secured, alternatively secured and unsecured pensions 2.50

From A-Day, pensions may either be secured, alternatively secured or unsecured. The meaning of these terms is summarised below:

- 'Secured' means a scheme entitlement which is backed by an employer or guaranteed by an annuity purchase.

- 'Alternatively secured' means an entitlement which is limited by income limits and annual reviews from being depleted too rapidly, and generally represents 70% of the amount that could be generated from applying an annuity rate for the member's age and sex up to age 75.

- 'Unsecured' means returns on designated widely invested funds which relate to a member. Payments may be made direct from a money purchase arrangement, or income paid from a short-term annuity contract purchased from such an arrangement, which deliver growth rather than security up to age 75. The maximum annual income withdrawal is 120% of the flat-rate single life annuity which could be bought out of the member's credit with five-yearly reviews. Alternatively, term-certain annuities may be purchased. Unsecured pension fund lump sum death benefits are lump sum benefits paid before age 75 from any unsecured pension fund of the member.

A more in-depth analysis is given below under the relevant subject headings.

HMRC consultation on actuarial tables 2.51

On 7 November 2005 HMRC published a consultation paper which concerns the underlying actuarial assumptions which are proposed by the Government Actuary's Department (GAD) for updated tables to determine the maximum annual income for member's and dependant's unsecured and alternatively secured pensions. The current tables will apply until A-Day. HMRC proposes to publish final tables at the beginning of March 2006.

Secured pension 2.52

A pension may be secured:

- direct from the scheme as a scheme pension; or

- by purchasing a lifetime annuity contract from an insurance company.

A lifetime annuity falls within benefit crystallisation event 4 (see **3.15** below). Failure to meet the statutory requirements will mean that the payment will be treated as an unauthorised member payment, unless the pension is another form of authorised pension payment and taxed as such.

The scheme rules will determine the method of securing benefits.

If a chargeable amount arises at a benefit crystallisation event (see **3.15** below) a secured pension may still be provided. The chargeable amount may be held in the scheme, to provide a scheme pension or to be used to purchase a lifetime annuity contract. The excess pension benefit/rights can be reduced to cover the lifetime allowance charge. This is an alternative to making a payment wholly as a lifetime allowance excess lump sum. The charge will be 25%, but a failure to cover the charge due will have a knock-on effect on the level of the chargeable amount arising (see RPSM11105220).

Open market option and lifetime annuities   2.53

A member must be given the opportunity to choose the insurance company from which a lifetime annuity is to be purchased. In the event that a member fails to select an insurance company, the administrator or trustees may select the insurance company.

Unsecured pension   2.54

An unsecured pension may be provided by a money purchase scheme if the rules permit. Pensions may be paid as combination of income withdrawal payments (see **2.58** below) and short-term annuity contracts, or by a series of short-term annuity contracts running concurrently. The amounts which may be paid apply to the total of all unsecured pension derived from the arrangement in question (whether paid through income withdrawals, short-term annuity contracts or a combination of both). The maximum amount is determined by using GAD tables (RPSM09102330 refers).

Alternatively secured pension (ASP)   2.55

Under the pre A-Day requirements for approved pension schemes, annuities had to be secured no later than age 75. This has been the matter of much debate, but the main requirement remains post A-Day. However, *Sch 28, Finance Act 2004*, provides that alternatively secured pensions are an alternative to a secured lifetime annuity or scheme pension by way of income withdrawal. It works as follows:

- ASP is a responsibility of the scheme, and it is effectively a continuation of income withdrawal which was in place before attaining age 75;

- the scheme must make income payments direct to the member;

- the annual maximum income that may be paid by the scheme shall be 70% of the amount that could be generated from applying an annuity rate determined by the Government Actuary's Department for the member's age and sex at age 75 (a minimum level of £1.00, or such higher amount as may be required by the DWP, shall apply);

- the initial limit calculated at the member's 75th birthday (or a later date, if entitlement arises after that date) applies only for the twelve-month period starting from that date; once set, the twelve-month pension year structure will not change;

- the pension years will continue until the member dies, with that last pension year ending when the member dies, unless a guarantee is being paid;

- benefits must be tested on an annual basis;

- if a scheme winds up, it shall be necessary to purchase an annuity;

- in the event of the death of a member, ASP must be applied firstly to secure dependants' pensions, and in the absence of dependants shall be returned to the scheme with the exception of any lump sum benefits to charities);

- it will be possible to provide value protection for secured pensions, facilitating the return of the balance of initial capital value of the pension (less any instalments paid up to the death of the member, if aged less than 75), subject to a tax charge of 35%. A guaranteed pension for a period not exceeding ten years may be offered as an alternative;

- where an existing pension is to be paid after the member's death for a period not exceeding the earlier of ten years or the last date of payment under the arrangement in force, this will be allowed to continue.

The government has expressed concerns about potential inheritance tax avoidance. Where a person who has opted for an alternatively secured pension dies after age 75 the member's estate will be increased by the undrawn fund, thus attracting tax. On death before age 75, before taking pension, undrawn funds could attract inheritance tax, in particular for older members. The matter is yet to be resolved.

The *Registered Pension Schemes Manual* (RPSM09103010) states:

'Once sums or assets have been "designated" into a member's alternatively secured pension fund any capital growth or income is treated as being part of that alternatively secured pension fund. Similarly, where assets are purchased at a later date from such funds those replacement assets also fall as part of the member's alternatively secured pension fund (as do any future growth or income generated by those assets). Any sums generated by the sale of assets held in those funds also form part of the alternatively secured pension fund. This is because that growth or income and those replacement assets are derived from that alternatively secured pension fund.

Any funds that are subsequently applied to purchase a *lifetime annuity* contract from an *insurance company*, or are applied to provide a *scheme pension*, will cease to be part of the alternatively secured pension fund.'

Annuity purchase   2.56

As from A-Day buy-out policies must be provided through a registered scheme, and will no longer be permitted to be free-standing. However, the monetary limits will be removed from policies and a tax-free lump sum of up to 25% of value may be paid. Any pre A-Day bought-out benefits shall remain subject to the limits that were written into those contracts. For the purpose of testing limits, defined contribution contracts must use a factor of 20:1.

Deferred annuity contracts   2.57

Deferred annuity contracts may only be offered by insurance companies, subject to any legislative relaxation.

Income withdrawal   2.58

Scheme rules may permit members to draw secured benefits in stages. The benefits drawn may be in the form of a lifetime annuity, or as a payment direct from the scheme. A tax-free pension commencement lump sum may be paid proportionate to the level of pension benefits being drawn.

The maximum income which can be withdrawn for the purpose of ASP and unsecured pension funds must be calculated not only on the initial sums and assets deposited, but also investment growth and any assets which are acquired to replace disposals.

Any uncrystallised funds which are held in a money purchase arrangement will remain invested within the fund (this is different to any unsecured pension fund where an unsecured pension is being provided – see **2.60** below). The funds may later be used, in full or in part, to provide a lifetime annuity contract or scheme pension, or designated to provide additional unsecured pension. This phasing of benefits under a money purchase arrangement can continue up until the member's 75th birthday. On the member's 75th birthday either a secured pension must be provided, or funds are retained within the arrangement to provide ASP.

The *Registered Pension Schemes Manual* (RPSM09101070 and RPSM09101060) gives the following examples:

'Example 1 – phased retirement in a defined benefits arrangement

Marion is a member of a *defined benefits* scheme. By the time she reaches her normal retirement date under the scheme (60) she is entitled to a pension for life of £15,000 per annum.

Marion does not wish to retire but wants to continue working for the company in a reduced capacity. As such she does not want to draw her full pension entitlement, but needs to draw some of that entitlement to supplement her reduced earnings.

As the scheme rules allow her to phase her pension benefits she decides to draw a *scheme pension* of £5,000 per annum from the scheme at age 60, deferring the start of the balance of £10,000 per annum pension until she fully retires.

Her *pension commencement lump sum* is linked to the pension she has become entitled to. So is based solely on the lower scheme pension level of £5,000 per annum.

The rules of the scheme allow for her deferred pension to be revalued to reflect the potentially reduced outlay to the scheme, as well as allowing for further accrual under the scheme in respect of her continuing employment with the company in her new reduced capacity.'

(There is no objection to those deferred benefits being augmented, as each separate entitlement will be valued separately for lifetime allowance purposes at the time they come into payment.)

'Example 2 – phased retirement in a money purchase arrangement

Peter is 55 years old and has £50,000 held in one *arrangement* under a *money purchase* scheme.

Peter leaves his current employer and takes up a new part-time job paying him a lower income. He decides he could do with a low pension income to supplement these reduced earnings, but wants to leave most of his pension pot untouched to provide for him later on when he fully retires.

Peter opts to use (designates) £20,000 of the funds held in his arrangement to provide him with pension benefits. He decides to draw the maximum tax-free *pension commencement lump sum* benefit (£5,000) and use the rest to purchase a small *lifetime annuity*. This annuity provides him with an income of £850 per annum for life.

The residual *uncrystallised funds* of £30,000 remain invested within the arrangement.

Five years later Peter retires from all employment. He chooses to draw all of the uncrystallised funds still held in the arrangement, which now totals £35,000 due to investment income growth.

Again Peter opts for the maximum pension commencement lump sum (£8,750) with the residual funds (£26,250) being used to purchase him an additional lifetime annuity contract (indexed to RPI this time). The initial annuity he receives is £1,200 per annum.

Peter now has a combined lifetime annuity income of £2,050 per annum (with £1,200 being indexed to *RPI*).'

Existing income drawdown arrangements 2.59

Existing income drawdown arrangements will become unsecured pensions. Each arrangement will be treated as having commenced on A-Day and valued at that date to establish the maximum that may be drawn. A two-year period from A-Day will be allowed for providers to review their arrangements.

Unsecured pensions 2.60

Where there are benefits in payment from unsecured funds at A-Day, and no new assets are designated into those funds from that date, there will be no crystallisation event for the purposes of the lifetime allowance or the tax-free lump sum.

On a benefit crystallisation event at age 75 for members with unsecured pensions, the amount crystallised will be the fund value less the amount crystallised when the fund was first created.

Documenting entitlements and scheme changes 2.61

Employers and trustees must be aware of the ever-developing rules and timescales that apply on modifying registered pension schemes.

Schedule 36, Pt 1, para 3, Finance Act 2004, conferred powers on the HMRC Board to modify schemes. This provision offers transitional protection to schemes if administrators or trustees had not amended the documentation to comply with the new tax regime. This transitional protection was to end on 6 April 2009 or on any earlier date of amendment, but this was extended to 6 April 2011 in the 2005 Budget, and included in the *Finance Act 2005.*

The *Registered Pension Schemes* (*Modification of the Rules of Existing Schemes*) *Regulations 2006* (*SI 2006/364*) give transitional protection to schemes if administrators or trustees do not amend their documentation to comply with the new tax regime. The transitional protection extends to 6 April 2011, or such later date as may be prescribed by regulations. The main effect of the regulations is to:

- provide that if an existing scheme's rules would otherwise require the trustees or managers of an existing scheme to make what, by virtue of the new tax regime, would be an unauthorised payment, the rules shall instead be construed as conferring on them a discretion to choose whether to make such a payment;

- preserve the effect of *s 590C, Income and Corporation Taxes Act 1988* (indexation of the permitted maximum) during the transitional period;

- make provision in the case of existing scheme rules where benefits are restricted by reference to the scheme's approval by the Inland Revenue or HMRC;

- provide that the rules of an existing scheme are to be read as authorising the reduction of a member's benefits in respect of the administrator's liability for the lifetime allowance charge.

Trustees who have not yet done so would be well advised to seek legal guidance on whether to continue to rely on the overriding legislation post A-Day.

There had to be compliance with *s 67, Pensions Act 1995,* in respect of any amendments which were made before A-Day. As from A-Day, *s 67* of the *Pensions Act 1995* has been substituted by *s 262* of the *Pensions Act 2004.* Schemes are now able to make a rule change that could have a detrimental effect on a member's subsisting rights at the date a rule change takes effect subject to certain conditions. The main subjects covered by the regulations are:

- exemptions to the provisions in the new *section 67* for prescribed schemes or schemes of a prescribed description;

- exemptions to the provisions in the new *section 67* for prescribed modifications;

- the qualifications and experience required of a person to be eligible to certify that the actuarial value of subsisting rights of members have been maintained;

- the requirements that must be met when calculating the actuarial value of subsisting rights of members.

Chapter 3
Tax-relievable allowance limits and benefit crystallisation

Introduction   3.1

The *Finance Act 2004* describes the new allowances within which tax-free payments may be made; namely the *annual allowance* and the *lifetime allowance*. The former is the maximum amount of input which may be made on the tax-allowable basis within a twelve-month period, the latter is the maximum amount of tax-free life savings which may be held in a pension scheme. For the purpose of the new legislation, the term 'approval' is replaced by the term 'registered'. The subjects of registration and non-registration are covered in **CHAPTERS 8** and **10** respectively. The two main allowances are described under the relevant headings below in this chapter.

The following important provisions are also described below:

* the pension input amount, as applied to the annual allowance;

* the annual allowance charge and the lifetime allowance charge on amounts in excess of the allowances;

* benefit crystallisation events, which require a testing of the lifetime allowance limit

* the various meanings of the term 'payment' under the *Finance Act 2004*;

* the effect of pension-splitting orders, early retirement, non-residency, low retirement ages and overseas transfers on the value of the lifetime allowance.

Annual allowance

Annual allowance limit   3.2

The new annual allowance is a limit on the tax-free level of annual input ('pension input amount') which may be put into or accumulated under a

49

registered pension scheme. The limit is the total aggregate increase in the member benefits during the year (determined in accordance with the relevant method shown in **3.3** below). The previous limits on employee contributions have been removed with effect from A-Day, and the allowance has been set at the levels shown in the table below. The limit is the aggregate of all other payments into registered schemes or arrangements for the same year. The ongoing level of the allowance is:

Tax year 2006/07	£215,000
Tax year 2007/08	£225,000
Tax year 2008/09	£235,000
Tax year 2009/10	£245,000
Tax year 2010/11	£255,000

Methods of calculation   3.3

The method of calculating the pension input amount depends on the type of scheme or arrangement concerned. This is because it is not possible to directly relate the total contributions which are paid into a defined benefits arrangement to the individual member, whereas this is generally possible for a money purchase scheme.

The contributions into a defined benefits arrangement are made for the purpose of funding the promised scale benefit for all the members of the scheme and are not linked directly to the level of the employer's and member's contributions on an individual basis. This meant that a new method of calculation had to be devised, based on the increase in the capital value of an individual's rights over the applicable pension input period. Examples of the elements which form the increased rights of a member over an applicable period include an increase in the amount of the member's pensionable service and/or pensionable earnings under the scheme provisions, and an augmentation of a member's benefit entitlement under the scheme. These increases are converted by using a factor of 10:1 to give an increased capital value, as shown under the relevant heading below.

The situation for money purchase arrangements is more straightforward. In effect, a factor of 1:1 is applied to the contributions which are received by the scheme. The opening value of the member's rights is deducted from the closing value, as shown under the relevant heading below. There are other categories included below, which seeks to offer a broad parity of treatment for other types of money purchase arrangement, and to make allowance for pension debits and credits on divorce or where transfers have taken place.

The pensions input period is determined by the *nominated date* (see the Glossary). There must be a pension input period in every tax year. A preferred end date may be chosen from inception (eg the end of the scheme accounting period or the end of the tax year). Detailed working examples are given in the *Registered Pension Schemes Manual* (see **3.4** below, and the comprehensive list of the contents of the manual in **APPENDIX 2**).

In all, four types of schemes or arrangements are identified under the *Finance Act 2004*.

Cash balance arrangement – pension input amount

The pension input amount is the increase in the value of an individual's rights in the pension input period. The increase is the difference between the pension value at the beginning of the opening period and the pension value at the end of the closing pension input period in the tax year concerned.

The opening value is the amount which would be available for the provision of benefits to or in respect of the individual on the assumption that the individual became entitled to the benefits at the beginning of the pension input period. This is uprated by RPI or 5%, whichever higher (or some other regulatory amount).

The closing value is the amount which would be available for the provision of benefits to or in respect of the individual on the assumption that the individual became entitled to the benefits at the end of the pension input period. Any pension debit in the period is added back (or deducted if the member received a pension credit). If there has been a transfer to a registered, or recognised overseas, scheme during the period, the amount of the sums transferred plus the market value of the assets is to be added (or deducted if there has been a transfer in). Any benefit that has crystallised in the period is to be added, unless the member has become entitled to the whole benefit or died. Any minimum payments under the *Pension Schemes Act 1993* are to be subtracted.

The glossary to the *Registered Pension Schemes Manual* states that benefits will be money purchase benefits, but:

> 'where the amount that will be available to provide those benefits is not calculated purely by reference to payments made under the arrangement by or on behalf of the member. This means that, in a cash balance arrangement, the capital amount available to provide benefits (the member's "pot") will not derive wholly from any actual contributions (or credits or transfers) made year on year.'

Other money purchase arrangement – pension input amount

The pension input amount is the increase in the value of an individual's rights in the pension input period. The increase is the total of any relievable pension contributions paid by or on behalf of the individual under the arrangement, and contributions paid in respect of the individual under the arrangement by an employer of the individual, at the end of the closing pension input period in the tax year concerned. *Section 233(3), Finance Act 2004*, states:

> 'when at any time contributions paid under a pension scheme by an employer otherwise than in respect of any individual become held for the purposes of the provision under an arrangement under the pension scheme of benefits to or in respect of an individual, they are to be treated as being contributions paid at that time in respect of the individual under the arrangement'.

Defined benefits arrangement – pension input amount

The pension input amount is the increase in the value of an individual's rights in the pension input period. The increase is the difference between the pension value at the beginning of the opening period and the pension value at the end of the closing pension input period in the tax year concerned.

Subsections 234(4) and *234(5), Finance Act 2004*, state:

'(4)   The opening value of the individual's rights under the arrangement is–

$(10 \times PB) + LSB$

where–

PB is the annual rate of the pension which would, on the valuation assumptions (see *section 277*), be payable to the individual under the arrangement if the individual became entitled to payment of it at the beginning of the pension input period, and

LSB is the amount of the lump sum to which the individual would, on the valuation assumptions, be entitled under the arrangement (otherwise than by commutation of pension) if the individual became entitled to the payment of it at that time.

(5)   The closing value of the individual's rights under the arrangement is–

$(10 \times PE) + LSE$

where–

PE is the annual rate of the pension which would, on the valuation assumptions, be payable to the individual under the arrangement if the individual became entitled to payment of it at the end of the pension input period, and

LSE is the amount of the lump sum to which the individual would, on the valuation assumptions, be entitled under the arrangement (otherwise than by commutation of pension) if the individual became entitled to the payment of it at that time.'

Any pension debit in the period is added back (or deducted if the member received a pension credit). If there has been a transfer to a registered, or recognised overseas, scheme during the period, the amount of the sums transferred plus the market value of the assets is to be added (or deducted if there has been a transfer in). Any benefit that has crystallised in the period is to be added, unless the member has become entitled to the whole benefit or died. Any minimum payments under the *Pension Schemes Act 1993* are to be subtracted.

The *Registered Pension Schemes (Uprating Percentages for Defined Benefits Arrangements and Enhanced Protection Limits) Regulations 2006 (SI 2006/130)* prescribe the alternative percentage by reference to which the opening value of defined benefits arrangements is calculated as the greatest of:

- 5%;

- the percentage by which RPI for the month in which the pension input period ends is higher than it was for the month in which it began; and

- the percentage to which regulations made by HMRC refer.

A defined benefits arrangement is one which provides all benefits in the form of defined benefits. Defined benefits means benefits, other than money purchase benefits, which are calculated by reference to earnings or service of the individual or any other factor other than an amount available for their provision.

Hybrid arrangement – pension input amount

The pension input amount is the greater or greatest of such of input amounts **A**, **B** and **C** as are relevant input amounts.

- **A** is what would be the pension input amount under *ss 230–232, Finance Act 2004*, if the benefits provided to or in respect of the individual under the arrangement were cash balance benefits.

- **B** is what would be the pension input amount under *s 233* if the benefits provided to or in respect of the individual under the arrangement were other money purchase benefits.

- **C** is what would be the pension input amount under *ss 234–236* if the benefits provided to or in respect of the individual under the arrangement were defined benefits.

HMRC worked examples   3.4

The pension input amounts arising from later periods which begin within the tax year but do not end within that tax year will not be tested for that tax year, but for the next. The *Registered Pension Schemes Manual* contains the following examples:

Example 1 (RPSM06105020)

'Calculating the pension input amount where the individual has two other money purchase arrangements and a defined benefit arrangement: an example

Patricia is a member of three registered pension schemes, under each of which she has one *arrangement* and wants to calculate whether she will face an *annual allowance charge* for the tax year ending 5 April 2007. Her details are as follows:

Arrangement	Type	Pension input period
1	Other Money purchase arrangement	6 April 2006 to 6 April 2007
2	Other Money purchase arrangement	1 January 2007 to 1 January 2008
3	Defined benefit arrangement	6 April 2006 to 31 March 2007 (would normally be an anniversary but for the first pension input period cannot begin earlier than 6 April 2006)

Arrangement 1

Patricia's arrangement received a *relievable pension contribution* of £200,000 from her employer on 5 April 2007 and a further £50,000 on 30 April 2007. These were the only contributions made between 6 April 2006 and 5 April 2008.

Arrangement 2

Patricia made a relievable pension contribution of £50,000 on 5 April 2007. This was the only contribution made between 6 April 2006 and 5 April 2008.

Arrangement 3

The arrangement provides benefits on a strict 60th basis. She had 25 years pensionable service on 6 April 2006 with earnings of £250,000. These had increased to £300,000 by 31 March 2007 and remained at £300,000 on 31 March 2008.

Arrangement 1, as the *pension input period* is from 6 April 2006 to 6 April 2007 only the sum of £200,000 will count towards the *annual allowance*. There are no adjustments to apply to this figure. So Patricia's pension input amount in respect of this arrangement is £200,000.

Arrangement 2, although £50,000 was paid on the same date as the employer's first contribution to arrangement 1 the pension input period for this arrangement is 1 January 2007 to 1 January 2008. This means the impact of this contribution will affect Patricia in the following tax year. Therefore there is no *pension input amount* to arise from this arrangement.

Arrangement 3, the pension input period is 6 April 2006 to 31 March 2007. In accordance with the criteria as set out in rpsm06103020, her pensionable entitlement on that date is £104,166.67. (25 x 1/60th x £250,000) and so her opening value before adjustment is £104,166.67.

By 31 March 2007 her pensionable entitlement is £130,000 (26 x 1/60th x £300,000) and so her closing value is £1,300,000.

Patricia's pension input amount in respect of this arrangement is therefore £258,333 (£1300,000-£1,041,667).

So the total *pension input amount* is £458,333 (£200,000 from arrangement 1 and £258,333 from arrangement 3). As the annual allowance for the tax year 2006–2007 is £215,000 Patricia will be taxed on the excess of £243,333. The annual allowance charge will be £97,333.20 (40% x £243,333).

The following year Patricia is again making the same calculation for the tax year ending 5 April 2008.

Arrangement 1, as the pension input period is from 6 April 2007 to 6 April 2008 the contribution of £50,000 on 30 April 2007 will count as a pension input amount.

Arrangement 2, although £50,000 was paid in the tax year ended 5 April 2007 the pension input period for this arrangement is 1 January 2007 to 1 January 2008. This means the impact of this contribution will affect Patricia in the tax year ended 5 April 2008. Therefore a pension input amount of £50,000 will arise from this arrangement.

Arrangement 3, the pension input period is 1 April 2007 to 1 April 2008. In accordance with the criteria as set out in rpsm06103020, her pensionable entitlement on that date is £130,000 (26 x 1/60th x £300,000).

On 1 April 2008 her pensionable entitlement is £135,000 (27 x 1/60th x £300,000) and so her closing value is £1,350,000.

Therefore in this case there is no "increase" and so there is no pension input amount.

In these circumstances the total pension input amount is £100,000 (£50,000 from arrangement 1, £50,000 from arrangement 2 and nil from arrangement 3).'

Examples 2 and 3 (RPSM06100070)

'End of the first pension input period

[s 238(1)]

The first *pension input period* will, unless otherwise changed, end at the anniversary of the start date. So a period starting on 1 June 2006 will end on 31 May 2007.

It can come to an end earlier than the anniversary if the scheme administrator, or in a *money purchase arrangement* that is not a *cash balance arrangement*, the scheme administrator or the member, opt to end it sooner. This earlier date is referred to as a *"nominated date"*.

A "nominated date" allows a change to be made to the fixed period relating solely to the anniversary of the member entering into the arrangement.

Example

"The scheme administrator operates with a scheme year for administrative purposes of 31 October. The scheme administrator may nominate that the pension input period which began on 1 June 2006, will cease on 31 October 2006 to facilitate alignment with the time of year when the scheme provides information to members."

In a money purchase arrangement, the member will have a statutory right under Department for Work and Pensions legislation to seek an illustration of benefits and other information about membership. Where a member puts in a request for an illustration, they may also want to obtain information about the amount being used to test against their *annual allowance*. If they do, they can (unless their arrangement is a cash balance arrangement) nominate a date upon which a pension input period will come to an end, so that the *pension input amount* is calculated over the same period as the illustration.

The nomination by either a scheme administrator or the member does not concern HMRC. A nomination by the scheme administrator is made by notice to the member concerned. And in the case of a money purchase arrangement where the member also has the right to nominate, the member should nominate by sending a notice to the scheme administrator.

If both parties make a nomination in relation to the first pension input period, the legislation provides that it is the first nomination made (which might not be the earlier of the dates nominated) that is the nominated date.

Example

"George is promoted to a new post with his employer on 29 January 2007. He is informed that he will be eligible to join the company's money purchase scheme and details will be forwarded to him in due course. George requests the 30 September 2007 be used as an illustration date and makes a nomination to that effect. The scheme administrator later nominates 30 April 2007 to fit in with the accounting year of the scheme. In these circumstances George's choice takes precedence even though the scheme administrator chose an earlier date." '

Example 4 (RPSM06100110)

'Annual allowance charge

[s 227]

The *annual allowance charge* is a tax charge on the individual. It arises where the *total pension input amount* for an individual in *pension input periods* which end in the tax year concerned exceeds the amount of the *annual allowance* for that tax year.

Where the total pension input amount exceeds the annual allowance, the annual allowance charge will be levied on the excess.

The amount of the annual allowance charge is 40% of the amount in excess of the allowance.

Example

"Heather is a member of 3 different schemes. Scheme A has a pension input period ending on 31 March, Scheme B 5 April and Scheme C 30 November. During the tax year ending 5 April 2008 she will have to amalgamate the pension input amounts for the periods ending on the following dates to arrive at her total pension input amount:

Scheme A	31 March 2008
Scheme B	5 April 2008
Scheme C	30 November 2007

The pension input amount in each fund is:

Scheme A	£54,000
Scheme B	£98,000
Scheme C	£98,000
Total pension input amount	£250,000

As the annual allowance for the tax year ending 5 April 2008 is £225,000 Heather will be taxed on the excess of £25,000. The annual allowance charge will therefore be £10,000 (40% x £25,000)." '

CHAPTER 4 describes the individual tax limits and charges which apply to employee and employer contributions.

Annual allowance charge, and additional exemptions from the annual allowance   3.5

In addition to the exemptions described in the four different methods of calculation of the pension input amount in **3.3** above, there are certain other elements which do not count towards the annual allowance. These are:

- any contributions which are in excess of a member's earnings that do not qualify for tax relief (see **CHAPTER 4**);

- the amount of any AVCs which are paid for the purpose of securing added years (these will be payable to a defined benefit scheme, typically a public sector pension scheme, or a public-sector type scheme, meaning that it is the increase in the member's benefits which will be counted);

- before the end of the year, where the individual has become entitled (meaning an actual right to draw) to all of the benefits;

- before the end of the tax year, where the individual has died.

The annual allowance charge is incurred if the total pension input amount is exceeded. The charge is payable by the member. If a member is liable for the charge, and has not been issued with a personal tax return, the individual should notify their tax office of the position. The charge is not treated as income for any of the purposes of the Taxes Acts. The rate chargeable is 40% (see **7.5** below) and it will be incurred whether or not the administrator or member are resident, ordinarily resident or domiciled in the UK. However, the excess monies may remain in the scheme subject to the ultimate lifetime allowance at retirement or earlier crystallisation. Any excessive tax withheld by the scheme may be refunded to the member.

If tax relief has already been given on an excess in the scheme, it will be clawed back from the fund. It will not be possible to offset the allowance from one year to another if the value of a defined benefit falls during the year, or against any other allowances, losses or reliefs.

Any excess amount will not count as pension income, or any other kind of income, for the purpose of the UK bilateral double taxation conventions.

Pension input period 3.6

The *Finance Act 2004* provides scope for the scheme to determine the pension input period which best suits them (the 'nominated date'). The nomination can be made by the administrator or, in the case of a money purchase arrangement other than a cash balance arrangement, the individual member or the administrator. The only other criterion is that there must be a pension input period in every tax year. The first pension input period will commence on the day that the member's pension rights begin to accrue under the registered scheme. A preferred end date may be chosen (for example, the end of the scheme accounting period, or the end of the tax year). The total of all pension input amounts paid in that tax year will be the amount which is tested against the annual allowance. Any excess will be subject to the annual allowance charge.

Regulatory sources 3.7

The following sources are relevant to the annual allowance under the *Finance Act 2004*:

- *s 152*: the calculation of the pension input amount;

- *s 227*: the annual allowance charge;

- *s 228*: the annual allowance;

- *ss 230–232*: the pension input amount for a cash balance arrangement;

- *s 233*: the pension input amount for another money purchase arrangement under *s 229*;

- *ss 234–236*: the pension input amount for a defined benefits arrangement;

- *s 237*: the pension input amount for a hybrid arrangement;

- *s 238*: the pension input period.

Lifetime allowance

Lifetime allowance limit 3.8

The lifetime allowance is a limit on the level of pension saving, when aggregated with all other similar savings under registered schemes or arrangements, that can benefit from tax reliefs in a fund during a member's lifetime (disregarding any dependant's pension which the member may be receiving). The limit is the gross value of benefits before the application of any lifetime allowance charge (see **3.10** below).

The membership qualifications for post A-Day tax-exempt pension schemes (which are classified as *registered schemes*) are much wider than under the previous rules, and greater access to benefits is provided, including for those who remain in service. Registered pension schemes are open to all, whatever the employment or residence status of the individual concerned, including the UK employed and self-employed. Additionally, a member may concurrently be a member of any type or any number of schemes (for example, occupational pension schemes and personal pension schemes). In all these circumstances there is a requirement to keep a record of the lifetime allowance of all members, and to make reports at specified times.

The previous limits on employee benefits have largely been removed (see **CHAPTER 2**). Transitional arrangements have been put in place to protect pre-existing rights as at A-Day. This is achieved mainly by giving a statutory entitlement to an enhanced personal level of lifetime allowance, in place of the standard lifetime allowance. The level of the standard lifetime allowance is:

Tax year 2006/07	£1,500,000
Tax year 2007/08	£1,600,000
Tax year 2008/09	£1,650,000
Tax year 2009/10	£1,750,000
Tax year 2010/11	£1,800,000

Thereafter, the limit is subject to five-yearly reviews. The allowance will not be set at a level lower than in the previous year.

Methods of calculation   3.9

As for the annual allowance, the method of calculating the limit depends on the type of scheme or arrangement concerned. However, the categories are not defined specifically for the lifetime allowance. For money purchase arrangements, funds will be measured at market value, and annuities valued at their cost. For defined benefits arrangements, funds must use a factor of 20:1 for valuing scheme pensions. A different factor must be agreed if the increases to benefits exceed RPI or a fixed 5% pa, or for survivors' benefits which in aggregate exceed the member's pension (the factor was chosen after representations had been made by the Association of Consulting Actuaries). Any lump sum entitlement which does not come from a commutation of the pension shall be added on afterwards.

Where a pension is in payment at A-Day, from whatever form of pension scheme, the capitalised value of the pension is determined by applying a factor of 25:1 to that pension.

For a cash balance arrangement, the measure will be the value of the fund which would be used to provide benefits if the entitlement to those benefits had arisen at age 75.

Lifetime allowance charge   3.10

The lifetime allowance must be tested each time a benefit crystallisation event (see **3.15** below) occurs, as each event will utilise all or part of the individual's lifetime allowance. The main events include when a person becomes entitled to a pension or lump sum; on transfers of funds being made to overseas schemes; and when any other reportable event occurs. HMRC must be notified of the amount of lifetime allowance used and the member must be notified, in annual benefit and tax statements, at A-Day, on subsequent augmentations and on the final vesting date. Once the full amount of the lifetime allowance has been used up, the lifetime allowance charge is payable.

The rate of the charge, where a pension is taken, is 25%. The rate, where a lump sum is taken, is 55%, which equates to the 25% charge, plus income tax at 40% (see **7.5** below). The scheme administrator may deduct the charge, and the member will normally declare the payment in his or her tax return, and offset the tax deducted.

The liability for the charge falls jointly and severally on the member and the administrator, or on the recipient in the case of a lump sum death benefit. The charge is payable whether or not the administrator or member are resident, ordinarily resident or domiciled in the UK. Any withholding tax accounted for by the scheme may be set against the member's liability. It is possible for the scheme administrator to reclaim excessive tax paid, and for benefits to be paid to the member as if the error had not occurred.

The method shown in *s 218, Finance Act 2004*, for calculating the lifetime allowance at the benefit crystallisation date where one or more lifetime allowance enhancement factors apply is by the formula:

SLA + (SLA x LAEF)

where:

SLA is the standard lifetime allowance at that date; and

LAEF is the lifetime allowance enhancement factor which operates at that date with regard to the event and the member.

The following example shows a straightforward method of testing the lifetime allowance on successive events.

Example – the effect of several crystallisation events

In this example, the member's lifetime allowance is the standard lifetime allowance:

Occasion 1

In the year 2006/07 the member crystallises £1,000,000 out of a standard lifetime allowance of £1,500,000.

Occasion 2

In the year 2010/11 the member crystallises £500,000 out of the balance of a standard lifetime allowance of £1,800,000. The result is:

- Amount already crystallised (£1,000,000 in 2006/07) = 66.67% of the standard lifetime allowance (the percentage of the member's allowance being used up is added to any percentage used up previously by the member, whether under the same scheme or a different registered pension scheme).

- Current value of the amount crystallised in the year 2006/07 is: £1,000,000 x 1,800,000/1,500,000 = 1,200,000.

- Lifetime allowance available in 2010/11 is therefore: 1,800,000 – 1,200,000 = £600,000.

Balance of lifetime allowance available in 2010/11, following Event 2, is £600,000 less £500,000 = £100,000.

HMRC worked example   3.11

The *Registered Pension Schemes Manual* (RPSM11100030) contains the following example of a test on each benefit crystallisation event:

> ' "Mike crystallises benefits with a capital value of £150,000. The standard lifetime allowance at that point is £1.5 million, so the percentage used up is 10%. If Mike had not crystallised any other benefits previously, he will have 90% of his lifetime allowance still available for the next BCE.
>
> The same process occurs when Mike crystallises benefits at a future date.
>
> This time Mike crystallises a further £500,000 when the standard lifetime allowance is £2 million. So Mike has used up a further 25% of the standard lifetime allowance. In total Mike has used up 35% (10% + 25%) of his lifetime allowance."

The percentage of the standard lifetime allowance used up at a particular BCE in a particular tax year remains constant year by year even though the standard lifetime allowance is increased in subsequent tax years. So the 10% of the standard lifetime allowance used up in the example above when the standard lifetime allowance is £1.5 million remains constant at 10% in the later year when the allowance has risen to £2 million. This process ensures that the original crystallisation amount of £150,000 maintains a fixed percentage, despite subsequent increases to the lifetime allowance.'

The administrator's responsibilities and actions   3.12

The *Registered Pension Schemes Manual* (RPSM11100030) states:

> 'When calculating the percentage of the standard lifetime allowance being used up at any BCE the *scheme administrator* need only be concerned with the benefits currently being tested under their particular scheme. They do not require specific details of any other benefits the member may have (which in turn avoids the need to

obtain details of other rights when the individual joins the scheme). However, in order to calculate whether the member has enough available lifetime allowance to cover the amount crystallising at that BCE (and whether or not a lifetime allowance charge is due) the scheme administrator may well require details from the member of the previous percentages of the "standard lifetime allowance" they have used up under other registered pension schemes at earlier BCEs.'

The manual identifies that the scheme administrator has three basic responsibilities before, at and after a benefit crystallisation event occurs in a member's lifetime:

(*a*) establishing whether a chargeable amount arises at the benefit crystallisation event;

(*b*) accounting to HMRC for the lifetime allowance charge due on any chargeable amount that arises at the benefit crystallisation event (on a quarterly basis); and

(*c*) providing the member after the benefit crystallisation event with a statement confirming the total level of the member's lifetime allowance that has been used up under the scheme, and if a chargeable amount arose at the benefit crystallisation event, a notice confirming:

- the level of chargeable amount that arose at the benefit crystallisation event;

- the lifetime allowance charge due; and

- whether or not they have accounted for the due charge, or intend to do so in due course.

There is no laid down regulatory method for establishing the available allowance at a benefit crystallisation event; schemes can adopt the method which best suits their design and operation.

The *Registered Pension Schemes Manual* (RPSM11100090) gives the following as a general guide as to how an administrator may wish to operate:

'On 9 October 2006, Judy decides to draw some of her benefits from a *registered pension scheme*. She wants to take the maximum lump sum and use the residual funds to purchase a *lifetime annuity*. The scheme administrator calculates the capital crystallised value of the level of benefits she wants to draw as being £750,000.

The scheme administrator writes to Judy telling her how much will crystallise for *lifetime allowance* purposes and the percentage of the current standard lifetime allowance this will represent (50% of the *standard lifetime allowance* for the 2006/07 tax year). They ask Judy to provide a statement within 1 month confirming the level of lifetime allowance she anticipates being available on the anticipated *BCE* date, and to say whether or not she anticipates any other BCE occurring either on or before that date under another scheme. They also ask her whether she is entitled to an enhanced lifetime allowance and, if so, to provide evidence of the certificate confirming the exact level of enhancement, as provided by HMRC.

Judy has not drawn any pension benefits from any other source previously and is subject to the standard lifetime allowance. She provides the requested statement confirming she has not used up any lifetime allowance previously and does not anticipate another BCE occurring either by or on the proposed date of the BCE.

The scheme administrator is satisfied that there is no *chargeable amount* and pays the benefits in full. They send Judy a statement verifying that she has used up 50% of the standard lifetime allowance at the BCE. Judy keeps this for future reference.

In the 2010/11 tax year Judy decides to draw the rest of her benefits under the scheme. The scheme administrator calculates the capital crystallised value of these remaining benefits as £180,000. The standard lifetime allowance is now £1.8 million so this second tranche of pension benefits represents 10% of the standard lifetime allowance at that time.

The scheme administrator writes to Judy outlining the above and asking her again about her anticipated available lifetime allowance at the time she wants to draw benefits. Judy still has 50% of her lifetime allowance available.

The new tranche of benefits will take Judy up to 60% of her lifetime allowance (50% plus 10%), so again there is no chargeable amount on this BCE. Judy declares to the scheme administrator that she has 50% of the standard lifetime allowance available at that time.

Benefits are paid out by the scheme administrator.

The scheme administrator sends a statement to Judy telling her she has now in aggregate used up 60% of her lifetime allowance (the standard lifetime allowance) through the scheme. Again, this certificate helps Judy keep track of the lifetime allowance she has used up, and evidence this fact where necessary'.

(The percentage expressed on the administrator's statement should go to two decimal places.)

Additional exemptions from the lifetime allowance 3.13

The exemptions include the following:

- any discretionary augmentations may be given across the board without testing for the allowance, if they apply to all pensions and there are at least 50 such persons in the scheme;

- partnership retirement annuities, but not other retirement annuities;

- where a member dies before transitionally protected benefits have fully vested, a lump sum may be paid in lieu of the pension that can no longer be paid. To the extent that the lump sum does not exceed the value of the protected pension rights, it will be free of the charge;

- a transfer to other registered schemes.

The administrator may be discharged of liability to the charge, if he or she acted in good faith, on application to HMRC. The *Registered Pension Schemes (Discharge of Liabilities) under Sections 267 and 268 of the Finance Act 2004) Regulations 2005 (SI 2005/3452)* have now supplemented the provisions of the *Finance Act 2004* and extended them to incapacitated persons. Transitional protection for existing rights is described in **CHAPTER 6**.

Regulatory sources 3.14

The following sources are the main ones that are relevant to the lifetime allowance under the *Finance Act 2004*:

- *s 214*: the lifetime allowance charge;

- *s 215*: the amount of the lifetime allowance charge;

- *s 216, Sch 32*: benefit crystallisation events and amounts crystallised;

- *ss 216* and *217* and *Sch 32, para 16, Finance Act 2004*: for a defined benefit scheme, a five-year guaranteed lump sum will be tax free if the sum is within the lifetime allowance;

- *s 217*: the persons liable to the lifetime allowance charge;

- *s 220*: pension credits;

- *ss 221–224*: non-residence;

- *ss 225* and *226*: overseas transfers;

- *ss 267* and *268*: the administrator may be discharged of liability to the charge, if he or she acted in good faith, on application to HMRC under the provisions of *s 267*;

● *Sch 36*: transitional protection.

Benefit crystallisation events   3.15

Benefit crystallisation events require a testing of the lifetime allowance limit. The reporting requirements are described in detail in **CHAPTER 8**. There are eight different testing events, and these are shown below. An individual cannot avoid the lifetime allowance charge by either simply not drawing benefits or taking them overseas. In the formulae which appear under three of the events, the following meanings apply:

● For the purposes of benefit crystallisation event 2, '**P**' is the amount of the pension which will be payable to the individual in the period of twelve months beginning with the day on which the individual becomes entitled to it (assuming that it remains payable throughout that period at the rate at which it is payable on that day).

● For the purposes of benefit crystallisation events 2, 3 and 5, '**RVF**' is the relevant valuation factor.

● For the purposes of benefit crystallisation event 3, '**XP**' is (subject to the above) the amount by which the increased annual rate of the pension exceeds the rate at which it was payable on the day on which the individual became entitled to it, as increased by the permitted margin.

● For the purposes of benefit crystallisation event 5, '**DP**' is the annual rate of the scheme pension to which the individual would be entitled if, on the date on which the individual reaches 75, the individual acquired an actual (rather than a prospective) right to receive it.

● For the purposes of benefit crystallisation event 5, '**DSLS**' is so much of any lump sum to which the individual would be entitled (otherwise than by way of commutation of pension) as would be paid to the individual if, on that date, the individual acquired an actual (rather than a prospective) right to receive it.

Event 1

This event is the designation of sums or assets held for the purposes of a money purchase arrangement under any of the relevant pension schemes as available for the payment of unsecured pension to the individual. The amount crystallised by the event is the aggregate of the amount of the sums and the market value of the assets designated.

Event 2

This event is the individual becoming entitled to a scheme pension under any of the relevant pension schemes. The amount crystallised is **RVF × P**.

Event 3

This event is the individual, having become so entitled, becoming entitled to payment of the scheme pension, otherwise than in excepted circumstances, at an increased annual rate which exceeds by more than the permitted margin the rate at which it was payable on the day on which the individual became entitled to it. The amount crystallised is **RVF × XP**.

Event 4

This event is the individual becoming entitled to a lifetime annuity purchased under a money purchase arrangement under any of the relevant pension schemes. The amount crystallised is the aggregate of the amount of such of the sums, and the market value of such of the assets, representing the individual's rights under the arrangement as are applied to purchase the lifetime annuity (and any related dependants' annuity).

Event 5

This event is the individual reaching the age of 75 when prospectively entitled to a scheme pension or a lump sum (or both) under a defined benefits arrangement under any of the relevant pension schemes. The amount crystallised is **(RVF × DP) + DSLS**.

Event 6

This event is the individual becoming entitled to a relevant lump sum under any of the relevant pension schemes. The amount crystallised is the amount of the lump sum (paid to the individual).

Event 7

This event is a person being paid a relevant lump sum death benefit in respect of the individual under any of the relevant pension schemes. The amount crystallised is the amount of the lump sum death benefit.

Event 8

This event is the transfer of sums or assets held for the purposes of, or representing accrued rights under, any of the relevant pension schemes so as to become held for the purposes of or to represent rights under a qualifying recognised overseas pension scheme in connection with the individual's membership of that pension scheme. The amount crystallised is the aggregate of the amount of any sums transferred and the market value of any assets transferred.

Meaning of the term 'payment' 3.16

The term 'payment' has special meaning under the *Finance Act 2004*. The main meanings ascribed to it are as follows:

- a transfer of assets or money's worth;

- a payment or benefit in respect of scheme assets;

- payments made to persons connected with the member or the sponsoring employer;

- payments made to persons who are not members or a sponsoring employer;

- certain assets, increases in value or reductions in liability of a member or sponsoring employer or connected person.

A 'connected person' has the meaning within *s 839, Income and Corporation Taxes Act 1988.*

A payment made by a registered pension scheme to a person who:

- is connected with a member or sponsoring employer (or was connected with a member at the date of the member's death); and

- is not a member or sponsoring employer;

is to be treated as made in respect of the member or sponsoring employer. Any asset held by a person connected with a member or sponsoring employer (or who was connected with a member at the date of the member's death) is to be treated as held for the benefit of the member or sponsoring employer.

The treatment of certain payments in specific circumstances is described under the relevant headings below.

Death benefits   3.17

Any lump sum monies which are not paid to the legal personal representatives in respect of unvested pensions must be notified to that person, who should be made aware of the amount of the lifetime allowance used up. Any lifetime allowance charge will fall on the beneficiary, not automatically on the legal personal representative. There will be no additional charge on pension payments. The member's personal representatives, not the scheme administrator, have responsibility for establishing whether or not any lifetime allowance charge is due, after the payments have been made.

A limit on the amount of dependants' benefits will be introduced in order to prevent avoidance of the lifetime allowance when it is valued incorporating an element for the dependants' pension.

Divorce   3.18

Where pension-splitting orders were in place as at A-Day, the value of the lifetime allowance may be ignored for the purpose of the allowance for both parties (a revision of the original proposals). A pension in payment which includes a pension credit as part of sharing on divorce will already have been tested against the lifetime allowance. In order to ensure that the pension credit is not tested again, the recipient's lifetime allowance may be increased by an appropriate pension credit factor to reflect the increased benefits the pension credit has provided. *Schedule 36, Part 2, para 18, Finance Act 2004*, describes the method of enhancement for pension credits.

For orders which are made after A-Day, pension credits will count against the recipient's allowance, but pension debits will not count against the donor's allowance. Where a pension credit is received that relates to a pension that is already in payment, and the credit relates to both crystallised and uncrystallised rights, only the crystallised element is taken into account.

The *Registered Pension Schemes Manual* (RPSM11101150) states that:

> 'no entitlement to a lifetime allowance enhancement factor will arise where an individual acquires pension credit rights on or after 6 April 2006 that were derived from:
>
> • an ex-spouse's pension that was in payment at the time of the pension sharing order but which came into payment before 6 April 2006; or
>
> • rights held by that ex-spouse that had not been crystallised at the time of the pension sharing order.'

Early retirement, and low normal retirement ages 3.19

An abatement percentage of 2.5% p a applies to the lifetime allowance for taking benefits before normal minimum pension age (see **2.37** above).

Non-UK members 3.20

Individuals who are not resident in the UK may retain membership of a registered pension scheme. During that time they may make contributions to, or accrue benefit rights within, a registered pension scheme that do not attract UK tax relief. In such cases, as the individual has not benefited from UK tax relief while not resident in the UK, the lifetime allowance applicable to that person may be increased, to the effect of ignoring those amounts that have not benefited from UK tax relief.

Transfers from overseas 3.21

Individuals who have built up rights within a recognised overseas pension scheme may transfer those rights into a UK-registered pension scheme. As their rights will have accumulated without the benefit of UK tax relief, there is provision to increase the lifetime allowance available to such individuals. This is subject to an adjustment for any amounts included in the transfer value which had previously benefited from UK tax relief.

Chapter 4
Membership
and contributions

Introduction 4.1

With effect from A-Day membership of registered pension schemes is open to virtually all, including the self-employed and most overseas employees. In addition to this significant relaxation, a much higher ceiling has been placed on the level of tax-relievable contributions which may be made to registered schemes (see **CHAPTER 8** for the meaning of this term). The maximum amount on which tax relief may be obtained is governed by the annual allowance. Spreading rules continue to apply to large contributions which are made by employers. In accordance with meeting the main requirements of the European IORPs Directive 2003/41/EC tax reliefs are extended to contributions made to recognised schemes (see **CHAPTER 9**).

Membership

Eligibility 4.2

There are very few references in the *Finance Act 2004* to the eligibility rules which apply from A-Day. The main reference is in *s 151,* which essentially defines the types of member a scheme or arrangement may have. There are no formal restrictions on the types of member, and UK residency is not a requirement. Members may be active members, pensioner members, deferred members or pension credit members.

The Treasury issued a consultation paper on its website, entitled 'Proposed Changes to the Eligibility Rules for Establishing a Pension Scheme', the consultation for which closed on 23 December 2005. The issues concern proposed changes to:

- the *Financial Services and Markets Act Regulated Activities Order,* to include a new regulated activity of setting up and running a personal pension scheme; and

- the *Finance Act 2004,* so that any person with permission to carry on this activity is eligible to establish a tax-privileged pension scheme.

The *Registered Pension Schemes Manual* contains greater guidance in this area, and some of the key information is summarised below.

Establishing employer bodies   4.3

The ability to establish registered pension schemes is far-reaching. From A-Day:

- a representative body that is itself an employer may establish a pension scheme for people who are employees in a particular industry; and

- one or more employers within a geographical area may set up a pension scheme for employees of theirs within that geographical area.

An employer (or employers) establishing a pension scheme may specify, for example, that the membership is for employees in a group of companies plus self-employed individuals who work with them.

Establishing providers   4.4

An application to register a pension scheme may be made only if the scheme is an occupational pension scheme or has been established by:

- an insurance company;

- a unit trust scheme manager;

- an operator, trustee or depositary of a recognised EEA collective investment scheme;

- an authorised open-ended investment company;

- a building society;

- a bank; or

- an EEA investment portfolio manager.

An occupational pension scheme will be established by:

- an employer – if the membership of the scheme is open to its own, or any other employees (such a scheme is an occupational pension scheme, even if other people may also join the scheme);

- more than one employer (collectively) – if the membership of the scheme is open to their own or any other employees (such a scheme is an occupational pension scheme, even if other people may also join the scheme); or

- government departments or ministers and UK parliamentary bodies (such a scheme will be a public service pension scheme).

(*Ch 2, ss 154* and *155, Finance Act 2004* refer.)

HM Treasury is currently in consultation with industry representatives and the FSA concerning proposed changes to the eligibility rules for establishing a pension scheme. This is based on proposed changes to the *Financial Services and Markets Act 2000 (Regulated Activities) Order 2001 (SI 2001/544)*, to include a new regulated activity of setting up and running a personal pension scheme.

Non-establishing employers 4.5

There is no HMRC requirement about the way that any employer, which is not the establishing employer, is allowed under the scheme rules to participate in an occupational pension scheme. But the employer will be recognised as a sponsoring employer where one or more of its employees are members and the scheme benefits for those members are directly related to their employment with the employers in question.

Multiple schemes 4.6

A member may concurrently be a member of any type or any number of schemes (for example, occupational pension schemes and personal pension schemes). The way is open for non-associated multi-employer schemes which can clearly benefit from economies of scale (*Ch 1, s 150, Finance Act 2004*).

HMRC, DWP and industry representatives, including the NAPF, have been working closely together to identify the main issues and how to address them. The issues include the Pension Protection Fund, cross-subsidies, funding and the consultation requirements.

Establishing and governing documentation 4.7

A pension scheme may be established by:

- a trust; or

- a contract; or

- a board's resolution; or

- a deed poll.

In other words, it is no longer necessary to establish a pension scheme under trust.

Contributions

Who may pay contributions 4.8

Members, employers and other persons may contribute to a registered pension scheme. There are no limits on the amounts which may be paid, only on the tax reliefs available. The persons who may contribute can be an individual, a corporate body or other legal entity. For tax purposes, a contribution made by other persons will be regarded as if it had been made by the scheme member. This means that the member should receive any tax relief due on the contribution, not the person who made the contribution. Guidance is set out in RPSM05101000, and a practical exception in the case of third-party contributions is given in RPSM0510320.

As maximum lump sum calculations will now be calculated at scheme level, it will become simpler to amalgamate additional voluntary contributions and other benefits within the same scheme.

Employer contributions 4.9

There is no limit on the amount of tax relief that an employer, including a former employer, may receive in respect of its contributions. However, tax relief is not automatic; it will be considered under the normal tax rules. The employer will receive relief against UK tax as trading or management expenses for contributions to a registered pension scheme (see **CHAPTER 8**) whether it is occupational or a series of arrangements. *Sections 196–200, Finance Act 2004*, describe the employer contribution rules and reliefs. In effect, the allowance of employers' contributions is restricted only by the £215,000 aggregate annual allowance on tax-relievable input.

No relief will be given to a non-registered scheme until the benefit is paid out (see **CHAPTER 10**). Also, rules will prevent routing the funding of non-registered schemes through a registered scheme in order to circumvent this requirement. As from A-day, employer contributions to unapproved schemes are not taxed on the employees or counted as employment income (*s 247, Finance Act 2004*).

There is some doubt as to whether payments of a capital nature, eg in specie at a commercial value, will be permitted. *Section 199, Finance Act 2004*, does not appear to debar them. The relevant pages in the *Registered Pension Schemes Manual* are under development, but they should provide definitive guidance when they are released.

Where an employer makes a statutory payment to cover deficiencies in the assets of a registered pension scheme under *s 75, Pensions Act 1995,* the payment is deemed to be a contribution and is allowable as a deduction against UK tax as trading or management expenses in the accounting period in which it is paid. If such a payment is made after an employer has ceased to trade, tax relief is given by treating any post-cessation contribution as a contribution paid by the employer on the last day of the trade.

Spreading employer contributions   4.10

The detailed tax-spreading rules for very large employer contributions are laid down in *ss 197* and *198, Finance Act 2004.* In brief, if contributions for an accounting period exceed 210% of the amount paid in the preceding year, unless the excess does not exceed £500,000 or there is a cessation of business, spreading will normally apply. As applied under the previous rules, spreading is intended to discourage employers from reducing the tax liability on their profits in a good year by making a large contribution to a registered pension scheme in the same year.

The following periods of spread apply:

Amount of excess	*How spread*
Between £500,000 and £1m	Over two years
Between £1m and £2m	Over three years
More than £2m	Over four years

An example of how the spread of tax relief on employer contributions works in practice is given below:

Example

ABC company pays the following contributions into its exempt approved pension scheme in each of its five accounting periods ended 30 April 2006:

£1m in year 2001/02

£1m in year 2002/03

£1m in year 2003/04

£1m in year 2004/05

£1m in year 2005/06

ABC company pays the following contributions into its registered pension scheme in its accounting period ended 30 April 2007:

£3m in year 2006/07

As the contribution of £3m exceeds 210% of the contribution of £1m paid in the accounting period ended 30 April 2006, the following spread will apply:

£750,000 will be allowed as a deduction in the year 2006/07

The balance of £2,250,000 will be spread forward and allowed as a deduction in each of the following years as follows:

£750,000 will be allowed as a deduction in the year 2007/08

£750,000 will be allowed as a deduction in the year 2008/09

£750,000 will be allowed as a deduction in the year 2009/10

The *Finance Act 2004* contains further provisions for adjusting the amount of a contribution to be spread if the previous and current accounting periods are not of equal length. *Schedule 36, Pt 4, para 42, Finance Act 2004,* describes the transitional arrangements for spreading employer contributions, which retain the status quo in relation to sums paid before A-Day (see **CHAPTER 6**).

As was the case previously, any contributions which are paid to fund a cost-of-living increase for pensioner members, or to fund or meet a future service liability for new entrants to a registered pension scheme, are excepted from the spreading requirement.

Where an employer permanently ceases to carry on a business during an accounting period to which a special contribution has been spread forward, a deduction may be allowed in an earlier accounting period. Employers may opt, taking into consideration their financial position, as to the accounting period into which they may have contributions spread.

Employer contributions – HMRC technical statement 4.11

In HMRC's September 'Pensions Tax Simplification Newsletter' it was confirmed that for the purposes of tax relief for employers' contributions the new rules in *ss 196–200, Finance Act 2004,* apply to accounting periods (or, for unincorporated businesses, periods of account) ending on or after 6 April 2006. So, for example, an accounting period that commenced on 1 July 2005 and will end on 30 June 2006 will be within the new rules. HMRC has since issued the following statement:

'This announcement has been mis-reported in the press as meaning that the Annual Allowance will apply to contributions made before A Day. This is not the case. The article in our September Newsletter dealt with tax relief for employer contributions only, and not with the Annual Allowance.

The annual allowance provisions in *ss 227–238, Finance Act 2004,* have no effect before 6 April 2006. The first 'pension input period' begins on the first date after 5 April 2006 when a contribution is made in respect of the individual (or, for defined benefits or cash balance arrangements, the first date after 5 April 2006 when rights accrue to the individual). So a contribution made before 6 April 2006 cannot count towards an individual's annual allowance or be subject to an annual allowance charge.

The different treatment for the annual allowance and employer contribution relief occurs because the annual allowance is an entirely new concept that does not exist before 6 April 2006, whilst relief for employers' contributions does exist before that date. So for an employer contribution we need to establish whether it falls within the old/pre A Day rules or the new/post A Day rules. This issue is determined by rules in *ICTA 1988* with the effect that the new rules apply to all employer contributions paid in accounting periods ending on or after 6 April 2006.'

Member contributions 4.12

Previously, tax relief and contributions were based on the earnings cap. This was abolished from A-Day and replaced by the annual allowance on contributions. The new qualification is that members will be able to receive full tax relief on contributions up to 100% of their annual earnings, or £3,600 if higher (at their marginal tax rate). For example, a member with UK earnings of £2,500 in 2006/07 may pay a contribution of £3,600 and obtain tax relief thereon. This reflects the previous threshold for contributions under stakeholder pension schemes. It is still possible for a third party to make contributions to a registered pension scheme up to £3,600 pa on behalf of a person resident in the UK who has no earnings, eg a minor or non-working spouse. This is an option for grandparents or working spouses, but the minor or non-working spouse will be unable to draw the accumulated retirement benefits from the registered pension scheme concerned until they reach age 55 (see **2.37** above).

As previously, it is possible for members to transfer certain shares acquired under an HMRC-approved employee share scheme to a member's scheme. The value of the shares will be treated as a contribution paid for the purposes of tax relief for members' contributions. Only shares from SAYE option schemes and share incentive plans may be transferred.

Any contributions over the tax-relief limits above may be paid into the pension scheme, but the member will not receive any tax relief on them, and the ceiling of the £215,000 aggregate annual allowance on tax-relievable input applies (see **3.2** above). Some examples are given below:

Example 1

The member has UK earnings in 2006/07 of £90,000.

He pays a contribution of £100,000 to his registered pension scheme in 2006/07.

He qualifies for tax relief on £90,000 of the contribution (100% of UK earnings), but the excess contribution of £10,000 does not attract tax relief.

The excess is not liable to the annual allowance charge of 40%, unless together with the qualifying contribution of £90,000 and the benefit of fund value accrual the annual allowance of £215,000 is exceeded.

Example 2

The member has UK earnings in 2006/07 of £265,750.

She pays a contribution of £247,000 to her registered pension scheme in 2006/07.

She qualifies for tax relief on £215,000 (the annual allowance for 2006/07).

The excess contribution of £32,000 is subject to the annual allowance charge of 40% on the scheme.

In any tax year in which a member takes their retirement benefits in full or a member dies, the annual allowance limit does not apply. So, a contribution may be made in excess of the annual allowance or 100% of earnings, perhaps from a golden handshake on loss of office, and attract tax relief. If the lifetime allowance is exceeded by such a contribution, the lifetime allowance charge will arise on the amount of the excess.

Tax reliefs on member contributions   4.13

Tax reliefs on member contributions will normally operate through the PAYE net pay system. There are alternative methods, but the member cannot choose the method which shall apply as it is determined by the method the pension scheme is allowed to operate under the legislation. Details are given in RPSM05101320 and RPSM05101370, and a summary is given below. The methods are as follows:

Relief at source (RAS)

Under RAS, an individual may make a relievable pension contribution after deducting a sum equal to the basic rate of income tax. The administrator may claim the payment from HMRC, which is credited to the pension fund. This means that the individual who makes a tax-relievable contribution of £100 would actually pay £78 to the pension scheme, at present rates. The amount of £22 can be claimed by the administrator who will then credit the member with a contribution of £100 into the scheme.

Higher-rate taxpayers must normally claim the extra relief through the self-assessment tax return system. Relief is given by extending the individual's basic rate limit by the amount of the contributions.

This method is used by individuals who are entitled to tax relief on a maximum of £3,600 of contributions because they have no relevant UK earnings chargeable to tax, or their relevant UK earnings chargeable to tax are less than the basic amount of £3,600.

Any person other than the employer or a former employer who contributes in respect of a member, where RAS is in point, shall gross the contribution up at standard tax rate (and higher relief will be available, where appropriate).

Net pay arrangements

The net pay arrangement has been in place for many years, and the present method is unchanged. This is the procedure whereby an employer deducts the contribution from an individual's employment taxable income before operating PAYE. There is a new term for such a contribution, which is 'relievable pension contribution'.

Tax relief is enjoyed by the individual at their marginal rate of income tax without needing to make an additional claim – unless, exceptionally, full relief cannot be given through the operation of net pay. So, if a member makes a relievable pension contribution of £100 the employer will deduct £100 from the individual's employment income and pay £100 into the pension scheme.

Relief on making a claim

This approach means that no relief is given to the member when the contribution is paid. The individual makes contributions to the scheme and claims tax relief on their relievable pension contributions. So, where an individual makes a relievable pension contribution of £100, £100 will be paid to the scheme. The individual then claims the tax relief from HMRC. Relief is given by way of a deduction from the individual's total income.

A person who contributes under a net pay arrangement can claim tax relief under self-assessment, PAYE coding or a repayment claim.

Contracting out   4.14

The pre A-Day tax treatment of payments which HMRC was required to make to an individual's appropriate personal pension scheme, ie because they have contracted out of S2P, will continue. The amount of the minimum contributions payable by HMRC is determined in accordance with DWP legislation.

Migrants   4.15

The overseas rules have been greatly relaxed, in keeping largely with the European IORPs Directive (see **CHAPTER 9**). Individuals who joined a scheme and who were resident in the UK at some time in the last five years will qualify for tax relief against UK chargeable earnings (*Ch 4, s 189, Finance Act 2004*). Where an employer makes a contribution to a qualifying overseas pension scheme in respect of migrant members, the contribution will be allowable as a deduction from the employer's profits liable to tax when the relevant benefits are paid to the employee or former employee.

Pension annuity contracts and retirement annuity contracts   4.16

Pension annuity contracts and retirement annuity contracts will be brought within PAYE from 6 April 2007.

Transfers of shares   4.17

The transfer of certain shares into a registered scheme may be treated as member contributions under *s 195*.

Electronic payment   4.18

Schedule 10, Finance Act 2005, inserts a new *s 255A* into the *Finance Act 2004* under the heading 'Electronic payment'. This states that: 'The Board of Inland

Revenue may give directions requiring specified persons to use electronic means for the making of specified payments required to be made under or by virtue of this Part'.

Chapter 5
Investments

Background sources to the investment rules

UK tax rules 5.1

The new simplified tax regime provides exciting new investment prospects for many pension schemes and arrangements with effect from A–Day. There is also transitional protection for existing investments held as at that date, as described in **CHAPTER 6**. However, although most investment restrictions, such as residential property, have now been removed for registered schemes (with an exception for self-directed schemes – see **5.18** below), there are still some which apply.

The new regime will impose few restrictions on the type of asset in which schemes can invest, although there will be tax charges in relation to certain types of investment; for example, those aimed at taking value out of the pension scheme. There will be a single set of investment rules for tax purposes, applying to all types of scheme.

Other UK law, and EU law 5.2

Investments are subject to the requirements of the DWP and any relevant EU constraints. There are important rules which must be taken into consideration. It is not possible to look at the tax rules in isolation in this field (see **5.4–5.33** below).

Trust law and the prudent man principle 5.3

General trust law requires the trustees to act prudently, conscientiously and honestly when making decisions in respect of a scheme of which they are trustees. Trustees should at all times act in the best interests of scheme members in their capacity as trustees and not as employees, shareholders etc. Additionally, investment actions must be taken on a commercial basis. For further information and guidance trustees should seek independent financial advice. HMRC has stated on the *Registered Pension Schemes Manual* website that it expects these principles to be upheld. Effectively, a fiduciary duty of care is expected to be exercised even though registered pension schemes need not be established under trust.

The prudent man principle under UK trust law also appears as an underlying principle in Article 18 of the IORPs Directive, wherein it is referred to as a 'prudent person approach' (see **5.32** below).

Tax reliefs   5.4

The pre A-Day tax reliefs on scheme funds continue post A-Day, with some modifications, for registered pension schemes (see **CHAPTER 8** for registration details). The relief provisions are described in *ss 186* and *187, Finance Act 2004*.

The main exemptions from income tax are as follows:

- income derived from investments or deposits held for the purposes of the scheme (*s 186, Finance Act 2004*);

- underwriting commissions applied for the purposes of the scheme if they would otherwise be chargeable to tax under Case VI of Schedule D (*s 186(1)(b), Finance Act 2004*);

- profits or gains arising from transactions in certificates of deposit (*s 56, Income and Corporation Taxes Act 1988*);

- profits from sale and repurchase agreements (repos) and manufactured payments (*Manufactured Payments and Transfer of Securities (Tax Relief) Regulations 1995 (SI 1995/3036)*).

The main exemption from capital gains tax is on gains arising from the disposal of investments held for the purposes of the scheme (*s 271, Taxation of Capital Gains Act 1992*). This includes income from futures contracts and options contracts (which are deemed to all be from investments, as is any income derived from transactions relating to futures contracts or options contracts (*s 186(3), Finance Act 2004*)).

Permitted and prohibited investments

Summary of the main rules   5.5

As from A-Day reliance is mainly placed on the prudence, and compliance with the statutory duties, of trustees or administrators, as the determining factor on new investments (see **5.3** above). The main rules are:

1. in accordance with the EU IORPs Directive 2003/41/EC, shareholdings in the sponsoring company and associated/connected companies continue to be limited to 5% of the fund value (see **5.32**(*f*) below). This was also the previous position under the *Occupational Pension Schemes (Investment of Scheme's Resources) Regulations 1992 (SI 1992/246)*;

2. the EU IORPs Directive contains certain exemptions for schemes with fewer than 100 members (see **5.32**–**5.33** below);

3. trading income is taxable under the self-assessment procedure (see **5.28** below);

4. underwriting commissions applied for the purposes of a scheme are not liable to income tax;

5. income derived from investments or deposits held as a member of a property investment LLP is liable to tax, as previously;

6. pre A-Day investments remain subject to the rules at the time (although any alteration to a loan will be treated as a new loan);

7. non-commercial use of assets by a member or associate will attract a benefit-in-kind charge on the member;

8. proportionate sanctions will be put in place to ensure compliance and for wind-up;

9. member loans are prohibited (this means that personal pension schemes and retirement annuities that have no sponsoring employer are unable to make loans to their members' businesses or partnerships where a partner is the scheme member) – loans to third parties are, however, permitted, but they must be on fully commercial terms;

10. borrowing must not exceed 50% of fund value (see *ss 182–185, Finance Act 2004*, the meaning of 'borrowing' in *s 163, Finance Act 2004*, and the conditions which are described in **5.6** below);

11. debts between the scheme, the employer or the member must be on commercial terms, and unpaid debts shall be taxed as unauthorised payments;

12. all investments, including loans to third parties, must be on commercial terms, not remove value from the fund, and annuities must not provide for a return of the balance of insurance funds on death except in circumstances described in **CHAPTER 2** – breaches shall be taxed as unauthorised payments;

13. *section 179, Finance Act 2004,* permits loans of up to 50% of fund value to the employer (but see **5.10** below).

Further details are given under the appropriate headings below.

Borrowing 5.6

There is no restriction on the source of any borrowing which may be undertaken by a scheme. Accordingly, monies can be borrowed from a member, or a person or business connected to the member, provided that this is done at a commercial rate.

The method of calculating the maximum level of scheme borrowing 5.7

The maximum level of 50% of the net market value of the fund is calculated prior to the borrowing event taking place. This must be aggregated with any borrowing previously taken, but the value of the fund need not include the investment that is to be purchased with the borrowing. Any excess amount of the loan that results will be subject to the schemes sanction charge (see **7.6** below). Any further restrictions which may be applied by the *Pensions Act 2004* see **5.32–5.33** below) shall also apply. The scheme sanction charge is chargeable upon the administrator.

Employer transactions with a scheme 5.8

An employer or member's business may transact with a registered pension scheme by purchasing or selling assets to or from that scheme provided that this is done on an arms-length commercial basis. If this condition is not met the unauthorised payment charge will be incurred.

Liquidity 5.9

The *Registered Pension Schemes Manual* (RPSM07101030) states the following:

'When deciding the scheme's investment policy, the administrators/ trustees will need to bear carefully in mind the need to have sufficient liquid funds to pay pension benefits?

For example, investment in land and buildings may be a good long-term investment when the *members* are many years from retirement but becomes less appropriate as their retirement approaches, particularly where the scheme has only one or two members. Even if the purchase of the member's, widow's/widower's or *dependant's* annuity is deferred, it is appropriate to ensure that the scheme is in a position to buy an annuity or provide benefits in the form of *Alternatively Secured Pension* without becoming involved in a forced sale of property. This is particularly so if the property purchased is an important part of the employer's own commercial premises or even the member's own residential property and thus potentially difficult to realise.'

This is commensurate with what is to be expected of trustees in the exercise of their fiduciary duty care under trust law. Of course, the new tax regime does not require schemes to be held under trust, and so it is important that the prudent man principle is separately stated, and this is further required by EU law.

Loans to the employer   5.10

Loans may be made to the sponsoring employer or any party unconnected to the member. Despite the availability of loans to the employer under the *Finance Act 2004*, the *Occupational Pension Schemes (Investment of Scheme's Resources) Regulations 1992 (SI 1992/246)* treated such loans as 'employer-related investments'. The *Occupational Pension Schemes (Investment) Regulations 1996 (SI 1996/3127)* further restricted employer-related investments (subject to certain investments, transitional provisions and loans that became employer-related and multi-employer schemes) to the effect that:

1. no more than 5% of the current market value of the resources of a scheme could at any time be invested in employer-related investments; and

2. none of the resources of a scheme could at any time be invested in any employer-related loan.

These regulations have now been revoked and are replaced by the *Occupational Pension Schemes (Investment) Regulations 2005 (SI 2005/3378)*. The way in which the EU IORPs Directive 2003/41/EC and the UK regulations apply in this area, including the small schemes exemption, is described in **5.32–5.33** below. The other requirements of the *Finance Act 2004* concerning such loans are:

- employer loans are permitted up to five years' duration – it may be rolled over once for a maximum period of five years, subject to **5.11** below;

- loans must be secured against assets of at least equal value;

- any amounts which exceed 50% of total fund value (or are otherwise unauthorised employer payments) will be taxed at 40%;

- under the *Registered Pension Schemes (Prescribed Interest Rates for Authorised Employer Loans) Regulations 2005 (SI 2005/3449)* a loan reference rate must be charged, being an average of the base rates of a specified group of banks (the rate is 1% more than the reference rate – high street bank rates – found on the reference date preceding the start of the period (that is, on 6 April)).

Employer loan roll-over 5.11

The facility to roll-over a loan which is described in **5.10** above may only be used in cases where an employer is having genuine difficulties making repayments and there is an amount of capital or interest outstanding at the end of the loan period.

No sponsoring employer 5.12

If the pension scheme is not an occupational pension scheme there will be no sponsoring employer. This means that any loans made by the scheme to an employer who is connected to the member will attract a tax charge on the member.

Pre A-Day loans to employer 5.13

Pre A-Day loans continue to be governed by their existing terms, provided that there are no changes to the repayment terms. If a change is made, any amount owing (including interest) is subject to the new rules.

Surcharges and sanctions 5.14

Surcharges and sanctions may be imposed if the provisions are abused and, where high levels of unauthorised payments are made, the registration of the scheme may be withdrawn (see **CHAPTER 7**).

Statutory sources 5.15

The main statutory sources are:

- *Schedule 30, Finance Act 2004*, contains various loan definitions and explains the treatment of unauthorised payments;

- *Schedule 36, Pt 4, para 38*, describes the transitional arrangements for loans;

- the meaning of a 'loan' is given in *s 162*.

Pension Protection Fund tax regulation 5.16

The *Pension Protection Fund (Tax) (2005–06) Regulations 2005 (SI 2005/1907)* came into force on 3 August 2005. Gains and losses accruing on disposals of investments held by the Board of the Pension Protection Fund for the purposes of the Pension Protection Fund or the Fraud Compensation Fund are not chargeable gains or allowable losses. This is because the Fund is treated in the same way as a tax-exempt scheme. Additionally, the transfer of the loan relationships held by the Pensions Compensation Board to the Board of the Pension Protection Fund has no tax consequences. The draft Pension Protection Fund (Tax) Regulations 2006 contain provisions for the required changes to be made to the tax legislation in order to accommodate the provisions of the Fund.

Property **5.17**

As stated in **5.1** above, there are new property investment prospects for schemes, including the removal of many restrictions, such as residential property purchases. The property rules and changes are described below.

1. If a residential property is let, the rent could (subject to the annual allowance and lifetime allowance) be invested in the member's scheme on a tax-free basis. It is possible that profit achieved by capital growth could also be invested in the fund without incurring capital gains tax. The member will, however, suffer a tax charge if he invests in his own residential property.

2. From 6 April 2004 disposals of assets, while retaining the ability to use them, attract income tax on the retained benefit. Although the changes are retrospective to 1986, there are some wider exemptions than were anticipated. There will be an exemption for spouses who now own the disposed property, and for taxpayers who receive full market value for a disposal in cash. Additionally, there are exemptions where an enjoyment is retained following a part disposal, such as the remaining in residence of a domestic property by an elderly parent.

3. Disposals of properties to trusts, in order to avoid inheritance tax by the person living in them, has previously been possible by way of home-loan schemes. The occupier sells the house to a trust, and receives an IOU from the trustees which he gives to heirs through another trust. He then continues to live in the house. It was stated in the Budget 2004 that these arrangements can be unscrambled. If they are not, income tax will be charged on the resident on the benefit-in-kind value of residency.

4. General care must be taken if scheme assets are enjoyed by a member or a member's family or household. Such a benefit is likely, subject to regulations, to be taxed as an unauthorised payment (see **5.19** below, and *s 173, Finance Act 2004*).

Residential property **5.18**

The government has certainly become a little uncomfortable with the effect of 'opening up' the residential property market from A-Day. This is reflected in the *Registered Pension Schemes Manual* (RPSM07101060), which states:

'Using a *registered pension scheme* to invest in a buy to let residential property or holiday home or any other type of residential property may have the following consequences:

- The property becomes an asset of the pension fund and there is a requirement to put all rental income into the pension fund so it is locked away and cannot be accessed until authorised benefits are paid.

- If the property is made available to a member of the scheme or members of their family it will give rise to a benefits in kind tax charge if a market rent is not paid (even if they choose not to use it).

- Any property bought by the pension fund in most cases will need to be sold before the pension can be drawn, to provide a secured income in retirement.

- Only 25% of the capital in the pension *arrangement* will be able to be extracted as a lump sum, the remainder will be locked in the pension to be drawn out over the period of retirement.

- Borrowing to fund a property purchase cannot exceed 50% of the value of the pension arrangement.

- Although any rental income or capital gains from the disposal of the property will be tax free in the pension fund when the money is paid as a pension it will be taxable at the members marginal rate of tax. Depending on the rate of tax this may well be higher than the rate that would be paid if the disposal were subject to the CGT [capital gains tax] regime after the property has been held for 7 years.

- Putting any previously-owned property into the pension scheme will trigger any unrealised chargeable gain on the property, and transaction costs such as stamp duty.

- Maximum tax relief on contributions made in any year is 100% of UK chargeable earnings, subject to an *annual allowance* set initially at £215,000. Tax relieved pension savings are also subject to a *lifetime allowance* initially set at £1.5 million.'

The main government concern is that many members could tie up most of their pension entitlement in a property which is vulnerable to market change, and will be catapulted onto the market at retirement date. Furthermore, the government stated in August 2005 that investment in residential property in SIPPs could result in individuals losing out. HMRC has stated that the concept was 'a realistic proposition for only those with the largest pension pots' and that, for most people, residential property will not be an appropriate investment. For those with very large funds, the assets can be widely diversified. Additionally, for schemes without trustees, there will be a need for the administrator to act in a prudent matter in such cases.

A recent survey by YouGov (on behalf of Instant Access Properties) found that almost two-fifths of Britons say they have lost faith in the private pension system and that it would take 'an act of God or the Government' to change their minds. However, as the research found also that approximately 44% believe that investing in property would provide the best return for retirement, the new opportunity to invest in property from A-Day may prove to be positive for new and ongoing pension provision.

The pre-Budget Report Technical Note, dated 5 December 2005, reflects the latest government thinking on simplification in respect of 'registered pension schemes which are self-directed'. This document is, in particular, largely seen as demonstrating a significant U-turn on the property investment opportunities of SIPPs and SSASs. The stated purpose of the change in direction is to avoid the misuse of schemes for buying second homes.

The main statement on tax avoidance in general observes that:

- SIPPs 'will be prohibited from obtaining tax advantages when investing in residential property and certain other assets such as fine wines' from A-Day;

- there will be changes to the disclosure of tax avoidance scheme regime, effective from A-Day;

- there will be further measures to tackle inheritance tax avoidance schemes, effective from 5 December 2005 (mainly concerning the purchase of second-hand interests in foreign trusts, and 'reverter-to-settlor' trust arrangements); and

- there will be changes to stop UK-resident individuals avoiding tax by exploiting offshore companies and trusts with effect from 5 December 2005.

Use of an asset by a member   5.19

Whereas there is no bar on a member or any of his or her family or household using a scheme asset, the asset will as a consequence of that usage be taxed as an unauthorised payment (any amount which the member may have paid towards the use of the asset, for example rent, will be taken into account when calculating the charge). The employer and/or the member can rent properties owned by the scheme at a commercial rate. If a commercial rate of rent is not paid an unauthorised payment tax charge will be incurred on the shortfall.

The meaning of a *member of family* includes:

- a member's spouse;

- a member's children and their spouses;

- a member's parents;

- a member's dependants.

The meaning of *member's of a household* is:

- a member's domestic staff;
- a member's guests.

It is the member who will be liable for any tax charge incurred.

Purchase of an asset from a pension scheme by a member   5.20

A member, or anyone connected with that member, may buy an asset from his or her pension scheme on an arms-length basis (meaning at a commercial rate). If this condition is not met an unauthorised payment charge will be levied on the difference between the amount paid and the actual value of the asset.

Reporting requirements

Reporting payments or enjoyment of benefits-in-kind   5.21

Where a member or other connected person enjoys use of an asset belonging to his or her scheme (eg living accommodation or vehicles) the benefit-in-kind is an unauthorised payment. The administrator is required to provide the member with details of any such payments by 7 July following the end of the tax year in which they are made. A cash equivalent is calculated in the same way as if an employer were providing the benefit-in-kind to the employee, which includes deducting from the unauthorised payment any amount which the member pays to the scheme for the use of the asset.

Reports to be made to the scheme administrator   5.22

The *Registered Pension Schemes Manual* provides details of reportable activities by the administrator. These are to be found in the links under RPSM12301000. Further details are given in **CHAPTER 8**. The main reports are identified as:

- all unauthorised payments, including details concerning any benefits-in-kind;

- the details which are required under a notice given by HMRC to make and deliver a registered pension scheme return, on which will need to be disclosed details of the following:

  - borrowing;

  - connected party transactions;

  - acquisition/disposal of shares held in a sponsoring employer;

  - acquisition/disposal of land/property to or from a connected party;

  - loans;

  - other assets acquired/disposed of at arms-length.

Where a tax charge becomes due the administrator must complete an accounting for tax return. This must be completed in each quarter in which a chargeable event occurs. A 'quarter' is a three-month period ending on the 31 March, 30 June, 30 September and 31 December. The final end date for the return and the tax due is 45 days from the end of the quarterly return period. This return does not apply to liability for the schemes sanction charge, for which an assessment will be raised by HMRC. Any other tax on scheme income will be payable through the scheme's self-assessment return.

The administrator must report all unauthorised payments to HMRC by 31 January following the end of the tax year in which the payment was made. Interest is due on any tax paid late and surcharges may also be due. There are also penalties for fraudulently or negligently making an incorrect return.

Reports required to be made by the employer   **5.23**

Where the administrator informs the employer that an unauthorised payment has been made to the employer, the employer must notify HMRC by no later than 31 January following the end of the tax year in which the payment was made.

The details required are:

- the scheme that made the payment;

- the nature of the payment;

- the amount of the payment;

- the date on which the payment was made.

This notice must be made to the office that deals with the corporation tax affairs of the company. Interest, surcharges and penalties may be incurred, as for the administrator in **5.22** above.

Reports of unauthorised payments by the member 5.24

Where a member receives an annual self-assessment tax return, he should declare any unauthorised payments on that return. If a member does not receive such a return, he should inform his local tax office by 5 October following the end of the tax year in which he received the unauthorised payment. If the deadline is missed any tax which has not been paid by the following 31 January will attract interest and penalties.

Sale of assets to scheme by a member 5.25

It is permitted for a member to sell an asset on a commercial basis to his or her pension scheme. If the sale is not done on an arms-length basis a tax charge may arise. Additionally, capital gains tax may be payable on the sale of asset and the transactions should be declared on the individual's self-assessment tax return. The HMRC leaflet CGT1 provides further information.

Shares 5.26

A scheme may freely invest in quoted or unquoted shares. The restriction which applies to the purchase of shares in the sponsoring employer means less than 5% of the net fund value at the date of purchase, whether or not the shares are quoted. Where there is more than one employer this 5% limit applies to each of them separately providing that the total invested is less than 20% of the fund. The *Registered Pension Schemes Manual* (RPSM07300100) states that: 'The scheme could own 100% of the shares in one employer provided that the cost of them equates to less than 5% of the net fund value. These limits would not apply to a scheme that is not an occupational scheme as there is no sponsoring employer and therefore no limit on share purchase.'

SSASs and SIPPs 5.27

Simplification has not been kind to new SSASs, in particular. The government feels that SSASs do not offer good protection for members in the event of the failure of the sponsoring business. Additionally, it sees no need to retain the special status of a pensioneer trustee for SSASs, although of course the social security legislation requires independent trustees to be appointed in some cases. However, the transitional rules ensure that existing investments of SSASs and SIPPs may be retained subject to the conditions described in **CHAPTER 6**, which indicates that the special expertise of pensioneer trustees will be required for some time to come.

On a more positive note for SSASs, the small schemes exemptions which are described in **5.32–5.33** below remain a considerable attraction, and the property investment opportunities go a long way to ensuring the survival of SIPPs in the marketplace. The exemptions that apply where all members are trustees (which mainly concern SSASs) will continue.

SIPPs were not previously permitted to hold unquoted shares unless they were acquired as a contribution from an approved share scheme. This facility has been carried over into the new pensions regime in respect of shares received from a SAYE. The absence of loan-back facilities will be a relevant consideration for current SSAS members who are considering transferring to a SIPPs.

SIPPs will also need to look carefully at their investments under the new freedoms; for example, they may find themselves liable for any health and safety violations at buy-to-let residential properties held in a SIPP after A-day. Also, some schemes, for example SIPPs, allow the member to direct how contributions are invested. Members may make choices about what assets are bought, leased or sold and decide when those assets are acquired or disposed of.

Trading   5.28

Registered schemes may undertake trading activities. Any income arising from such activity is not categorised as investment income or income from deposits. Accordingly, tax exemptions, including those relating to capital gains on assets used by a scheme for trading purposes, do not apply. This means that the scheme will be liable to pay tax on any income derived from a trading activity.

The *Registered Pension Schemes Manual* (RPSM07101050) states:

> 'Whether a transaction constitutes trading transaction is a question of fact and HMRC will not normally give a view on this in advance of a transaction being carried out. Trading income of a registered pension scheme must be returned on a Self-Assessment Tax Return.'

Value shifting   5.29

Where a scheme transacts with a connected party (eg the member or employer) at less than commercial rate the unauthorised payment charge will be incurred. If the method of passing value from a scheme is adopted without making any payments the charge will still be incurred.

It is envisaged that value shifting can be achieved in a number of ways, including increasing the value of an asset or decreasing the liability of a member or employer without creating a payment. The main concern is transactions which are made on a *non arms-length* basis. The meaning of this term is tied in with that of the meaning of *connected parties*. There are three connected parties which must be brought in for the arms-length test. These are categories A, B or C. The meaning of these terms is as follows:

- *Category A:* transactions between the scheme, the member or the sponsoring employer.

- *Category B:* transactions between the scheme and persons connected with members and/or connected employers (*connected* means as defined in *s 839, Income and Corporation Taxes Act 1988*).

- *Category C:* transactions between the scheme and a third party which is directly or indirectly for the benefit of the member or sponsoring employer.

HMRC requires scheme trustees to ensure that when connected party transactions are made they take a sensible, commercial and prudent course and obtain relevant valuations from suitably qualified valuers. A working example is given in the *Registered Pension Schemes Manual* (RPSM07102130) as follows:

'A scheme sells an asset worth £1m to a member at a price of £500,000. There is value passed to the member of £500,000 and this amount will be taxed as an unauthorised payment.'

Waivers of debt   5.30

Any member debt which is waived will be treated as a loan to the member and will be taxed as an unauthorised payment.

Wasting assets   5.31

A tax charge may be incurred if a scheme invests in wasting assets. A wasting asset is described in **7.6** below. If a member or any of his or her household have personal use of such an asset, it is the scheme administrator who will be liable for the tax charge (the scheme sanction charge). The scheme member shall also be subject to a tax charge on the receipt of the benefit.

DWP and EU pension investment requirements

The Occupational Pensions Schemes (Investment) Regulations 2005   5.32

On 21 March 2005 the DWP issued a consultative document entitled *Pensions: Investment Requirements*. This document related to the draft Occupational

Pensions Schemes (Investment) Regulations 2005. These regulations have now been made, and are entitled the *Occupational Pension Schemes (Investment) Regulations 2005 (SI 2005/3378)*. They revoke the *Occupational Pension Schemes (Investment) Regulations 1996 (SI 1996/3127)*, and supplement changes made to the *Pensions Act 1995* by the *Pensions Act 2004*.

The purpose of the consultation was to seek views on proposals to implement certain requirements of the EU Directive on the Activities and Supervision of Institutions for Occupational Retirement Provision (IORPs) 2003/41/EC. The main topics were:

- a 'prudent person approach', as the underlying principle for capital investment, in accordance with Article 18 of the IORPs Directive;

- a written statement of investment policy principles, under Article 12 (*s 35, Pensions Act 1995* refers);

- investment restrictions and requirements, including where there is more than one employer.

The regulations contain appropriate provisions, including:

(*a*)   Assets must be invested in the best interests of members and beneficiaries; and in the case of a potential conflict of interest, in the sole interest of members and beneficiaries.

(*b*)   The powers of investment, or the discretion, must be exercised in a manner calculated to ensure the security, quality, liquidity and profitability of the portfolio as a whole.

(*c*)   Assets must consist predominantly of investments admitted to trading on regulated markets, and other investments must be kept to a prudent level. There must also be diversification of assets, and special rules apply to derivatives and collective investment schemes.

(*d*)   The requirements of the IORPs Directive are adopted in a proportionate and flexible manner, where appropriate using the 'small scheme exemption' which is contained in Article 5. Schemes with fewer than 100 active and deferred members are exempted from much of the requirements of the regulations, but are still required to have regard to the need for diversification on investment rule.

(*e*)   A triennial review of the statement of investment principles is required. The previous requirements on the statement's contents are largely restated.

(*f*)   Trustees must consider 'proper advice' on the suitability of a proposed investment, and there are specific requirements in relation to borrowing and a restriction on investment in the 'sponsors' undertaking' to no more than 5% of the portfolio (where a group is concerned, the percentage is no greater than 20%).

The Occupational Pension Schemes (Trust and Retirement Benefits Exemption) Regulations 2005

5.33

The *Occupational Pension Schemes (Trust and Retirement Benefits Exemption) Regulations 2005 (SI 2005/2360)* have been made. They prescribe the description of schemes which are exempt from:

1.   the requirement in s 252(2), *Pensions Act 2004*, that trustees or managers of an occupational pension scheme with its main administration in the UK must not accept funding payments unless the scheme is established under irrevocable trust;

2.   the requirement in s 255(1) of the Act that an occupational pension scheme with its main administration in the UK must be limited to retirement benefit activities.

Section 252(2) transposes Article 8 of the EU Directive on the Activities and Supervision of Institutions for Occupational Retirement Provision (IORPs) 2003/41/EC (Article 8 requires legal separation of the assets of an occupational pension scheme and those of a sponsoring employer).

Section 255(1) transposes Article 7 of the Directive (Article 7 requires that occupational pension schemes are limited to retirement benefit activities).

Chapter 6
Protection for pre
A-Day rights

Introduction
6.1

One of the criticisms of the pre A-Day pension tax rules was that every time they were changed, the change only applied to employees joining an occupational scheme after the date of the change, thereby creating a complexity and inequality that the *Finance Act 2004* now seeks to do away with. Unlike previous Finance Acts which introduced new occupational pension tax regimes, the *Finance Act 2004* does *not* allow those who enjoyed benefit accrual under a previous tax regime to continue to be pensioned under that basis in the future.

Given that the pension provisions of the *Finance Act 2004* are effectively retrospective, it was recognised that some protection for rights already accrued would have to be introduced. Two general protection principles were devised.

Enhanced protection and primary protection – general overview
6.2

Enhanced protection would allow scheme members to retain, subject to conditions, their accrued rights without fear of penalty under the new lifetime and annual allowances. Those conditions, however, include a requirement that no further relevant benefit, as defined, accrues to them.

Primary protection on the other hand would allow members to accrue further benefits and would provide a simple protection on accrued rights by offering an uplift to an individual's lifetime allowance in the form of a lifetime allowance enhancement factor based on the amount of pension rights already accrued at A-Day.

Protection for lump sums – general overview
6.3

In addition to these rules on the amount of protected pension, some form of protection for accrued tax-free lump sums was also called for. The treatment of lump sum entitlements will depend on the size of the lump sum and whether an individual has primary protection, enhanced protection or no pension protection at all.

Protection for accrued rights – general overview   6.4

Finally, there were some other types of accrued benefit rights which would exist on 5 April 2006 but which would be adversely affected under the new tax regime if nothing was done to protect them. These are described at the end of this chapter.

The regulatory sources   6.5

The major transitional protections are found in *Sch 36, Finance Act 2004*, as amended by the *Finance Act 2005*, statutory instruments issued under that *Schedule*, and Chapter 3 of the *Registered Pension Schemes Manual*.

Primary protection

Conditions for protection   6.6

Primary protection is available for any individual if the amount of their relevant pension rights exceeded £1.5m on 5 April 2006 and they have notified HMRC of their intention to rely on primary protection before 6 April 2009.

Pension rights are relevant if they derive from:

(a) a retirement benefit scheme approved under *Ch I, Part XIV, Income and Corporation Taxes Act 1988*;

(b) a scheme formerly approved under *s 208, Income and Corporation Taxes Act 1970*;

(c) a relevant statutory scheme;

(d) a *s 32* policy;

(e) a parliamentary pension fund;

(f) a retirement annuity contract (also known as a *s 226* annuity); or

(g) a personal pension scheme approved under *Ch IV, Part XIV, Income and Corporation Taxes Act 1988*.

Rights built up in a pre A-Day funded or unfunded unapproved retirement benefit scheme (FURBS or UURBS) do not count as relevant pension rights, nor does any entitlement to a pension which arises upon the death of another. Furthermore, the value of uncrystallised relevant pension rights must not exceed the maximum approvable limit by reference to the appropriate tax regime applicable to each of an individual's occupational pension scheme rights on 5 April 2006 (see below).

Valuation of rights at A-Day 6.7

The method by which existing rights are valued depends on whether or not they have come into payment. Where rights have come into payment, they are valued as 25 times the annual rate of pension that is being paid. Note that any lump sum already paid is not taken into account; this is already catered for by multiplying the pension in payment by 25 instead of 20. There is no need to test pensions in payment against HMRC pre A-Day limits as this will already have been done when the benefits were brought into payment.

Where the rights in payment are in the form of income drawdown, they are valued as 25 times the maximum annual rate of drawdown that could be received on 5 April 2006. For this purpose it is not necessary to obtain a new drawdown valuation as at 5 April 2006; the maximum rate established at the last review is sufficient. The following two examples are reproduced from RPSM03101040:

'Example 1

An individual is drawing a pension of £5,000 under drawdown, but the maximum annual rate of this pension is £10,000. The value of the crystallised rights in these circumstances is £250,000 (25 x £10,000 = £250,000).

The same principle applies in the case of an individual taking income withdrawal from a personal pension scheme.

Example 2

Alan had a fund of £1.6 million. He took a lump sum of £400,000 in January 2006. From the remaining fund of £1.2 million he takes a pension of £91,200 a year under income drawdown. This is the maximum pension that could have been taken under income drawdown. (Alan is assumed to be age 60 and gilt yields are assumed to be 4.5% per annum.)

Alan's pension is therefore valued at £2,280,000 (25 x £91,200 = £2,280,000).'

The valuation of rights which have not yet come into payment depends on the type of arrangement from which they derive (money purchase, cash balance, defined benefits or hybrid – see **3.3** above).

For money purchase arrangements, which includes both personal pensions and occupational defined contribution schemes, the value of a member's uncrystallised rights is the sum of any cash held under the scheme and the market value of the other assets held to provide the member's benefits on 5 April 2006.

For a cash balance scheme, the value of a member's uncrystallised rights is the amount that would be available for the provision of immediate benefit if the member had been entitled to receive it on 5 April 2006. For this purpose it is assumed that the member is in good physical and mental health and has reached either age 60, or, if a different age was specified in the arrangement at 10 December 2003 as the minimum age at which benefits could be paid without reduction, that age.

For a defined benefits arrangement, the value of a member's uncrystallised rights is calculated by the formula:

(RVF x ARP) + LS

where:

RVF is the relevant valuation factor (ie 20);

ARP is the annual rate of pension the member would be entitled to if he or she acquired an actual rather than a prospective right to receive it on 5 April 2006; and

LS is the amount of lump sum the member would have received otherwise than by commutation (ie only if the scheme provides separate pension and lump sum).

As for cash balance arrangements, it is assumed that the member is in good physical and mental health and has reached either age 60, or, if a different age was specified in the arrangement at 10 December 2003 as the minimum age at which benefits could be paid without reduction, that age.

In a hybrid arrangement the value of uncrystallised rights is simply calculated on whichever of the bases produces the highest result.

Note, however, that the value of uncrystallised rights must be restricted to comply with pre A-Day HMRC limits where those rights derive from an occupational pension scheme in the following list:

(*a*)   a retirement benefit scheme approved for the purpose of *Ch I, Pt XIV, Income and Corporation Taxes Act 1988*;

(b)   a scheme formerly approved under *s 208, Income and Corporation Taxes Act 1970*;

(c)   a relevant statutory scheme as defined in *s 611A, Income and Corporation Taxes Act 1988*, or a pension scheme treated by HMRC as if it were such a scheme; or

(d)   an deferred annuity contract securing benefits under any of the three types of scheme above.

The restriction is expressed by the formula:

20 x MPP

where:

MPP is the maximum permitted pension that could be paid to the individual on 5 April 2006 under the arrangement without giving HMRC grounds for withdrawing tax approval.

In arriving at MPP it is assumed that the member is in good physical and mental health and has reached either age 60, or, if a different age was specified in the arrangement at 10 December 2003 as the minimum age at which benefits could be paid without reduction, that age. For a member still in service on 5 April 2006, it is assumed that he or she left employment on that date.

As an example, if a member of a defined benefit scheme was subject to the pre-1987 regime, was still in service on 5 April 2006, had 30 years' potential service to his normal retirement date and had 20 years' service accrued to 5 April 2006, his HMRC maximum permitted pension at 5 April 2006 would be calculated as the higher of:

(a) $20/60$ x final remuneration; and

(b) $20/30$ x (($40/60$ x final remuneration) – retained benefits).

In this case the member has more than 10 years' service to his normal retirement date, and, as the pre-1987 regime applies, he can therefore count on the uplifted 60ths scale, which gives him a maximum pension ('**P**') of $40/60$. Retained benefits must then be deducted, if necessary, and the result multiplied by **N/NS**, where **N** is service accrued, in this case, to 5 April 2006, and **NS** is potential service to normal retirement date (20 years and 30 years respectively in this example). (See para 7.47 of the Practice Notes IR12 (2001).)

Retained benefits do not have to be taken into account if the member's P60 earnings from pensionable employment did not exceed £50,000 in the 2004/05 tax year, even for controlling directors. If pensionable service did not continue for the whole of the 2004/05 tax year, a pro rata calculation applies. If pensionable service ceased before 6 April 2004, retained benefits do not have to be taken into account if P60 earnings in the last complete tax year before the date of leaving did not exceed £25,000. Retained benefits may also be ignored under the administrative easements described in paras 7.5–7.7 of the Practice Notes.

Note that HMRC limits are subject to the requirements of the preservation legislation. This means that it will not always be possible to restrict **MPP** to the **N/60** or **N/NS x (P-RB)** formulae above. This is an especially important consideration for members of occupational money purchase pension schemes. For example, the maximum permitted pension for a member of such a scheme approved after 1991 would be the pension he could have received if he had retired on ill-health grounds at the date of leaving, i e using potential service up to his normal retirement date.

In an occupational money purchase pension scheme the calculation of **MPP** should be carried out on the appropriate preservation basis depending on when the scheme was approved. The appropriate preservation basis will be the version of HMRC's limits calculation that was set out in the Practice Notes IR12 at the time of approval. There are three versions for this calculation and the following extracts are taken from RPSM03101550, RPSM03101560 and RPSM03101570:

Version 1 – schemes approved before 1 October 1989

'A scheme of the type to which Regulation 5 of the Occupational Pension Schemes (Preservation of Benefit) (No2) Regulations 1973 (SI 1973 No 1784) applies (whether or not in existence on 6 April 1974), i.e. a scheme providing benefits based on final remuneration but funded by means of a policy or policies with level annual premiums securing benefits based on current remuneration, may give a member leaving service the amount of deferred pension actually secured by premiums paid up to date of his withdrawal even if this is somewhat in excess of the amount calculated under N/NS x P formula. A money purchase scheme, or a scheme using earmarked policies must test leaving benefits against the N/NS x P formula unless

(a)   the member's earnings while a member of the scheme have not exceeded £5,000 in any year or

(b)   at the time of leaving he is less than 45 years of age or

(c)   such a restriction would infringe the preservation requirements of the Social Security Act 1973

When calculating the limit above, final remuneration shall be determined by reference to the maximum amount of earnings allowed under the rules of the scheme for the purposes of calculating the maximum retirement benefits for that individual.'

Version 2 – schemes approved after 30 September 1989 and before 1 September 1991

'Because of the preservation requirements of the Social Security Act 1973 it may not be possible for certain schemes to restrict the benefits of an early leaver by reference to the 1/60th of final remuneration or N/NS x P formula, namely:

(*a*)   scheme giving a benefit of a constant proportion of final or average earnings for each year of service, at an accrual rate greater than 1/60th.

(*b*)   money purchase schemes and insured level annual pension premium schemes set up before 6 April 1974

(*c*)   "proceeds of policy" schemes

When calculating the limit above, final remuneration shall be determined by reference to the maximum amount of earnings allowed under the rules of the scheme for the purposes of calculating the maximum retirement benefits for that individual.'

Version 3 – schemes approved on or after 1 September 1991

'The maximum benefits an approved money purchase scheme may provide at normal retirement date for a member who left pensionable service prior to that date, is a deferred pension (including the pension equivalent of any deferred lump sum benefits) of the greater of:

(*a*)   1/60th of final remuneration for each year of service (up to 40 years) increased at a fixed rate not exceeding 5% per annum compound, or by a greater percentage but restricted so as not to exceed the increase in the retail prices index during the period of deferment. And

(*b*)   the total benefit the member could have expected to receive at normal retirement date calculated on the same basis as applies for incapacity together with any statutory revaluation increases required by the relevant DWP pensions legislation. (The basis that applies for incapacity benefits is retirement benefits may be paid by the fraction of final remuneration the employee could have received had he or she remained in service until normal retirement date less the pension debit where necessary).

When calculating the limit above, final remuneration shall be determined by reference to the maximum amount of earnings allowed under the rules of the scheme for the purposes of calculating the maximum retirement benefits for that individual.'

Under primary protection where the value of uncrystallised rights is greater than **20 x MPP**, note that the excess over **20 x MPP** is not lost, nor does it have to be surrendered (as it would for enhanced protection). **20 x MPP** is simply the maximum value that can be taken into account when calculating the lifetime allowance enhancement factor. The excess rights remain in the scheme, but would obviously be more likely to be subject to a lifetime allowance charge.

Valuation of lump sum rights at A-Day 6.8

The method of valuing lump sum rights on 5 April 2006 is the same for both primary protection and enhanced protection and is expressed by the formula:

VCPR/4 + VULSR

where:

VCPR is the value of relevant crystallised pension rights; and

VULSR is the value of relevant uncrystallised lump sum rights.

VCPR is calculated as 25 times the annual rate at which any existing pension (or the sum if more than one) is currently payable on April 2006 from one or more of the following:

(*a*)   a retirement benefit scheme approved under *Ch I, Pt XIV, Income and Corporation Taxes Act 1988*;

(*b*)   a scheme formerly approved under *s 208, Income and Corporation Taxes Act 1970*;

(*c*)   a relevant statutory scheme;

(*d*)   a *s 32* policy;

(*e*)   a parliamentary pension fund;

(*f*)   a retirement annuity contract (also known as a *s 226* annuity);

(*g*)   a personal pension scheme approved under *Ch IV, Pt XIV, Income and Corporation Taxes Act 1988*; or

(*h*)   a right to make income withdrawals under *s 634A, Income and Corporation Taxes Act 1988*.

Any dependant's pension paid as a result of the death of another person is not to be taken into account. If an individual is taking income drawdown, it is valued as 25 times the maximum annual rate that could be taken. Calculating **VCPR** in this way will obviously differ from the lump sum that may actually have been taken from the arrangement in question, but is done in the interest of simplicity.

VULSR is calculated as if the member had become entitled on 5 April 2006 to the present payment of any lump sum payable under the rules of any of the arrangements mentioned in (*a*)–(*g*) above. For this purpose it is assumed that the member is in good physical and mental health and has reached either age 60, or, if a different age was specified in the arrangement at 10 December 2003 as the minimum age at which benefits could be paid without reduction, that age.

The exception is that a lump sum from a retirement annuity contract will be limited to 25% of the funds held for the purpose of the arrangement on 5 April 2006, even though a lump sum percentage higher than 25% could have been paid.

For members of occupational pension schemes the value of the lump sum is restricted by reference to the HMRC limits which applied before A-Day. For a member still in service on 5 April 2006, it is assumed that he left employment on that date. As an example, if a member was subject to the pre-1987 regime, was still in service on 5 April 2006, had 30 years' potential service to his normal retirement date and had 20 years' service accrued to 5 April 2006, his HMRC maximum lump sum at 5 April 2006 would be calculated as the higher of:

(*a*)   3/80 x 20 x final remuneration; and

(*b*)   20/30 x ((120/80 x final remuneration) – lump sum retained benefits).

In this case the member has more than 20 years' service to his normal retirement date, and, as the pre-1987 regime applies, he can therefore count on the uplifted 80ths scale, which gives him a maximum lump sum of 120/80. Lump sum retained benefits must then be deducted, if necessary, and the result multiplied by N/NS, where N is service accrued, in this case, to 5 April 2006, and **NS** is potential service to normal retirement date (20 years and 30 years respectively in this example).

Retained benefits do not have to be taken into account if the member's P60 earnings from pensionable employment did not exceed £50,000 in the 2004/05 tax year, even for controlling directors. If pensionable service did not continue for the whole of the 2004/05 tax year, a pro rata calculation applies. If pensionable service ceased before 6 April 2004, retained benefits do not have to be taken into account if P60 earnings in the last complete tax year before the date of leaving did not exceed £25,000. Retained benefits may also be ignored in the usual circumstances set out in the Practice Notes IR12 (2001). Note that consideration of retained benefits is only necessary for pre-1987 members. Lump sum retained benefits do not need to be considered for 1987–1989 regime members or for post-1989 regime members.

If lump sum rights are valued at more than £375,000 they may be included in the notification to HMRC to rely on primary and/or enhanced protection.

Calculation of enhancement factor 6.9

The lifetime allowance enhancement factor is calculated by the formula:

(RR − SLA) / SLA

where:

RR is the value of pension rights on 5 April 2006;

SLA is the standard lifetime allowance for the 2006/07 tax year (£1.5m).

For example, if the value of an individual's pension rights on 5 April 2006 was £1,830,000, his lifetime allowance enhancement factor would be 0.22:

(1,830,000 − 1,500,000) / 1,500,000 = 0.22

This means he would be entitled to a personal lifetime allowance 22% greater than the standard lifetime allowance at the time he takes benefits.

Note, however, that if primary protection applies and an individual's pension rights are decreased by a pension debit as a result of pension sharing on divorce, the lifetime allowance enhancement factor needs to be recalculated by reference to the value of rights that remain after the pension debit is deducted. If this reduces the value of rights below £1.5m then primary protection is lost and the individual will be subject to the standard £1.5m lifetime allowance.

Registration 6.10

Notification of a member's intention to rely on primary protection must be made by him or her on the appropriate form to reach HMRC by 5 April 2009. Alternatively, notification can be made online by visiting: http://www.hmrc.gov.uk. Notification of intention to rely on enhanced protection as well as on primary protection can be made at the same time, and the form will include space for notifying HMRC of lump sum entitlements greater than £375,000 on 5 April 2006. Records relating to the protection notification must be kept for at least six years.

If the form is completed by someone else on the individual's behalf, the individual must still sign the form unless he or she is physically or mentally incapable of doing so. An individual's personal representative may also sign the form if the individual has died. Once HMRC has processed the form it will issue a certificate showing the enhanced lifetime allowance.

At the time of writing the appropriate notification forms remain in draft.

Payment of pension benefits   **6.11**

The amount of a benefit crystallised at a benefit crystallisation event is usually tested against the standard lifetime allowance at the time of crystallisation. Under primary protection the crystallised amount is tested against an individual's personal lifetime allowance ie the standard lifetime allowance as increased by his or her lifetime allowance enhancement factor.

To take an example, if the standard lifetime allowance were £1.8m, an individual had an enhancement factor of 0.22, and he crystallised benefits valued at £2.1m, he would still escape the lifetime allowance charge:

Personal lifetime allowance = 1,800,000 x 1.22 = £2,196,000, which is greater than the crystallised amount of £2,100,000.

If an individual vests benefits at different times, the application of the personal lifetime allowance is operated in the same way as the standard lifetime allowance. The following example is taken from RPSM03102030:

> ### Example – protection from the lifetime allowance charge – taking benefits at different times
>
> 'Jacob had £3 million of pension rights protected under primary protection on 5 April 2006, giving an additional lifetime allowance factor of 1.
>
> He took benefits worth £1.8 million in 2011 when the standard lifetime allowance was £1.8 million. At that time, Jacob's primary protection was worth £3.6 million (standard lifetime allowance of £1.8 million plus additional lifetime allowance factor of £1.8 million). So Jacob used up 50% of his personal lifetime allowance.
>
> In 2023 Jacob took the rest of his benefits that were worth £2 million. The standard lifetime allowance (SLA) in 2023 was £2.1 million. Jacob's primary protection was then worth £4.2 million (SLA plus a factor of 1).
>
> Jacob has already used up 50% of his protection so has £2.1 million available. In taking £2 million Jacob has no *lifetime allowance charge* to pay. This is because the amount taken is within the amount of protection still available to him.'

Payment of lump sum benefits greater than £375,000   **6.12**

Where an individual has applied for primary protection and has registered lump sum rights at 5 April 2006 which are greater than £375,000, the normal

rules for calculating pension commencement lump sums at a benefit crystallisation event do not apply. Instead, the pension commencement lump sum is
calculated as the amount registered at A-Day increased by the rise in the
standard lifetime allowance between A-Day and the year in which benefits are
vested.

For example, if lump sum rights of £400,000 were registered at A-Day, and in
the year of vesting, 2010/11 say, the standard lifetime allowance had increased
to £1.8m, the maximum lump sum that could be paid is:

£400,000 x (1,800,000 / 1,500,000) = £480,000

Note that the sum registered at A-Day relates to the aggregate of all lump sum
rights that an individual may have under several pension arrangements. If lump
sums are taken from two different schemes at two different times, the protected
lump sum amount will have to be adjusted to take account of the first lump
sum paid. This is done by increasing the first lump sum in line with increases in
the standard lifetime allowance, and then deducting it from the increased
protected lump sum amount at the second payment date.

In the example above, if a £200,000 lump sum had been paid in the 2007/08
tax year when the standard lifetime allowance was £1.6m, then the maximum
lump sum that could be paid on vesting in 2010/11 would be:

(£400,000 x (1,800,000 / 1,500,000)) – (£200,000 x (1,800,000 / 1,600,000))
= £255,000

With lump sum protection under primary protection it may be possible to
transfer protected lump sum allowance from one scheme to another, and even
commute the benefits entirely from one scheme if this would still be within the
protected lump sum allowance. This of course would be subject to scheme
rules permitting such commutation. This is illustrated by the following
example from RPSM03105160:

Example – protection of lump sums with primary protection: taking benefits at more than one time – some lump sum benefits are not tax free

'Sally has lump sum rights of £1 million on 5 April 2006 and has
primary protection on pension rights of £5 million. She has rights in
two arrangements. Her lump sum rights are payable by commuting
pension rights.

She takes benefits on 3 April 2011 from the smaller of the two
arrangements. The *standard lifetime allowance* in 2010–2011 is £1.8
million. The amounts of her protected pension and lump sum have
increased in line with the increase in the standard lifetime allowance
to £6 million and £1.2 million (each amount being multiplied by
£1.8 million/£1.5 million).

As the smaller arrangement, a *money purchase arrangement*, is valued at £600,000 she chooses to take all her benefit as a lump sum.

Sally takes benefits from her second arrangement in 2017 when the standard lifetime allowance is £2.1 million. The amounts of her protected pension and lump sum have increased in line with the increase in the standard lifetime allowance to £7 million and £1.4 million (each being multiplied by £2.1 million/£1.5 million).

Sally has taken benefits previously so the amounts of benefits currently protected must be reduced by the value of the earlier benefits. The value of the earlier benefits must be increased in line with the increase in the standard lifetime allowance from its value when the benefits were taken to its current value. In this example, the standard lifetime allowance has increased from £1.8 million to £2.1 million. The value of the £600,000 lump sum taken in 2011 is therefore £700,000 (£600,000 x £2.1/1.8 million).

Sally's available protected pension and lump sum are therefore £6.3 million (£7 million-£700,000) and £700,000 (£1.4 million-£700,000) respectively.

Her second arrangement is a money purchase arrangement worth £8.3 million. She takes a *pension commencement lump sum* of £700,000 and uses the remainder of her protected pension rights, £5.6 million, to buy a *lifetime annuity*.

The residue of £2 million in the arrangement (£8.3 million less protected pension rights of £6.3 million) is liable to the *lifetime allowance charge*. From this residue she takes a lump sum of £900,000 after tax of £1.1 million.'

The amount of lump sum payable tax free must not exceed the amount of lifetime allowance available. This applies for lump sums paid under primary protection as for ordinary pension commencement lump sums. It is therefore very important to take great care over the timing of different lump sum payments to ensure that valuable tax-free lump sum rights are still within the lifetime allowance available. Consider the following two examples from RPSM03105170 and RPSM03105180:

Example – protection of lump sums with primary protection: taking benefits at more than one time – some lump sum benefits are not tax free

'Jane has primary protection for her pension rights, and her lump sum rights on 5 April 2006 exceeded £375,000. She has already taken some benefits after 5 April 2006 under primary protection.

Her remaining rights are in a *money purchase arrangement*, which are valued at £1 million. Her available protected pension rights are valued at £600,000, which means her available personal lifetime allowance is £600,000. The amount of protected lump sum is £700,000 – her protected lump sum rights are greater than her available personal lifetime allowance.

Jane decides to take all of her benefits as a lump sum. She takes a *pension commencement lump sum* of £700,000, using up all of her available lifetime allowance. She takes the balance of the £1 million (£300,000), as a *lifetime allowance excess lump sum*. £600,000 of her pension commencement lump sum is free of income tax, but £100,000 is liable to the *lifetime allowance charge* under section 215 Finance Act 2004. So she receives £600,000 tax-free and £180,000 after tax under the lifetime allowance charge.

Jane cannot take all of her protected lump sum amount tax-free because the maximum amount of pension commencement lump sum exceeds the amount of her available lifetime allowance.

Because Jane took too little lump sum when she took her earlier benefits, the full aggregate lump sum available under protection was not paid entirely free of income tax.'

Example – Protection of lump sums with primary protection: taking benefits at more than one time, some lump sum benefits are not tax free

'Dean had registered pension rights of £3 million and lump sum rights of £800,000 by commutation under primary protection on 5 April 2006. £3 million was the equivalent of the *standard lifetime allowance* (£1.5 million) plus an additional factor of 1.

In 2011, Dean took pension rights worth £3 million plus a lump sum of £600,000. In 2011 the standard lifetime allowance was £1.8 million. So Dean's personal lifetime allowance is £3.6 million (this being the standard lifetime allowance of £1.8 million at the time plus a factor of 1) and his maximum protected lump sum is £960,000 (£800,000 x £1.8 million/£1.5 million). Dean has now used up all of his personal lifetime allowance.

In 2013, Dean took further benefits including a lump sum, and paid a *lifetime allowance charge* on the whole of the benefits that he took.

Although Dean originally had a lump sum right of £800,000, he did not use this up whilst he had some personal lifetime allowance remaining. The result is that any lump sum taken after his personal lifetime allowance has been used up in full is subject to the lifetime allowance charge. The lump sum paid after his personal lifetime allowance had been used up is a *lifetime allowance excess lump sum*.'

Payment of death benefits . 6.13

Payment of a defined benefit lump sum death benefit and an uncrystallised funds lump sum death benefit are tested against an individual's lifetime allowance. If the lump sum exceeds the available lifetime allowance, it is subject to the 55% charge. Excess amounts over the available lifetime allowance will not be subject to a lifetime allowance charge if they are paid in the form of dependants' pensions.

The situation does not change under primary protection except that, instead of the lump sum amount being tested against the standard lifetime allowance, it is tested against the individual's personal lifetime allowance i e as increased by the application of the lifetime allowance enhancement factor.

The following examples are taken from RPSM03109020 for illustration:

Examples – primary protection and death benefits

'Example 1

Joe has pension rights at 5 April 2006 worth £2 million, which he protects. He has death in service benefits of 4 x his salary of £200,000 a year (a lump sum of £800,000).

If Joe dies, the death benefit will be tested against his *lifetime allowance* of £2m. If Joe has not taken any benefits the £800,000 will be within his lifetime allowance and so no tax charge will be due.

But if Joe had already taken some benefits and used up all his lifetime allowance, the £800,000 may still be paid but any amount of benefit above the lifetime allowance will be taxed.

Example 2

Josephine has a *money purchase fund* worth £2 million at 5 April 2006 plus a term life policy of £800,000. She has claimed primary protection on the £2 million. If she dies during the period of the term life policy, any capital sum paid from it will be tested against her lifetime allowance, but any *dependants'* pensions will not.'

Enhanced protection

Conditions for protection   6.14

There are two conditions for enhanced protection to apply. The first is that an individual must have given notice to HMRC of his or her intention to rely on it. The second is that the valuation of his or her uncrystallised rights derived from all occupational pension schemes on 5 April 2006 does not exceed an amount calculated as **20 x MPP**, where **MPP** is, broadly, the maximum permitted pension that would be allowed by reference to the appropriate tax regime in force before 6 April 2006.

For an explanation of **MPP** and information on the valuation of uncrystallised rights on 5 April 2006, please refer to **6.7** above. The same benefit valuation methods and calculation of **MPP** apply for enhanced protection as for primary protection.

If an individual's uncrystallised occupational pension scheme rights on 5 April 2006 exceed 20 x **MPP** then the excess has to be surrendered if enhanced protection is to be relied on. This is addressed by the *Registered Pension Schemes (Surrender of Relevant Excess) Regulations 2006 (SI 2006/211)* which were laid on 2 February 2006.

These regulations modify the rules of a pension scheme so as to allow members to be able to surrender those rights in excess of 20 x **MPP**. The regulations also provide that payment of the excess amount to the member in question would not be an unauthorised payment and would therefore only be subject to income tax if it were paid to the member.

Registration   6.15

Notification of a member's intention to rely on enhanced protection must be made by him or her on the appropriate form to reach HMRC by 5 April 2009. However, because an application for enhanced protection involves making certain decisions about the accrual of benefit beyond A-Day, most people will not be able to wait until 2009 and will need to have considered their position before A-Day.

Notification can also be made online by visiting: http://www.hmrc.gov.uk. Notification of intention to rely on primary protection can be made at the same time as a notification for enhanced protection, as long as an individual's rights are valued at more than £1.5m on 5 April 2006. In fact, an individual with A-Day rights greater than £1.5m who registers for enhanced protection would be well advised to register for primary protection as well. If enhanced protection is ever lost, then at least primary protection would provide a fall back position. The notification form will also include a section for notifying

HMRC of lump sum entitlements greater than £375,000 on 5 April 2006. Records relating to the protection notification must be kept for at least six years.

If the form is completed by someone else on the individual's behalf, the individual must still sign the form unless he or she is physically or mentally incapable of so doing. An individual's personal representative may also sign the form if the individual has died. Once HMRC has processed the form it will issue a certificate giving details of the enhanced protection.

At the time of writing the appropriate notification forms remain in draft.

Permitted transfers and impermissible transfers   6.16

Enhanced protection will be lost in the following circumstances:

(*a*)   where a transfer is made from any arrangement holding rights for the individual in a registered pension scheme and that transfer is not a permitted transfer;

(*b*)   where a new arrangement is made under a registered pension scheme otherwise than to receive a permitted transfer;

(*c*)   where an arrangement receives an impermissible transfer.

Benefits must not have been transferred out of the scheme at the member's request on or after A-Day. However, this is a complex issue and further details are given in **6.26** below.

Transfers made under the following circumstances will be permitted transfers and will not occasion loss of protection:

(*a*)   All sums and assets or all pension rights relating to the individual under the arrangement are transferred. A partial transfer where some rights or assets remain will *not* be a permitted transfer.

(*b*)   The sums and assets or pension rights are transferred to form all or part of the assets of one or more money purchase arrangements under a registered pension scheme or recognised overseas pension scheme. But where the transfer is in connection with the winding up of a registered pension scheme under which the individual has defined benefit or cash balance rights, such rights can be transferred to another cash balance or defined benefits arrangement for the individual. This is subject to the receiving cash balance or defined benefits arrangement being held in a registered pension scheme or recognised overseas pension scheme relating to the same employment as the wound-up arrangement.

(c)   Where defined benefit or cash balance pension rights are transferred to a money purchase arrangement, the value of the sums and assets received by the money purchase arrangement are actuarially equivalent to the rights being transferred.

Transfers in the following situations will be impermissible transfers and will occasion the loss of enhanced protection:

(a)   The transfer of any sums or assets from a registered pension scheme not relating to the individual into a money purchase scheme (except a cash balance scheme) relating to the individual.

(b)   The transfer of any sums or assets into an individual's money purchase arrangement (except a cash balance arrangement) which were held otherwise than by a pension scheme. A transfer from a pension scheme that is not a registered pension scheme will cause loss of enhanced protection.

(c)   The payment of a transfer lump sum death benefit into an individual's arrangement.

(d)   The transfer at any time after 5 April 2006 of a type mentioned above to an individual's hybrid arrangement and that hybrid arrangement subsequently becoming a money purchase arrangement that is not a cash balance arrangement.

(e)   An individual's defined benefits or cash balance arrangement becoming, at any time after 5 April 2006, a money purchase arrangement that is not a cash balance arrangement.

A transfer of rights to another scheme for an ex-spouse following a pension sharing order may still be made. Such a transfer does not affect enhanced protection.

Relevant benefit accrual   6.17

For enhanced protection to remain valid there must be no relevant benefit accrual on or after A-Day. If relevant benefit accrual occurs, enhanced protection will be lost at the time of its occurrence.

Relevant benefit accrual occurs under a money purchase arrangement (but not a cash balance arrangement) if a contribution is paid which is:

(a)   a tax-relievable contribution paid by or on behalf of the individual;

(b)   a contribution in respect of the individual by his or her employer;

(c)   any other contribution which becomes held for the benefit of the individual.

Minimum contracting-out payments may be made and it was intended that these would not jeopardise enhanced protection. However, the drafting of the legislation would appear only to refer to the flat-rate contracted-out rebate, which means that payment of age-related rebates might unintentionally jeopardise enhanced protection. It is anticipated that this will be amended so that all types of contracted-out rebate would be allowed.

Relevant benefit accrual occurs under a cash balance or defined benefits arrangement if, at the time when a benefit payment is made (or upon a permitted transfer to a money purchase arrangement), the crystallised value of the benefit exceeds the appropriate limit. The appropriate limit is the higher of (1) and (2) below.

1. The value of an individual's rights on 5 April 2006 increased to the date of payment by the highest of:

    (*a*)   5% compound;

    (*b*)   the increase in the Retail Prices Index;

    (*c*)   an increase specified in the statutory order applicable to contracted-out rights.

2. The benefit derived by using pensionable service to 5 April 2006, the scheme's accrual rate, and the amount of pensionable earnings at the actual date of payment, which may be some time after A-Day.

Naturally, there are some restrictions on the earnings that can be used under option 2. The elements included in earnings must be the same elements that were pensionable prior to A-Day.

If the member was subject to the post-1989 regime on 5 April 2006, his or her earnings are limited to the highest earnings in any consecutive twelve-month period in the three years before retirement or 7.5% of the standard lifetime allowance if that is lower.

If the member was not subject to the post-1989 regime on 5 April 2006, his or her earnings are similarly calculated as the highest earnings in any consecutive twelve-month period in the three years before retirement, but if they exceed 7.5% of the standard lifetime allowance they must be restricted to a three-year average or to 7.5% of the standard lifetime allowance, whichever is greater.

This means that it is perfectly feasible for defined benefits to continue to accrue post A-Day as long as the eventual amount crystallised on retirement does not exceed the appropriate limit set out above. This allows for modest pay rises to the date of retirement, but, more importantly, it allows for normal accrual to continue and for early retirement to be taken where the early retirement reduction factor takes the value of the actual benefit paid under the appropriate limit.

The following three examples are taken from RPSM03104590, RPSM03104600 and RPSM03104610, and illustrate when benefit accrual in a defined benefits arrangement would, and would not, occasion the loss of enhanced protection:

Example 1 – relevant benefit accrual in defined benefit schemes and cash balance arrangements

'David is a member of a *defined benefits scheme* with an accrual rate of one sixtieth for each year of service. On 5 April 2006, David has 30 years' service and his pensionable earnings are £120,000. He takes benefits from the scheme in April 2011. The scheme uses the 20:1 valuation factor in section 276 Finance Act 2004.

Step 1

On 5 April 2006, David's rights are valued at £1.2 million (30/60 x £120,000 x 20).

Step 2

Calculate the "appropriate limit" using the value from Step 1. Two calculations need to be done: the higher of the two is the "appropriate limit".

The first calculation is increasing £1.2 million by an indexation figure. The indexation figure is the highest figure obtained from a calculation over the period between 6 April 2006 and the date of the relevant event. The indexation figure is the highest of

- 5% annual compound interest over the period,

- $[RPI(2) - RPI(1)] / RPI(1)$

where RPI(2) is the **RPI** for the month in which the relevant event occurs and RPI(1) is the RPI for April 2006; or

- for contracted-out rights, some other figure specified in The Registered Pension Schemes (Defined Benefit Arrangements– Uprated Opening Value) Regulations [not yet laid] that HMRC makes in regulations.

Assume the highest figure is arrived at by using 5% compound for the five years between April 2005 and April 2011. Indexing £1.2 million in this way gives a figure of £1,531,538.

The second calculation is to use David's pensionable earnings in April 2011 and apply David's accrual rate under the scheme to this. In this instance, the scheme rules would not apply an early retirement factor to David's pension rights when they come into payment in 2011.

David's pensionable earnings are now £160,000. Assume that this pensionable earnings figure does not exceed the limit on "post-commencement earnings". David's pre 6 April 2006 rights have a value of £1.6 million (30/60 x £160,000 x 20).

The amount of £1.6 million from the earnings re-calculation is higher than £1,531,400 figure from the indexation calculation. So the "appropriate limit" is £1.6 million.

Step 3

Compare the value of the *benefit crystallisation event* in April 2011 with the "appropriate limit".

Scenario 1: The benefit crystallisation event in April 2011 is worth £1.75 million. Enhanced protection is lost but there is no *lifetime allowance charge* because the *standard lifetime allowance* is £1.8 million.

Scenario 2: The benefit crystallisation event in April 2011 is worth £2 million. Enhanced protection is lost and there is a lifetime allowance charge.'

Examples of benefit increases after 5 April 2006 that are not relevant benefit accruals

The two examples below show where 'relevant benefit accrual' as defined in *para 13, Sch 36, Finance Act 2004*, has not occurred and consequently the individual has not lost enhanced protection.

Example 2 – accrual after 5 April 2006, but low salary increases

'Anthony had 30 years service on 5 April 2006. The scheme's accrual rate was 1/60th for each year of service. His final pensionable salary, as defined on that day in the scheme documentation, was £240,000. He therefore registered £2.4 million (£120,000 x 20) for enhanced protection.

Anthony remained an active member of the pension scheme for another five years until he reached normal retirement age. By this time, his final pensionable salary had grown to £252,000 giving a pension of £147,000 (35/60 x £252,000). The value of the *benefit crystallisation event* is £2.94 million (£147,000 x 20).

The test for relevant benefit accrual is whether the value of the benefit crystallisation event is greater than the value of the appropriate limit.

The appropriate limit is the greater of

- indexation of £2.4 million (x 5% compound, *RPI* or the percentage rate specified in The Registered Pension Schemes (Defined Benefit Arrangements – Uprated Opening Value) Regulations [not yet laid], and

- a recalculation of the pension accrued at 5 April 2006 reflecting current final pensionable salary and the scheme early retirement factor (where appropriate) for the current age and a valuation factor of 20.

For the purposes of this example it has been assumed that indexation at 5% compound gives a higher figure than the recalculation.

The value of the appropriate limit is £3,063,076 (£2.4 million indexed at 5%) which is less than the value of the benefit crystallisation event (£2.94 million). Therefore relevant benefit accrual has not occurred and enhanced protection is retained.'

Example 3 – early reduction factor where the member retires before normal retirement date

'Matthew had 30 years' service on 5 April 2006. The scheme's accrual rate was 1/60th for each year of service. His final pensionable salary, as defined on that day in the scheme documentation, was £240,000. He therefore registered for enhanced protection.

He remained an active member of the pension scheme for another five years until age 55. His final salary grew to £300,000. The scheme operated a normal retirement age of 60. If the accrued pension had been taken as a deferred pension at age 60 the scheme would have paid £175,000 per annum (35/60 x £300,000). However Matthew wanted an immediate pension. The scheme applied its own early retirement factor of 4% per annum for each year that benefits were taken before age 60. Matthew was therefore paid a pension of £140,000, which has a capital value of £2.8 million (£140,000 x 20).

The test for relevant benefit accrual as in example 1 in rpsm03104600 meant that a pension of £153,154 per annum (valued at £3,063,076) could have been paid without causing the loss of enhanced protection. Matthew retains enhanced protection.'

Payment of pension benefits 6.18

As long as an individual retains enhanced protection he or she will have no liability for the lifetime allowance charge at any benefit crystallisation event. It will also not be possible for him or her to receive payment of a lifetime allowance excess lump sum. While enhanced protection is in place, an individual will not be subject to any annual allowance charge.

Payment of lump sum benefits greater than £375,000
6.19

Where an individual has applied for enhanced protection and has registered lump sum rights at 5 April 2006 which are greater than £375,000, the normal rules for calculating pension commencement lump sums do not apply. Instead, the pension commencement lump sum is calculated as the same percentage of rights being crystallised at the vesting date as the percentage arrived at by dividing uncrystallised lump sum rights at A-Day by the value of uncrystallised rights at A-Day and multiplying by 100. This is best demonstrated by an example:

At A-Day

If:	the value of uncrystallised lump sum rights on 5 April 2006 = £400,000
And:	the value of uncrystallised rights on 5 April 2006 = £2,000,000
Then:	the lump sum percentage on 5 April 2006 = (£400,000 / £2,000,000) x 100 = 20%

At retirement

If:	the value of rights crystallised at retirement = £2,400,000
Then:	the maximum lump sum at retirement = 20% x £2,400,000 = £480,000

The position is more complicated when enhanced protection covers more than one registered pension scheme, as this example from RPSM03105210 shows:

Protection of lump sum rights with enhanced protection

'Sally has uncrystallised lump sum rights of £400,000 and uncrystallised pension rights of £2 million on 5 April 2006. This gives (VULSR ÷ VUR) of 20%. She takes benefits from three schemes on different dates whilst retaining enhanced protection.

Sally takes benefits from the first scheme, which are worth £1 million, by taking unsecured pension using income withdrawal. She designates assets valued at £800,000 for the payment of her unsecured pension and takes a lump sum benefit of £200,000. This is the maximum permitted by (VULSR ÷ VUR) multiplied by the value of the funds designated for the payment of unsecured pension plus the lump sum – paragraph 29 (2) of Schedule 36 Finance Act 2004.

Sally takes benefits from the second scheme worth £750,000 in the form of a *lifetime annuity* bought for £600,000 and a lump sum benefit of £150,000. This is the maximum permitted by (VULSR ÷ VUR) multiplied by the value of the annuity purchase price plus the lump sum – paragraph 29 (2) of Schedule 36 Finance Act 2004.

Sally takes benefits from the third scheme as a *scheme pension* of £20,000 plus a lump sum benefit of £100,000. The scheme pension is valued at £400,000 (20 x the annual pension of £20,000). And the lump sum is the maximum permitted by (VULSR ÷ VUR) multiplied by the value of the scheme pension plus the lump sum – paragraph 29 (2) of Schedule 36 Finance Act 2004.

If one of Sally's schemes paid her a lump sum of 15% of the combined value of her lump sum and pension benefits (because scheme rules did not permit a larger lump sum) her other schemes could not pay her a lump sum greater than 20% to make up the "shortfall".'

VULSR is the value of uncrystallised lump sum rights on 5 April 2006; and

VUR is the value of uncrystallised rights on 5 April 2006.

Payment of death benefits   6.20

Whether the payment of a lump sum death benefit would jeopardise enhanced protection depends on the type of arrangement from which it is paid.

A defined benefit pension scheme would typically pay a death-in-service lump sum calculated as a multiple of salary at date of death. Such cover can continue to be provided under enhanced protection even though salary may have increased greatly since A-Day, but since payment of the lump sum is a benefit crystallisation event under a defined benefits arrangement, it must be tested against the appropriate limit to determine whether relevant benefit accrual has occurred (see **6.17** above). If relevant benefit accrual has not occurred, enhanced protection continues to apply and there is no liability to a lifetime allowance charge.

For example, if pension rights at A-Day were valued at £2,000,000 (based on, say, a salary of £200,000, service of 30 years and an accrual rate of 1/60ths = £200,000 x (30/60) x 20 = £2,000,000), then a death benefit paid later on based on four times a salary of, say, £300,000, would be 4 x £300,000 = £1,200,000 and still well within the appropriate limit for a lump sum payment in this case. Any dependants' pensions paid in addition would not be taken into account as they do not constitute a benefit crystallisation event.

In the case of a money purchase arrangement, an uncrystallised funds lump sum death benefit may be paid equal to the accumulated value of the assets in a member's pension fund at the date of death, and enhanced protection would not be lost.

The situation becomes complicated, however, if an insured lump sum is payable. If the proceeds of a life assurance policy would form part of the member's overall fund and the scheme rules simply provide for a death benefit calculated as a return of fund, as opposed to a targeted amount (eg 4 x salary), then the total fund including the life policy proceeds can be paid as a lump sum without jeopardising enhanced protection. Care needs to be taken with such insurance; if any premiums paid qualify for tax relief, then enhanced protection would be lost. However, HMRC confirmed in Pensions Tax Simplification Newsletter No. 8 that if such premiums were paid out of the existing assets of a member's scheme, then this would not jeopardise enhanced protection.

If the proceeds of a life assurance policy back the promise of a targeted amount, then a cash balance arrangement exists in tandem with the money purchase arrangement. Such an insured arrangement may form part of the main pension scheme, as in an occupational scheme, or may be a separate group life scheme sitting alongside a group personal pension. In either case, premiums paid to the cash balance life cover arrangement would not jeopardise enhanced protection, but payment of a lump sum death benefit would. Since payment of the lump sum is a benefit crystallisation event under a cash balance arrangement, it must be tested against the appropriate limit to determine whether relevant benefit accrual has occurred (see **6.17** above). Relevant benefit accrual will definitely have occurred since the value of the cash balance arrangement at A-Day was nil. If the benefit was paid in the form of dependants' pensions, enhanced protection would not be lost as this would not constitute a benefit crystallisation event.

HMRC received many queries about the treatment of life cover under enhanced protection, and they finally produced further explanation to try to clarify this very grey area of the new tax regime. Their understanding of the position was set out in Pensions Tax Simplification Newsletter No. 8, published on 23 December 2005. The relevant extract is reproduced below.

'Life assurance and enhanced protection

In Newsletter No 4 item 4a on Enhanced protection and contributions for life cover we explained that some arrangements providing death benefits using life cover policies are other money purchase arrangements. We have subsequently received a number of queries about this article and we are now providing further clarification.

Not all arrangements in registered pension schemes containing life cover policies will be other money purchase arrangements. The type of arrangement is determined not by whether life cover is provided but by the nature of the promise to the member under the arrangement.

The guidance on the different types of arrangement a member of a registered pension scheme may have is set out in RPSM09100200 to RPSM09100260. This article provides more detail. To find out the type of arrangement in any particular scheme you need to go to the scheme documentation to see what benefits have been promised to the member. A policy providing life cover may deliver other money purchase benefits, cash balance benefits or defined benefits depending on the terms of the arrangement.

You should first decide whether under the terms of the individual's arrangement the benefits to be provided are to be calculated by reference to a pot of money that will be made available for their provision (what the legislation calls "an amount available"). If the answer is no, then the arrangement is a defined benefits arrangement. If the answer is yes, then the arrangement is a money purchase arrangement, and you then have to go on to decide whether it is a cash balance or an other money purchase arrangement.

The difference between cash balance and other money purchase arrangements is set out in RPSM09100255. Under a cash balance arrangement the benefits are calculated by reference to a specified pot, which will be made available regardless of the amount of any actual payments to and investment growth in the pension fund. Whereas under an other money purchase arrangement the benefits are calculated by reference to a pot, the amount of which is not specified in advance but is simply the amount of payments into the pot and investment growth up to the date of the calculation of the benefits. The investment growth can include the proceeds of a life cover policy held under a scheme for the member.

It is the actual terms of the scheme documentation that are important. For example, a scheme may contain a life cover policy for £500,000 for an individual member. However the terms of the scheme state that the scheme will pay a lump sum death benefit of the return of the member's fund. The proceeds of the life cover policy will form part of the funds in the member's arrangement. As the scheme documentation does not promise a set monetary amount will be available to provide benefits the benefits are other money purchase benefits and the arrangement will be an other money purchase arrangement.

Contracts approved under S621(1)(b) ICTA 1988, commonly known as S226A policies, will automatically become registered pension schemes on 6 April 2006. For these schemes the only asset is a life cover policy and the scheme documentation will be the life policy. The amount provided by the policy is dependent on the premiums that have been paid. The benefits provided are calculated by reference to a pot, which is itself calculated "... wholly by reference to payments made under the arrangement". As such S226A policies are other money purchase arrangements.

It is possible for a scheme to contain more than one type of arrangement. For example a scheme may provide a member with retirement benefits on an other money purchase basis and also provide benefits on death in service of 4 x salary. The retirement benefits are other money purchase benefits and the death benefit is a defined benefit. So the scheme contains two types of arrangement – an other money purchase arrangement for the retirement benefits and a defined benefits arrangement for the death benefits.

To summarise

- DB benefits: the form and amount of the benefit promised is fixed. For example the member is promised a pension of one 60th of final salary for each year of pensionable service, or that a lump sum death benefit of, say, £100,000, or 4 times salary, will be paid if he dies in service.

- CB benefits: the promised value of pot that will provide the benefit is fixed, but the form and/or amount of the benefit is not. For example the member is promised that when she retires a pot of £200,000 will be made available to provide her with benefits, or, if she dies in service, a pot of £200,000 will be made available to provide death benefits (whether pension or lump sum).

- Other money purchase benefits: the benefits are calculated by reference to a pot, the amount in which will be determined by the value of the member's pension fund at the date of calculation. For example, the member is promised that the current value of his pot will be made available to provide benefits on retirement, or, if he dies in service, the current value of the pot, including the proceeds of any life cover policy held by the trustees in relation to him, will be made available to provide death benefits (whether pension or lump sum).

If a contribution is paid to an other money purchase arrangement after A day enhanced protection will be lost. However where a premium for a life policy is paid for from funds in the arrangement on 5 April 2006 enhanced protection will not be lost.

Benefits paid from an other money purchase arrangement will not cause enhanced protection to be lost. This is because there is no relevant benefit accrual test on benefit payment from an other money purchase arrangement.

The payment of lump sum death benefits from a cash balance or defined benefits arrangement may cause enhanced protection to be lost. This is because a benefit paid from a cash balance or defined benefits arrangement that is a benefit crystallisation event will trigger a relevant benefit accrual test. You should test the total value of benefits provided from cash balance and defined benefits arrangements for an employment against the appropriate limit of the value of the benefits protected at A day. This is explained in RPSM03109510 to RPSM03109550. Where the total benefits paid in respect of an employment are more than the appropriate limit enhanced protection will be lost and any lump sum benefit provided over the member's available lifetime allowance will be taxable at a rate of 55%.

Example 1

Bill has benefits provided from a defined benefits arrangement for his employment with X plc. He protected £3.2 million of retirement benefits for this employment using enhanced protection and primary protection. Five years later Bill dies and his scheme provides a lump sum death benefit of 4 x his salary of £700,000, i.e. £2.8 million. This lump sum is less than the amount of his protected benefits so Bill retains enhanced protection. The lump sum can be paid tax free.

Example 2

As above except Bill's retirement benefits are provided from an other money purchase arrangement and his death benefits are provided from a defined benefits arrangement. Death benefits have a Nil value for protection purposes. So for the relevant benefit accrual test for the defined benefits arrangement the appropriate limit is Nil. The payment of the £2.8 million lump sum death benefit from the defined benefit arrangement causes Bill to lose enhanced protection for all rights in all his registered pension schemes. As Bill had registered for primary protection as well as enhanced protection he reverts to primary protection and his available lifetime allowance is now £4 million. This means total tax free lump sum death benefits of £4 million can be paid form both his defined benefits and other money purchase arrangement. However if Bill had not registered for primary protection the amount over the standard lifetime allowance would be taxable. So if the lifetime allowance is £1.8 million any amount over £1.8 million would be taxable at 55%.'

In addition to the above, the following three examples, taken from RPSM03109530, RPSM03109540 and RPSM03109550, further illustrate the permutations that would, or would not, cause enhanced protection to be lost upon the payment of death benefits:

Enhanced protection: money purchase rights and loss of enhanced protection

'Alec has several *personal pension arrangements* valued at £4 million at 5 April 2006. He also has a life assurance policy (a section 226A contract) giving him life cover of £1 million. The value of his rights at 5 April 2006 for the purposes of enhanced protection is £4 million.

Alec dies some years later without having taken any benefits.

Lump sums subsequently paid from the (former) personal pension arrangements total £5.2 million, which was the entire value of the funds in the contracts when the payment was made.

The proceeds from the life assurance policy are £1.2 million. The amount of cover had been increased before Alec's death.

If all the proceeds are used to provide pensions for Alec's *dependants*, enhanced protection will not be affected. If part or all of the proceeds are used to pay a lump sum (which will be an uncrystallised funds lump sum death benefit under a *cash balance arrangement*), enhanced protection will be lost immediately.

This is because the lump sum death benefit is a *benefit crystallisation event* with a value of the amount of the lump sum. The payment of the lump sum is also a relevant event, for the purposes of enhanced protection, which triggers a test against the appropriate limit.

The value of the life assurance policy on 5 April 2006 was zero for the purposes of the appropriate limit. The payment of any lump sum benefit from the proceeds of the policy causes enhanced protection to be lost.'

Enhanced protection: defined benefit lump sum death benefits paid without loss of enhanced protection

'Julia was a member of a *defined benefits arrangement* that had an accrual rate of one sixtieth of pensionable earnings for each year of service. On 5 April 2006, she had 20 years service and her pensionable earnings were £300,000. Her rights were valued at £2 million.

(20/60 x £300,000 x 20). The scheme had provision to pay a lump sum on death in service of 4 x pensionable earnings.

When Julia died in 2011, her pensionable earnings were £425,000, so the scheme wished to pay a lump sum of £1.7 million. Julia had taken no benefits from any *registered pension scheme*, so the £1.7 million was compared with current value of her pension rights on 5 April 2006 (the "appropriate limit"). As her pensionable earnings had increased significantly since 2006, the appropriate limit was calculated using the earnings re-calculation value. This gave a value of £2,833,333 for the appropriate limit (20/60 x £425,000 x 20).

(There was no adjustment to the promised value of her benefits, as she died just before her normal retirement date.) Enhanced protection was retained.

Where the payment of a lump sum death benefit is the first relevant event that occurs in the arrangement the earnings re-calculation value should be determined using the deceased's age when they died (the assumption in paragraph 15(6)(a) Schedule 36, Finance Act 2004 refers).'

Enhanced protection: defined benefit lump sum death benefit paid which causes loss of enhanced protection

'Palbinder was a member of a *defined benefits arrangement* that had an accrual rate of one sixtieth of pensionable earnings for each year of service. On 5 April 2006, she had 20 years service and her pensionable earnings were £300,000. The scheme used a factor of 20:1 to value Palbinder's pension rights, so these were valued at £2 million (20/60 x £300,000 x 20). The scheme had provision to pay a lump sum on death in service of 4 x pensionable earnings.

When Palbinder died in 2011, her pensionable earnings were £320,000. The scheme had by now increased its death in service lump sums to 10 x pensionable earnings, so it paid a lump sum of £3.2 million. Palbinder had taken no benefits from any *registered pension scheme* so the £3.2 million was compared with the current value of her pension rights on 5 April 2006 (the "appropriate limit"). The most favourable basis for calculation of the appropriate limit was to index it at 5% compound. This gave a value of £2,552,000. As this was lower than the lump sum paid, enhanced protection was lost immediately. The lump sum death benefit therefore became potentially subject to the *lifetime allowance charge*. Palbinder had also claimed primary protection and reverted to that form of protection when enhanced protection was lost. The value of the primary protection was £2.6 million at the payment of the lump sum death benefit. As the lump sum paid was £3.2 million there was a lifetime allowance charge.'

Protection of tax-free lump sum entitlements

The tax-free lump sums payable from defined benefit, cash balance and money purchase arrangements in the normal course of events are described in **CHAPTER 2**. Under the new tax regime the vast majority of members of defined benefit schemes are able to receive, subject to scheme rules, a tax-free lump sum significantly in excess of the pre A-Day maximum permitted lump sum. For members of personal pension schemes the position has not altered significantly, as their lump sum entitlements remain to be calculated effectively as 25% of their fund values. However, members of occupational money purchase schemes may well find that the lump sum formula of the new tax regime is less than the 3n/80 or uplifted 80ths formula they enjoyed previously. The main reason for this is the lower level of contributions that tend to be made for many members in money purchase arrangements; 25% of a member's fund value may well be less than a sum calculated as 3/80ths of final remuneration for each year of service. Where this is the case, protection is granted for such members under *paras 31–34, Sch 36, Finance Act 2004*. If the protection conditions are met, the normal lump sum formulae described in **CHAPTER 2** are replaced with the ones below.

Conditions for lump sum protection 6.22

It had been mooted in HMRC consultation that members with existing lump sum entitlements in excess of 25% of existing rights at A-Day would have to register with HMRC for their lump sum protection. However, once the *Finance Act 2004* was published, this was seen not to be the case; if a member had an entitlement to a lump sum exceeding 25% of rights at A-Day, he or she continues to be entitled to that lump sum, and trustees of occupational money purchase pension schemes will need to ensure that they hold sufficient data to be able to give effect to members' lump sum entitlements when they come to retire.

All of the following conditions must be met for lump sum protection to apply:

- the member must become entitled to all pensions payable to him or her under the scheme on the same date;

- the pension scheme must have been an approved occupational pension scheme (see note below);

- the value of the member's uncrystallised lump sum rights on 5 April 2006 must have exceeded 25% of the value of his or her uncrystallised rights on 5 April 2006;

- if the lump sum entitlement at A-Day exceeded £375,000, the member must not have given notice to HMRC of intention to rely on either primary or enhanced protection;

- the member's benefits must not have been transferred out of the scheme at his or her request on or after 6 April 2006.

Note: an approved occupational pension scheme is a retirement benefits scheme approved under *Ch I, Pt XIV, Income and Corporation Taxes Act 1988,* a relevant statutory scheme, a parliamentary fund, a *section 32* policy or a former approved superannuation fund under *s 208, Income and Corporation Taxes Act 1970.*

Even if an individual has registered for primary and/or enhanced protection, he or she may still be able to benefit from lump sum protection as described here if his or her uncrystallised lump sum rights at A–Day exceeded 25% but did not exceed £375,000.

Valuation of lump sum rights at A-Day 6.23

Whether lump sum rights exceed 25% on 5 April 2006 is determined by the formula:

VULSR / VUR x 100

where:

VULSR is the value of uncrystallised lump sum rights on 5 April 2006; and

VUR is the value of uncrystallised rights on 5 April 2006.

In the case of a retirement annuity contract (also known as a *s 226* policy), the lump sum is valued as 25% of the funds held for the purpose of the arrangement on 5 April 2006, even though a lump sum percentage higher than 25% could have been paid from such an arrangement.

In any other case the lump sum is calculated as if the member had become entitled to the present payment of the lump sum under the rules on 5 April 2006. For this purpose it is assumed that the member is in good physical and mental health and has reached either age 60, or, if a different age was specified in the arrangement at 10 December 2003 as the minimum age at which benefits could be paid without reduction, that age.

For members of occupational pension schemes the value of the lump sum is restricted by reference to the HMRC limits which applied before A-Day. For past early leavers this would be the HMRC maximum lump sum calculated at their date of leaving, revalued up to 5 April 2006 in line with increases in the Retail Prices Index (see paras 10.15–10.18 of the Practice Notes IR12 (2001)). For a member still in service on 5 April 2006, it is assumed that he or she left employment on that date. As an example, if a member was subject to the pre-1987 regime, was still in service on 5 April 2006, had 30 years' potential service to his normal retirement date and had 20 years' service accrued to 5 April 2006, his HMRC maximum lump sum at 5 April 2006 would be calculated as the higher of:

(*a*)   3/80 x 20 x final remuneration; and

(*b*)   20/30 x ((120/80 x final remuneration) – lump sum retained benefits).

In this case the member has more than 20 years' service to his normal retirement date and, as the pre-1987 regime applies, he can therefore count on the uplifted 80ths scale, which gives him a maximum lump sum of 120/80. Lump sum retained benefits must then be deducted, if necessary, and the result multiplied by **N/NS**, where **N** is service accrued, in this case, to 5 April 2006, and **NS** is potential service to normal retirement date (20 years and 30 years respectively in this example). See para 8.37 of the Practice Notes IR12 (2001).

Retained benefits do not have to be taken into account if the member's P60 earnings from pensionable employment did not exceed £50,000 in the 2004/05 tax year, even for controlling directors. If pensionable service did not continue for the whole of the 2004/05 tax year, a pro rata calculation applies. If pensionable service ceased before 6 April 2004, retained benefits do not have to be taken into account if P60 earnings in the last complete tax year before the date of leaving did not exceed £25,000. Retained benefits may also be ignored in the usual circumstances set out in the Practice Notes IR12 (2001). Note that consideration of retained benefits is only necessary for pre-1987 members. Lump sum retained benefits do not need to be considered for 1987–1989 regime members or for post-1989 regime members.

Valuation of pension rights at A-Day   6.24

In a similar way, the value of uncrystallised rights on 5 April 2006 is calculated as if the member had become entitled to the present payment of those rights. The value is expressed in the following formula:

(RVF x ARP) + LS

where:

RVF is the relevant valuation factor (ie 20);

ARP is the annual rate of pension that the member would have received if he or she had become immediately entitled to it without reduction; and

LS is the amount of lump sum that the member would have received otherwise than by commutation (ie in a scheme which provides a separate pension and lump sum).

The value of uncrystallised rights must also be restricted by reference to the HMRC limits which applied on 5 April 2006. The limit is expressed in the formula:

20 x MPP

where:

MPP is the maximum permitted pension calculated under pre-1987, 1987–1989 or post-1989 regime rules as appropriate.

As before, it is assumed that the member is in good physical and mental health and has reached either age 60 or, if a different age was specified in the arrangement at 10 December 2003 as the minimum age at which benefits could be paid without reduction, that age. If the member was still in service on 5 April 2006, it is assumed that he or she left employment at that date. The maximum permitted pension for the member in the previous example would be calculated as the higher of:

(*a*)   20/60 x final remuneration; and

(*b*)   20/30 x ((40/60 x final remuneration) − retained benefits).

As before, retained benefits may be ignored where P60 earnings do not exceed £50,000 in the 2004/05 tax year, or £25,000 in the last tax year before leaving if the member left before 6 April 2004. Although lump sum retained benefits are not taken into account for 1987–1989 regime and post-1989 regime members, retained pension benefits do have to be taken into account for such members, unless one of the easements above or one of the easements in the Practice Notes IR12 (2001) applies.

More than one scheme relating to the same employment 6.25

As if this was not complicated enough, the situation is different again where an individual has benefits under two or more occupational pension schemes relating to the same employment. In this case the HMRC limits on lump sum and maximum permitted pension apply to the employment as a whole, and if the aggregate lump sums or the aggregate pension rights from all schemes relating to the employment exceed the limit, then each benefit must be reduced in proportion to the excess of aggregate rights.

This could mean that if lump sum rights are excessive in total, then lump sum rights greater than 25% under one or more schemes could be reduced to below 25% in each scheme. Conversely, if total pension rights are excessive, their value may have to be restricted, which means that lump sum values might then be greater than 25% where they were not before. The following examples are taken from RPSM03105560 and RPSM03105570 respectively and illustrate the issue:

Valuing lump sum benefits exceeding 25%: lump sum benefits on 5 April 2006 exceed 'HMRC limits'

'Asif has pension and lump sum rights for a single employment on 5 April 2006. His total pension rights are £210,000 and total lump sum rights are £60,000. These rights are held in three schemes. His rights are held in a single *arrangement* under each scheme.

Asif's "maximum permitted lump sum" for the employment under "HMRC limits" was calculated as £54,000. His "maximum permitted pension" under "HMRC limits" was greater than £210,000.

Therefore VULSR must be adjusted whilst VUR remains the same.

The position before adjustment was as follows

- Scheme 1 – pension rights of £60,000; lump sum £15,000; lump sum percentage 25%

- Scheme 2 – pension rights of £60,000 ; lump sum £20,000; lump sum percentage 33.33%

- Scheme 3 – pension rights of £90,000; lump sum £25,000; lump sum percentage 27.78%

The reduction in Asif's lump sum rights from £60,000 to £54,000 must be apportioned amongst the three schemes. In scheme 1 the lump sum rights are adjusted as follows, £15,000-(£6,000 x £15,000 ÷ £60,000) which gives a figure of £13,500.

After adjustment, Asif's lump sum percentage from each of the three schemes becomes

- Scheme 1 – pension rights of £60,000; lump sum £13,500; scheme percentage 22.5%

- Scheme 2 – pension rights of £60,000; lump sum £18,000; scheme percentage 30%

- Scheme 3 – pension rights of £90,000; lump sum £22,500; scheme percentage 25%

So after the required adjustment, only the rights in Scheme 2 qualify for protection as the lump percentage exceeds 25% of the uncrystallised pension rights in that scheme.

Rights in schemes 1 and 3 may be taken at 25% because the normal rules for *pension commencement lump sums* in Schedule 29 Finance Act 2004 apply to the rights under those two schemes.'

Valuing lump sum benefits exceeding 25%: pension benefits on 5 April 2006 exceed 'HMRC limits'

'An adjustment to the value of an individual's uncrystallised pension rights also triggers a re-calculation of the lump sum percentage available in multiple schemes.

Lesley has pension and lump sum rights in two schemes for a sole employment on 5 April 2006. She has total pension rights of

£200,000 and her lump sum rights are £44,000. Her rights are held in a single *arrangement* under each scheme. The £44,000 is less than her "maximum permitted lump sum" under "HMRC limits" but her "maximum permitted pension" under "HMRC limits" is valued at £160,000.

The position before adjustment was as follows

- Scheme A – pension rights of £80,000; lump sum £20,000; lump sum percentage 25%

- Scheme B – pension rights of £120,000; lump sum £24,000; lump sum percentage 20%

The reduction in Lesley's pension rights from £200,000 to £160,000 must be apportioned between the two schemes. In scheme A, the value of the pension rights is adjusted as follows, £80,000-(£40,000 x £80,000 ÷ £200,000) which gives a figure of £64,000.

After adjustment, Lesley's lump sum percentages from the two schemes become

- Scheme A – pension rights of £64,000; lump sum £20,000; lump sum percentage 31.25%

- Scheme B – pension rights of £96,000; lump sum £24,000; lump sum percentage 25%

So after the required adjustment, the rights in Scheme A qualify for protection, as the lump sum percentage exceeds 25% of Lesley's uncrystallised pension rights in that scheme.'

Block transfers   6.26

One of the conditions of enhanced protection referred to in **6.16** above was that benefits must not have been transferred out of the scheme at the member's request on or after A-Day. This is understating the complexity of the matter. Originally the protection would have been lost on any transfer of rights from the original scheme after A-Day unless it was part of a block transfer to another pension scheme. A *block transfer* is defined in the *Registered Pension Schemes Manual* glossary as:

'The transfer in a single transaction of all the sums and assets held for the purposes of (or representing accrued rights under) the *arrangements* under the *pension scheme* from which the transfer is made, which relate to the member in question and at least one other member of that pension scheme, where before the transfer either the member was not a member of the pension scheme to which the transfer is made, or he has been a member of that pension scheme for no longer than such period as is prescribed by regulations (not laid yet). (Note Paragraph 4C of the Technical Note which appeared on the Inland Revenue website on 16 February 2005 explained that a transfer will still be a block transfer if at the time of the transfer, the member had not been a member of the receiving scheme for more than one year).'

The block transfer easement was originally introduced to ensure that pension transactions as a result of a corporate reconstruction were not adversely affected. Amendments in the *Finance Act 2005* and the draft Pension Schemes (Block Transfers) (Permitted Membership Period) Regulations 2005 would allow members to keep their lump sum protection if two or more transferred at the same time (voluntarily or not) to another pension arrangement within twelve months of joining that other arrangement. Originally such members would only have been allowed to do this once before losing their protection, but now this can be done any number of times as long as the block transfer conditions continue to be met on each occasion. Note that this could be a transfer to either a personal pension arrangement or an occupational pension scheme. For this to be effective the right to the lump sum must have existed on 10 December 2003 and be available to the member on 5 April 2006. Unfortunately, the scheme could easily have been restructured as a result of corporate activity between these two dates, and so additional provisions, in a draft Pension Schemes (Transitional Provisions) Order 2005, have been made to extend protection to this situation.

Furthermore, if, upon the winding up of a pension scheme, a member's rights are transferred to an individual buy-out policy in his or her own name, this would not have met the conditions for a block transfer, as the buy-out policy would effectively be a single life scheme. So draft legislation has been laid (a draft Pension Schemes (Transitional Provisions) Order 2005) to try to continue such members' protection on wind-up. The lump sum protection continues to apply if 'all the rights of the member have been discharged by purchasing one annuity which meets the conditions specified in *s 74(3)(c), Pensions Act 1995*', i e a policy of insurance that meets certain prescribed conditions. Note that all rights relating to one member under the scheme being wound up have to be transferred to the same policy. Note also that transfer to a personal pension as an option on wind-up would invalidate the lump sum protection. It is not clear whether a subsequent transfer from the buy-out policy to another pension arrangement would invalidate the lump sum protection.

Payment of protected lump sums   6.27

If relevant benefit accrual (as defined for enhanced protection above) *does not* occur post A-Day, the protected tax-free lump sum at retirement is calculated as the lump sum entitlement on 5 April 2006 increased by the rise in the lifetime allowance since A-Day. It is expressed in the following formula:

VULSR x CSLA / FSLA

where:

VULSR is the value of uncrystallised lump sum rights on 5 April 2006, limited to the maximum approvable lump sum;

CSLA is the standard lifetime allowance applicable at the date of vesting; and

FSLA is the standard lifetime allowance for the 2006/07 tax year (ie £1.5m).

If relevant benefit accrual *does* occur post A-Day, then an additional lump sum may be given based on the increase of the fund post A-Day over and above increases in the lifetime allowance. The *total* lump sum is expressed in the following formula:

(VULSR x CSLA / FSLA) + 1/4 x (LS + AC − VUR x CSLA / FSLA)

where:

VULSR, CSLA and **FSLA** are as before;

LS is the lump sum being paid; and

AC is the amount crystallised by the connected pension coming into payment.

Note: if **1/4 x (LS + AC − VUR x (CSLA / FSLA))** produces a result which is less than zero, it is taken to be zero.

This formula is reproduced from the *Finance Act 2004* and appears rather complicated, especially with the inclusion of the lump sum amount itself (**'LS'**) in the lump sum formula. However, as this protection will apply predominantly to members of occupational money purchase schemes, and the Finance Act 2006 is intended to amend the lump sum calculation for money purchase arrangements to be no more than 25% (even where 'scheme pension' is paid), we can perhaps express it a little more simply, for money purchase arrangements, as:

$$LS_A \text{ x } (LTA_V / LTA_A) + 1/4 \text{ x } (FV_V − FV_A \text{ x } (LTA_V / LTA_A))$$

where:

LS_A is the lump sum entitlement at A-Day;

LTA_V is the lifetime allowance at the date of vesting;

LTA_A is the lifetime allowance at A-Day;

FV_V is the fund value at the date of vesting; and

FV_A is the fund value at A-Day.

Recalculation on partial transfer   6.28

If any part of a member's benefit is transferred out of the pension scheme in which he or she has lump sum protection under *Sch 36, paras 31–34, Finance Act 2004*, then the protected lump sum amount needs to be recalculated so as to relate only to that part of the benefit left behind.

Schedule 36, para 34, Finance Act 2004, modifies the normal lump sum calculation for members with lump sum entitlements greater than 25% at A-Day. In what is fast becoming one of the most complicated pieces of pensions legislation, recently laid draft legislation (the draft Finance Act 2004 (Part 4) (Transitional Provisions) Order 2005) would apply a modification to this modification to achieve the required recalculation of the protected lump sum amount upon a partial transfer.

If relevant benefit accrual has occurred and a transfer, other than a block transfer, of money or assets is made to another arrangement, then the protected lump sum amount is recalculated using the following formula:

VULSR x (CSLA / FSLA) + 1/4 x (LS + AC – VUR x (CSLA / FSLA)) – 1/4 x TV

where:

VULSR, CSLA, FSLA, LS, AC and **VUR** have the same meanings as before; and

TV is the value of all sums and assets held for the purposes of, or representing accrued rights under, the pension scheme which have been transferred out.

If relevant benefit accrual has not occurred, then the formula is simply:

VULSR x (CSLA / FSLA) – 1/4 x TV.

Interaction with the overall limit   6.29

The normal lump sum formulae contained in *Sch 29, Finance Act 2004*, contain a restriction on the overall amount of pension commencement lump sum that can be paid. The lump sum is restricted to one-quarter of an individual's available lifetime allowance and expressed in the formula:

1/4 x (CSLA – AAC x (CSLA / PSLA))

where:

CSLA is the standard lifetime allowance at the date of vesting;

AAC is the aggregate of the amounts crystallised by previous benefit vestings; and

PSLA is the standard lifetime allowance at each respective previous crystallisation event.

Note that the calculation for protected lump sums greater than 25% in an arrangement overrides this restriction. It would therefore be possible for a member of a pension arrangement who does not register for primary or enhanced protection to continue to have a lump sum entitlement greater than £375,000 if that entitlement was greater than 25% of the value of his or her rights at A-Day, and as long as he or she meets the other protection conditions in *paras 31–34, Sch 36, Finance Act 2004*. It would even appear that an additional lump sum could be paid in respect of post A-Day increases in fund value if relevant benefit accrual, as defined, occurs. Whether this will still be the case once HMRC has finished all of its legislative amendments remains to be seen.

However, this does not help someone who has exhausted their lifetime allowance. A pension commencement lump sum is payable only when some or all of an individual's lifetime allowance is available at the date of vesting. Therefore, even if a lump sum is protected because it exceeded 25% at A-Day, if it exceeds the available lifetime allowance at retirement, the excess is subject to a lifetime allowance charge. This is illustrated by an example in RPSM03105620:

How to pay protected lump sum benefits exceeding 25%: there is not enough available lifetime allowance

'Peter has a proposed lump sum benefit of £50,000 under a *registered pension scheme*.

The lump sum is calculated on the basis of Peter's protected lump sum rights in the scheme.

Immediately before taking benefits from this scheme, his available *lifetime allowance* is valued at £20,000. The maximum Peter can take as a *pension commencement lump sum* is £50,000. If he does, £20,000 of his pension commencement lump sum is free of income tax – but £30,000 is subject to the *lifetime allowance charge* under section 215 Finance Act 2004.'

Other protections

Pension credit rights 6.30

There are two protections available for any individual who has pension credit rights arising as a result of pension sharing on divorce. The first relates to pension credit rights acquired before A-Day. The second relates to pension credit rights acquired on or after A-Day in respect of a pension which came into payment on or after A-Day. Although this second type is not an existing right at A-Day, we are covering it here for completeness.

The two protections operate by allowing members with such pension credit rights to claim a lifetime allowance enhancement factor. The enhancement factor increases the standard lifetime allowance for such members in the same way as provided for under primary protection.

Pension credit rights acquired before A-Day

Before A-Day a member with pension credit rights would not be subject to HMRC benefit limits. Instead, the HMRC maximum benefit of the person whose pension was being shared was subject to a reduction equivalent to the value of the pension credit rights.

Anyone seeking to claim an enhancement factor for their pre A-Day pension credit rights must give notice to HMRC on or before 5 April 2009. The enhancement factor itself is calculated according to the following formula:

IAPC / SLA

where:

IAPC is the appropriate amount of the pension credit rights at the date they were acquired (ie that part of the original member's cash equivalent transfer value which was split in favour of the ex-spouse); and

SLA is the standard lifetime allowance for the 2006/07 tax year (£1.5m).

In determining the amount of **IAPC**, it is increased in line with increases in the Retail Prices Index from the month in which the pension credit rights were acquired up to April 2006.

Note, however, that a lifetime allowance enhancement factor cannot be claimed for pre-A-Day pension credit rights if the pension credit member has also made a claim for primary protection.

Pension credit rights acquired on or after A-Day

This protection can only be claimed if the pension being shared came into payment on or after A-Day. As the pension being shared would have been tested against the lifetime allowance when it was brought into payment, it would be unfair to test part of it against the lifetime allowance a second time.

Anyone seeking to claim an enhancement factor for these pension credit rights must give notice to HMRC by 31 January five years after 31 January following the tax year in which the pension sharing order or provision took effect. The enhancement factor is calculated according to the following formula:

APC / SLA

where:

APC is the appropriate amount of the pension credit rights at the date they were acquired (ie that part of the original member's cash equivalent transfer value which was split in favour of the ex-spouse); and

SLA is the standard lifetime allowance at the time when the pension credit rights were acquired.

Five-year guarantees   6.31

Once in payment, a pension from an occupational pension scheme, whether defined benefit or money purchase, may be guaranteed to continue in payment for up to ten years, notwithstanding the death of the member within that period. In respect of guarantees of five years or less, however, the balance of instalments between the date of death and the end of the five-year period may be paid as a tax-free lump sum.

Under the new tax regime it would appear that a defined benefits pension arrangement, which pays a lump sum death benefit equal to the balance of the five-year guarantee, could continue to make this payment tax free, albeit subject to the lifetime allowance, if death occurs before age 75. A similar payment from a money purchase arrangement, however, would be subject to 35% tax as an annuity protection lump sum death benefit.

Legislation would seek to ensure that where a pension came into payment before A-Day and there was an attaching right for payment of the guarantee balance as a lump sum, that lump sum could continue to be paid tax free on death after A-Day within the guarantee period and regardless of whether the pensioner was over age 75 at date of death.

Children's pensions 6.32

Under the new tax regime pensions paid to dependent children (other than those paid as a result of incapacity) must cease by age 23. Draft legislation (a draft Finance Act 2004 (Transitional Provisions) Order 2005) would seek to ensure that a right to a child's pension pre A-Day would continue post A-Day and the pension would be payable until the later of the child reaching age 23 and ceasing full-time education or vocational training. For this protection to apply one of the following three conditions must be met:

Condition 1

(*a*)   the pension was in payment to a child of the member on 5 April 2006 or the member had died on or before 5 April 2006 and a pension was due to come into payment to the child; and

(*b*)   the rules of the pension scheme allowed a pension to be paid to a child of the member following the death of that member until the child ceased full-time education or vocational training.

Condition 2

(*a*)   the pension was in payment to a member on 5 April 2006;

(*b*)   the rules of the pension scheme allowed a pension to be paid to a child of the member following the death of that member until the child ceased full-time education or vocational training; and

(*c*)   the child was born on or before 5 April 2007.

Condition 3

(*a*)   the rules of the pension scheme allowed an irrevocable election to be made designating part of the sums or assets representing the member's rights as available for the payment of a pension to a child of the member following the death of that member until the child ceased full-time education or vocational training; and

(*b*)   such an election had been made by the member and accepted by the scheme administrator on or before 9 December 2003.

Funeral expenses 6.33

The rules of some occupational pension schemes allow a one-off tax-free payment to be made upon the death of a member in order to fund funeral expenses. Under the new tax regime such payments would not have been authorised payments if the member were aged 75 or over at the date of death.

Draft legislation (a draft Pension Schemes (Transitional Provisions) Order 2005) has been laid to allow these payments to continue to be paid tax free where a right to receive them existed on 10 December 2003 and the member retired before A-Day. This is achieved by adding another type of benefit, called a 'life cover lump sum', to the list of authorised lump sum death benefits in *s 168, Finance Act 2004*.

A lump sum death benefit is a life cover lump sum if:

(*a*) the member had reached the age of 75 before he or she died; and

(*b*) payment of the sum would not have prejudiced approval of the scheme for the purposes of *Ch I, Part XIV, Income and Corporation Taxes Act 1988*, if it had been made on 5 April 2006.

The conditions to be met for a life cover lump sum to be paid are as follows:

(*a*) the registered pension scheme was, immediately before A Day, a retirement benefit scheme approved for the purposes of *Ch I, Part XIV, Income and Corporation Taxes Act 1988*;

(*b*) the member had a right under the pension scheme to a life cover lump sum on 5 April 2006;

(*c*) the rules of the pension scheme on 10 December 2003 included provision conferring such a right on some or all of the persons who were then members of the pension scheme, and such a right was either then conferred on the member or would have been had the member been a member of the scheme on that date;

(*d*) the rules of the scheme in relation to life cover lump sums have not been changed since 10 December 2003; and

(*e*) the member was in receipt of benefits from the scheme on or before 5 April 2006.

A life cover lump sum is exempted from income tax by adding it to the list of exemptions in *s 636A, Income Tax (Earnings and Pensions) Act 2003* (exemption for certain lump sums under registered pension schemes). A life cover lump sum would also appear not to be subject to the lifetime allowance, as it is not defined as a relevant lump sum death benefit for the purpose of benefit crystallisation events (*s 216* and *Sch 32, Finance Act 2004*).

Lump sums held over until after A-Day   6.34

There may be occasions where a member will become entitled to a lump sum payment before A-Day but, for some reason, it is not paid until on or after A-Day. To avoid the scenario where such lump sums would fall to be treated under the new tax regime, amending legislation will ensure that the pre A-Day rules continue to apply to such lump sum payments.

Cash-only schemes 6.35

There are a number of schemes which were approved pre A-Day as occupational retirement benefit schemes, but which provide only a tax-free lump sum on retirement (e g 3/80 x final remuneration). The first problem is that a pension commencement lump sum can only be paid in connection with a relevant pension (*para 1(1)(a), Sch 29, Finance Act 2004*). Draft legislation (a draft Pension Schemes (Part 4 of the Finance Act 2004 Transitional [and Transitory] Provisions) Order 2005) would modify this so that such lump sums can continue to be paid even though there is no connected pension payment, but there would be conditions attaching to the protection. The second problem is how to calculate such lump sums at retirement.

For an individual to benefit from this protection, the following conditions should be met:

(*a*) relevant benefit accrual as defined for enhanced protection must not have occurred under the pension scheme in relation to the individual on or after the A-Day;

(*b*) the individual's rights under the pension scheme on A-Day consist only of uncrystallised lump sum rights; and

(*c*) all of the individual's uncrystallised rights under the scheme will come into payment at a single benefit crystallisation event.

The protected tax-free lump sum at retirement would be calculated as the lump sum entitlement on 5 April 2006 increased by the rise in the lifetime allowance since A-Day. It is expressed in the following formula:

VULSR x CSLA / FSLA

where:

VULSR is the value of uncrystallised lump sum rights on 5 April 2006, limited to the maximum approvable lump sum;

CSLA is the standard lifetime allowance applicable at the date of vesting; and

FSLA is the standard lifetime allowance for the 2006/07 tax year (i e £1.5m).

Note that the protection conditions above may be slightly different for an individual who has either primary or enhanced protection.

Rights to retire below the normal minimum pension age

6.36

Except in cases of ill-health the normal minimum pension age at which benefits may come into payment under the new tax regime is 50 until 5 April 2010, and 55 thereafter. Members may have rights to take benefits below these ages in two situations. The first is that they belong to a scheme with a low normal retirement age (under 50), such schemes normally being for sportspersons or those in hazardous occupations. The second is where they may be entitled to early payment of pension from age 50 as of right in certain conditions (eg redundancy).

Right to low normal retirement age (below 50)

Members of personal pension schemes and retirement annuity contracts will be able to retain their low normal retirement age if they had an unqualified right to take a pension before age 50, they become entitled to all of their uncrystallised pension and/or lump sum rights under the scheme on the same day and they held an occupation as one of the following:

(*a*)   Athlete

(*b*)   Badminton Player

(*c*)   Boxer

(*d*)   Cricketer

(*e*)   Cyclist

(*f*)   Dancer

(*g*)   Diver (Saturation, Deep Sea and Free Swimming)

(*h*)   Footballer

(*i*)   Golfer

(*j*)   Ice Hockey Player

(*k*)   Jockey – Flat Racing

(*l*)   Jockey – National Hunt

(*m*)   Member of the Reserve Forces

(*n*)   Model

(*o*)   Motor Cycle Rider (Motocross or Road Racing)

(*p*)   Motor Racing Driver

(*q*)   Rugby League Player

(*r*)   Rugby Union Player

(s)   Skier (Downhill)

(t)   Snooker or Billiards Player

(u)   Speedway Rider

(v)   Squash Player

(w)   Table Tennis Player

(x)   Tennis Player (including Real Tennis)

(y)   Trapeze Artiste

(z)   Wrestler

Note that if the pension scheme relates to an employment, the member must have left employment before being able to benefit from the lower normal retirement age. Additionally, where a block transfer is made, members with a right to a low normal retirement age may continue to hold that right under the new arrangement. The conditions for a block transfer are described at **6.26** above.

Members of occupational pension schemes or deferred annuity contracts with a low normal retirement age will be able to retain that right if the following conditions are met:

(a)   the member must have had the right on 5 April 2006 to take a pension and/or lump sum before the age of 55;

(b)   the right must be unqualified (in that no other party need consent to the individual's request before it becomes binding upon the scheme or contract holder);

(c)   the provision to take benefits before age 55 must have been set out in the governing documentation of the retirement benefit scheme or deferred annuity contract on 10 December 2003;

(d)   the member must have either:

    (i)   had the right under the scheme or contract on 10 December 2003; or

    (ii)   acquired the right in accordance with the scheme provisions as they were on 10 December 2003 upon joining the scheme after that date;

(e)   the member must have become entitled to all of his or her uncrystallised pension and/or lump sum rights under the scheme on the same day; and

(f)   the member must have left the employment to which the scheme relates.

Note that where a block transfer is made, members with a right to a low normal retirement age may continue to hold that right under the new arrangement.

Although individuals with a low normal retirement age may continue to enjoy this right under transitional protection, their lifetime allowance will be reduced if they do decide to exercise their right to retire before age 50. Their lifetime allowance will be reduced by 2.5% for each complete year between the date of the benefit crystallisation event and the date on which they would have reached normal minimum pension age (50 or 55 depending). The 2.5% reduction will not apply, however, if an individual is taking his or her benefits from one of the following schemes:

(*a*)   the Armed Forces Pension Scheme;

(*b*)   the British Transport Police Force Superannuation Fund;

(*c*)   the Firefighters' Pension Scheme;

(*d*)   the Firemen's Pension Scheme (Northern Ireland);

(*e*)   the Police Pension Scheme;

(*f*)   the Police Service of Northern Ireland Pension Scheme;

(*g*)   the Police Service of Northern Ireland Full Time Reserve Pension Scheme; or

(*h*)   a scheme established solely for the receipt of additional voluntary pension contributions from members of the schemes above.

Right to early retirement age (over 50 and below 55)

For a member of an occupational pension scheme or deferred annuity contract to retain his or her right to take benefits from an age after 50 but before 55, the following conditions must apply:

(*a*)   the member must have had the right on 5 April 2006 to take a pension and/or lump sum at a minimum age from 50 to 54;

(*b*)   the right must be unqualified (in that no other party need consent to the individual's request before it becomes binding upon the scheme or contract holder);

(*c*)   the provision to pay benefits before age 55 must have been set out in the governing documentation of the retirement benefit scheme or deferred annuity contract on 10 December 2003;

(*d*)   the member must have either:

    (i)   had the right under the scheme or contract on 10 December 2003; or

    (ii)   acquired the right in accordance with the scheme provisions as they were on 10 December 2003 upon joining the scheme after that date;

(*e*)   the member must have become entitled to all of his or her uncrystallised pension and/or lump sum rights under the scheme on the same day; and

(*f*)   the member must have left the employment to which the scheme relates.

Note that where a block transfer is made, members with a right to an early retirement age below the normal minimum retirement age may continue to hold that right under the new arrangement. The conditions for a block transfer are described at **6.26** above.

Chapter 7
Tax charges and penalties

Introduction 7.1

The new simplified pensions regime is founded on the basis of compliance with the statutory legislation. The former discretionary pensions regime in *Pt XIV, Income and Corporation Taxes Act 1988,* with few sanctions against transgressions, has been abolished. Instead, all of HMRC's requirements for registered pension schemes are now enshrined in statute and strict adherence thereto has been required since A-Day. There are no detailed discretionary practice notes. These have been replaced to some extent by the *Registered Pension Schemes Manual* (see **1.24** above), but the manual is a direct interpretation of the statutory provisions and does not permit any deviation therefrom without incurring a tax charge and/or penalty.

The regime requires compliance by scheme administrators, employers and members, with specified reporting requirements to HMRC and compliance audit carried out by HMRC staff to ensure compliance has taken place. Breaches of the legislation notified to HMRC, or of which HMRC becomes aware via the reporting process or compliance audit, will result in a range of tax charges, some quite substantial, being imposed on scheme administrators and members rather than de-registration of the pension scheme, although this sanction may be used. Penalties, which again can be quite substantial, may also be sought for other transgressions of statute. This is the way in which HMRC intends to prevent abuses of the benefits obtained from the tax reliefs and exemptions afforded to registered pension schemes from A-Day.

This chapter describes the various tax charges and penalties that may be imposed, the circumstances giving rise to them, the rates of tax chargeable and the persons liable to pay them.

Tax charges

The unauthorised payments charge 7.2

This tax charge is provided for in *s 208, Finance Act 2004.* It is imposed on payments from registered pension schemes to a member or sponsoring employer that are not authorised by the scheme rules. Tax is chargeable at 40%

on the amount of the unauthorised payment and is payable by the member, the recipient or the sponsoring employer according to the circumstances. Unauthorised payments include:

(*a*)   benefits taken before age 50 from A–Day and age 55 from 2010;

(*b*)   cash lump sum benefits in excess of the permitted maximum;

(*c*)   assignments or surrenders of pension;

(*d*)   reductions or stopping of a pension;

(*e*)   lump sum death benefits paid to a person not in existence at the death of a member;

(*f*)   deceased member's rights used to increase the rights of a connected person;

(*g*)   dependant's pension in excess of the member pension limit;

(*h*)   transfers to non-registered pension schemes;

(*i*)   unauthorised loans;

(*j*)   winding-up lump sum death benefits paid to non-dependants;

(*k*)   trivial commutation in excess of 1% of the fund;

(*l*)   payments to migrant members who have benefited from UK tax relief;

(*m*)   value shifting from a registered pension scheme to a member or to a sponsored employer (see **5.29** above);

(*n*)   debts payable by members to a scheme which are not on arm's-length terms (including debts payable by a person connected with the member).

Use (*n*) of a scheme asset by a member or any of his or her family or household will be treated as an unauthorised payment, but taxed as a benefit-in-kind (see **7.10** below).

Where an unauthorised payments charge arises on funds which were previously liberated from a member's pensions savings because the member was duped into liberating the funds, and the funds are repatriated, *s 266A, Finance Act 2004*, provides relief from the unauthorised payments charge. The member concerned has to claim the relief within a year of the repatriation of the funds.

Where a pension is reduced (see (*d*) above), the unauthorised payments charge is applied once only, under *Sch 28, para 2, Finance Act 2004*, on the first occasion when there is a reduction. This measure ensures that the lump sum rules are not manipulated by inflating a pension to increase the level of the tax-free cash lump sum and then reducing or stopping the pension.

The unauthorised payments surcharge   7.3

This tax charge is provided for in *s 227, Finance Act 2004*. It is payable in addition to the unauthorised payments charge in **7.2**. The surcharge arises if the amount of the unauthorised payment to the member (*s 210(7), Finance Act 2004*) or sponsoring employer (*s 213(7), Finance Act 2004*) is 25% or more of the fund value or if more than one unauthorised payment is made to a member (*s 210(2), Finance Act 2004*) or sponsoring employer (*s 213(2), Finance Act 2004*) in a specified period. The rate of the surcharge is 15% of the amount of the unauthorised surchargeable payment and is payable by the member, the recipient or the sponsoring employer according to the circumstances. This would bring the total payable by the member or employer in any such instance to 55% of the value of the unauthorised payment.

Where an unauthorised payments surcharge arises on funds which were previously liberated from a member's pensions savings because a member was duped into liberating the funds, and the funds are repatriated, *s 266A, Finance Act 2004*, also provides relief from the unauthorised payments surcharge. Once again, the member concerned has to claim the relief within a year of the repatriation of the funds.

The annual allowance charge   7.4

This tax charge is provided for in *s 227, Finance Act 2004*. It is payable if a member's total pension input for a given tax year exceeds the annual allowance for that year. The rate of tax chargeable is 40% of the amount by which the total amount of the pension input exceeds the annual allowance. The charge is payable by the member concerned via self-assessment.

The lifetime allowance charge   7.5

This charge is provided for in *s 214, Finance Act 2004*. It is payable if an individual's total pension savings exceed the lifetime allowance for any year in which they are wholly or partly vested. This may include instances where primary protection has been registered or where benefits vest on the death of a member. The rate of tax chargeable is 25% of the amount of the excess over the lifetime allowance if a pension is paid. However, if a cash lump sum is paid, the rate of tax chargeable is increased to 55% by *s 215(2), Finance Act 2004*. The charge is payable under *s 215(9), Finance Act 2004* by the scheme administrator, the member or a beneficiary.

The scheme sanction charge   7.6

This charge is provided for in *s 239, Finance Act 2004*. It arises if the administrator of a registered pension scheme makes one or more scheme chargeable payments in any year. Scheme chargeable payments are defined in *s 41(1), Finance Act 2004*, either as an unauthorised payment as in **7.2** above or as unauthorised borrowings. The rate of tax chargeable is 40% of the amount of the scheme chargeable payment. *Section 240(2), Finance Act 2004*, provides that, where the scheme chargeable payment is an unauthorised payment on which the unauthorised payments charge at **7.2** has already been paid, a reduction is made to the amount of tax that would otherwise be chargeable. This reduction is limited to the lower of:

(*a*)   25% of the scheme chargeable payments on which tax was paid under the unauthorised payments charge; and

(*b*)   the actual amount of tax paid on the unauthorised payment.

The charge is payable by the scheme administrator.

Unauthorised payments may include the use of assets to provide benefits where those assets are wasting assets (*s 44, Taxation of Chargeable Gains Act 1992*, states that a wasting asset is one which has an anticipated life of less than 50 years). Such assets will include properties with less than 50-year leases, cars, race-horses, plant and machinery etc. The unauthorised payments charge is not due where tax charges are made in respect of benefits-in-kind on non-wasting assets.

Where a scheme sanction charge arises on funds which were previously liberated from a member's pensions savings because a member was duped into liberating the funds, and the funds are repatriated, *s 266B, Finance Act 2004*, provides relief from the scheme sanction charge. The scheme administrator has to claim the relief within a year of the repatriation of the funds.

The de-registration charge   7.7

This charge is provided for in *s 242, Finance Act 2004*. It will be incurred where, exceptionally, registration of a scheme is withdrawn. This will happen in circumstances where HMRC considers that a pension scheme has failed to meet certain statutory requirements. The rate of tax chargeable is 40% of the value of the whole fund. The charge is payable by the person who was the scheme administrator immediately before HMRC de-registered the scheme.

The special lump sum death benefits charge   7.8

This charge is provided for in *s 206, Finance Act 2004*. It arises where a member dies before their 75th birthday and:

(*a*)   an annuity lump sum death benefit is payable; or

(b)   the member was in receipt of an unsecured pension from the whole or part of their pension fund.

The charge is payable on either the value of the annuity lump sum death benefit or on the value of the member's fund supporting the unsecured pension in payment at their death. The rate of tax chargeable in either instance is 35%. The charge is payable by the scheme administrator. If an insurance company pays a lump sum death benefit to the deceased member's nominee, the insurance company is liable under *s 273A, Finance Act 2004*, for the tax charge.

The authorised surplus payments charge   7.9

This charge is provided for in *s 207, Finance Act 2004*. It applies where an authorised surplus payment is made by a registered pension scheme to a sponsoring employer. The charge is payable on the amount of any surplus payment authorised by HMRC to be repaid to a sponsoring employer. The rate of tax chargeable is 35% on the amount of the surplus to be repaid. *Section 177, Finance Act 2004,* provides for regulations to be published covering the calculation of surpluses. These regulations have not yet been finalised.

The tax charge on benefits-in-kind   7.10

This charge is provided for in *s 173, Finance Act 2004*. It arises where members or their relatives occupy residential property or enjoy the use of a pride-in-possession asset owned by a registered pension scheme at less than a commercial rent. An unauthorised payment, as in **7.2** above, arises on the value of the benefit-in-kind so enjoyed. The rate of tax chargeable is 40%. The charge is payable by the member enjoying the benefit or any other recipient of the benefit at the rate of 40%, regardless of their effective rate of tax.

Non-UK schemes – application of certain charges   7.11

Some of the member payment charges mentioned at **7.2–7.10** above and elsewhere apply to, or are deemed to apply to, a tax-relieved UK scheme member of a relevant non-UK scheme or to a transfer member of such a scheme under *Sch 34, Finance Act 2004*. Under *Sch 34, para 1(3)*, these charges include:

(a)   the unauthorised payments charge at **7.2**;

(b)   the unauthorised payments surcharge at **7.3**;

(c)   the short service refund lump sum charge;

(*d*)   the special lump sum death benefits charge at **7.8**;

(*e*)   the trivial commutation lump sum charge.

7.12

Under *Sch 34, para 1(5), Finance Act 2004*, the scheme is a 'relevant non-UK scheme' if:

(*a*)   migrant member relief has been given;

(*b*)   double taxation relief has been given post A-Day;

(*c*)   members have been exempted under *s 307, Income Tax (Earnings and Pensions) Act 2003*, from tax liability relating to pension or death benefit provision at any time after A-Day when the scheme was an overseas scheme; and

(*d*)   there has been a relevant transfer from a UK scheme after A-Day when the scheme was a qualifying recognised overseas scheme.

7.13

Under *Sch 34, para 2, Finance Act 2004*, the member payment charge only applies to transfers where the member was resident in the UK at the time the transfer was made or had been resident within any of the preceding five years. The rate of tax payable and the person liable to pay the tax relating to a member payment charge are the same as for the relevant payment charge concerned.

The annual allowance charge at **7.4** above must be adjusted under *Sch 34, paras 8–12, Finance Act 2004*, where it applies to currently-relieved members of currently-relieved non-UK pension schemes ie the conditions in **7.12**(*a*)–(*d*) above apply. Formulae for calculating the annual allowance charge in these circumstances are provided in *Sch 34, paras 9–11, Finance Act 2004*.

The lifetime allowance charge at **7.5** above also has to be adjusted under *Sch 34, paras 13–19, Finance Act 2004*, where it applies to currently-relieved members of currently-relieved non-UK pension schemes. Provision is made in *Sch 34, para 14, Finance Act 2004*, for calculating the lifetime allowance charge on vesting, that takes non-UK pension scheme benefits into account. Members can elect under *Sch 34, para 15(1), Finance Act 2004*, to notify HMRC of the appropriate date of vesting. Under *Sch 34, para 16(2), Finance Act 2004*, transfers count as benefit crystallisation events unless they form part of a block transfer.

Penalties

Introduction 7.14

Separately from, and sometimes in addition to, the foregoing tax charges under the new regime, HMRC has the power in *ss 257–266, Finance Act 2004*, to seek penalties, substantial in some instances, for failure to provide information and the provision of false information.

Pension scheme returns 7.15

The failure to provide a pension scheme return can render the scheme administrator liable under *s 257(1), Finance Act 2004*, to a penalty of £100 and under *s 257(2), Finance Act 2004*, to a continuing penalty of up to £60 per day for the continuing failure. If the administrator makes an incorrect return or delivers incorrect accounts, they become liable to a penalty under *s 257(4), Finance Act 2004*, not exceeding £3,000.

Provision of information 7.16

Section 98, Taxes Management Act 1970, has been amended by *s 258(1), Finance Act 2004*, to allow for penalties to be imposed for failure to provide information or providing false information. If a person fails to preserve documents where required, they may be liable to a penalty under *s 258(2), Finance Act 2004*, not exceeding £3,000.

Provision of documents or particulars 7.17

If a person fails to comply with a notice requiring documents or particulars, a penalty not exceeding £300 under *s 259(1), Finance Act 2004*, may be imposed, with a continuing penalty up to £60 per day under *s 259(2), Finance Act 2004*, for the continuing failure. If a person fraudulently or negligently produces or makes available for inspection any incorrect documents, or provides any incorrect particulars, a penalty not exceeding £3,000 under *s 259(4), Finance Act 2004*, may be imposed.

Accounting return 7.18

If a scheme administrator fails to make a return of tax charged, they may be liable to a penalty under *s 260, Finance Act 2004*, calculated according to the tax payable and to the number of persons whose particulars should be included in the return. If the return is incorrect through fraud or negligence, further penalties under *s 260(6), Finance Act 2004*, may be imposed.

Registration of enhanced lifetime allowance 7.19

Some individuals are entitled to a different level of lifetime allowance (see **CHAPTER 6** above). They must produce or make available certain documents, certificates and information when registering such a non-standard lifetime allowance. If they provide or make available incorrect or false documents, certificates or information when registering an enhanced lifetime allowance, HMRC has the power in *s 261, Finance Act 2004*, to impose a penalty of up to 25% of the excess allowance claimed on the individual concerned.

Regulations laid under *s 262, Finance Act 2004*, which have yet to be finalised, will allow HMRC to request information to verify an individual's registration for an enhanced lifetime allowance. If these information requirements are not complied with, the individual concerned may be liable to a penalty under *s 262, Finance Act 2004*, of up to £3,000.

Failure to notify benefits accruing 7.20

As discussed in **CHAPTER 6**, individuals may protect their funds and rights arising before A-Day by registering a claim for enhanced protection. They cannot then accrue retirement benefits after A-Day, and if they do, they must notify HMRC. Failure to notify HMRC within 90 days of benefits accruing can render the individual concerned liable to a penalty under *s 263, Finance Act 2004*, of up to £3,000.

False statements 7.21

If someone fraudulently or negligently makes a statement or representation to enable themselves or someone else to obtain relief from tax, a tax repayment, or to benefit from an unauthorised payment, they may be liable to a penalty under *s 264(1), Finance Act 2004*, not exceeding £3,000. If someone assists or helps in the provision of incorrect information which may result in an unauthorised payment, they may also be liable under *s 264(2), Finance Act 2004*, to a similar penalty.

Benefits on winding up 7.22

If a registered pension scheme is deliberately wound up to provide winding-up lump sums to the members or winding-up lump sum death benefits to others, the scheme administrator is liable to a penalty under *s 265, Finance Act 2004*, not exceeding £3,000 in respect of each member to whom a winding-up lump sum, and in respect of whom a winding-up lump sum death benefit, is paid. Additionally, the scheme may be de-registered and suffer a 40% tax charge.

Transfers to the appropriate person   7.23

A penalty of up to £3,000 may be imposed under *s 266, Finance Act 2004*, on any scheme administrator who does not ensure that transfers, which are made to another registered pension scheme that invests in insurance policies, are made to the appropriate person. This is to encourage compliance with transfer procedures and minimise the risk of misdirecting transfers.

Discharge from liability   7.24

Scheme administrators will have to rely on information provided by scheme members to determine whether or not the lifetime allowance has been exceeded. There will be other occasions when it would not be just or reasonable to impose a tax charge on administrators eg the unauthorised payments surcharge at **7.3** above or the scheme sanction charge at **7.6** above. So scheme administrators can seek a discharge from HMRC under *s 267, Finance Act 2004*, from a lifetime allowance charge where they reasonably believe there was no such liability and it would be just and reasonable to discharge the liability. Scheme administrators can similarly seek a discharge under *s 268, Finance Act 2004*, from liability to pay an unauthorised payments surcharge or a scheme sanction charge if, in all the circumstances of the case, it would not be just and reasonable to impose either charge. If HMRC refuses to discharge a scheme administrator from liability in any of these instances, an appeal can be made under *s 269, Finance Act 2004*, to the General or Special Commissioners within 30 days of HMRC's notification of refusal.

The administrator and other persons generally will need to demonstrate that they acted in good faith or on grounds of reasonableness.

Under the *Registered Pension Schemes (Unauthorised Payments by Existing Schemes) Regulations 2006 (SI 2006/365)* a payment falling within *para 1(1), Sch 36, Finance Act 2004*, on or after 6 April 2006, is exempt from being treated as a scheme chargeable payment for the purposes of *s 241(2)* of that Act if it is a payment that is referable to subsisting rights which have accrued under defined benefits arrangements before that day, or to contributions which have been paid to a scheme under money purchase arrangements before that day. This will avoid being subject to the otherwise relevant charges described above. However, the exemption is limited in the case of a payment which is a refund of additional voluntary contributions.

Surpluses 7.25

It is still possible for employers to extract surplus monies from pension schemes subject to the fixed tax charge of 35% (*ss 177* and *207, Finance Act 2004*). In order to determine whether a surplus arises in a defined benefit scheme, DWP rules will be laid down, and legislation will also be passed for money purchase schemes. This means that, with effect from A-Day, all the previous legislation and practice which related to the reduction of surpluses, the regular reviews for surpluses etc have ceased. Any earlier periods must be administered under the old rules.

Value shifting 7.26

Chapter 3, s 174, Finance Act 2004, describes the concept of 'value shifting' (see **7.2**(*m*) above), which is aimed at preventing transactions which pass value from a registered scheme to a member without creating a payment. Such transactions can be deemed to be unauthorised payments. There will also be new rules which prevent the reallocation of investments and benefits for the purpose of tax avoidance.

Appeals 7.27

The following appeals against HMRC action may be made to the General Commissioners or the Special Commissioners, normally within 30 days of the relevant event:

- against a failure to register a scheme;

- against an action to de-register a scheme;

- against a decision to exclude a recognised overseas pension scheme;

- against notices requiring documents or particulars; and

- in respect of the discharge of the lifetime allowance charge.

The main appeals procedures which were in place pre A-Day remain. The order that makes the necessary modifications to reflect the transfer of powers to HMRC is entitled the *Taxes Management Act 1970 (Modifications to Schedule 3 for Pension Scheme Appeals) Order 2005 (SI 2005/3457)*.

Audit and compliance 7.28

The government intends an audit programme to be operated on a random selection basis and also on a risk-assessment basis. Audits will cover a wide perspective in connection with scheme administration, contributions (including the valuation of 'in specie'), investment (including benefits-in-kind), payments, the lifetime allowance, and other activities. In the event of non-compliance, penalties and sanctions may be imposed, and appropriate sanctions will be set for false claims to transitional relief and for payments which are not made in accordance with the agreed transitional rules for the member concerned. HMRC is discussing post-simplification audit objectives with industry representatives.

There will normally be a pre-inspection visit.

The *Registered Pension Schemes (Accounting and Assessment) Regulations 2005 (SI 2005/3454)* and the *Registered Pension Schemes (Audited Accounts) (Specified Persons) Regulations 2005 (SI 2005/3456)* apply.

Inheritance tax 7.29

The pre A-Day inheritance tax exemptions for approved schemes held under discretionary trusts continue post A-Day. However, for non-registered schemes, *Sch 36, paras 56–58, Finance Act 2004*, describe the inheritance tax exemptions for schemes with no post A-Day contributions, and those with post A-Day contributions (see **CHAPTER 10** for details of the application of the new rules). Effectively, the relief will remain on the accumulated fund as at A-Day if no further contributions are paid, but will be restricted where contributions are made – and further accrual will not be tax exempt. *Section 203, Finance Act 2004*, amends the *Inheritance Tax Act 1984* in order to accommodate the above changes.

The general tax avoidance rules 7.30

Part 7, Finance Act 2004, covers general tax avoidance. However, it could apply to tax avoidance arrangements in relation to pension schemes if anything is done in breach of prescribed circumstances. A summary of the main disclosure requirements is given below.

Notifiable overseas arrangements, and promoters 7.31

Section 306, Finance Act 2004, concerns notifiable arrangements and notifiable proposals under tax-avoidance schemes. Such arrangements are those which fall within any description prescribed by the Treasury by regulations. They enable a person to gain a tax advantage by means of the main, or one of the main, benefits of the arrangement.

A promoter of such an arrangement is described in *s 307, Finance Act 2004*, as follows:

'a person is a promoter–

(*a*)   in relation to a notifiable proposal if, in the course of a "relevant business"–

(i)   he is to any extent responsible for the design of the proposed arrangements, or

(ii)   he makes the notifiable proposal available for implementation by other persons, and

(*b*)   in relation to notifiable arrangements, if he is by virtue of paragraph (*a*)(ii) a promoter in relation to a notifiable proposal which is implemented by those arrangements or if, in the course of a relevant business, he is to any extent responsible for–

(i)   the design of the arrangements, or

(ii)   the organisation or management of the arrangements.'

'Relevant business' means any trade, profession or business which either involves the provision to other persons of services relating to taxation, or is carried on by a bank, as defined by *s 840A, Income and Corporation taxes Act 1988*, or by a securities house, as defined by *s 209A(4)* of that Act.

A person is not to be treated as a promoter for the purposes by reason of anything done in prescribed circumstances. By way of a relaxation, the government stated on 24 June 2004 that only those at the heart of the scheme or arrangement, who are capable of meeting its obligations, will be treated as the promoter.

Under *s 308, Finance Act 2004*, the promoter must provide information to HMRC within a prescribed period after the date on which he or she makes a notifiable proposal, or the date on which he or she first becomes aware of any transaction forming part of the proposed arrangements. This applies under *s 319* to post-17 March 2004 relevant dates and transactions.

Under *s 309* the duty falls on any client who enters into any transaction forming part of any notifiable arrangements in relation to which a promoter is resident outside the UK, and no promoter is resident in the UK. Under *s 310* the duty extends to any other person who enters into any transaction forming part of any notifiable arrangements in similar circumstances. *Sections 309* and *310* apply, by virtue of *s 319*, to post-22 April 2004 transactions.

Penalties for non-compliance 7.32

Under *s 312, Finance Act 2004*, the promoter must provide information to the client within 30 days in relation to the arrangements. There are penalties for non-compliance – *s 315, Finance Act 2004*, inserts *s 98C* into the *Taxes Management Act 1970*. A penalty not exceeding £5,000 will be imposed on a promoter, with penalties of £600 a day for continuing non-compliance. Any person who is a party to the arrangement who fails to comply will be fined £100 per scheme, or £500 or £1,000 if he or she has previously failed to comply during the preceding period of 36 months on one or more occasions (respectively).

Disclosure 7.33

Disclosures must be made on the forms on the HMRC website, which were published on 28 May 2004. These are S292 for UK promoters, S293 for users where there is an overseas promoter and S294 for users where there is no external promoter. Various 'tax avoidance' and 'tackling tax avoidance' regulations have been drafted.

The statutory rules are not only very wide; they almost impossible to understand. The intended meanings of 'avoidance' and 'promoter' in the *Finance Act 2004* are unclear. It is hoped that clarification will be received at a future date. The new rules potentially impact on employment terms, securities, financial products, premium fees and confidentiality testing – which will widely affect disclosure rules for employers, advisers and others.

Chapter 8
Administration, registration and reporting

The scheme administrator   8.1

The scheme administrator of a registered scheme has an important role in scheme registration and reporting. The administrator is defined in *s 270, Finance Act 2004*. The administrator must be:

- a resident of the UK or another state which is an EU member state or a non-member EEA state; and

- a person who has made an appropriate declaration to HMRC.

The administrator must also be a legal person (for example, a corporate body, but not a partnership) and must register individually. Tax charges, penalties and interest can all fall on the administrator on a failure to comply.

Administration payments   8.2

Chapter 3, ss 171 and *180, Finance Act 2004*, state that payments for administration or management to members and employers (respectively) which exceed those which might be expected to be paid to a person at arm's length, and loans to a sponsoring employer, are not deemed to be administration expenses.

HMRC has also issued guidance on management expenses which fall under *s 75, Income and Corporation Taxes Act 1988*, on its website. The meaning of, and the liability of, the administrator are to be found in *Ch 7, ss 270–274*, and *Sch 36, Pt 1, paras 4* and *6, Finance Act 2004*. Where a scheme is used by a member, an expense is not treated as an unauthorised payment if it is a benefit received by reason of an employment; for example, where an employee is provided with a company car.

In general, allowable scheme administration employer payments include the payment of wages, salaries or fees to persons engaged in scheme administration and payments for the purchase of assets. Payments made for the acquisition of shares in the sponsoring employer are not scheme administration employer payments if the market value of such shares held by the scheme is 5% or greater of the fund. In the case of more than one employer in the scheme, the threshold is 20% or greater (*s 180(5)*, *Finance Act 2004*).

Authorised practitioner   8.3

A new role of 'authorised practitioner' has been introduced, whom the administrator can authorise to perform certain tasks (with the exception of registration). The administrator may authorise different authorised practitioners for specific roles.

Sub-divided schemes   8.4

In certain sub-divided schemes, such as the Local Government Scheme, it will be permitted to treat each division as a separate scheme for the purpose of tax administration. *Schedule 10, Finance Act 2005*, inserts a new *s 274A* into the *Finance Act 2004* which empowers HMRC to make regulations for and in connection with treating registered pension schemes as if they were a number of separate registered pension schemes.

Registration

General   8.5

Under the new tax regime from A-Day, previously exempt approved schemes and public sector pension schemes have automatically been registered (see **8.11** below), unless they have opted out of the new regime (see **CHAPTER 10**). Schemes and arrangements which are set up on or after A-Day need to apply if they are to register, and core information is required. The new simplification forms are under discussion with industry representatives and are on the HMRC website, as is the 'Protection of Existing Rights' draft form.

Section 153, Finance Act 2004, describes the registration procedure and opting out of registration. *Schedule 36, Pt 1, paras 1* and *2*, cover the deemed registration of schemes in existence immediately before A-Day, and a 40% charge on opting out of registration at any time before A-Day (see **10.9** below). Under *s 154, Finance Act 2004*, an application to register may be made only if the pension scheme is an occupational pension scheme or has been established by a provider (see **4.4** above).

Compliance   8.6

Sections 250 and *251, Finance Act 2004,* contain details of all compliance procedures, including the information that is required on registration.

Non-standard communications or submissions of information will be accepted in written form, by post, telephone and email. The secure electronic delivery mechanism will apply unless a specific request for posted mail is received or there is no email address.

Documentation   8.7

It is not necessary to submit scheme documentation as there is freedom of choice in scheme design under the new tax regime from A-Day.

The main information requirements   8.8

The main information requirements of registration are:

- the legal structure (a trust is not essential);

- size of membership in bands of 0, 1–10, 11–50, 51–10,000 and over 10,000 (the perception is that small schemes may carry more risk than large ones);

- degree of member control over assets;

- the establisher of the scheme (the perception is that schemes established by a connected employer may carry more risk than 'off-the-shelf' products);

- details of the administrator;

- a declaration of compliance and understanding from the administrator or authorised practitioner;

- registration for relief at source (RAS), where applicable;

- registration with the Pensions Regulator, where there is more than one member;

- election to contract-out of S2P, where required;

- registration of a stakeholder plan, where applicable.

The registration forms are described in **APPENDIX 5**. The administrator must make the registration application. There is a twelve-month period in which HMRC may raise any queries, although this can be extended if information is withheld or falsely given. The intent is that standard forms should be completed online. However, HMRC announced on 14 November 2005 that it has delayed compulsory online pensions administration plans which had required that pension reporting must be carried out electronically from A-Day. There is expected to be a six-month delay, during which time schemes will be allowed to submit paper reports until the new system is operational.

There will be a choice of written application for contracting-out forms. The scheme return SA970 is not available online at present.

The available tax reliefs   8.9

The available tax reliefs for a registered scheme are significant. They are summarised below, and described in greater detail under the relevant subject headings in this book.

Summary:

- contributions made by, and on behalf of, members (with the exception of payments made by employers) receive tax reliefs up to the higher of £3,600 and 100% of earnings;

- any increase in pension benefits which are promised in defined benefits arrangements up to the limit of the annual allowance do not attract a charge;

- contributions made by the employer are tax relievable;

- investment income is free of income tax;

- investment gains are free of capital gains tax;

- lump sum benefits, in specified circumstances, are paid free of income tax;

- pension business – such of a company's life assurance business as is referable to contracts entered into for the purposes of a registered pension scheme, or is the re-insurance of such business, is not taxable.

Tax relief on contributions will commence from the date that HMRC acknowledges registration. In effect, tax-efficient contributions and benefit accrual will cease after A-Day once the lifetime allowance is exceeded.

Opting out of registering a scheme which exists at 5 April 2006   8.10

The rules which apply on opting out of registering a scheme which exists at 5 April 2006 are described in **10.9** below.

Registering a scheme which existed at 5 April 2006 8.11

The main procedures for registering a scheme which existed at 5 April 2006 are described in *paras 1(1)(a), (b), (c), (e), (f), (g), Sch 36, Finance Act 2004*. *Paragraphs 1* and *2* cover the deemed registration of schemes in existence immediately before A-Day, and the 40% charge on opting out of registration at any time before A-Day (see **10.9** below). Under *s 154* of the Act, an application to register may be made only if the pension scheme is an occupational pension scheme, or has been established by a provider (see **4.4** above).

In addition to exempt approved schemes, certain other tax-privileged schemes or contracts are automatically treated as registered. A registered pension scheme is any scheme that, on 5 April 2006, falls within any of the following categories:

- A retirement benefit scheme approved under *Ch 1, Pt XIV, Income and Corporation Taxes Act 1988 (ICTA 1988)* (ie an approved occupational pension scheme). This includes AVC schemes.

- Split-approved schemes, under *s 611, ICTA 1988*, only in respect of the part which was so approved.

- A personal pension scheme approved under *Ch IV, Pt XIV, ICTA 1988* (ie an approved personal pension scheme – including an approved stakeholder pension scheme – or an approved group personal pension scheme).

- A retirement annuity contract or retirement annuity trust scheme approved before 1 July 1988 under *Ch III, Pt XIV, ICTA 1988* (contracts for the self-employed or employees in non-pensionable employment). These policyholders are still able to contribute to these arrangements.

- Relevant statutory schemes (ie public sector pension schemes), which are not approved schemes. Examples include schemes such as those for employees of the NHS, Civil Service, police, fire, armed forces, teachers, Parliament and National Assemblies, and also schemes not established by statute but which have been treated as statutory schemes.

- Former approved superannuation funds (ie 'old code' schemes). These are schemes which were approved before 1970, but which had not been re-approved as 'new code' occupational pension schemes under *Ch I, Pt XIV, ICTA 1988*. However, they have retained their former approved status if no contributions have been made to the scheme since 5 April 1980.

- Certain deferred annuity contracts, although they were not approved pension schemes prior to 6 April 2006, are automatically treated as registered pension schemes.

Registering a scheme which is set up on or after A-Day – form of application 8.12

The main procedures for registering a scheme which is set up on or after A-Day are described in *sub-s 153(2)* and *(3)*, *Finance Act 2004*. The administrator must submit to HMRC:

1. A fully completed application in the form specified by HMRC.

2. A declaration that the person making the application understands that they are responsible for discharging the functions conferred or imposed on the administrator by the tax legislation and intends to discharge those functions at all times, no matter whether resident in the UK, any other EU member state or non-EU EEA member state.

3. Such declarations as HMRC reasonably requires.

The current requirements of (3) above are a declaration that:

● the scheme meets all the conditions to be a registered pension scheme;

● the information supplied in the application is correct and complete; and

● the administrator understands that false statements may lead to a penalty and/or prosecution.

Further details on making an online transaction will be provided by HMRC later. The web source is the Pension Schemes Service Online at: http://www.hmrc.gov.uk.

Once the pension scheme is registered, the scheme administrator can authorise one or more practitioners to carry out certain administrative tasks in relation to that scheme.

The *Registered Pension Schemes Manual* (RPSM02101030) states:

'Once the scheme administrator has gone through the entire application process and all the data given has been validated, the on-line service will automatically register the *pension scheme*. It is therefore now envisaged that HMRC will not issue many (if any) notifications advising that they have decided not to register the pension scheme.'

The application process

HMRC has stated that it will handle applications on a 'process now and check later' basis. This reflects the general approach which is being taken by HMRC on all pension matters, and it heralds a removal of advice by the HMRC in advance of actions being taken. HMRC considers that the law requires the administrator to be responsible for ensuring that they and the scheme meet the conditions for registration before making the relevant declaration(s).

In most cases, a scheme will be registered instantly, and HMRC must inform the administrator of the decision. This will, once in place, be by electronic notification, unless the administrator has elected not to receive electronic communications (in which case, they will receive the acknowledgement of registration and confirmation of the date from which it is effective by post).

The notification must state the date from which the scheme was registered. The scheme qualifies for tax relief from this date. In practice, this is the date that the valid online application is made. Should any contributions have been made prior to this date, they will not qualify for relief. HMRC has the power to enquire into the scheme's affairs at a later date and may withdraw the scheme's registration from a later date. The grounds on which HMRC can consider withdrawing registration include the discovery that any information or declaration given in the registration application was materially incorrect or false.

Schemes applying for registration from a date on or after 6 April 2006 – registration refused 8.13

The circumstances which may lead to a refusal by HMRC to register a scheme are described in **10.2** below. *Section 157(1), Finance Act 2004*, describes the de-registration procedure by HMRC.

Schemes which exist at 5 April 2006 – application received on or after 6 April 2006, but approval required from a date before 6 April 2006 8.14

Under the approval rules prior to A-Day, HMRC could approve some occupational pension schemes with effect from an earlier date than the date the approval letter was actually issued. The general rule was that, where an application for approval was made before the end of a six-month application period, HMRC would backdate approval to the date when the scheme was set up. Under this concession, approval could be backdated even if the scheme's establishment date was in an earlier tax year.

This power is retained beyond A-Day under *Sch 36, para 1(4), Income and Corporation Taxes Act 1988*, where approval is to be given from a date prior to 6 April 2006. The period for which such a concession will continue to apply is still to be confirmed. Any applications received after such date will be considered on a case-by-case basis.

Such a scheme will be treated as satisfying the registration conditions automatically from A-Day and will be treated as a registered scheme from that date. Any opt out must have been notified to HMRC by the administrator by 5 April 2006 at the latest. So, if an application for approval from a date before A-Day is received on or after that date, it is too late for the scheme to then opt out of the new regime.

Further guidance will be issued by HMRC in due course.

Transitional protection   8.15

The information that is required in respect of a claim for protection from the standard lifetime allowance, or for transitional protection, should be provided online on the system once this is ready (see **8.5** above). Payment of taxes and dues should be made by epayment/BACS etc; appropriate methods are still being formulated. HMRC will make post-registration compliance checks.

Reporting requirements

Forms   8.16

HMRC has issued draft forms for consultation to industry representatives (see **APPENDIX 5**). These are:

- Registration for tax relief and exemptions
- Registration for relief at source
- Contracting out (industry wide schemes)
- Contracting out (other schemes)
- Event report
- Accounting for tax return
- Registered pension scheme return
- Protection of existing rights
- Enhanced lifetime allowance (pension credit rights)
- Enhanced lifetime allowance (international)
- Declare as a scheme administrator of a deferred annuity contract.

In addition to the above, HMRC has also published some of the maintenance forms:

- Cessation of scheme administrator

- Pre-register as a scheme administrator
- Notify scheme administrator details
- Change of scheme administrator/practitioner details
- Authorising a practitioner
- Add scheme administrator
- Amend scheme details

The HMRC Pensions Tax Simplification Newsletters contain details of the available forms. Newsletter No. 6 explains the delay referred to in **APPENDIX 5**.

Annual statements and self-assessment   8.17

The intention is that members of defined benefit schemes should receive automatic annual benefit statements. Many of the pre A-Day reporting requirements have been removed, and the new process has adopted the self-assessment principle, and penalty and appeals regime, wherever possible. The lifetime allowance will need to be stated wherever appropriate.

The main areas which are likely to be relevant are: the Self-Assessment Return, which will include various questions on fund value, membership, transfers etc; the Event Report form; the Registered Pension Scheme Return; and the Accounting for Tax Return.

Fines   8.18

There are fines for failures to provide information. The information which may be required from members, scheme administrators and associated employers of registered pension schemes, qualifying overseas pension schemes and qualifying recognised overseas pension schemes, can include:

- the mandatory provision of information without first being asked by HMRC;
- provision of information following the issue of a notice from HMRC;
- provision of documents/particulars in response to a notice from HMRC;
- the preservation of particular documents.

The penalties are:

- Failure to provide information required by regulations: a penalty in accordance with *s 98, Taxes Management Act 1970*. That is a penalty not exceeding £300. Where failure continues: a further penalty not exceeding £60 for each day failure continues.

- Fraudulently or negligently providing incorrect information required by regulations: a penalty not exceeding £3,000.

- Failure to preserve documents as required by regulations: a penalty not exceeding £3,000.

- Failure to submit a registered pension scheme return: a penalty of £100. Where failure continues: a further penalty not exceeding £60 for each day on which failure continues.

- Fraudulently or negligently submitting an incorrect registered pension scheme return and/or associated documents: a penalty not exceeding £3,000.

- Failure to produce documents and particulars as required by *s 252, Finance Act 2004*: a penalty not exceeding £300. Where failure continues: a further penalty not exceeding £60 for each day on which failure continues.

- Fraudulently or negligently producing incorrect documents or particulars in response to a Notice under *s 252, Finance Act 2004*: a penalty not exceeding £3,000.

- Failure to submit an Accounting for Tax form: where the number of persons whose particulars should be included in the return is ten or fewer: a penalty of £100 for each quarter, or part quarter from which failure continues up to and including the fourth quarter. Where the number of persons whose particulars should be included in the return is more than ten: a penalty of £100 for each ten persons or part thereof (for example, 25 persons = £300 penalty) for each quarter or part quarter from which failure continues up to and including the fourth quarter. Regardless of the number of persons whose particulars should be included in the return, from the fifth quarter: a penalty not exceeding the amount of income tax (excluding scheme sanction charge) for the quarter that the return was not made.

- Fraudulently or negligently producing an incorrect Accounting for Tax form: a penalty not exceeding the difference between the amount of the tax shown on the form and the amount of tax which should have been shown on the form. Where no tax is shown on the form: the amount of tax which should have been shown.

Draft regulations   8.19

The draft Registered Pension Schemes (Provision of Information) Regulations 2005 include the administrator's general duty to report certain events to

HMRC and other parties. They were due to come into effect on A-Day. Most reports must be made after 5 April of the year following the relevant event, and before the following 31 January.

The main subjects which are covered by the reportable events are summarised below:

- any changes in control of the scheme or its assets;
- rule changes permitting unauthorised payments;
- changes to legal structure;
- crystallisation events involving enhanced protection;
- changes in membership bands;
- a change from split-approval status;
- unauthorised payments;
- payment of certain pension commencement lump sums;
- deaths where more than 50% of the lifetime allowance has been paid out gross;
- suspension of an ill-health pension;
- pension and lump sums certificate number if sums in excess of the normal lifetime allowance or lump sum limit are paid out;
- overseas transfers;
- payment of early retirement benefits or ill-health lump sums to connected parties;
- winding up;
- lump sums greater than £100,000 and more that 25% of rights and less than 25% of the lifetime allowance.

Further details are given under the specific headings which are used to describe the reportable events below.

Alternatively secured pension   8.20

This is where sums or assets in respect of at least one member meet *Condition A* or *B* in *para 11, Sch 28, Finance Act 2004*, for the first time during the reporting year.

The information to be given by the administrator to HMRC is the number of members who, having met Condition A or Condition B for the first time during the reporting year, fall within each of the following bands in respect of the funds or the assets held.

The bands are:

£1.00 – £50,000

£50,001 – £100,000

£100,001 – £250,000

£250,001 – £500,000

more than £500,000

Paragraph 11, Sch 28, Finance Act 2004, as amended, contains the following wording concerning Conditions A and B:

'(1)   For the purposes of this Part the member's alternatively secured pension fund in respect of an arrangement consists of such of the sums and assets held for the purposes of the arrangement as–

    (a)   meet condition A or condition B, and

    (b)   have not been subsequently applied towards the provision of a scheme pension.

(2)   Condition A is that they–

    (a)   were part of the member's unsecured pension fund in respect of the arrangement when the member reached the age of 75, or

    (b)   arise, or (directly or indirectly) derive, from sums or assets within paragraph (a) or which so arise or derive.

(3)   Condition B is that they–

    (a)   became held for the purposes of the arrangement after the member reached the age of 75 or arise, or (directly or indirectly) derive, from sums or assets which became so held or which so arise or derive, or

    (b)   if the arrangement is a relevant arrangement, have at any time since the member reached that age been designated as available for the payment of alternatively secured pension to the member or arise, or (directly or indirectly) derive, from sums or assets which have been so designated or which so arise or derive.

(4)   A relevant arrangement is an arrangement which became a money purchase arrangement after the member reached the age of 75 (having previously been a hybrid arrangement under which, in certain circumstances, defined benefits were payable).

(5)   If any sums or assets representing the member's alternatively secured pension fund in respect of an arrangement under the

pension scheme would (apart from this sub-paragraph) come to be taken to represent another alternatively secured pension fund of his under the pension scheme, or a dependant's alternatively secured pension fund of his under the pension scheme, they are to be treated as not doing so.'

Benefit crystallisation events, and enhanced lifetime allowance or enhanced protection   8.21

A reporting requirement arises where a benefit crystallisation event occurs in relation to a member in respect of the scheme and:

(*a*)   the amount crystallised by the event:

- exceeds the standard lifetime allowance; or

- together with the amounts crystallised by other events in relation to that member, exceeds the standard lifetime allowance;

for the year in which the event occurs; and

(*b*)   the member relies on the entitlement to either an enhanced lifetime allowance or enhanced protection in order to reduce or eliminate liability to the lifetime allowance charge.

The information to be given by the administrator to HMRC is:

(*a*)   name, date of birth, address and NI number of the member;

(*b*)   amount and date of the event;

(*c*)   reference number given by HMRC under the enhanced lifetime allowance regulations.

Calculation of the percentage of standard lifetime allowance crystallised on the happening of a benefit crystallisation event

When computing the cumulative total percentage of the standard lifetime allowance, the amount crystallised on the happening of each event shall be expressed as a percentage found by the application of the formula:

AC/RSLA x 100/1

where:

AC is the amount crystallised on the happening of the benefit crystallisation event; and

RSLA is the relevant standard lifetime allowance at the time of that event.

The cumulative total percentage of the allowance crystallised by previous events is the sum of the percentages found above in respect of benefit crystallisation events in respect of the member.

Change in the legal structure of a scheme   8.22

This is where the legal structure of the scheme changes from one of the following categories to another:

(a)   a single trust under which all the assets are held for the benefit of all the members of the scheme;

(b)   an overall trust within which there are individual trusts supplying the benefit of each member;

(c)   an overall trust within which specific assets are held as, or within, sub-funds for each member;

(d)   an annuity contract;

(e)   a body corporate; and

(f)   other.

The information to be given by the administrator to HMRC is the date on which the change took effect, together with:

(i)   the new category which applies to the scheme;

(ii)   in the case of a change falling within category (f), a brief description of the new category or legal structure of the scheme.

Change in number of members   8.23

This is where the number of members falls within a different band at the end of the tax year from that within which it fell at the beginning of the previous tax year. The bands are:

nil members

1 – 10 members

11 – 50 members

51 – 10,000 members

more than 10,000 members

The information to be provided is the new band which applies to the number of applicable members.

Changes to scheme rules   8.24

This is where a scheme changes its rules in order to permit:

(*a*)   the making of unauthorised member payments;

(*b*)   the making of unauthorised employer payments; or

(*c*)   investments, other than in policies or insurance.

The information to be given by the administrator to HMRC is the fact of the change and the date on which the change takes effect.

Changes to the rules of pre-commencement schemes treated as more than one scheme   8.25

This is where a scheme, being one which immediately before A-Day was treated in accordance with *s 611, Income and Corporation Taxes Act 1988*, as two or more separate schemes, changes its rules in any way.

The information required is the fact of the change and the date on which the change takes effect.

Early provision of benefits   8.26

This is where the scheme provides benefits to a member who is under normal pension age, and before the benefits were provided the member was, either in the year they were provided or any of the preceding six years:

(*a*)   in relation to the sponsoring employer, or an associated company of that employer, a director or person connected with a director; or

(*b*)   whether alone or with others, the sponsoring employer; or

(*c*)   a person connected with the sponsoring employer.

The information is to be given by the administrator to HMRC.

Events statements to members   8.27

Where an arising entitlement to a scheme pension triggers an 'event 2' benefit crystallisation event (see **3.15** above) the administrator must provide the individual with a statement confirming the level of lifetime allowance that individual has used up in total under that scheme (expressed as a percentage of the standard lifetime allowance). They must then send the individual such a statement every tax year until the pension stops.

Where a lifetime annuity contract is purchased, the insurance company from which the contract is purchased must similarly provide the individual with the same annual statement, but only in relation to the amount crystallising in relation to that contract. To enable them to do this the scheme administrator has to provide the insurance company with certain information. These requirements are explained in RPSM11103320.

Lump sum payment after the death of a member aged 75 or over   8.28

This is where a lump sum payment is made in respect of a member after the member has died after reaching the age of 75.

The information to be given by the administrator to HMRC is:

(*a*)   the name;

(*b*)   the date of birth; and

(*c*)   the last known address and National Insurance number;

of the deceased member, together with:

(*d*)   the name and address of the person to whom the lump sum payment was made; and

(*e*)   the amount, and nature and date, of the payment.

Overseas matters   8.29

The main overseas requirements are explained in **CHAPTER 9**. The regulations which concern overseas events are the *Pension Schemes (Information Requirements – Qualifying Overseas Pension Schemes, Qualifying Recognised Overseas Pension Schemes and Corresponding Relief) Regulations 2006 (SI 2006/208)*.

The lifetime allowance must be checked at the time of an overseas transfer and a report made to HMRC by 31 January following the year in which the event took place. A report must be made by the administrator to HMRC by 31 January following the year in which any other benefit crystallisation event took place in respect of funds which have received, or are receiving, UK tax relief. If enhanced protection is in point, any transfers of unvested rights between registered schemes after A-Day must be accompanied by a certificate stating that either the transfer does not contain post A-Day contributions or that the individual has been 'inactive' since A-Day.

The application of the lifetime allowance and the lifetime allowance charge to overseas schemes is complex. The relevant application of European law to the free movement of capital and transfers without incurring tax, and of existing tax treaties, still awaits full clarification.

Member able to control scheme assets   8.30

This is where a member, either alone or with others, gains or loses the ability to control the way in which the scheme assets are used to provide benefits.

The information to be given by the administrator to HMRC is:

(*a*)   the dates on which at least one member becomes able to exercise control where none had been able to do so immediately before; and

(*b*)   no member is able to exercise control, where at least one had been able to do so immediately before.

Pension commencement lump sum   8.31

Reports are required when payment is made of a pension commencement lump sum which:

(*a*)   when added to the crystallised amount, on becoming entitled to the pension with which the lump sum is associated, exceeds 25% of the total; and

(*b*)   is more than 7.5%, but less than 25%, of the current standard lifetime allowance.

The information to be given by the administrator to HMRC is:

(*a*)   the name, date of birth, address and NI number of the member;

(*b*)   the amount and date of the lump sum; and

(*c*)   the amount crystallised on the member.

Pension commencement lump sum – primary and enhanced protection 8.32

Primary and enhanced protection are described in **CHAPTER 6**. Where lump sums exceed £375,000 (under *paras 24–30, Sch 36, Finance Act 2004*), the information to be given by the administrator to HMRC is:

(*a*)   the name, date of birth, address and NI number of the member;

(*b*)   the amount and date of the payment;

(*c*)   the reference number given by HMRC under the enhanced lifetime allowance regulations.

Serious ill-health lump sum 8.33

This is where the scheme pays a member a serious ill-health lump sum and before that payment was made the member was, either within the year in which the benefits were provided or any of the preceding six years:

(*a*)   in relation to the sponsoring employer, or an associated company of that employer, a director or person connected with a director; or

(*b*)   whether alone or with others, the sponsoring employer; or

(*c*)   a person connected with the sponsoring employer.

(*Schedule 36, Finance Act 2004*).

The information to be given by the administrator to HMRC is:

(*a*)   the name;

(*b*)   the address;

(*c*)   the date of birth; and

(*d*)   the National Insurance number;

of the member; and

(*e*)   the date and the amount of the payment.

Suspension of an ill-health pension 8.34

This is where an ill-health pension, which has been paid pursuant to pension rule 1 of *s 165, Finance Act 2004,* is not now paid because the ill-health condition is no longer met.

The information to be provided by the administrator to HMRC is:

(a)   the name;

(b)   the address;

(c)   the date of birth; and

(d)   the National Insurance number;

of the member to whom the pension has been paid; and

(e)   the date on which the period of non-payment began;

(f)   the annual rate of the pension to a which a member was entitled immediately before that period began.

Transfer lump sum death benefit   8.35

This is where at least one transfer lump sum death benefit is paid during the reporting year.

The information to be given by the administrator to HMRC is the number of transfer lump sum death benefits paid during the reporting year, the value of which falls in each of the bands shown below:

£1.00 – £50,000

£50,001 – £100,000

£100,001 – £250,000

£250,001 – £500,000

more than £500,000

Transfers to a qualified and recognised overseas pension scheme   8.36

This is where a scheme makes a recognised transfer to a qualified, recognised, overseas pension scheme which is not a registered scheme.

The information to be given by the administrator to HMRC is:

(a)   the name;

(b)   the address;

(c)   the date of birth; and

(d)   the National Insurance number;

of the member; and

(*e*)   the amount of the sums or assets transferred;

(*f*)   the date of the transfer together with the name of the qualified and recognised overseas pensions scheme and the country or territory under the law of which it is established and regulated.

Unauthorised payments by members or employers
8.37

These are payments made by members or employers which are not authorised by the rules which apply to registered schemes. The information to be given by the administrator to HMRC is:

(*a*)   the name;

(*b*)   the date of birth (if applicable);

(*c*)   the address; and

(*d*)   the National Insurance or company registration number;

of the person to whom the payment was made, together with;

(e)   the nature, amount and date of the payment.

Provision of information between a scheme administrator and a member on the enhanced lifetime allowance
8.38

If an enhanced lifetime allowance or enhanced protection is to apply under s 256(1), *Finance Act 2004*, the member must supply the administrator with the reference number given by HMRC under the enhanced lifetime allowance regulations.

If the scheme administrator makes a payment on account of his liability to pay for the lifetime allowance charge, he shall, within three months of the crystallisation event, give details to the member of:

(*a*)   the chargeable amount on which the charge arises;

(*b*)   how the chargeable amount is calculated;

(*c*)   the amount of the tax charge; and

(*d*)   whether he has accounted for the tax or intends to do so.

Provision of information by the administrator on a scheme wind-up 8.39

On a scheme wind-up, the administrator shall give notice to HMRC of that fact, and the date on which the winding-up was concluded. It is not necessary to give notice in respect of an annuity contract which is treated as a registered pension scheme, a former approved superannuation fund or an annuity contract or trust scheme approved under *ss 620* or *621, Income and Corporation Taxes Act 1988.*

The prescribed time for making the notice is any time on or before:

(*a*) the last day of the period of three months beginning on the day on which the winding-up is completed; or

(*b*) the last day otherwise prescribed by the regulations for the purpose of that information;

whichever is the earlier.

Provision of information by the administrator to another administrator 8.40

This applies where part or all of a member's pension rights are transferred from one scheme to another (scheme A to scheme B).

The administrator of scheme A must provide the administrator of scheme B, within three months of the transfer, with a cumulative total percentage of the standard lifetime allowance crystallised by the event in respect of scheme A and any scheme from which that scheme has received directly or indirectly a transfer payment.

Provision of information by the administrator to HMRC on ceasing to be the administrator 8.41

The person who was, and has now ceased to be, an administrator must notify HMRC of the termination of his or her appointment, together with the date on which termination took effect, within 30 days of the event.

Provision of information by the administrator to the member about benefit crystallisation events 8.42

The administrator must provide to each member:

(*a*) to whom a pension is being paid, at least once in each tax year; or

(*b*) in respect of whom a benefit crystallisation event has occurred, within three months of that event;

a statement of the cumulative total percentage of the lifetime allowance crystallised, at the date of the statement, by the events in respect of the scheme and any other scheme from which that scheme has received, whether directly or indirectly, a transfer payment.

Provision of information by the administrator to the member about unauthorised payments 8.43

Where a scheme has made an unauthorised payment to a member, the administrator must provide the member before 7 July following the tax year in which the event took place with the following information:

(*a*) the nature of the benefit provided;

(*b*) the amount of the unauthorised payment which is being treated as being made by the provision of the benefit; and

(*c*) the date on which the benefit was provided.

Provision of information by the administrator of annuities in payment – provided to and by the administrator, insurance company and annuitant 8.44

If, on the crystallisation of a member's pension rights, an insurance company is provided with funds to provide a lifetime annuity, the scheme administrator shall, within three months of annuity purchase, provide the insurance company with details of the percentage of the standard lifetime allowance crystallised both before and after such a purchase.

At least annually, the insurance company shall provide the annuitant with a statement of the percentage of the standard lifetime allowance crystallised at the date of the statement in respect of the annuity.

Provision of information by the administrator to the personal representatives 8.45

The administrator must provide the following information on the death of a member:

(*a*)   the percentage of the standard lifetime allowance crystallised by, and the amount and date of payment of, a relevant lump sum death benefit paid by the scheme in relation to the member (no later than the last day of the period of three months beginning with the day on which the final such payment was made);

(*b*)   the cumulative total percentage crystallised, at the date of the statement, by benefit crystallisation events in respect of the deceased member under the scheme or any schemes from which assets have been transferred (whether directly or indirectly), in respect of the deceased member's pension rights, but excluding any amount in respect of any relevant lump sum death benefit payment in respect of the deceased member (this information shall be provided no later than the last day of the period of two months beginning with the day on which a request for it is received from the member's personal representatives).

Provision of information by the employer company 8.46

Where an unauthorised employer payment is made to a company, that company shall provide the following information:

(*a*)   details of the scheme that made the payment;

(*b*)   the nature of the payment;

(*c*)   the amount of the payment;

(*d*)   the date on which the payment was made.

The information must be provided to HMRC no later than 31 January following the tax year in which the payment was made.

Provision of information by an insurance company etc to personal representatives on death 8.47

Where an insurance company or similar provider has paid an annuity from the assets of the scheme and the person concerned has died, the provider shall on request provide the following information to the personal representatives:

(a)   the date the annuity was purchased;

(b)   the amount crystallised as a percentage of the standard lifetime allowance;

within two months of the request.

Provision of information by personal representatives to HMRC   8.48

Where a relevant lump sum death benefit is paid and, either alone or when aggregated with other similar payments, this results in a lifetime allowance charge, the following information must be provided to HMRC by the personal representatives:

(a)   the name of the scheme and the name and address of the administrator;

(b)   the name of the deceased member;

(c)   the amount and date of the payment; and

(d)   the chargeable amount on which the charge arises;

within 13 months of the death of the member, or 30 days from the date that the personal representatives became aware of the event giving rise to the charge.

If a requirement to report arises after expiration of the above period, the information must be provided within 30 months of the death of the member. On the discovery of further information after the expiry of such a period, a report must be made within three months of discovery.

Retention of records   8.49

Generally, administrators and related persons, trustees, employers or directors must keep records for a period of six years.

Registered pension scheme return   8.50

The Registered Pension Scheme Return is separate from the self-assessment return. HMRC may require, by giving notice, the completion of a scheme return for any year, together with the provision of any information which is reasonably required. The main details which must be entered on the pension scheme return by the scheme administrator are:

(a)   payments (contributions, transfers, payments out and borrowing);

(*b*)   assets/connected party information (shares, property, loans etc);

(*c*)   cash/bank balances, non-connected party transactions;

(*d*)   a declaration signed by the administrator or authorised practitioner.

The deadline for submitting the return will normally be 31 January following the relevant tax year. However, the period will be three months after any notice which is given after 31 October in the relevant tax year, or three months from the completion of the winding up of a scheme which wound up before that date.

The penalty for a failure to deliver a return is £300, plus £60 per day for continued non-compliance. In cases of fraud or negligence, fines of up to £3,000 may be imposed (this includes a failure to retain prescribed information for a prescribed period).

Tax due, and other reports   8.51

There is a form for Accounting for Tax by the administrator. Schemes must make reports on lifetime allowance charges (see *s 254, Finance Act 2004*). Payment must be made quarterly and is due within 45 days of quarter end. Additionally, charges on lump sum refunds, death benefits, surplus refunds and de-registration must be made on the form. There are fines for non-compliance.

Further reports must be made to members by the scheme (which may attract penalties if missed), including the fund value at vesting, the percentage of the lifetime allowance used (in future to be included on the P60 form) and any benefits-in-kind (by 19 July following the relevant tax-year end). Reports must also be made by members to the scheme, including a transfer certificate if contributions ceased at A-Day.

Section 251, Finance Act 2004, contains details of the information that must be provided automatically, and *s 252* contains details of information which may be called for by way of a notice. Appeals may be made against notices under *s 253*.

The main legislative sources   8.52

The following legislation contains the relevant reporting references:

(*a*)   *Chapter 7, s 250, Finance Act 2004*, states that a notice may be issued for a return to be made, and contains a list of the information which may be required;

(*b*)   *Chapter 7, s 251*, contains details of the information that must be provided automatically;

(*c*)   *Chapter 7, s 252*, contains details of information which may be called for by way of a notice;

(*d*)   appeals may be made against notices under *Ch 7, s 253*;

(*e*)   the information requirements under *ss 605* and *651, Income and Corporation Taxes Act 1988*, and attaching regulations, continue in respect of information which relates to periods prior to A–Day (*Sch 4, para 50*);

(*f*)   the *Registered Pension Schemes (Accounting and Assessment) Regulations 2005 (SI 2005/3454)* and the *Registered Pension Schemes (Audited Accounts) (Specified Persons) Regulations 2005 (SI 2005/3456)*.

Chapter 9
Transfers, overseas considerations and RPSM extracts

Introduction
9.1

The matters of transfers and overseas considerations have given rise to a great deal of HMRC publications and draft legislation. The main impact of these sources is described in **9.2–9.20** below. The description provided is only a summary, which is provided in order to give an overview on these wide-ranging subjects. The main source for a comprehensive view of how these matters work in detail is the *Registered Pension Schemes Manual* (RPSM). In view of the importance of following the very detailed instructions carefully, the main relevant text from the manual has been extracted and appears under **9.21–9.49** below.

Transfers
9.2

The new tax regime will greatly ease transfers between relevant schemes. Registered schemes may:

(*a*) transfer to other registered schemes without restriction, and without having to test for the lifetime allowance; and

(*b*) transfer to a scheme in another country which is recognised and regulated in that country as a pension scheme (*s 169, Finance Act 2004*, states that 'a registered scheme may make a transfer out to any recognised overseas pension scheme').

Any other transfers will be unauthorised payments, and a tax charge will be levied unless the scheme made the transfer in good faith which is based on false or incorrect information from the member. A registered scheme may also:

(*c*) receive a direct transfer from other registered schemes (including any under *s 615, Income and Corporation Taxes Act 1988* (now *ss 647–654, Income Tax (Earnings and Pensions) Act 2003*);

(d) disregard transfers from schemes which are described in (a) and (b) above from the annual allowance (the position with regard to transfers from other schemes requires clarification); and

(e) disregard transfers from schemes described in (b) above from the lifetime allowance if they do not include monies which have received UK tax relief.

Any transfers made into an insurance company receiving scheme or to a third party administrator must be made directly to that person. Any monies which are received from other schemes will be treated as contributions and count towards the annual allowance and by way of benefits against the lifetime allowance.

The easement in the transfer requirements has led to HMRC terminating its reciprocal agreements with the Republic of Ireland, Jersey, Guernsey and the Isle of Man for the transfer of pension rights with effect from A-Day. No longer do individuals have to meet any conditions as was the case under the pre A-Day tax rules and the reciprocal agreements. HMRC has announced that the new rules will make it easier to make transfers than the previous bilateral arrangements, and all parties to the agreements therefore agreed that they should be terminated.

Bulk transfers   9.3

The definition of 'bulk transfer' requires members in a bulk transfer not to have been members of the receiving scheme prior to the transfer of the sums and assets relating to the transfer. This restriction applies only if the member had been a member of the receiving scheme for one year or longer.

Enhanced protection   9.4

If enhanced protection is in point, any transfers of unvested rights between registered schemes post A-Day must be accompanied by a certificate stating that either:

(a) the transfer does not contain post A-Day contributions; or

(b) the individual has been 'inactive' since A-Day.

In specie transfers, and social security legislation   9.5

Generally, the *Pension Schemes Act 1993* gives a member the right to the cash equivalent of their accrued rights. HMRC has pointed out that this does not mean that the assets transferred must be cash. Other forms of asset may be transferred, provided they have the appropriate cash value.

Lump sum transfers – fragmentation   9.6

Pensions Update No. 147, dated 9 June 2004, explains that special rules may be applied to fragmented lump sum transfers for regulated individuals which are used to obtain a higher lump sum when made to a new regime scheme.

Member payment charges   9.7

Certain member payments charges apply to, or are deemed to apply to, a tax-relieved UK scheme member of a relevant UK scheme or a transfer member of such a scheme under *Sch 34, Finance Act 2004*. These charges include:

(*a*)   the unauthorised payments charge;

(*b*)   the unauthorised payments surcharge;

(*c*)   the short service refund lump sum charge;

(*d*)   the special lump sum death benefits charge; and

(*e*)   the trivial commutation, winding-up lump sums and lump sums death benefits charges.

This includes transfers to a relevant non-UK scheme. As stated in **7.12** above, a scheme is a relevant non-UK scheme if:

●   migrant member relief has been given;

●   post-5 April 2006 double taxation relief has been given;

●   members have been exempted from tax liability under *s 307, Income Tax (Earnings and Pensions) Act 2003*, in respect of pension or death benefit provision at any time after 5 April 2006 when the scheme was an overseas scheme; or

●   there has been a relevant transfer from a UK scheme after 5 April 2006 when the scheme was a qualifying recognised overseas scheme.

The member payment charge only applies to a transfer if the member was resident in the UK when the transfer was made, or had been so within any of the preceding five years (see **7.13** above). The rate of tax payable and the person liable to pay the tax in relation to member payment charges are the same as for the relevant payment charge involved.

There are wide powers in *Sch 34, Finance Act 2004*, to make regulations which may discount elements of the fund from which the payment is applied, discharge or repay any amounts from which tax is incurred overseas from monies emerging from the transfer, and introduce further provisions and relaxations etc. The *Registered Pension Schemes (Discharge of Liabilities under Sections 267 and 268 of the Finance Act 2004) Regulations 2005 (SI 2005/3452)* have now been made, which update the 2004 draft regulations and enable some charges to be discharged in certain circumstances.

Pensions in payment 9.8

Transfers in service are permissible, and pensions in payment may be transferred as long as there is no change to their terms.

Reasons for making a transfer 9.9

RPSM14100020 lists the possible reasons for making a transfer as including the following:

- 'the member may no longer be employed by the employer which set up that scheme, and may prefer all benefits to be provided by a registered scheme of their new employer;

- the member may have been divorced and has agreed as part of the divorce settlement that part of their fund is to be re-allocated to their *ex-spouse*, who does not want the re-allocated fund to remain in the same registered scheme;

- where a person has made their own private pension arrangements through joining a registered pension scheme of a provider of their own choice, they may later identify an alternative registered pension scheme which they consider to be better than the one they are currently a member of the pension scheme may be being wound up;

- the member is going to live overseas and wishes to move their pension to a scheme in the country they are moving to'.

Accrued benefit rights shall generally be moved to registered or recognised schemes without adverse tax conditions.

Section 615 schemes 9.10

Schemes under *s 615, Income and Corporation Taxes Act 1988* (now *ss 647–654, Income Tax (Earnings and Pensions) Act 2003* schemes), generally being for non-residents who are in overseas employment, were no longer to be permitted as the government did not consider that they were necessary once the new regime was in place. However, the government was prepared to listen to representations and *s 615(3)*, schemes now appear under *Ch 6, ss 245(5)* and *249(3), Finance Act 2004* – so indicating that they may continue.

Tax charges 9.11

Transfers overseas to a qualifying recognised overseas pension scheme will be tested against the lifetime allowance and any amounts transferred above the individual's lifetime allowance will be subject to a tax charge of 25%. Transfers below the lifetime allowance will not attract a tax charge. The individual will not have to emigrate to transfer-out. After the transfer, other charges may also be applicable, because certain payments made out of overseas schemes containing funds which have benefited from UK tax reliefs may be liable to UK tax charges such as the annual allowance, lifetime allowance and unauthorised payment charges.

Transfers to an overseas pension scheme that is not a qualifying recognised overseas pension scheme are treated as unauthorised payments and will be subject to tax charges.

The new rules provide details of certain tax charges that arise in respect of 'relevant non-UK schemes', where UK tax relief has been given on contributions under migrant member relief, or under the terms of a Double Taxation Treaty, or where a transfer has been made from a UK registered scheme to an overseas scheme.

Transfers – contracting out 9.12

The *Contracting-out, Protected Rights and Safeguarded Rights (Transfer Payment) Amendment Regulations 2005 (SI 2005/555)* are effective from 6 April 2005. The main purpose is to remove the requirement for the trustees of a transferring scheme to satisfy themselves that a member has permanently emigrated before making a transfer payment of contracted-out or safeguarded pension rights to an overseas pension scheme or arrangement. Other small changes bring the detailed provisions applying to different types of contracted-out and safeguarded rights into line with one another.

Transfer regulations for overseas recognised schemes 9.13

There are currently four sets of UK regulations which concern recognised overseas schemes, and transfers which may be made to such schemes and relevant migrant members. They are reproduced in **APPENDIX 4**, and are as follows:

- the *Pension Schemes (Categories of Country and Requirements for Overseas Pension Schemes and Recognised Overseas Pension Schemes) Regulations 2006 (SI 2006/206)*;

- the *Pension Schemes (Application for UK Provisions to Relevant Non-UK Schemes) Regulations 2006 (SI 2006/207)*;

- the *Pension Schemes (Information Requirements – Qualifying Overseas Pension Schemes, Qualifying Recognised Overseas Pensions Schemes and Corresponding Relief) Regulations 2006 (SI 2006/208)*;

- the *Pension Schemes (Relevant Migrant Members) Regulations 2006 (SI 2006/212)*.

A 'relevant non-UK scheme' is as described in **7.12** above.

Schedule 34, paras 8–12, Finance Act 2004, describe the annual allowance charge, which applies to currently-relieved members of 'currently-relieved non-UK pension schemes'. 'Currently-relieved non-UK pension schemes' are schemes under which:

- migrant member relief has been given;

- post-5 April 2006 double taxation relief has been given; or

- members have been exempted from tax liability under *s 307, Income Tax (Earnings and Pensions) Act 2003*.

Formulae are provided for the purpose of calculating the charge, which take into account the amount of taxable earnings within the meaning of *s 10(2), ITEPA 2003*.

Schedule 34, paras 13–19, Finance Act 2004, describe the lifetime allowance charge, which applies to currently-relieved members of 'currently-relieved non-UK pension schemes'. The paragraphs apply to benefit crystallisation events. A member may elect to notify HMRC of the applicable date of a benefit crystallisation event in a form specified by HMRC. Transfers will count as benefit crystallisation events unless they form part of a block transfer.

Winding up 9.14

A transfer may be made to another registered scheme which is in wind-up, or (alternatively) the member may be issued with a contract under a registered scheme. Winding-up lump sums from former approved superannuation funds are covered by *Sch 36, Pt 3, para 35, Finance Act 2004*.

If the requirements of HMRC or the DWP on winding up are not met, payments will be treated as unauthorised payments. Additionally, the scheme may be de-registered and suffer a 40% tax charge. *Chapter 7, s 265, Finance*

Act 2004, empowers HMRC to impose a penalty if a transfer is made on winding up wholly or mainly to provide lump sums to the members or dependants.

Overseas considerations 9.15

In addition to the transfer requirements listed above, there are new overseas rules for members. These are described below.

Migrants 9.16

Migrants who come to the UK will be given tax relief on their contributions in place of the previous corresponding relief provisions. This is known as 'migrant member relief'. The main provisions are in *Sch 33, Finance Act 2004*. The new rules are more flexible than the previous corresponding relief rules. During the parliamentary debates on the proposed new tax regime pre A-Day, and in answer to a question concerning the extent of the intended migrant member relief, the following statement was issued:

> 'under the current rules for corresponding relief, individuals can only claim relief when they are not domiciled in the UK and are employed by an overseas employer. There is transitional protection for relief on employee and employer contributions where someone entitled to corresponding relief as at A-Day does not qualify for migrant relief. There will be no lifetime allowance charge in respect of corresponding relief given for contributions made before A-Day.

> The new rules no longer take the individual's domicile into account and there is no restriction on where the scheme has to be established.

> The scheme has to be regulated as a pension scheme in the country where it is established and undertake to provide certain specified information in respect of the member. This makes it a flexible relief for those whose careers bring them to the UK, as existing members of a local pension scheme, who wish to continue to pay contributions to that scheme and benefit from tax relief on those contributions'.

Migrant member relief 9.17

Migrant member relief will be available where an individual:

(a)   is resident in the UK but was not resident in the UK at the time he or she joined a qualifying overseas pension scheme;

(b)   comes to the UK as a member of that scheme, and remains a member of the overseas scheme;

(c)   notifies the scheme manager that he or she intends to claim migrant member relief (UK tax relief against UK earnings on contributions paid to the overseas scheme);

(d)   has earnings chargeable in the UK; and

(e)   was eligible for tax relief on contributions to the overseas scheme in the country in which he or she was resident immediate before coming to the UK, or meets such other conditions as may be prescribed by regulations.

The EC sent a formal request to the UK to change its original legislation as it considered that the beneficial tax treatment of domestic pension schemes was incompatible with the freedoms mentioned in the EC Treaty. The EC required the UK to amend its legislation by extending the favourable tax treatment to contributions paid to schemes not fulfilling specific national requirements. The *Finance Act 2004* was subsequently reviewed. The wording 'or meets such other conditions as may be prescribed by regulations' in (e) above was inserted by *Sch 10, Finance Act 2005*. The *Pension Schemes (Relevant Migrant Members) Regulations 2006 (SI 2006/212)* have since added an alternative condition to the requirement in (e) above. The alternative is where a member had received tax relief on contributions paid to the pension scheme in the country of residence at any time in the ten years prior to coming to the UK.

The overseas scheme must either be EEC registered, or one that generally corresponds with a UK scheme, and must:

*   notify HMRC that it is an overseas pension scheme, providing supporting evidence if required;

*   undertake to notify HMRC if it stops being an overseas pension scheme;

*   undertake to provide HMRC with certain information in accordance with regulations; and

*   notify any member claiming migrant member relief that it has undertaken to comply with the information requirements.

Employers may claim a deduction for contributions paid to a qualifying overseas pension scheme in respect of employees who are eligible for migrant member relief.

Crystallisation date   9.18

There is an optional benefit crystallisation event for claimants of migrant member relief, and for claimants of relief under double taxation agreements, that will enable the claimant to elect that a benefit crystallisation event occurs when tax relief is no longer claimed. Credit against UK tax due under the member payments charge will be available for foreign taxes paid in respect of the same payments. There is flexibility built into the new rules to allow for modified application of the normal UK rules for overseas schemes if they would be impractical or inappropriate; for example, where a term used in the legislation has a different or irrelevant meaning under the overseas scheme's own rules.

Finance (No 2) Act 2005   9.19

The *Finance Act 2004* received royal assent on 22 July 2004 and has subsequently been revised by the *Finance Act 2005*. *Sections 149–284* and *Schedules 28–36* concern pension schemes. The *Finance (No.2) Act 2005* restored some of the provisions of the original Finance Bill, together with adding some new provisions. There are provisions to counter the avoidance of capital gains tax by temporary non-residents (that is, persons who are absent for fewer than five years), the avoidance of such tax by trustees changing their residence and disposing of settled property, and matters involving the disposal of assets overseas by residents and non-residents.

EU Directive   9.20

HMRC has published a version of the European Union Savings Directive Guidance Notes on its website to combat tax evasion on cross-border savings income (see http://www.hmrc.gov.uk/esd-guidance/guidance.htm).

A consultative document on the Occupational Pension Schemes (Exemption) Regulations 2006 was issued in October 2005. Under *s 253, Pensions Act 2004*, occupational pensions schemes with their main administration outside the member states of the EU must be established as irrevocable trusts if they are to receive contributions from either employers based in the UK (wherever their employees work) or from employers in respect of their employees who work in the UK. The government pointed out:

1. That certain occupational pension schemes with their main administration outside the member states which do not have UK resident members are currently exempt from the provisions of the pensions legislation because there is no UK interest in these schemes. As such schemes will be defined as occupational pension schemes from A-Day the draft regulations ensure that such schemes which are not tax registered and have no UK resident members continue to be outside the jurisdiction of UK pensions legislation, and are exempt from the trust requirement and other requirements of pensions legislation, including the need of having a UK-based trustee.

2. Occupational pension schemes with their main administration outside the EU member states are exempt from: the internal dispute resolution

procedures; the requirement to appoint professional advisers; the requirement to produce a payment schedule (in this specific circumstance the
regulations also amend the definition of occupational pension schemes
with fewer than twelve members to bring it into line with that used in
other sets of regulations); the jurisdiction of the Pensions Ombudsman;
the employer debt measures for defined benefit schemes on wind-up or
insolvency; member-nominated trusteeship; subsisting rights under *s 67,
Pensions Act 1995*; scheme funding requirements; and the employer's
requirement to consult. All of these exemptions are reliant on the fact
that such schemes are not tax registered.

The outcome of the latest consultative process is still awaited.

The HMRC RPSM guidance on transfers and overseas matters

RPSM technical page extracts 9.21

The technical pages in the *Registered Pension Schemes Manual* for transfers and
overseas matters are brought together below. Paragraphs **9.22–9.45** concern
transfers, while paragraphs **9.46–9.49** concern international matters.

The following is a list of the main subjects which are covered by the manual in
these areas. This is then followed by the details and extracts which appear in the
manual:

- Annual allowance, lifetime allowance and recognised transfers from
  registered schemes

- Non-recognised transfers from registered schemes

- Transfer to a non-registered overseas pension scheme which is not a
  qualifying recognised overseas pension scheme

- Transfer from another registered pension scheme

- Transfer from a recognised overseas pension scheme

- Transfer received from a non-registered pension scheme which is not a
  recognised overseas pension scheme

- Member with enhanced protection

- Member with primary protection

- Lump sum protection in transferring scheme: member with primary
  protection

- Lump sum protection in transferring scheme: member with enhanced
  protection

- Member entitled to lump sum of more than 25% of rights

- Member has protected low pension age

- Member has a protected low normal retirement age

- Entitlement to take pension before normal retirement age

- Transfer of crystallised rights

- Transfer to an insurance company of pension in payment

- Transfer to an insurance company of an annuity in payment

- Transfer of rights where previous entitlement to the payment of unsecured pension or alternatively secured pension

- Pensions in payment or rights where there is already an entitlement to benefits

- Transfers must be made between pension schemes

- Form of transferred rights

- Fragmentation – splitting rights between recipient schemes

- Partial transfers

- Reporting transfers to HMRC.

Annual allowance, lifetime allowance and recognised transfers from registered schemes (RPSM14101010)   9.22

'Transfer to another registered pension scheme

[Section 169(1)(a)]

A transfer from a *registered pension scheme* to another registered pension scheme is a "recognised transfer". A recognised transfer is a type of authorised payment. No tax charges or sanctions apply to recognised transfers.

Tax relief

[Section 188(5)]

A *recognised transfer* from one registered pension scheme to another is not a contribution, so no tax relief is due in respect of the transfer. The contributions to the transferring scheme would usually have received tax relief when originally made to that scheme, and the transfer is merely re-locating the pension rights represented by those contributions to a different registered pension scheme.

Annual allowance

[Sections 188(5), 230–234 & 236]

The treatment of the value transferred for the purpose of the *member's annual allowance* calculation for the year in which the transfer takes place is as follows.

- Defined benefit arrangements

    - Where the transferring scheme is one under which the member has a *defined benefit arrangement*, the amounts transferred, and the *market value*s of any assets transferred in the *pension input period* are to be included in the member's closing value in the arrangement (so they are added back in at their values at the time of the transfer).

    - Where the receiving scheme is one under which the member has a defined benefit arrangement, the amounts transferred, and the market values of any assets transferred in the pension input period are to be deducted from the member's closing value in the arrangement (so they are subtracted at their values at the time of the transfer).

- Money purchase arrangement

    - *cash balance arrangement*, as for defined benefit arrangement, see above.

    - any other *money purchase arrangement* – the transfer is not a contribution (see above), so no tax relief is due and the transfer value is not to be included in the individual's annual allowance calculation for the receiving arrangement.

Lifetime allowance

A recognised transfer from one registered pension scheme to another is not a *benefit crystallisation event* for the purpose of applying the *lifetime allowance*. But if, for example, the transfer is of funds from which the member had not already started to draw benefits, there will be a benefit crystallisation event for the lifetime allowance when the benefits are taken in the receiving scheme.'

Non-recognised transfers from registered schemes (RPSM14102010) 9.23

'**Transfer to a non-registered UK pension scheme**

[Section 169(1)]

A transfer to a UK pension scheme that is not a *registered pension scheme* is not a *recognised transfer*.

It is therefore an *unauthorised member payment.*

Tax charges

[Section 160(5)]

Such a transfer incurs a tax charge on the *member* at a rate of 40% of the payment.

This tax charge – broadly speaking – recoups the tax relief already given in respect of the contributions made by or on behalf of the member, and the income from the investment of those contributions. If the transfer payment and any other unauthorised payments to the member in a 12 month period exceeds 25% of the member's fund, the member is liable to an unauthorised payment surcharge of a further 15% of the payment.

A *scheme sanction charge* of up to 40% may also apply, for which the *scheme administrator* is liable. If the scheme administrator has deducted the member's tax charge from the transfer payment and paid the tax charge to HMRC on the member's behalf, the scheme administrator may reduce the amount of the scheme sanction charge by the lesser of 25% and the amount of member's tax charge deducted as a proportion of the transfer payment.

In addition, if the amounts transferred equate to 25% or more of the scheme fund value, HMRC may withdraw the transferring scheme's registration. This involves a de-registration charge of 40% (see rpsm02105050).

Tax relief

[Section 188(5)]

The transfer is not a contribution and no tax relief is due.

Annual allowance

If the transfer was made from a *cash balance arrangement*, or from a *defined benefit arrangement*, the amount transferred is not to be included in the closing value when calculating the member's *pension input amount* for the transferring arrangement. (See rpsm06101020 and rpsm06103010.) The closing value is not adjusted where the transfer is not to a registered pension scheme or a qualifying recognised overseas pension scheme.

In a *money purchase arrangement* that is not a cash balance arrangement, the amount transferred in itself is not included when calculating the member's pension input amount, as only contributions are counted for the pension input amount in such an arrangement.

Lifetime allowance

[Section 216]

The transfer is not a *benefit crystallisation event* for the purpose of the member's lifetime allowance and so is not taken into account for the member's lifetime allowance either on the occasion of the transfer, or on any future crystallisation of other benefits the member might take from registered pension schemes.

Reporting requirement

The transferring *scheme administrator* must report such a transfer (as an *unauthorised member payment*) on the Event Report [RPSM1230xxxx]'.

Transfer to a non–registered overseas pension scheme which is not a qualifying recognised overseas pension scheme (RPSM14102020) 9.24

'Transfer to a non–registered overseas pension scheme which is not a qualifying recognised overseas pension scheme

A transfer from a *registered pension scheme* to a non–UK pension scheme that is not a *qualifying recognised overseas pension scheme* is not a *recognised transfer*. Such a transfer is an *unauthorised member payment*.

See rpsm14101030 and rpsm14101040 for the conditions for a *recognised overseas pension scheme*.

Tax charges

The *member* incurs a tax charge of 40% on the amount of the payment.

This tax charge, broadly speaking, recoups the tax relief already given in respect of the contributions made by the member or on their behalf, and the income from the investment of those contributions. If the transfer payment and any other unauthorised payments to the member in a 12 month period exceeds 25% of the member's fund, the member is liable to an unauthorised payment surcharge of a further 15% of the payment.

A scheme sanction charge of up to 40% may also apply for which the *scheme administrator* is liable. If the scheme administrator has deducted the member's tax charge from the transfer payment and paid the tax charge to HMRC on the member's behalf, the scheme administrator may reduce the amount of the scheme sanction charge by the lesser of 25% and the amount of member's tax charge deducted as a proportion of the transfer payment.

In addition, if the amounts transferred equate to 25% or more of the scheme fund value, HMRC may withdraw the transferring scheme's registration. This involves a de-registration charge of 40% (see rpsm02105050).

Tax relief

[Sections 188(5) & 232]

Tax relief is only given on contributions to *registered pension* schemes. A transfer is not a contribution. The payment is not being made to a registered pension scheme. No UK tax relief is due to the receiving scheme.

Annual allowance

If the transfer is made from a *cash balance arrangement*, or from a *defined benefit arrangement*, the amount transferred is not to be included in the closing value when calculating the member's *pension input amount* for the transferring arrangement (See rpsm06101020 and RPSM0610310). The closing value is not adjusted where the transfer is not a registered pension scheme or a qualifying recognised overseas pension scheme.

In a *money purchase arrangement* that is not a cash balance arrangement, the amount transferred in itself is not included when calculating the member's pension input amount, as only contributions are counted for the pension input amount in such a scheme.

Lifetime Allowance

The transfer is not a *benefit crystallisation event* for the purpose of the member's *lifetime allowance* and is not taken into account for the member's lifetime allowance either on the occasion of the transfer or on any future crystallisation of other benefits the member might take from registered pension schemes.

Reporting requirement

The scheme administrator of the transferring scheme must report the transfer (as an *unauthorised member payment*) to HMRC on the Event Report [RPSM1230xxxx].'

Recognised transfers to registered pension schemes: transfer from another registered pension scheme (RPSM14103010)

9.25

'Transfer from another registered pension scheme

[section 169(1)(a)]

A transfer of a member's pension rights from a *registered pension scheme* to another registered pension scheme is a *recognised transfer*, (see rpsm14101010).

Although a transfer may be a recognised transfer for tax purposes, if there are contracted-out rights involved, Department for Work and Pensions (DWP) legislation provides that the transfer can only go ahead if the receiving scheme is eligible to hold those rights.'

Recognised transfers to registered pension schemes: transfer from a recognised overseas pension scheme (RPSM14103020)

9.26

'Transfer from a recognised overseas pension scheme

[section 188(5) and sections 224–226]

A transfer to a *registered pension scheme* from a *recognised overseas pension scheme* that is not a registered pension scheme is not a *recognised transfer*. But it is not an unauthorised payment either, because unauthorised payments are payments from registered pension schemes. And the legislation specifically states that an amount received by transfer from another pension scheme is not a contribution, so it does not qualify for tax relief on being received by a registered pension scheme.

Instead, special treatment is given to the *lifetime allowance* of a *member* who transfers-in funds from a recognised overseas pension scheme that is not registered, to a pension scheme that is registered (see RPSM1310xxxx).

No UK tax relief has been received, so it would be unfair if the transferred amount were to use up the member's available lifetime allowance. But, broadly, any part of an amount transferred that relates to UK tax relieved contributions made after 5 April 2006 will count against the member's lifetime allowance.

As explained in rpsm11101050, the member's lifetime allowance is increased, or "enhanced", by an appropriate factor, from the date of the transfer. The member must claim this enhancement no later than five years after 31 January following the tax year in which the transfer is made, and register the amount with HMRC. This process enables HMRC to verify the amount claimed in appropriate cases.

For the member's *annual allowance*, the treatment of the transfer value depends on the type of scheme receiving the transfer. If the receiving scheme is either a *defined benefit* scheme or a *cash balance* scheme, subtract the transfer value from the closing value. If the receiving scheme is any other type of *money purchase* scheme, the transfer is not included, as only contributions are included for the annual allowance.'

Non-recognised transfers to registered pension schemes (RPSM14104010) 9.27

'Transfer received from a non-registered pension scheme which is not a recognised overseas pension scheme

A *registered pension scheme* may receive a transfer payment from another scheme that is neither a registered pension scheme nor a *recognised overseas pension scheme*, for example

- an employer financed retirement benefits scheme, or

- a pension scheme abroad that does not satisfy the requirements to be treated as a recognised overseas pension scheme.

Tax relief

A transfer payment is not a contribution, because section 188(5) specifically excludes transfer payments between pension schemes from being considered as contributions for tax relief purposes (regardless of whether or not the pension schemes concerned are registered or recognised).

No tax relief is due on the transfer payment on receipt. However, any investment income or gain in relation to the funds in the receiving scheme is free of income tax and capital gains tax.

Member's annual allowance

If the rights are being transferred into a *defined benefit arrangement* or a *cash balance arrangement*, the value of the transfer payment should be deducted from the closing value of the member's rights.

If the rights are being transferred into any other type of *money purchase arrangement*, the transfer payment is not included for the annual allowance. This is because, for *annual allowance* purposes, in a money purchase arrangement only contributions are counted, and a transfer payment is not a contribution.

Member's lifetime allowance

A transfer into a registered pension scheme is not a *benefit crystallisation event (BCE)* for *lifetime allowance* purposes. When the member eventually takes benefits, there will be a benefit crystallisation event at that point, and the lifetime allowance test must be carried out.

Where the transfer to a registered pension scheme has come from a scheme abroad, the member's lifetime allowance should only be enhanced if the transferring scheme is a recognised overseas pension scheme. In any other case, the *standard lifetime allowance* applies on a BCE, unless the member qualifies for an enhancement due to other special circumstances.'

Transfer of a member's rights where the member has protection from tax charges: member with enhanced protection (RPSM14105010) 9.28

'Member with enhanced protection

[Schedule 36 Part 2, Para 12]

A *member* with enhanced protection is entitled to crystallise their benefits in full from the protected funds without incurring a tax charge, regardless of whether in doing so they exceed the *standard lifetime allowance*.

When a member applies to transfer benefit rights which have enhanced protection, the enhanced protection will be lost unless the transfer is a permitted transfer (see rpsm03104090).'

Transfer of a member's rights where the member has protection from tax charges: member with primary protection (RPSM14105020) 9.29

'Member with primary protection

A scheme *member* who is entitled to primary protection (see rpsm03100050), but transfers their pension rights out of the pension scheme of which they were a member at 5 April 2006, retains any primary protection obtained in relation to those pension rights. This retention of primary protection also applies on any subsequent transfer.

This means that for such an individual, the *standard lifetime allowance* (at the time the benefits that have primary protection are crystallised) is increased by the same proportion by which the individual's benefits exceeded £1,500,000 on 5 April 2006.

Example

The value of the member's benefits at 5 April 2006 was £2 million.

This is one third more than £1.5 million, the standard lifetime allowance at the start of the new tax regime for pension schemes.

The member is entitled to primary protection on crystallising benefits of up to one third more than the standard lifetime allowance at any time, even if those benefits have been transferred to other schemes.

If those benefits were eventually paid in 2010–11, when the standard lifetime allowance is £1.8 million, the member's lifetime allowance at that time would be increased by one third, to £2.4 million – regardless of the benefits being paid by a different pension scheme to that which originally calculated the value of the benefits at 5 April 2006.

If the amount being crystallised in 2010–11 was £2.5 million, the *lifetime allowance tax charge* would apply to only £100,000 of that payment.

If the amount being crystallised in 2010–11 was £2.35 million, no lifetime allowance tax charge would apply on that crystallisation.'

Transfer of a member's rights where the member has protection from tax charges: lump sum protection in transferring scheme: member with primary protection (RPSM14105030)   9.30

'Lump sum protection in transferring scheme: member with primary protection

Where a scheme *member* who is entitled to primary protection (see rpsm03100050) transfers their pension rights out of a pension scheme of which they were a member at 5 April 2006, they retain any primary protection in relation to those pension rights.

The way in which the lump sum protection works is explained in rpsm03105000.'

Transfer of a member's rights where the member has protection from tax charges: lump sum protection in transferring scheme: member with enhanced protection (RPSM14105040) **9.31**

'Lump sum protection in transferring scheme: member with enhanced protection

Where a *member* is entitled to enhanced protection (see rpsm03100040), they retain that protection on transfer providing the transfer is a permitted transfer (see rpsm03104090).

If the transfer is not a permitted transfer, the member loses enhanced protection and the member's lump sum entitlement reverts to

- primary protection, if they have claimed this (see rpsm03100060), or

- 25% of the *standard lifetime allowance* for the tax year in question, if the member only claimed enhanced protection.'

Transfer of a member's rights where the member has protection from tax charges: lump sum protection in transferring scheme (RPSM14105050) **9.32**

'Member entitled to lump sum of more than 25% of rights

Where a *member's* lump sum rights in a *registered pension scheme* qualify for lump sum protection under the rules at rpsm03105510, the member retains that protection on transferring those rights, providing the conditions set out in rpsm03105520 are met.

If the transfer is made in other circumstances, the protection is lost. The member's lump sum entitlement reverts to a maximum of 25% of the *standard lifetime allowance* for the tax year in question.'

Transfer of a member's rights where the member has protection from tax charges, member has protected low pension age (RPSM14105060) 9.33

'Member has protected low pension age

[paragraph 21 and 23 Schedule 36 Finance Act 2004]

A *member* may qualify for low pension age protection in their pension scheme. They may also qualify to retain their low pension age after transferring into another scheme if certain circumstances prevail. These are that

- the transferring scheme, immediately before 6 April 2006, was either

  - a tax approved personal pension scheme or

  - a tax approved retirement annuity contract, and

- the low pension age which applied to the member on 5 April 2006 was an age under 50, and

- the member's occupation on 5 April 2006 was or had been a *prescribed occupation*, and

- the transfer is part of a *block transfer* (transferring from a retirement annuity contract may not satisfy condition if there is only one member at the time of the transfer).

This is also subject to the new scheme's rules allowing payment of benefits at an age earlier than the normal minimum pension age.

When the member crystallises benefits from the scheme they transferred into, the benefit payments will not be treated as unauthorised payments even though they are being paid earlier than normal minimum pension age.

But the member will be treated as receiving an unauthorised payment on crystallisation at the earlier age unless he becomes entitled to all uncrystallised rights under the receiving scheme at the same time.'

Transfer of a member's rights where the member has protection from tax charges: member has a protected low normal retirement age (RPSM14105070) 9.34

'Member has a protected low normal retirement age

[paragraph 21 and 22 Schedule 36 Finance Act 2004]

A *member* may be entitled to low normal retirement age (NRA) protection in the scheme they were a member of on 5 April 2006. They may also qualify to retain this protection after transferring out of that pension scheme.

The member qualifies to retain their low NRA after transfer to another *registered pension scheme* if

- the transferring scheme, immediately before 6 April 2006, was either

    - a tax approved retirement benefits scheme, or

    - a deferred annuity contract, or

    - a former approved superannuation fund, or

    - a statutory pension scheme, or

    - a Parliamentary pension scheme, and

- the member's NRA under that scheme on 5 April 2006 was an age less than 55, and

- that scheme's rules on 10 December 2003 conferred this NRA on at least some members of the scheme, and

- this included the member now transferring from that scheme (or would have done if he had been a scheme member on that date), and

- the transfer is part of a *block transfer*.

Payment of benefits at the protected age will also depend on the rules of the receiving scheme allowing this.

When the member crystallises benefits from the scheme they transferred into, the benefit payments will not be treated as unauthorised payments even though they are being paid earlier than the normal minimum pension age, providing

- the member becomes entitled to all benefits under that scheme at the same time, and

- the member is not employed by a *sponsoring employer* in relation to that scheme after becoming entitled to a pension from that scheme.'

Transfer of a member's rights where the member has protection from tax charges: entitlement to take pension before normal retirement age (RPSM14105080) 9.35

'Entitlement to take pension before normal retirement age

[paragraph 21 and 22 Schedule 36 Finance Act 2004]

A *member* may have been entitled to receive benefits before normal retirement age (NRA) in the scheme they were a member of on

5 April 2006. (For example, they may be entitled to receive benefits at an age up to 10 years before NRA in the scheme, and NRA in the scheme may be age 60). The member may qualify to retain this entitlement after transferring out of that *registered pension scheme*.

The member qualifies to retain this right after transfer to another registered pension scheme if

- the transferring scheme, immediately before 6 April 2006, was either

    - a tax approved retirement benefits scheme, or

    - a deferred annuity contract, or

    - a former approved superannuation fund, or

    - a statutory pension scheme, or

    - a Parliamentary pension scheme, and

- the member was entitled under that scheme on 5 April 2006 to crystallise benefits before age 55, and

- that scheme's rules on 10 December 2003 conferred this right on at least some members of the scheme, and

- this included the member now transferring from that scheme (or would have done if he had been a scheme member on that date), and

- the transfer is part of a *block transfer*.

Payment of benefits at the earlier age will also depend on the rules of the receiving scheme allowing it.

When the member crystallises benefits from the scheme they have transferred into, the benefit payments will not be treated as unauthorised payments even though they are being paid earlier than the normal minimum pension age, providing

- the member becomes entitled to all benefits under that scheme at the same time, and

- the member is not employed by a *sponsoring employer* in relation to that scheme after becoming entitled to a pension from that scheme.'

Transfers of pensions in payment, or rights where there is already an entitlement to benefits: transfer of crystallised rights (RPSM14106010)   **9.36**

'Transfer of crystallised rights

Section 169(1B) to (1E)

It is possible within the tax rules on authorised payments to make a transfer from a *registered pension scheme* relating to a pension which is already in payment, or in the case of an unsecured or *alternatively secured pension fund*, where an entitlement to benefits has already arisen.

A pension in payment under a registered pension scheme, is capable of being transferred to another registered pension scheme and being regarded as a *recognised transfer*. This applies to any of the following

- member's *scheme pension*
- member's *unsecured pension*
- member's *alternatively secured pension*
- dependant's *scheme pension*
- dependant's *unsecured pension* or
- dependant's *alternatively secured pension*.

If the provision of benefits derived from the transfer meet certain conditions, then the benefits paid from the transfer in the receiving registered pension scheme are capable of being within the pension rules and being authorised payments. Any failure to meet the conditions will result in the amount transferred being regarded as an unauthorised payment.

The conditions will be set out in forthcoming regulations.'

Transfers of pensions in payment, or rights where there is already an entitlement to benefits: transfer to an insurance company of pension in payment (RPSM14106020)   **9.37**

'Transfer to an insurance company of pension in payment (Section 169(1A))

Scheme pension

It is possible within the tax rules on authorised payments for a *scheme pension* in payment under a *registered pension scheme* to be transferred to an *insurance company*.

Such a transfer is capable of being a recognised transfer provided certain conditions are met. The main condition is that, although the insurance company is not acting within a registered pension scheme, the transfer as received is nonetheless applied to provide a pension which conforms to the pension rules for a member's scheme pension.

For example, if a registered pension scheme is paying scheme pensions and the scheme is later winding-up, it is possible for the sums and assets representing the rights concerned to be transferred to an insurance company to provide for those pensions. Whereas an insurance company acting outside of a registered pension scheme would not otherwise be able to pay a scheme pension, the continuation of the pension rules on a scheme pension will be possible such that the on-going pension is capable of being an authorised payment.

Failure to be within the pension rules applying to an on-going scheme pension will mean that the amount transferred will be regarded as an unauthorised payment. Continuation of the pension rules for a scheme pension by the receiving insurance company means that, for example, the transfer should not be used as an event to stop or reduce the pension other than permitted under the usual pension rules. Forthcoming regulations will set out the precise conditions.'

Transfers of pensions in payment, or rights where there is already an entitlement to benefits: transfer to an insurance company of an annuity in payment (RPSM14106030)   9.38

'Transfer to an insurance company of an annuity in payment

Schedule 28 para 3(2B), 6(1B) and para 17(3) and 20(1B)

Where an *insurance company* is paying a

- *lifetime annuity*

- *dependant's annuity*

- *short-term annuity* or

- *dependant's short-term annuity*

it is not doing so directly under a *registered pension scheme* but following the application of sums and assets formerly held under a registered pension scheme.

If a transfer of an annuity took place, given that no registered pension scheme is involved, it would not be a *recognised transfer*. Nor therefore would such a transfer fall within the provisions within the tax rules relating to transfers of pensions in payment under registered pension schemes. Nonetheless, it is possible within the tax rules for authorised payments for a lifetime annuity or dependant's annuity in payment to be transferred from one insurance company to another.

Certain conditions must be met. If they are not, then the amount transferred will be regarded as an unauthorised payment.

The conditions will be specified in regulations.'

Transfers of pensions in payment, or rights where there is already an entitlement to benefits: transfer of rights where previous entitlement to the payment of unsecured pension or alternatively secured pension (RPSM14106040) 9.39

'Transfer of rights where previous entitlement to the payment of unsecured pension or alternatively secured pension

Section 169(1D) and (1E)

It is possible within the tax rules on authorised payments for an *unsecured pension* or an *alternatively secured pension* under a *registered pension scheme* (whether payable to the *member* or a *dependant*) to be transferred to another registered pension scheme. This also applies where entitlement to an unsecured or alternatively secured pension exists but no payments of pension were actually being drawn under the transferring scheme.

More details will follow when regulations have been laid. The regulations are likely to include conditions that no *benefit crystallisation event* is regarded as taking place directly as a result of the transfer and no new entitlement to a *pension commencement lump sum* arises.'

Transfers of pensions in payment, or rights where there is already an entitlement to benefits: transfer within a registered pension scheme (RPSM14106050)   **9.40**

'Pensions in payment or rights where there is already an entitlement to benefits

Schedule 28

It may happen that a *scheme administrator* of *registered pension scheme* makes a transfer from one unsecured pension fund of a member to another unsecured pension fund of the same member within the same registered pension scheme.

For the purpose of the tax rules, such a transfer within a registered pension scheme is disregarded. That is, under the tax rules, the sums and assets transferred continue to be treated as part of the original arrangement. This is to counter the use of a transfer as a means of circumventing the pension rules as would have applied if a transfer did not take place.

This condition applies to transfers within a registered pension scheme of

- member's *alternatively secured pension* fund (Schedule 28 paragraph 11(5))

- member's *unsecured pension* fund (Schedule 28 paragraph 8(4))

- *dependant's unsecured pension* fund (Schedule 28 paragraph 22(3))

- *dependant's alternatively secured pension* fund (Schedule 28 paragraph 25(4)).

The above applies equally to transfers between funds for the same individual, whether those funds are held in respect of that individual as a member or as a dependant.'

General points for transfers: transfers must be made between pension schemes (RPSM14107010)   **9.41**

'Transfers must be made between pension schemes

[section 266]

A *scheme administrator* of a *registered pension scheme* should make sure that the person to whom they are transferring funds is someone with a position of responsibility in the receiving scheme.

A transfer is not a *recognised transfer* unless it is

- between registered pension schemes or

- from a registered pension scheme to a *qualifying recognised overseas pension scheme.*

Non-recognised transfers incur tax charges.

Where the receiving scheme is an "insured scheme", but the transfer payment is not made directly to the scheme administrator or an *insurance company* which issues policies under the receiving scheme, the scheme administrator of the transferring registered pension scheme is liable to a maximum penalty of £3,000.

An "insured scheme" is a pension scheme where all the income and other assets are invested in policies of insurance.'

General points for transfers: form of transferred rights (RPSM14107020) 9.42

'Form of transferred rights

Subject to the rules of the pension schemes concerned, either assets (which includes insurance policies) or cash funds, or a combination of the two, can be transferred provided they represent the full value of the member's rights to be transferred.'

General points for transfers: fragmentation – splitting rights between recipient schemes (RPSM14107030) 9.43

'Fragmentation – splitting rights between recipient schemes

If the rules of the schemes involved allow this, and benefits are not yet in payment, a transfer value may be split and each part transferred to separate destination schemes.

Where an individual has enhanced protection, the normal rules on permitted transfers apply (see rpsm03104090). So if the transfer is not a permitted transfer, the *member* loses enhanced protection.'

General points for transfers: partial transfers (RPSM14107040)   **9.44**

'Partial transfers

A transfer of part of a member's pension rights in a *registered pension scheme* leaving the remaining rights in the scheme is a recognised transfer providing

- it is made to either another registered pension scheme or a *qualifying recognised overseas pension scheme*, and

- the pension rights are uncrystallised.'

General points for transfers: reporting transfers to HMRC (RPSM14107050)   **9.45**

'Reporting transfers to HMRC

Registered Pension Scheme Return

The Registered Pension Scheme Return is for a *scheme administrator* to complete, but this should only be done at HMRC's request. The Return can be submitted through the Pension Schemes Service Online, which can be found on the HMRC website.

If completing the Registered Pension Scheme Return, the scheme administrator must report the following information concerning transfers to HMRC on it

- the amount transferred to other *pension schemes* that tax year

- the amount received as transfers from other pension schemes that tax year.

The Registered Pension Scheme Return must be received by HMRC by 31 January following the tax year it relates to.

See RPSM1230xxxx for further guidance on the Registered Pension Scheme Return.

Event Report

A scheme administrator must report to HMRC, using the online Event Report

- a transfer to a *qualifying recognised overseas pension scheme*

- any transfer which is an *unauthorised member payment* (for example, a transfer to an employer-financed retirement benefits scheme).

The Event Report must be received by HMRC by 31 January following the end of the tax year in which the transfer took place (but see RPSM12xxxxxx where the scheme is wound up).

Unlike the Registered Pension Scheme Return, the Event Report is to be completed in all cases, without HMRC requesting it.

See RPSM1230xxxx for further guidance on the Event Report.'

The extracts below concern the following overseas matters:

- Application of charges to non-UK schemes: lifetime allowance: general.
- General principles of international enhancement.
- Application of charges to non-UK scheme: basic principles.
- Eligibility for membership of a registered pension scheme.

The new overseas rules are very complex, and a full list of the *Registered Pension Schemes Manual* points of reference can be found in **APPENDIX 2**.

International: application of charges to non-UK schemes: lifetime allowance: general (RPSM13102510)   9.46

'General

[Paras 13–19, Schedule 34]

Paragraphs 13 to 19 of schedule 34 modify the *lifetime allowance* provisions so as to apply the *lifetime allowance charge* to members of overseas pension schemes that are not *registered pension schemes* in certain circumstances. The lifetime allowance provisions are explained in detail at rpsm11100000. You should read that section before continuing with the following description of what schedule 34 does.

Broadly, under the lifetime allowance provisions every individual has a lifetime allowance which is the total capital value of benefits that they can draw from registered pension schemes without triggering a lifetime allowance tax charge. The lifetime allowance also covers transfers to certain *overseas pension schemes*. When an individual's benefits crystallise the capital value of those benefits is tested against their lifetime allowance. Their lifetime allowance is used up or reduced as a consequence, and the capital value of any benefits that crystallise after that will be tested against any remaining allowance.

The lifetime allowance charge is intended to recoup excess UK tax relief that an individual has received. So it has to apply to an individual's benefits from overseas pension schemes that have attracted UK tax relief, as well as to benefits from registered pension schemes.

Schedule 34 applies the lifetime allowance provisions to an individual who is a relieved member (rpsm13102140 refers) of a relieved non-UK pension scheme (rpsm13102520 refers) as if the scheme were a registered pension scheme.

This part explains what relieved non-UK pension schemes are, who relieved members are, and how the lifetime allowance charge provisions apply to them.'

International: enhancement: general principles (RPSM13100040)   **9.47**

'General principles of international enhancement

[s 221–226]

The *lifetime allowance* is an overall ceiling on the amount of UK tax-relieved pension savings that an individual can draw from *registered pension scheme*s and certain overseas pension schemes. If when a *benefit crystallisation event* occurs (see example at rpsm11102040) the total value of an individual's benefits exceeds their unused lifetime allowance then that individual will be subject to a *lifetime allowance charge* (rpsm11103000 refers).

Everyone is entitled to the *standard lifetime allowance*, which is £1.5 million in the 2005/06 tax year and will increase in subsequent years. However, in certain circumstances an individual can notify HMRC that they are entitled to a lifetime allowance that is higher than the standard amount: an "enhanced" lifetime allowance. If so, a lifetime allowance charge would only arise when a benefit crystallisation event occurred if the total value of that individual's benefits exceeded their unused enhanced lifetime allowance.

An individual can notify HMRC of an entitlement to enhance their lifetime allowance in two international situations in which benefits in a registered pension scheme are built up without UK tax relief. These are

1.   membership of a registered pension scheme whilst a *relevant overseas individual* (see rpsm13100100 to rpsm13100310), and

2. transfer to a registered pension scheme from a recognised *overseas pension scheme* (see rpsm13100410 to rpsm13100570)

Even if an individual is entitled to enhance their lifetime allowance they may not need to do so. A notification will be beneficial where the total value of an individual's UK tax-relieved pension scheme benefits is likely to exceed the standard lifetime allowance.'

International: application of charges to non-UK scheme: basic principles (RPSM13102020)   **9.48**

'Basic principles

[Sch 34 and related regulations – not yet laid]

Schedule 34 provides for certain charging provisions in Part 4 of the Finance Act 2004 to apply in certain circumstances to members of non-UK pension schemes that are not *registered pension schemes*.

This is necessary because there are circumstances in which an *overseas pension scheme* that is not a registered pension scheme will contain funds that have benefited from UK tax relief. For example, where a migrant individual comes to the UK as a member of an overseas pension scheme, any subsequent contributions to their overseas scheme may benefit from UK tax relief just like contributions to a registered pension scheme. Also, funds in an overseas pension scheme which have built up in a registered pension scheme before being transferred to the overseas pension scheme may equally have benefited from UK tax relief.

The schedule applies three main types of charge to members of non-UK schemes. These are the various charges referred to as the member payment charges (see rpsm13102100), the *annual allowance charge* (see rpsm13102300) and the *lifetime allowance charge* (rpsm13102500).

However, for members of non-UK pension schemes, these charges are targeted only at payments that relate to the part of the member's overseas pension fund that has benefited from UK tax relief.

Schedule 34 modifies the way the charges operate to facilitate their application to these non-UK schemes, and further modifications are contained in The Pension Schemes (Application of UK Provisions to Relevant Non-UK Schemes) Regulations 2005 – not yet laid.

This chapter explains how these charges apply to certain members of non-UK pension schemes as if they were members of registered pension schemes. The schedule 34 modifications of the charging provisions are described in rpsm13102100 to rpsm13102600. The modifications provided for in the regulations referred to above are described in rpsm13102700 onwards.'

International: overseas membership of a registered pension scheme: eligibility (RPSM13103010)   9.49

'Eligibility for membership of a registered pension scheme

After 5 April 2006 membership of a *registered pension scheme* is open to anyone regardless of where they are resident or of where their employer (if any) is resident. Nor is there any restriction on the amount that can be contributed by an overseas resident individual or by an employer in respect of them. But relief from UK income tax may not be available, or may be restricted on such contributions in certain circumstances.

Overseas resident members of a registered pension scheme are subject to the annual and lifetime allowances and their associated charges (see rpsm13103040), and to other charges under Part 4, such as the unauthorised payments charge (see rpsm04104500).'

EC and Swiss Confederation Co-operation Agreement   9.50

The *European Communities (Definition of Treaties) (Cooperation Agreement between the European Community and its Member States and the Swiss Confederation to Combat Fraud) Order 2006 (SI 2006/307)* came into effect on 14 February 2006. The explanatory note states:

'This Order declares the Cooperation Agreement between the European Community and its Member States, of the one part, and the Swiss Confederation, of the other part, to combat fraud and any other illegal activity to the detriment of their financial interests to be a Community Treaty as defined in section 1(2) of the European Communities Act 1972.

The object of the Agreement is to extend administrative and judicial assistance in order to combat illegal activities in customs; agricultural legislation; value added tax, special taxes on consumption, and excise duties; the charging and retention of funds from the budgets of the parties to the Agreement or from budgets managed by them or on their behalf; and procedures for the award of contracts by them.

The principal effect of declaring this Agreement to be a Community Treaty is that the provisions of section 2 of the European Communities Act 1972 (which provide for the general implementation of Community Treaties) apply to it.'

Chapter 10

Non-registered/ unapproved schemes

Introduction

This chapter firstly describes the treatment of schemes which are refused registration or have their registration status withdrawn, followed by the treatment of schemes which opt out of registration, new employer-financed retirement benefits schemes (EFRBS) (as described in s 393A, ITEPA 2003) and registering or maintaining previously unapproved schemes (FURBS and UURBS). The different circumstances which are currently known to apply are described under the appropriate headings below.

At the time of writing HMRC had not yet codified how FURBS and UURBS would be treated from A-Day, but it had stated that details would appear in its *Trusts, Settlements and Estates Manual*. The current guidance under this manual is summarised in **10.18** below, and it can be seen that the post A-Day amendments are still awaited. However, there is a great deal of material in HMRC's internal *Employment Income Manual* (EIM) and some useful extracts appear at the end of this chapter (see **10.12** below, and the extracts in **10.21–10.25**).

The *Employer-Financed Retirement Benefits Schemes (Provision of Information) Regulations 2005 (SI 2005/3453)* came into force on A-Day (see **10.12** below).

Registration refused

10.2

Under s 156, *Finance Act 2004*, if HMRC decides not to register the scheme, the scheme administrator may appeal within 30 days against the decision. The appeal may be made to the General Commissioners or the Special Commissioners. Under ss 157 and 158, *Finance Act 2004*, HMRC may withdraw registration if it appears:

- that the amount of the scheme chargeable payments from the pension scheme during any period of twelve months exceeds the de-registration threshold (of 25% chargeable payments);

- that the scheme administrator fails to pay a substantial amount of tax (or interest on tax) due from the scheme administrator;

- that the scheme administrator fails to provide information required to be provided to HMRC and the failure is significant;

- that any information contained in the application to register the pension scheme or otherwise provided to HMRC is incorrect in a material particular;

- that any declaration accompanying that application or the provision of other information to HMRC is false in a material particular; or

- that there is no scheme administrator.

Registration withdrawn   10.3

It would be exceptional for HMRC to withdraw registration from an entire pension scheme, and not from an arrangement or arrangements within the scheme.

De-registration threshold   10.4

Section 158(2)–(4), Finance Act 2004, stipulates a de-registration threshold. The threshold is exceeded if the total of the percentages of the fund used up by each scheme chargeable payment in any twelve-month period is 25% or more. The percentage of the fund used up is determined by the following formula:

$$\frac{Scheme\ chargeable\ payment}{Value\ of\ scheme\ funds} \times \frac{100}{1}$$

The value of the scheme funds is the market value of the assets held for the purposes of the scheme plus the amount of the sums held for the purposes of the scheme, both taken at the time of the payment.

RPSM02105030 provides the following worked example:

Example

'Two scheme chargeable payments have been made within a 12-month period. The payments were of £14,000 and £10,000. The fund value at the time of the first payment comprised assets with a market value of £80,000 and cash of £20,000 giving a total value of £100,000.

The percentage of the scheme fund used up at the time of the first scheme chargeable payment is:

$$\frac{£14,000}{£100,000} \times \frac{100}{1} = 14\%$$

The fund was valued at £88,000 at the time of the second payment, which was of £10,000:

$$\frac{£10,000}{£88,000} \times \frac{100}{1} = 11\%$$

Add together 14% and 11% and the aggregate is 25%. The de-registration threshold is exceeded. This means there are grounds for HMRC to de-register the scheme'.

Actions on de-registration   10.5

Under *s 158(2)–(4), Finance Act 2004*, when HMRC de-registers a scheme it must notify the administrator (or, if there is no administrator, the person(s) who has/have responsibility for the scheme and whom it is reasonably practicable for HMRC to identify) stating the date on and after which the scheme will not be registered. HMRC will also notify the Pensions Regulator that the scheme has been de-registered.

Under *s 242, Finance Act 2004*, a tax charge will be incurred (see 7.7 above) of an amount equal to 40% of the total of:

- the scheme market value, immediately before it ceased to be registered, of the assets held; plus

- the sums held immediately before registration ceased.

The administrator is liable for the charge, regardless of that scheme administrator's residence or domicile status for UK tax purposes. If more than one person is the administrator, each person is jointly and severally liable for the tax due.

Scheme taxation   10.6

The tax reliefs on the scheme are lost and, unless the scheme is wound up, it may continue as a non-registered pension scheme (see **10.11** below). This means that, if it is an occupational pension scheme, it may become subject to the provisions relating to employer-financed retirement benefits schemes. Any life assurance business will cease to be pension business at the beginning of the company's period of account in which the scheme loses its registration status.

Unauthorised payment   10.7

If there is an unauthorised payment, there is a tax charge on either the member or the sponsoring employer, as appropriate. Where the payment relates to a deceased member, the charge is on another person instead of the member. There may also be a tax charge on the scheme administrator.

Appeals   10.8

Appeals may be made against a decision to de-register, under *s 159, Finance Act 2004* (*s 242* describes the 40% scheme de-registration charge). The appeal must be made by the end of the 30th day beginning with the day on which the appellant was notified of the decision. The appeal will usually be made to the General Commissioners, although the appellant may elect for the appeal to be heard instead by the Special Commissioners.

A Commissioners' decision can be appealed by way of case stated.

Existing pension schemes at 5 April 2006 which opt out of registration   10.9

Under *Sch 36, para 2(1), Finance Act 2004,* an approved scheme which did not wish to be automatically registered had formally to opt out. To achieve this, the administrator must have advised HMRC in writing before A-Day. There is no special form for advising HMRC that a scheme is to be treated as having opted out.

As from A-Day the only way for an ongoing scheme to become unregistered is for HMRC to withdraw registration.

Tax position on opting out   10.10

Under *paras 2(2)–2(4)* and *2(6), Sch 36, Finance Act 2004,* a tax charge is incurred on opting out. The charge is 40% of the market value of the pension fund, being assets or other sums held for the purposes of the scheme immediately before A-Day. Any life assurance ceases to be pension business at the beginning of the company's period of account in which the pension scheme opts out. The date of opting out for this purpose is A-Day.

The relevant administrator (for the type of scheme or arrangement concerned) is liable for the charge. If more than one person is the administrator, each person is jointly and severally liable for the tax due.

A scheme which is established for the benefit of particular employees will be taxed as an employer-financed retirement benefits scheme (see **10.12** below). As from A-day, employer contributions to unapproved schemes are not taxed on the employees or be counted as employment income (*s 247, Finance Act 2004*).

Pension schemes set up on or after A-Day which do not wish to be registered 10.11

Where a pension scheme, which was set up on or after A-Day, does not wish to be registered, HMRC SPSS does not need to know about such a scheme. Nevertheless, HMRC is reviewing its information requirements for such arrangements, and guidance on its general practice is expected in due course.

The manual envisages that such a scheme is likely to be an 'employer-financed retirement benefits scheme' for the purposes of the tax legislation.

Employer-financed retirement benefits schemes 10.12

Unapproved schemes are treated as employer-financed retirement benefits schemes (EFRBS) from A-Day and do not receive any privileged tax treatment, except under transitional arrangements.

The *Employer-Financed Retirement Benefits Schemes (Provision of Information) Regulations 2005 (SI 2005/3453)* came into force on A-Day and require a 'responsible person', within the meaning of *s 399A, ITEPA 2003*, to report any EFRBS which provides relevant benefits within the meaning of *s 393B* of that Act. Information for the first year of establishment of such a scheme must be sent by 31 January following the tax year in which the scheme was set up. Information concerning the recipient of any relevant benefit must be sent by 7 July following the tax year in which the payment was made.

The main rules are as follows:

- There is an extension to the persons who are responsible for certain actions under the *Taxes Management Act 1970* beyond that of the scheme administrator to 'responsible persons' where assessments are due on certain payments or actions.

- Employers will not receive relief on contributions and administration expenses until benefits come into payment (*ss 245* and *246, Finance Act 2004*, respectively).

- An employer's cost of insuring benefits against employer insolvency is chargeable to the member as a benefit-in-kind. The employer can claim the cost as an expense against profits at the time that it is paid.

- For investment gains, capital gains tax will be taxable at the rate applicable to trusts (RAT), which increased from 34% to 40% on 6 April 2004, and amounts held in the fund will not be included in the lifetime allowance.

- The basic rate of tax applies on the first £500 of gains from 6 April 2005, which removes one-third of trusts from the RAT (tax returns are only likely to be issued every five years in such cases, although taxable income should be declared if it arises).

- Elections for the new regime must have been made by 6 April 2006 if they are to apply from 6 April 2004.

- Income tax on the fund for unapproved schemes increased from 22% to 40% from 6 April 2004.

- Lump sum death benefits will be charged to inheritance tax.

- It is understood that there will be no NIC charge on any benefits paid out of non-registered schemes, provided that they are within the limits of benefits that could be paid out of a registered scheme and all employer and connected employer relationships have ceased.

The *Employer-Financed Retirement Benefits Schemes (Excluded Benefits for Tax Purposes) Regulations 2006 (SI 2006/210)* provide transitional protection for benefits which were already provided for at A-Day and for lump sums paid in circumstances of non-accidental death while in service.

HMRC's Employment Income Manual

The *Registered Pension Schemes Manual* draws attention to HMRC's *Employment Income Manual* for details of how a trust-based employer-financed retirement benefits scheme is treated for tax purposes. This provides the following additional information:

- only 'relevant benefits' count as employment income under *s 394, Income Tax (Earnings and Pensions) Act 2003*;

- the charge on lump sums paid out may be reduced where prior employer contributions have been taxed and where the employee has made contributions;

- a pension is charged separately as pension income under *Pt 9, Income Tax (Earnings and Pensions) Act 2003 (Pt 9* charges pensions income to tax).

In the above:

- 'relevant benefits' means any lump sum, gratuity or other benefit provided:
  - on retirement or on death; or
  - in anticipation of retirement; or
  - after retirement or death in connection with past service; or
  - on or in anticipation of or in connection with any change in the nature of the employee's service; or
  - by virtue of a pension sharing order or provision.

  This includes a non-cash benefit, but not:
  - pension income within *Pt 9, Income Tax (Earnings and Pensions) Act 2003*;
  - benefits chargeable under *Sch 34, Finance Act 2004*;

- 'excluded benefits' are benefits:
  - in respect of ill-health or disablement of an employee during service;
  - in respect of death by accident of an employee during service;
  - under a 'relevant life policy' (guidance on the meaning of this will be made available in the *Policyholder Taxation Manual* (IPTM)).

Guidance on how annuities, annual payments and non-cash receipts are dealt with is given in EIM15100, and some EIM extracts are provided in **10.21–10.25** below.

Foreign pensions 10.13

Section 573, Income Tax (Earnings and Pensions) Act 2003 (ITEPA 2003), applies to any pension paid by or on behalf of a person who is outside the UK to a person who is resident in the UK. It does not apply to any pensions charged by any of the provisions in *Part 9, Chapters 5–14, ITEPA 2003*. EIM74001 on the HMRC website provides further details.

Section 574, ITEPA 2003, extends the charge under *s 573* to a pension that is paid voluntarily or is capable of being discontinued if the following conditions are met:

- the pension is paid to a former employee or office holder or to their widow, widower, child, relative or dependant;

- the payment is paid by or on behalf of the person who employed the former employee (or the person under whom the office was held) or by the successors of that person.

Section 575, ITEPA 2003, provides that the taxable amount of a foreign pension is 90% of the actual amount arising in the tax year unless the income is charged on the remittance basis. As foreign pensions are treated as relevant foreign income, there is provision for claims to remittance basis, deductions and reliefs and unremittable income. IM1580 on the HMRC website provides further details.

Extra-Statutory Concession A10   10.14

The basic aim of the concession is to give exemption or relief from tax similar to that for foreign service in relation to s 401, ITEPA 2003. The concession applies to lump sum relevant benefits, which includes both lump sums received under the rules of an overseas scheme and lump sums received in commutation of pension rights under such a scheme.

Any charge to tax under s 394, ITEPA 2003, will therefore be reduced or eliminated under the terms of that concession if the employee has foreign service in the relevant employment.

The wording of the concession is as follows:

'Income tax is not charged on lump sum relevant benefits receivable by an employee (or by his personal representatives or any dependant of his) from an Overseas Retirement Benefits Scheme or an Overseas Provident Fund where the employee's overseas service comprises

(a) not less than 75 per cent of his total service in that employment; or

(b) the whole of the last 10 years of his service in that employment, where total service exceeds 10 years; or

(c) not less than 50 per cent of his total service in that employment, including any 10 of the last 20 years, where total service exceeds 20 years.

If the employee's overseas service is less than described above, relief from income tax will be given by reducing the amount of the lump sum which would otherwise be chargeable by the same proportion as the overseas service bears to the employee's total service in that employment.

In addition, income tax is not charged on lump sum relevant benefits receivable by an employee (or by his personal representatives or any dependant of his) from any superannuation fund accepted as being within Section 615 ICTA 1988.

For the purposes of this concession, the term "relevant benefits" has the meaning given in Section 612(1) ICTA 1988 and the term "overseas service" shall be construed in accordance with the definition of "foreign service" found at Paragraph 10 Schedule 11 ICTA 1988.'

A period of service falling after 5 April 2003 is 'foreign service' if either:

- the emoluments from the employment are not chargeable under Case I of Schedule E. This will be the case where:

  - the employee is not 'resident and ordinarily resident' in the UK. So, for example, if the employee is not resident, the employee is not chargeable under Case I, so during that period the employee's service is 'foreign service'; or

  - the employee is resident and ordinarily resident in the UK but is not domiciled in the UK, is working for a foreign employer and is carrying out all the duties of the employment outside the UK; or

- the employee is eligible for 100% foreign earnings from the emoluments.

If there is a period of service when there are no earnings from the employment, it is possible to apply the above rules in the same way as if there were.

The concession is currently being reviewed in connection with employer-financed retirement benefits schemes. HMRC *Pensions Tax Simplification Newsletter No. 7* stated that the effect of the concession would continue from A-Day. The concession will be interpreted in the following ways in the light of the new simplified tax legislation:

- 'overseas retirement benefits scheme' and 'overseas provident fund' will be interpreted as overseas employer financed retirement benefits schemes, as defined in *s 393A, ITEPA 2003*;

- the concession will continue to apply to lump sums received from schemes within *s 615(6), ICTA 1988*;

- 'relevant benefits' will be defined in accordance with *s 393B, ITEPA 2003*;

- the concession will not apply to any benefits chargeable under *Sch 34, Finance Act 2004.*

Section 249, Finance Act 2004, contains various legislative amendments relating to the taxation of non-pension benefits from funded unapproved schemes. *Schedule 35, Finance Act 2004*, contains minor and consequential amendments to various Acts and brings in the various changes to FURBS which are described below. Further changes are anticipated once HMRC has reviewed the tax position of employer-financed retirement benefits schemes for the post A-Day regime.

Registering FURBS and UURBS which exist at 5 April 2006   10.15

Funded unapproved retirement benefit schemes (FURBS) or unfunded unapproved retirement benefit schemes (UURBS) were traditionally set up as 'top-up schemes' for individuals who were subject to the earnings cap from the year 1989. If such a scheme applies for registration, HMRC will register the scheme and it will become subject to the tax regime for registered pension schemes from the date of its registration.

Schemes which lost approval before A-Day   10.16

A scheme which lost approval before A-Day may apply to become a registered pension scheme at any time from that date onwards if its scheme administrator applies for registration for the scheme and satisfies the registration conditions.

Existing FURBS and UURBS   10.17

Under pre A-Day tax legislation all FURBS benefits could be paid out tax free if a member had been taxed on the employer contributions paid into the scheme. If FURBS and UURBS do not register they will be treated, under *ss 245–249, Finance Act 2004*, as Employer-Financed Retirement Benefits Schemes as described in **10.12** above. The government does not believe that FURBS and UURBS are essential 'unless the aim is to provide benefits that would not be allowed under a non-registered scheme'. There is transitional protection for monies which were already held in FURBS as at A-Day and for promises made under UURBS:

1. The value of a pension promise under an UURBS will not be included in the annual allowance or lifetime allowance.

2. It is still possible to back an UURBS benefit (where appropriate) by an asset or security but the member must pay a benefit-in-kind tax charge on the cost to the employer of providing security and or underwriting.

3. It is possible to insure UURBS promises against employer default if the premiums are taxed on the member as a benefit-in-kind.

4. Under *Sch 36, Pt 4, Finance Act 2004*, it was possible to consolidate any pre-existing UURBS and roll them into the new regime before A-Day (this will not count towards the annual allowance, only the lifetime allowance, unless the deadline was missed – in which case both elements will be counted).

5. It is possible to make contributions to FURBS post A-Day, and for the tax-free lump sum to be adjusted to take account of the earlier tax-free elements (see point 6 below).

6. Pre-existing FURBS enjoy the protection of a tax-free lump sum element, plus indexation, on values up to A-Day where such payments have qualified for relief either by virtue of the taxation of employer contributions on the member or the taxation of all income and gains under the fund.

7. The value of the fund as at A-Day is calculated by the application of an 'appropriate fraction', and the appropriate fraction is determined from the market value of the assets had the scheme been wound up on that date.

8. The normal inheritance tax exemptions apply to pre A-Day assets in FURBS which are under a discretionary trust (for schemes with no post A-Day contributions, and those with post A-Day contributions, the IHT treatment for the former shall be that in place as at 5 April 2006, and limited relief shall be given in the latter case for pre A-Day funds inclusive of indexation).

9. IHT exemptions will not apply to post A-Day assets.

10. *Schedule 36, paras 52–56, Finance Act 2004*, protect tax-free payments from FURBS where the contributions were taxed under *s 595, Income and Corporation Taxes Act 1988* or *s 386, Income Tax (Earnings and Pensions) Act 2003*, before A-Day.

11. No additional tax charge will arise on the fund/lump sum for a FURBS which ceased contributions/input before A-Day.

12. A registered scheme would, of course, be caught by 25% of the lifetime allowance and, for UURBS, it appears that the maximum pension that can be given up for cash, in order to reduce or avoid a NIC charge, is 25%.

Trusts, Settlements and Estates Manual   10.18

HMRC's internal *Trusts, Settlements and Estates Manual* is due to be revised in respect of unapproved schemes (see **10.1** above).

Pre A-Day, new FURBS and UURBS were submitted for consideration to HMRC Trusts, Bootle. If a scheme lost approval because resident trustees had been replaced by non-residents the case was referred to CNR (Non-Resident Trusts) – all other cases were proper to HMRC Trusts, Nottingham.

An extract from the existing guidance in the manual is given below.

FURBS: resident trustees (EBT2)   **10.19**

The internal memo contains information, advice and action points for:

- the Trust Office dealing with the FURBS trust;

- the tax office for the company; and

- the employment income tax office.

The main actions are:

'The Trust Office

Liability on income

Initial action Issue returns annually to the trustees.

Information Income arising from the invested contributions is charge-able at the lower/basic/Sch F rate only. It is not chargeable at the rate applicable to trusts/Schedule F trust rate. This is because the scheme provides for "Relevant Benefits" (defined in S612 ICTA 1988) only. The exemption is in S686 (2)(c) ICTA 1988 [*Author's note: see* **10.12** *above – this only applies historically*].

Action The exemption does not apply, and the trustees are chargeable at the rate applicable to trusts/Schedule F trust rate, if any of the situations below applies. If you discover such a situation, advise the trustees they are liable at the rate applicable to trusts/Schedule F trust rate. The trustees

- are chargeable Case I Schedule D on trading profits

- invest the contributions in a way that does not give a commercial return, for example

   – non–commercial rate loans

   – investing a significant part of the funds in non–income producing assets.

Advice Refer any objection to HMRC Trusts Bootle.

Action If the trustees use the contributions to provide benefits that are not within the definition of Relevant Benefits, for example

- non–commercial rate loans to a member

- occupation of a trust property either rent free or below the open market rent

- free use of a trust asset

the S686 exemption may not apply, or it may be an indication that a member is the settlor, in which case the Settlements legislation may treat the scheme's income as the settlor's. If you become aware that any of the above three points applies, submit the case to HMRC Trusts Bootle.

The Settlements Legislation

Information The Settlements Legislation in Part XV ICTA 1988 will not apply if the scheme is operating on normal commercial lines as part of an employment package. But in certain circumstances you may consider whether the Settlements legislation applies to charge the FURBS trust's income and gains on a director.

Action Both the Settlements Legislation and the CG equivalent provisions can apply if the trust is apparently not genuinely to provide retirement benefits. Apply the following guidelines when examining trust returns and accounts, and liaise with the tax office for the company and the employment income tax office, or submit to HMRC Trusts Bootle, as necessary.

- The Settlements Legislation will not apply where only the employer makes contributions – unless the contributions are

  - made by a close company which a member controls or

  - unrealistically large by normal commercial standards.

  For example, if there is only one director who is also the sole shareholder of the employing company, and substantial contributions are made into the FURBS, you may consider whether the Settlements legislation applies to treat the director/shareholder as the settlor. If you think this may be the case, you must liaise with the tax office for the company. They will consider whether to deny a deduction for the contributions.

- The Settlements Legislation will not apply if a member makes contributions and these are reasonable compared with the member's salary. As a rule of thumb contributions not exceeding 15% of remuneration (excluding the payments) are reasonable. If you consider the Settlements Legislation may apply, submit your papers to HMRC Trusts Bootle.

- The Settlements legislation may apply if the relief provided by S686 (2)(c) ICTA 1988 has been disallowed. See "Liability on income" above.

The Tax Office for the Company

Contributions

Information Guidance on whether the contributions into the scheme are allowable is at IM8410 onwards. S76 FA 1989 deals with the timing of any deductions due (see IM8412).

The employer's contributions are allowable only if they are chargeable as employment or pension income on a member or another person. Where due, a deduction is given for the period in which the employer makes the contribution (S76 (4)). This ensures the payer's relief matches the employee's charge as to both time and amount.

Advice If you cannot resolve a problem about this, refer the case to Business Tax 1 (Schedule D).

Action There may be tax avoidance opportunities if a company is "close" and a member is a participator with a significant interest in the company. You may want to consider whether amounts put into the scheme by the employer are commensurate with a normal commercial provision for the employee concerned.

Action If a schedule D deduction has been successfully denied because the contribution has not been wholly and exclusively expended for the purposes of the employer's trade, submit the file for the employer to HMRC Trusts Bootle so that they can consider whether the Settlements Legislation applies.

The Employment Income Tax Office

Initial action Put a sub folder in the 46 file to house relevant correspondence. Ask each participating employer for an annual report on form P11D. The report should state the amount of contributions into the scheme to provide benefits for a member. It is then possible to check if all liability under s386 ITEPA 2003 has been met.

Contributions

Information A member is chargeable on the amount of contributions into the scheme as employment income under s386 ITEPA 2003. The charge is for each year of assessment in which there are contributions. Costs of creating or administering the scheme are not chargeable on the member.

Advice Refer any problem about the application of s386 ITEPA 2003 to Personal Tax (Technical).

Pensions

Information Pensions that the trustees pay are chargeable as pension income by virtue of s569 ITEPA 2003 (because of s393(2) ITEPA 2003).

Advice Refer any problem to Personal Tax (Technical).

Lump sum benefit

Information s393 ITEPA 2003 deals with lump sum benefits that trustees pay. A benefit may be chargeable or may be exempt. In particular s395(4) ITEPA 2003 exempts from tax lump sums if the contributions are charged under s386 ITEPA 2003.

Advice Refer any problem to Personal Tax (Technical).

Action Inform IR Capital Taxes, Technical Group, Meldrum House, Drumsheugh Gardens, Edinburgh where a member of a FURBS has died, giving full name and date of death.

National Insurance contributions (NICs) position

For information about the NICs position on:

- an employer's payments into a FURBS; and

- payments out of a FURBS,

see NIM02155 – NIM02163 and SCS98/03.

For advice, contact your NICs Technical Support Manager.'

FURBS: non–resident trustees (NRT40)   **10.20**

There is also a memo for FURBS where the trustees are non-resident. This is the NRT40. Similar tax requirements apply to those stated above.

Extracts from HMRC's Employment Income Manual (EIM)   **10.21**

'EIM15010 – Non-approved and employer-financed retirement benefits schemes: introduction

Sections 386–400 ITEPA 2003 (as amended by Section 249 FA 2004 for receipts after 5 April 2006)

In general terms, a retirement benefits scheme is one that provides for benefits on an employee's retirement or death (for the full definitions see EIM15020).

Retirement benefits schemes can be granted approval, or after 5 April 2006 be registered, by IBS Directorate (APSS). These and some other similar schemes (see EIM15030), receive significant tax advantages. For example, their investment income is not taxed, contributions to the scheme can qualify for tax relief and lump sum benefits (not pensions) are exempt from tax. Consequently, there is detailed legislation governing such schemes and the guidance in respect of them is in the Pensions Manual (EIM guidance does not deal with these schemes).

None of those tax advantages apply if the scheme is not one of those schemes (identified in EIM15030), so that legislation does not apply. Before 6 April 2006 such schemes are known as "non-approved" (or unapproved) and after 5 April 2006 as "employer-financed". The differences in tax treatment of these two types are indicated in the following guidance.

If the receipt being considered is received after 5 April 2006 follow those parts of the guidance that refer to employer-financed schemes to determine its taxation. Otherwise, follow the guidance for non-approved schemes, but remember that an employer-financed scheme may have been a non-approved scheme before 6 April 2006 and so there may be transitional rules to follow (see EIM15121).

These schemes exist, both for individual employees and groups, mainly because what an approved or registered scheme can provide is limited by legislation. For example, in calculating retirement benefits that can be taken from an approved scheme before 6 April 2006, any salary above a certain sum cannot be taken into account (see EIM15172 for figures). So a non-approved scheme is often set up to provide benefits based on salary in excess of that sum.

The general structure of the legislation for non-approved and employer-financed schemes is to tax as follows:

- For non-approved schemes, employer's contributions to the scheme made before 6 April 2006 count as employment income (see EIM00512) of the employee under Section 386 ITEPA 2003 (see EIM15040). There is no equivalent charge for contributions to an employer-financed scheme made after 5 April 2006

- All lump sum payments (including commutations: see EIM15150) out of non-approved schemes count as employment income (see EIM00512) of the recipient under Section 394 ITEPA 2003 (see EIM15100). For employer-financed schemes, only "relevant benefits" (see EIM15021) count as employment income under Section 394 ITEPA 2003.

- For both non-approved and employer-financed schemes, the charge on lump sums paid out may be reduced where prior employer contributions have been taxed (see EIM15125) and where the employee has made contributions (see EIM15123 and EIM15126 for non-approved and employer-financed schemes respectively).

- A pension from any of these schemes is charged separately as pension income under Part 9 ITEPA 2003 (see EIM74001).

- See EIM15100 for guidance on how annuities, annual payments and non-cash receipts are dealt with.

See EIM15020 for the definition of non-approved and employer-financed retirement benefits schemes.'

10.22

'EIM15020 – Non-approved and employer-financed retirement benefits schemes: general definitions

Non-approved: Section 387 ITEPA 2003, Sections 611 & 612(1) ICTA 1988. Employer-financed: Section 393A ITEPA 2003 as amended by Section 249(3) FA 2004

Employers frequently make financial provision for the retirement or death of their employees by setting up a pension scheme or fund or similar arrangement. The employer may make contributions in advance in order to fund the benefits (a funded scheme) or simply pay benefits on retirement or death (an unfunded scheme). All such arrangements are retirement benefits schemes (see definitions below).

A receipt after 5 April 2006 is chargeable under this legislation only if it is provided under an employer-financed retirement benefits scheme. So when dealing with such a receipt do not try to apply guidance that deals with non-approved schemes.

A retirement benefits scheme is defined for the purposes of both non-approved and employer- financed schemes as a scheme that consists of or includes relevant benefits (Section 611(1) ICTA 1988 ICTA88 and Section 393A(1) ITEPA 2003).

"**Scheme**" is defined in the same way for both non-approved and employer-financed schemes as including a "deed, agreement, series of agreements or other arrangements". It does not have to be a formal document and schemes do not have to adopt any particular form. See EIM15028 for more information.

However, the definition of **"Relevant benefits"** differs for non-approved and employer-financed schemes (see EIM15021).'

10.23

'**EIM15015 – Non-approved and employer-financed retirement benefits schemes: tax charges**

Sections 386, 393 and 394(1) ITEPA 2003

A tax charge arises where there is a lump sum receipt:

- **From** a non-approved scheme (see definition in EIM15020) before 6 April 2006 or

- **From** an employer-financed scheme (see definition in EIM15020) after 5 April 2006 **provided** that it is a "relevant benefit" (see EIM15021)

and where an employer makes a contribution **to** a non-approved scheme before 6 April 2006 (see EIM15040).

The above guidance is subject to the following qualifications:

- Pension income is always charged under Part 9 ITEPA 2003 (see EIM74000 and subsequent guidance)

- If the total amount of the benefits received by an individual from an employer-financed scheme in a tax year is £100 or less, there is no charge (Section 394(1A) ITEPA 2003). If the total exceeds that sum, it is all charged (that is, not just the excess over £100)

- Some receipts are excluded from charge in whole or in part (see EIM15121)

- "Transitional" rules may apply where there have been employer contributions to the scheme before 6 April 2006 (whether or not there are such contributions on or after that date): see EIM15121

- Contributions by the employee may need to be taken into account (see EIM15123 and EIM15126 for non-approved and employee-financed schemes respectively).'

10.24

'**EIM15050 – Non-approved and employer-financed retirement benefits schemes: contributions made by employer excluded from charge**

Sections 389 and 390 ITEPA 2003

Note: Section 386 is repealed with effect from 6 April 2006 by Section 247 FA 2004. Any contributions on or after that date are not taxable under Section 386 (see EIM15015).

There are some situations in which an employer's contribution to a non-approved retirement benefits scheme is not chargeable under Section 386 ITEPA 2003 on the employee:

- where the earnings from the employment (see EIM00515) are charged on remittance (see EIM40002) or would be if there were any. Earnings are charged on remittance if they are taxable earnings under Section 22 or Section 26 ITEPA 2003 (see EIM40002). Section 22 applies to chargeable overseas earnings for a year when the employee is resident and ordinarily resident but not domiciled in the UK. Section 26 applies to foreign earnings for a year when the employee is resident but not ordinarily resident in the UK.

- where:

  - the earnings from the employment are from a non resident employer to someone not domiciled in the UK (see EIM40031) **and**

  - the retirement benefits scheme is a "corresponding" scheme. (This refers to non- UK schemes that have the characteristics of a UK exempt approved scheme (see EIM15030). IBS Directorate (APSS) is responsible for deciding whether a scheme has "corresponding" status).

- in practice, where a 100% deduction is allowable against earnings under Section 341 ITEPA 2003 (see EIM33000 and subsequent guidance).

However, a charge may still arise under Section 394 ITEPA 2003 in respect of lump sums, etc subsequently paid **out of** the scheme (see EIM15100).'

10.25

'**EIM15051 – Non-approved and employer-financed retirement benefits schemes: contributions made by employee**

For non-approved schemes (see EIM15020):

Contributions made by an employee to a non-approved retirement benefits scheme:

- are not assessable on the employee

- do not qualify for tax relief. The only exception to this is in relation to a scheme that has received corresponding approval status from IBS Directorate (APSS), see EIM32661.

- do not give rise to a charge under Section 394 ITEPA 2003 (other than as a pension under Part 9 ITEPA 2003 see EIM15100).

For employer-financed schemes (see EIM15010):

- Where a lump sum is received from an employer-financed scheme and an employee has made contributions towards its provision, the taxable sum is reduced by the total of those contributions.

- Once a contribution has reduced a charge, that same contribution cannot be used to reduce any other charge later on.

It is the taxpayer's responsibility to show that contributions qualify.'

Old code schemes   10.26

Any remaining *s 608, Income and Corporation Taxes Act 1988*, schemes fall under the new tax regime unless they choose to opt out. As such, the annual allowance and the lifetime allowance apply from A-Day. If such schemes choose to opt out they will be treated in the same way as non-registered schemes. By way of an alternative, *s 608* schemes (as revised by the *Income Tax (Earnings and Pensions) Act 2003*) may choose to wind up if their rules so permit, commuting all benefits to a lump sum with a 25% tax-free element. This option is only available for the first year following A-Day.

Appendix I

HMRC regulations and orders

The main regulations and orders are listed below, and are in draft form unless the SI number is given.

- The Employer-Financed Retirement Benefits (Excluded Benefits for Tax Purposes) Regulations 2006 (SI 2006/210)

- The Employer-Financed Retirement Benefits Schemes (Provision of Information) Regulations 2005 (SI 2005/3453)

- Establishment of Schemes Regulations 2006

- The Finance Act 2004, Part 4 (Pension Schemes – Transitional and Transitory Provisions and Savings: Pipeline Lump Sums) Order 2006

- The Finance (No 2) Act 2005, Section 45 (Appointed Day) Order 2005 (SI 2005/3337)

- The Pension Benefits (Insurance Company Liable as Scheme Administrator) Regulations 2006 (SI 2006/136)

- The Pension Protection Fund (Tax) (2005–06) Regulations 2005 (SI 2005/1907)

- The Pension Protection Fund (Tax) Regulations 2006

- The Pension Schemes (Part 4 of the Finance Act 2004 Transitional and Transitory Provisions) Order 2005

- The Pension Schemes (Reduction in Pension Rates) Regulations 2006 (SI 2006/138)

- The Registered Pension Schemes (Accounting and Assessment) Regulations 2005 (SI 2005/3454)

- The Registered Pension Schemes and Employer-Financed Retirement Benefits Schemes (Information) (Prescribed Descriptions of Persons) Regulations 2005 (SI 2005/3455)

- The Registered Pension Schemes and Overseas Pension Schemes (Electronic Communication of Returns and Information) Regulations 2005

- The Registered Pension Schemes (Authorised Member Payments) Regulations 2006 (SI 2006/137) for demutualisation of insurance companies and members of qualifying pension schemes

- The Registered Pension Schemes (Authorised Payments) Regulations 2006 (SI 2006/209)

- The Registered Pension Schemes (Authorised Payments) (Transfers to the Pension Protection Fund) Regulations 2006 (SI 2006/134)

- The Registered Pension Schemes (Audited Accounts) (Specified Persons) Regulations 2005 (SI 2005/3456)

- The Registered Pension Schemes (Co-ownership of Living Accommodation) Regulations 2006 (SI 2006/133)

- The Registered Pension Schemes (Defined Benefits Arrangements and Money Purchase Arrangements – Uprating) Regulations 2005

- The Registered Pension Schemes (Discharge of Liabilities under Sections 267 and 268 of the Finance Act 2004) Regulations 2005 (SI 2005/3542)

- The Registered Pension Schemes (Enhanced Lifetime Allowance) Regulations 2006 (SI 2006/131)

- The Registered Pension Schemes (Meaning of Pension Commencement Lump Sum) Regulations 2006 (SI 2006/135)

- The Registered Pension Schemes (Minimum Contributions) Regulations 2005 (SI 2005/3450)

- The Registered Pension Schemes (Modification of the Rules of Existing Schemes) Regulations 2006 (SI 2006/364)

- The Registered Pension Schemes (Prescribed Interest Rates for Authorised Employer Loans) Regulations 2005 (SI 2005/3449)

- The Registered Pension Schemes (Prescribed Schemes and Occupations) Regulations 2005 (SI 2005/3541)

- The Registered Pension Schemes (Provision of Information) Regulations 2005

- The Registered Pension Schemes (Relevant Annuities) Regulations 2006 (SI 2006/129)

- The Registered Pension Schemes (Relief at Source) Regulations 2005 (SI 2005/3448)

- The Registered Pension Schemes (Restriction of Employer's Relief) Regulations 2005 (SI 2005/3548)

- The Registered Pension Schemes (Surrender of Relevant Excess) Regulations 2006 (SI 2006/211)

- The Registered Pension Schemes (Unauthorised Payments by Existing Schemes) Regulations 2006 (SI 2006/365)

- The Registered Pension Schemes (Uprating Percentages for Defined Benefits Arrangements and Enhanced Protection Limits) 2006 (SI 2006/130)

- The Registered Pensions (Splitting of Schemes) Regulations 2006
- The Taxes Management Act (Modifications to Schedule 3 for Pension Scheme Appeals) Order 2005 (SI 2005/3457)
- Transitional Provision Order: Pre A-Day Assets 2005
- Transitional Provision Order: Protection of Large Lump Sums under Enhanced Protection 2005
- Transitional Provision Order: Scheme Specific Lump Sums 2005
- Transitional Provision Order: Transfer of Crystallised Rights With Enhanced Protection 2005
- Transitional Provision Order: Transfers and Wind-ups Secured by Individual Contracts of Insurance 2005
- Transitional Provision Order: Transitional Protection for Lump Sum Only Schemes 2005
- Transitional Provision Order: Lump Sum Death Benefit 2005
- Transitional Provision Order: Lump Sum Only Contracts Becoming Registered Pension Schemes 2005

The HMRC regulations for overseas matters are:

- The Pensions Schemes (Application of UK Provisions to Relevant Non-UK Schemes) Regulations 2006 (SI 2006/207)
- The Pension Schemes (Categories of Country and Requirements for Overseas Pension Schemes and Recognised Overseas Pension Schemes) Regulations 2006 (SI 2006/206)
- The Pension Schemes (Information Requirements – Qualifying Overseas Pension Schemes, Qualifying Recognised Overseas Pension Schemes and Corresponding Relief) Regulations 2006 (SI 2006/208)
- The Pension Schemes (Relevant Migrant Members) Regulations 2006 (SI 2006/212)

These four regulations are reproduced in full in **APPENDIX 4**.

The other relevant regulations, draft regulations and orders are:

- The Civil Partnership Act 2004 (Commencement No 2) Order 2005 (SI 2005/3175)
- The Civil Partnership (Amendment to Registration Provisions) Order 2005 (SI 2005/2000)
- The Civil Partnership (Contracted-out Occupational and Appropriate Personal Pension Schemes) (Surviving Civil Partners) Order 2005 (SI 2005/2050)

- The Civil Partnership (Miscellaneous and Consequential Provisions) Order 2005 (SI 2005/3029)

- The Civil Partnership (Pensions and Benefit Payments) (Consequential, etc. Provisions) Order 2005 (SI 2005/2053)

- The Civil Partnership (Pensions, Social Security and Child Support) (Consequential, etc Provisions) Order 2005 (SI 2005/2877)

- The Contracting-out, Protected Rights and Safeguarded Rights (Transfer Payment) Amendment Regulations 2005 (SI 2005/555)

- The Financial Assistance Scheme (Appeals) Regulations 2005 (SI 2005/3273)

- The Financial Assistance Scheme (Internal Review) Regulations 2005 (SI 2005/1994)

- The Financial Assistance Scheme (Modifications and Miscellaneous Amendments) Regulations 2005 (SI 2005/3256)

- The Financial Assistance Scheme (Provision of Information and Administration of Payments) Regulations 2005 (SI 2005/2189)

- The Financial Assistance Scheme Regulations 2005 (SI 2005/1986)

- The Financial Services and Markets Act 2000 (Financial Promotion) (Amendment) Order 2005 (SI 2005/3392)

- The Information and Consultation of Employees (Amendment) Regulations 2006

- The Local Government Pension Scheme (Civil Partnership) (Amendment) (England and Wales) Regulations 2005 (SI 2005/3069)

- The Occupational and Personal Pension Schemes (Civil Partnership) (Miscellaneous Amendments) Regulations 2005 (SI 2005/3164)

- The Occupational and Personal Pension Schemes (Consultation by Employers and Miscellaneous Amendment) Regulations 2006 (SI 2006/349)

- The Occupational and Personal Pension Schemes (Disclosure of Information) Amendment Regulations 2002 (SI 2002/1383)

- The Occupational and Personal Pension Schemes (General Levy) Regulations 2005 (SI 2005/626)

- The Occupational and Personal Pension Schemes (Pension Liberation) Regulations 2005 (SI 2005/992)

- The Occupational Pension Schemes and Pension Protection Fund (Amendment) Regulations 2005 (SI 2005/993)

- The Occupational Pension Schemes (Administration and Audited Accounts) (Amendment) Regulations 2005 (SI 2005/2426)

- The Occupational Pension Schemes (Consultation by Employers) (Modification for Multi-employer Schemes) Regulations 2006 (SI 2006/16)

- The Occupational Pension Schemes (Contracting-out) (Amount Required for Restoring State Scheme Rights) Amendment Regulations 2005 (SI 2005/891)

- The Occupational Pension Schemes (Cross-border Activities) Regulations 2005 (SI 2005/3381)

- The Occupational Pension Schemes (Disclosure of Information) Regulations 2006

- The Occupational Pension Schemes (Disclosure of Information) Amendment Regulations 2005

- The Occupational Pension Schemes (Early Leavers: Cash Transfer Sums and Contribution Refunds) Regulations 2006 (SI 2006/33)

- The Occupational Pension Schemes (Employer Debt) Regulations 2005 (SI 2005/678)

- The Occupational Pension Schemes (Employer Debt etc) Regulations 2005 (SI 2005/2224)

- The Occupational Pension Scheme (Equal Treatment) (Amendment) Regulations 2005 (SI 2005/1923)

- The Occupational Pension Schemes (Exemption) Regulations 2006

- The Occupational Pension Schemes (Fraud Compensation Levy) Regulations 2006

- The Occupational Pension Schemes (Fraud Compensation Payments and Miscellaneous Amendments) Regulations 2005 (SI 2005/2184)

- The Occupational Pension Schemes (Independent Trustee) Regulations 2005 (SI 2005/703)

- The Occupational Pension Schemes (Internal Controls) Regulations 2005 (SI 2005/3379)

- The Occupational Pension Schemes (Internal Dispute Resolution Procedures) Regulations 2005

- The Occupational Pension Schemes (Investment) Regulations 2005 (SI 2005/3378)

- The Occupational Pension Schemes (Levies) Regulations 2005 (SI 2005/842)

- The Occupational Pension Schemes (Levies) (Amendment) Regulations 2006

- The Occupational Pension Schemes (Levy Ceiling) Order 2006

- The Occupational Pension Schemes (Member-Nominated Trustees and Directors) Regulations 2006

- The Occupational Pension Schemes (Minimum Funding Requirement and Actuarial Valuations) Amendment Regulations 2004 (SI 2004/3031)

- The Occupational Pension Schemes (Miscellaneous Amendments) Regulations 2005 (SI 2005/2113)

- The Occupational Pension Schemes (Modification of Pension Protection Provisions) Regulations 2005 (SI 2005/705)

- The Occupational Pension Schemes (Modification of Subsisting Rights) Regulations 2006

- The Occupational Pension Schemes (Pension Protection Levy and Miscellaneous Amendment) Regulations 2006

- The Occupational Pension Schemes (Regulatory Own Funds) Regulations 2005 (SI 2005/3380)

- The Occupational Pension Schemes (Scheme Funding) Regulations 2005 (SI 2005/3377), and the Regulator's Code of Practice

- The Occupational Pension Schemes (Transfer Values and Miscellaneous Amendments) Regulations 2003 (SI 2003/1727)

- The Occupational Pension Schemes (Trust Exemptions) Regulations 2005

- The Occupational Pension Schemes (Trust and Retirement Benefits Exemption) Regulations 2005 (SI 2005/2360)

- The Occupational Pension Schemes (Trustees Knowledge and Understanding) Regulations 2005

- The Occupational Pension Schemes (Winding Up and Deficiency on Winding Up etc) (Amendment) Regulations 2004 (SI 2004/403)

- The Occupational Pension Schemes (Winding Up, Deficiency on Winding Up and Transfer Values) (Amendment) Regulations 2004 (SI 2005/72)

- The Occupational Pension Schemes (Winding up etc.) Regulations 2005 (SI 2005/706)

- The Occupational Pension Schemes (Winding Up) (Modification for Multi-employer Schemes and Miscellaneous Amendments) Regulations 2005 (SI 2005/2159)

- The Occupational Pension Schemes (Winding Up Notices and Reports etc.) Regulations (SI 2002/459)

- The Pension Protection Fund (Appointment of Ordinary Members) Regulations (SI 2005/616)

- The Pension Protection Fund (Assumption of Responsibility, Discharge of Liabilities and Equal Treatment) Regulations 2006

- The Pension Protection Fund (Compensation) Regulations 2005 (SI 2005/670)

- The Pension Protection Fund (Compensation) (Amendment) Regulations 2006

- The Pension Protection Fund (Eligible Schemes) Appointed Day Order 2005 (SI 2005/599)

- The Pension Protection Fund (Entry Rules) Amendment Regulations 2005 (SI 2005/2153)

- The Pension Protection Fund (Entry Rules) Amendment Regulations 2006

- The Pension Protection Fund (Entry Rules) Regulations 2005 (SI 2005/590)

- The Pension Protection Fund (Hybrid Schemes) (Modification) Regulations (2005/449)

- The Pension Protection Fund (Insolvent Partnerships) (Amendment of Insolvency Events) Order 2005 (SI 2005/2893)

- The Pension Protection Fund (Investigation by PPF Ombudsman of Complaints of Maladministration) Regulations 2005 (SI 2005/2025)

- The Pension Protection Fund (Limit on Borrowing) Order 2005 (SI 2005/339)

- The Pension Protection Fund (Maladministration) Regulations 2005 (SI 2005/650)

- The Pension Protection Fund (Multi-employer Schemes) (Modification) Regulations 2005 (SI 2005/441)

- The Pension Protection Fund (Partially Guaranteed Schemes) (Modification) Regulations 2005 (SI 2005/277)

- The Pension Protection Fund (Payments to meet Investment Costs) Regulations 2005 (SI 2005/1610)

- The Pension Protection Fund (Pension Compensation Cap) Order 2005 (SI 2005/825)

- The Pension Protection Fund (Pension Compensation Cap) Order 2006 (SI 2006/347)

- The Pension Protection Fund (Pension Protection Levies Consultation) Regulations 2005 (SI 2005/1440)

- The Pension Protection Fund (PPF Ombudsman) Order 2005 (SI 2005/824)

- The Pension Protection Fund (Provision of Information) Regulations 2005 (SI 2005/674)

- The Pension Protection Fund (Provision of Information) (Amendment) Regulations 2006

- The Pension Protection Fund (Reference of Reviewable Matters to the PPF Ombudsman) Regulations 2005 (SI 2005/2024)

- The Pension Protection Fund (Reviewable Ill Health Pensions) Regulations 2005 (SI 2005/652)

- The Pension Protection Fund (Reviewable Matters) Regulations 2005 (SI 2005/600)

- The Pension Protection Fund (Reviewable Matters) and (Review and Reconsideration of Reviewable Matters) (Amendment) Regulations 2006

- The Pension Protection Fund (Review and Reconsideration of Reviewable Matters) Regulations 2005 (SI 2005/669)

- The Pension Protection Fund (Risk-based Pension Protection Levy) Regulations 2006

- The Pension Protection Fund (Statement of Investment Principles) Regulations (SI 2005/675)

- The Pension Protection Fund (Valuation) Regulations 2005 (SI 2005/672)

- The Pension Protection Fund (Valuation of the Pension Protection Fund) Regulations 2006

- The Pension Schemes (Categories) Regulations 2005 (SI 2005/2401)

- The Pensions Act 2004 (Commencement No 1 and Consequential and Transitional Provisions) Order 2004 (SI 2004/3350)

- The Pensions Act 2004 (Commencement No. 2, Transitional Provisions and Consequential Amendments) Order 2005 (SI 2005/275)

- The Pensions Act 2004 (Commencement No. 3, Transitional Provisions and Amendment) Order 2005 (SI 2005/695)

- The Pensions Act 2004 (Commencement No 4 and Amendment) Order 2005 (SI 2005/1108)

- The Pensions Act 2004 (Commencement No 5) Order 2005 (SI 2005/1436)

- The Pensions Act 2004 (Commencement No 6 Transitional Provisions and Savings) Order 2005 (SI 2005/1720)

- The Pensions Act 2004 (Commencement No 7) Order 2005 (SI 2005/2447)

- The Pensions Act 2004 (Commencement No 8) Order 2005 (SI 2005/3331)

- The Pensions Act 2004 (Consultation by Employers) (Protections for Nominated Representatives) Regulations 2006

- The Pensions Act 2004 (Funding Defined Benefits) Appointed Day Order 2006 (SI 2006/337)

- The Pensions Act 2004 (PPF Payments and FAS Payments) (Consequential Provisions) Order 2006 (SI 2006/343)

- The Pensions Appeal Tribunals (England and Wales) (Amendment) Rules 2005 (SI 2005/1029)

- The Pensions Appeal Tribunals (Posthumous Appeals) (Amendment Order) 2005 (2005/245)

- The Pensions Ombudsman (Disclosure of Information) (Amendment of Specified Person) Order 2005 (SI 2005/2743)

- The Pensions Regulator (Contribution Notices and Restoration Orders) Regulations 2005 (SI 2005/931)

- The Pensions Regulator (Freezing Orders and Consequential Amendments) Regulations 2005 (SI 2005/686)

- The Pensions Regulator (Financial Support Directions etc) Regulations 2005 (SI 2005/2188)

- The Pensions Regulator (Notifiable Events) Regulations 2005 (SI 2005/900)

- The Pensions Regulator Tribunal (Legal Assistance Scheme) Regulations 2005 (SI 2005/781)

- The Pensions Regulator Tribunal (Legal Assistance Scheme – Costs) Regulations 2005 (SI 2005/782)

- The Pensions Regulator Tribunal Rules 2005 (SI 2005/690)

- The Personal and Occupational Pension Schemes (Indexation and Disclosure of Information) (Miscellaneous Amendments) Regulations 2005 (SI 2005/704)

- The Personal Pension Schemes (Appropriate Schemes) (Amendment) Regulations 2006 (SI 2006/147)

- The Protected Rights (Transfer Payment) (Amendment) Regulations 2005 (SI 2005/2906)

- The Register of Occupational and Personal Pension Schemes Regulations 2005 (SI 2005/597)

- The Social Security (Civil Partnership) (Consequential Amendments) Regulations 2005 (SI 2005/2878)

- The Social Security (Deferral of Retirement Pensions, Shared Additional Pension and Graduated Retirement Benefit) (Miscellaneous Provisions) Regulations 2005 (SI 2005/2677)

- The Social Security (Deferral of Retirement Pensions) Regulations 2005 (SI 2005/453)

- The Social Security (Graduated Retirement Benefit) Regulations 2005 (SI 2005/454)

- The Social Security (Inherited SERPS) (Amendment) Regulations 2005 (SI 2005/811)

- The Social Security (Inherited SERPS) (Amendments relating to Civil Partnership) Regulations 2005 (SI 2005/3030)

- The Stakeholder Pension Schemes (Amendment) Regulations 2005 (SI 2005/577)

- The Transfer of Employment (Pension Protection) Regulations 2005 (SI 2005/649)

- The Transfer of Undertakings (Protection of Employment) Regulations 2006 (SI 2006/246)

The HMRC Registered Pension Schemes Manual contents

The HMRC *Registered Pension Schemes Manual* runs to many volumes. It covers the new tax regime, and protection for existing rights. As soon as a chapter becomes available it becomes accessible through the online contents pages, at: http://www.hmrc.gov.uk/manuals/rpsmmanual/index.htm.

The sections of the manual are listed below and the sub-division pages are shown, where these have been published.

Technical pages (coded RPSM00100000)

RPSM01100000   **About this manual**

RPSM01000010
Welcome to the Registered Pension Schemes Manual

RPSM01000020
Who this manual is for

RPSM01000030
How this manual is updated

RPSM01000040
Before you start

RPSM01000050
How to use the manual

RPSM01000060
Page numbering explained

RPSM01000070
Hyperlinks

RPSM01000080
Navigation aids

RPSM14107000
General points for transfers

RPSM20000000   **Glossary – A comprehensive alphabetical list of definitions**

Member pages (coded RPSM00200000)

RPSM01200000   **About this manual**

RPSM01000010
Welcome to the Registered Pension Schemes Manual

RPSM01000020
Who this manual is for

RPSM01000030
How this manual is updated

RPSM01000040
Before you start

RPSM01000050
How to use the manual

RPSM01000060
Page numbering explained

RPSM01000070
Hyperlinks

RPSM01000080
Navigation aids

RPSM01000090
Helpful contacts

RPSM02200000   **Registering a pension scheme with HMRC**

RPSM02200010
What is a pension scheme?

RPSM02201000
Can I set up my own pension scheme?

RPSM02202000
What is a registered pension scheme?

RPSM02203000
What is a de-registered pension scheme?

RPSM02204000
Where can I find more information?

Scheme Administrator pages (coded RPSM00300000)

RPSM07300000 **Investments**

RPSM07300010
What investments may be made by registered pension schemes?

RPSM07300020
Can a registered pension scheme invest in residential property?

RPSM07300030
Can a member or employer transact with their own registered pension scheme?

RPSM07300040
Can a member use an asset owned by his or her registered pension scheme?

RPSM07300050
Can an employer use an asset owned by their pension scheme?

RPSM07300060
What is a wasting asset?

RPSM07300070
Can a registered pension scheme make a loan?

RPSM07300080
What borrowing restrictions are there for registered pension schemes?

RPSM07300090
Who can lend money to a registered pension scheme?

RPSM07300100
Can a registered pension scheme invest in shares?

RPSM07300110
What is value shifting?

RPSM07300120
What tax charges are there?

RPSM07300130
When will a tax charge be due?

RPSM07300140
What investments may lead to other tax charges?

RPSM07300150
How should the scheme administrator account to HMRC for tax due?

Employer pages (coded **RPSM00400000**)

Defined terms – tax legislation sources

The main list of defined terms in contained in *s 280, Finance Act 2004*. Further definitions appear in:

- *Sch 10, Finance Act 2005*;

- regulations or draft regulations which have been made in pursuance of the *Finance Act 2004*;

- the glossary in HMRC's *Registered Pension Schemes Manual* (RPSM) (reproduced in the glossary in this Guide).

A list of the most commonly occuring terms is given below, after a list of the abbreviations of statutes used within it.

Abbreviations of statutes – mainly drawn from the list in section 280, Finance Act 2004

FA 2004	Finance Act 2004
FA 2005	Finance Act 2005
FSMA 2000	Financial Services and Markets Act 2000
ICTA 1970	Income and Corporation Taxes Act 1970
ICTA	Income and Corporation Taxes Act 1988
ITEPA 2003	Income Tax (Earnings and Pensions) Act 2003
NIA 1965	National Insurance Act 1965
NIA(NI) 1966	National Insurance Act (Northern Ireland) 1966
PSA 1993	Pension Schemes Act 1993
SSCBA 1992	Social Security Contributions and Benefits Act 1992
SSCB(NI)A 1992	Social Security Contributions and Benefits (Northern Ireland) Act 1992
TCGA 1992	Taxation of Chargeable Gains Act 1992
TMA 1970	Taxes Management Act 1970

WRPA 1999 Welfare Reform and Pensions Act 1999

WRP(NI)O 1999 Welfare Reform and Pensions (Northern Ireland) Order 1999 (SI 1999/3147)

General index

Definition	*Statute or source (Finance Act 2004, unless otherwise stated)*
Accounting period	Section 834(1), ICTA
Accounting return	Section 260
Active member (of a pension scheme)	Section 151(2)
Active membership period (in sections 221 to 223)	Section 221(4) and (5)
Alternatively secured pension	Paragraphs 12, 13, Schedule 28, and RPSM
Alternatively secured pension fund	Paragraphs 11, Schedule 28, and RPSM
Amount crystallised	Section 216
Annual allowance	Section 228
Annual allowance charge	Section 227(1)
Annual amount	The Registered Pension Schemes (Relevant Annuities) Regulations 2006 (SI 2006/129)
Annuity protection lump sum death benefit	Paragraph 16, Schedule 29
Applicable amount limit	Paragraph 3, Schedule 29 (revised by Sch 10, FA 2005)
Appropriate portion	Paragraphs 16B(4), 16C(15), Schedule 28 (inserted by Schedule 10, FA 2005)
Arms length bargain	RPSM
Arrangement	Section 152(1), RPSM
Associated company	Section 716, ICTA, and the draft Pension Schemes (Provision of Information) Regulations 2005
Authorised employer loan	Section 179
Authorised member payments	Section 164

Definition	*Statute or source (Finance Act 2004, unless otherwise stated)*
Authorised open-ended investment company	Section 262, FSMA 2000, and RPSM
Authorised pensions	Section 204, Schedule 28, 31 (revised by Schedule 10, FA 2005)
Authorised lump sums	Section 204, Schedule 28, 31 (revised by Schedule 10, FA 2005)
Authorised surplus payment	Section 177
Authorised surplus payments charge	Section 208
Available (in relation to a persons lifetime allowance)	Section 219
Bank	Section 840A(1)(b), ICTA, and RPSM
Basic rate	Section 832(1), ICTA
Basic rate limit	Section 832(1), ICTA
Basis amount	Paragraph 10, Schedule 28 (revised by Schedule 10, FA 2005), RPSM
Benefits (provided by pension scheme	Section 279(2)
Benefit crystallisation event	Section 216, Schedule 32 (revised by Schedule 10, FA 2005), and RPSM
Benefit crystallisation events: supplementary	Schedule 32 (revised by Schedule 10, FA 2005)
Block transfer	RPSM
the Board of Inland Revenue	Section 279(1)
Borrowing	Section 163
Building society	Building Societies Act 1986, and RPSM
Cash balance arrangement	Sections 152(3), 230, and RPSM
Cash balance benefits	Section 152(5)
Category 1; category 2; category 3 (differing types of overseas recognised schemes)	The Pensions Schemes (Categories of Country and Requirements for Overseas Pension Schemes and Recognised Overseas Pension Schemes) Regulations 2006 (SI 2006/206)
Chargeable amount	RPSM

Definition	Statute or source (*Finance Act 2004, unless otherwise stated*)
Chargeable gain	Section 832(1), ICTA
Charity	Section 279(1)
Charity lump sum death benefit	RPSM
Company	Section 832(1), ICTA
Compensation payment	Section 178
Contracts of long-term insurance	Section 278
Contribution	Sections 188(4)–(6) and 195
Deferred member	RPSM
Defined benefits	Section 152(7), and RPSM
Defined benefit occupational pension scheme	Awaiting definition (RPSM)
Defined benefits arrangement	Sections 152(6), 234, and RPSM
Defined benefits lump sum death benefit	Paragraph 13, Schedule 29, and RPSM
Dependant	Paragraph 15, Schedule 28 (revised by Schedule 10, FA 2005), and RPSM
Dependants' alternatively secured pension	Paragraphs 26, 27, Schedule 28 (revised by Schedule 10, FA 2005), and RPSM
Dependants' alternatively secured pension fund	Paragraph 25, Schedule 28 (revised by Schedule 10, FA 2005), and RPSM
Dependants' annuity	Paragraph 17, Schedule 28 (Schedule 10, FA 2005, two inserts), and RPSM
Dependants' scheme pension	Paragraph 16, Schedule 28 (revised by Schedule 10, FA 2005), and RPSM
Dependants' short-term annuity	Paragraph 20, Schedule 28 (inserted by Schedule 10, FA 2005), and RPSM
Dependants' unsecured pension	Paragraphs 20, 23, 24, Schedule 28 (revised by Schedule 10, FA 2005), and RPSM
Dependants' unsecured pension fund	Paragraph 22, Schedule 28 (revised by Schedule 10, FA 2005), and RPSM
De-registration charge	Section 242

Definition	Statute or source (*Finance Act 2004, unless otherwise stated*)
Director	Section 716, ICTA, and the draft Pension Schemes (Provision of Information) Regulations 2005
Electronic payment	Section 255A (inserted by Schedule 10, FA 2005)
Employee and employer (**and employment**)	Section 279(1)
Employer-financed retirement benefits scheme	Section 245, and section 393(a), ITEPA 2003, and the Employer-Financed Retirement Benefits Schemes (Provision of Information) Regulations 2005 (SI 2005/3453)
Employer loan	Schedule 30
Employment income	Section 7(2), ITEPA 2003
Enhanced lifetime allowance regulations	Sections 256(2), 261, 262, 263
Enhanced protection	Paragraphs 12−17, Schedule 36 (revised by Schedule 10, FA 2005)
Entitled (**in relation to a lump sum**)	Section 166(2)
Entitled (**in relation to a pension**)	Section 165(3)
European Economic Area (EEA) investment portfolio manager	Schedule 3, FSMA 2000, and RPSM
Excepted circumstances	Paragraph 10, Schedule 32, FA 2005, paragraph 16C(3), Schedule 28 (inserted by Schedule 10, FA 2005
Exceptional circumstances amount	Paragraph 16C(13), Schedule 28 (inserted by Sch 10, FA 2005
Ex-spouse	RPSM
FSAVCS	Section 592(1)(h), ICTA, and RPSM
GAD	RPSM
GAD tables	RPSM
GMPs	PSA 1993, and RPSM
Higher rate	Section 832(1), ICTA

277

Definition	*Statute or source (Finance Act 2004, unless otherwise stated)*
Hybrid arrangement	Sections 152(8), 237, and RPSM
Ill-health condition	Paragraph 1, Schedule 28
the individual (in sections 215 to 219)	Section 214(5)
Initial member pension limit	Paragraph 16B(3), Schedule 28, (inserted by Schedule 10, FA 2005)
the Inland Revenue	Section 279(1)
Insurance company	Section 275, Part 4 and Schedules 3, 15, FSMA 2000, and RPSM
Investments (in relation to a pension scheme)	Section 186(3) and (4)
Liability	Section 163
Lifetime allowance (in relation to a person)	Section 218, and RPSM
Lifetime allowance charge	Section 214(1), 267, and RPSM
Lifetime allowance enhancement factors	Section 218(5)
Lifetime allowance excess lump sum	Paragraph 11, Schedule 29, and RPSM
Lifetime annuity	Paragraph 3, Schedule 28, and RPSM
Loan	Section 162, Schedule 30 (revised by Schedule 10, FA 2005)
Lump sum death benefit	Section 168(1)
Lump sum death benefit rule	Section 168(2)
Market value	Section 278, and RPSM
Member (of a pension scheme)	Section 151(1)
Member payment charges	Paragraphs 1–7 Schedule 34
Members' alternatively secured pension fund	Paragraph 11, Schedule 28 (paragraph 8 of Schedule 28, revised by Schedule 10, FA 2005)
Members' unsecured pension fund	Paragraph 8, Schedule 28 (revised by Schedule 10, FA 2005)
Migrant member relief	Section 243

Definition	*Statute or source (Finance Act 2004, unless otherwise stated)*
Money purchase	RPSM
Money purchase arrangement	Sections 152(2), 233, and RPSM
Money purchase benefits	Section 152(4)
Net pay pension scheme	Section 191(9)
New dependants' scheme pension	Section 169 (inserted by Schedule 10, FA 2005)
New scheme pension	Section 169 (inserted by Schedule 10, FA 2005)
Normal minimum pension age	Section 279(1)
Notional repayment amount	The Registered Pension Schemes (Minimum Contributions) Regulations 2005 (SI 2005/3450)
Occupational pension scheme	Section 150(5), and RPSM
the Old arrangement	Section 169 (inserted by Schedule 10, FA 2005)
Operative date	The Registered Pension Schemes (Prescribed Interest Rates for Authorised Employer Loans) Regulations 2005 (SI 2005/3449)
Original dependants' scheme pension	Section 169 (inserted by Schedule 10, FA 2005)
Original pension scheme	Paragraph 23(5), Schedule 36 (inserted by Schedule 10, FA 2005)
Original scheme pension	Section 169 (inserted by Schedule 10, FA 2005)
Other money purchase arrangement	RPSM
Overseas arrangement active membership period	Section 224(7), (8), and RPSM
Overseas pension scheme	Section 150(7), and RPSM
Payment	Section 161
Payments (made by pension scheme)	Section 279(2)
Pension	Section 165(2)

Definition	Statute or source (*Finance Act 2004, unless otherwise stated*)
Pension commencement lump sum	Paragraphs 1–3, Schedule 29 (revised by Schedule 10, FA 2005), and RPSM
Pension commencement lump sum: applicable amount	Paragraph 3, Schedule 29 (revised by Schedule 10, FA 2005)
Pension commencement lump sum: deduction from applicable amount in case of scheme pension	Paragraph 3(8), Schedule 29 (revised by Schedule 10, FA 2005)
Pension credit and pension debit	Section 279(1), WRPA 1999, Schedule 10, Finance Act 1999, and RPSM
Pension death benefit rules	Section 167
Pension input amount	Section 229
Pension input period	Section 238
Pension protection lump sum death benefit	Paragraphs 14, 16, Schedule 29, and RPSM
Pension scheme	Section 150(1), and RPSM
the Pension scheme (in sections 215 to 219)	Section 214(5)
Pension sharing event	Paragraph 24(8A), Schedule 28 (inserted by Schedule 10, FA 2005)
Pension sharing order	Section 28(1), WRPA 1999, and SI 1999/3147 in Northern Ireland
Pension sharing order or provision	Section 279(1), and RPSM
Pension year	RPSM
Pensioner member (of a pension scheme)	Section 151(3)
Period of account	Section 832(1), ICTA
Permitted margin	Paragraph 11, Schedule 32, paragraph 16C(7), Schedule 28 (inserted by Schedule 10, FA 2005)
the Permitted maximum	Section 172C (inserted by Schedule 10, FA 2005)
Personal representatives	Section 279(1), and RPSM

Definition	Statute or source (*Finance Act 2004, unless otherwise stated*)
Power to split schemes	Section 274A (inserted by Schedule 10, FA 2005)
Prescribed occupation	The Registered Pension Schemes (Prescribed Schemes and Occupations) Regulations 2005 (SI 2005/3451)
Prescribed person	Section 399A, ITEPA 2003, and the Employer-Financed Retirement Benefits Schemes (Provision of Information) Regulations 2005 (SI 2005/3453)
Prescribed rate of interest	Section 179, and the Pension Schemes (Prescribed Interest Rates for Authorised Employer Loans) Regulations 2005 (SI 2005/3449)
Prescribed scheme	The Registered Pension Schemes (Prescribed Schemes and Occupations) Regulations 2005 (SI 2005/3451)
Primary protection	Paragraphs 7–11, Schedule 36, (revised by Schedule 10, FA 2005)
Property investment LLP	Section 842(B), ICTA, and RPSM
Protected rights	RPSM
Public service pension scheme	Section 150(3)
Public service scheme payment	Section 176
Qualifying overseas pension scheme	Paragraph 3, Schedule 33, and RPSM
Qualifying recognised overseas pension scheme	Section 169(2), and RPSM
Recognised European Economic Area (EEA) collective investment scheme	Section 235, FSMA 2000, and RPSM
Recognised for tax purposes	The Pensions Schemes (Categories of Country and Requirements for Overseas Pension Schemes and Recognised Overseas Pension Schemes) Regulations 2006 (SI 2006/206)
Recognised overseas pension scheme	Section 150(8), and RPSM

281

Definition	Statute or source (*Finance Act 2004, unless otherwise stated*)
Recognised overseas scheme arrangement	Section 224(2), (3)
Recognised transfer(s)	Section 169 (revised by Schedule 10, FA 2005), and RPSM
Reference date	The Registered Pension Schemes (Prescribed Interest Rates for Authorised Employer Loans) Regulations 2005 (SI 2005/3449)
Refund of excess contributions lump sum	RPSM
Registered pension scheme	Section 150(2), and RPSM
Registered pension scheme return	Section 250
Registration	Section 153
Relevant annual percentage rate	Para 11, Schedule 32, FA 2005
Relevant annuity	The Registered Pension Schemes (Relevant Annuities) Regulations 2006 (SI 2006/129)
Relevant associated persons	Section 278
Relevant benefits	Section 393(a), ITEPA 2003, and the Employer-Financed Retirement Benefits Schemes (Provision of Information) Regulations 2005 (SI 2005/3453)
Relevant existing pension	Paragraph 16C(5), Schedule 28 (inserted by Schedule 10, FA 2005)
Relevant lump sum	Paragraph 15, Schedule 32, FA 2005,
Relevant lump sum death benefit	Paragraph 16, Schedule 32, FA 2005, and the draft Pension Schemes (Provision of Information) Regulations 2005
Relevant member	The Pension Schemes (Information Requirements – Qualifying Overseas Pension Schemes, Qualifying Recognised Overseas Pension Schemes and Corresponding Relief) Regulations 2006 (SI 2006/208)

Definition	*Statute or source (Finance Act 2004, unless otherwise stated)*
Relevant migrant member	Paragraph 3, Schedule 33, and paragraph 4(c) (inserted by Schedule 10, FA 2005)
Relevant non-UK scheme	Paragraph 1, Schedule 34
Relevant overseas individual	Sections 178, 221(3), and RPSM
Relevant pension schemes	Paragraph 1, Schedule 32, FA 2005,
Relevant uncrystallised funds	Paragraph 8, Schedule 28 (revised by Schedule 10, FA 2005)
Relevant UK earnings	Section 189(2), and RPSM
Relevant UK individual	Section 189, and RPSM
Relevant valuation factor	Section 276
Relief at source	Section 192
Relievable pension contributions	Section 188(2), (3), and RPSM
Reportable event	Section 251, and the draft Pension Schemes (Provision of Information) Regulations 2005
Responsible person	Section 399A, ITEPA 2003; the Employer-Financed Retirement Benefits Schemes (Provision of Information) Regulations 2005 (SI 2005/3453) and the Registered Pension Schemes and Employer-Financed Retirement Benefits Schemes (Information) (Prescribed Descriptions of Persons) Regulations 2005 (SI 2005/3455)
Retail prices index	Section 279(1)
Retirement benefit scheme	Chapter I, Part XIV, ICTA, or statutory scheme (or one treated as such), or old code scheme, and as described in RPSM
Scheme administration employer payments	Section 180
Scheme administration member payments	Section 171
Scheme administrator	Section 270 (but see also sections 271–274)

Definition	Statute or source (*Finance Act 2004, unless otherwise stated*)
Scheme chargeable payment	Section 241
Scheme manager	Section 169(3)
Scheme pension	Paragraph 2, Schedule 28, and RPSM
Scheme sanction charge	Sections 239(1), 268
Section 9(2B) Rights	Section 9(2B), PSA 1993, and RPSM
Secured pension	RPSM
Serious ill-health lump sum	Paragraph 4, Schedule 29
Short service refund lump sum	Paragraph 5, Schedule 29
Short service refund lump sum charge	Section 205(1)
Short-term annuity	Paragraph 6, Schedule 28 (inserted by Schedule 10, FA 2005), and RPSM
Special lump sum death benefits charge	Section 206(1)
Split approval	Section 274A (inserted by Schedule 10, FA 2005)
Sponsoring employer	Section 150(6)
Standard lifetime allowance	Section 218(2), (3), and RPSM
Sums and assets held for the purposes of an arrangement	Section 279(3)
Tax year	Section 279(1)
the Tax year 2006–07 etc	Section 279(1)
Total income	Section 835, ICTA
Total pension input amount	Section 229
Transfer lump sum death benefit	Paragraph 19, Schedule 29, and RPSM
Transferee pension scheme	Paragraphs 22, 23(5), Schedule 36 (inserted by Schedule 10, FA 2005)
Trivial commutation lump sum	Paragraphs 7–9, Schedule 29, and RPSM
Trivial commutation lump sum death benefit	Paragraph 20, Schedule 29, and RPSM

Definition	*Statute or source (Finance Act 2004, unless otherwise stated)*
Unauthorised borrowing	Section 182
Unauthorised employer payment	Section 160(4)
Unauthorised member payment	Section 160(2)
Unauthorised payment	Section 160(5)
Unauthorised payments charge	Section 208(1)
Unauthorised payments surcharge	Sections 209(1), 268
Uncrystallised funds lump sum death benefit	Paragraph 15, Schedule 29
Unit trust scheme manager	Part 4, FSMA 2000, or Schedule 4, FSMA 2000, as explained in RPSM
Unsecured pension	RPSM
Unsecured pension fund lump sum death benefit	Paragraph 17, Schedule 29, and RPSM
Unsecured pension years etc	Paragraphs 10, 24, Schedule 28 (revised by Schedule 10, FA 2005)
Unvested funds	RPSM
Unvested funds lump sum death benefit	RPSM
Valuation assumptions (in relation to a person)	Section 277, and RPSM
Value shifting	Section 181
Winding-up lump sum	Paragraph 10, Schedule 29, and RPSM
Winding-up lump sum death benefit	Paragraph 21, Schedule 29, and RPSM
Working day	The Pension Schemes (Prescribed Interest Rates for Authorised Employer Loans) Regulations 2005 (SI 2005/3449)

The overseas regulations

There are four sets of regulations that apply to overseas matters. These are reproduced below in order that they may be read alongside **CHAPTER 9**:

- the *Pension Schemes (Categories of Country and Requirements for Overseas Pension Schemes and Recognised Overseas Pension Schemes) Regulations 2006 (SI 2006/206)*;

- the *Pensions Schemes (Application of UK Provisions to Relevant Non-UK Schemes) Regulations 2006 (SI 2006/207)*;

- the *Pension Schemes (Information Requirements – Qualifying Overseas Pension Schemes, Qualifying Recognised Overseas Pension Schemes and Corresponding Relief) Regulations 2006 (SI 2006/208)*;

- the *Pension Schemes (Relevant Migrant Members) Regulations 2006 (SI 2006/212)*.

Pension Schemes (Categories of Country and Requirements for Overseas Pension Schemes and Recognised Overseas Pension Schemes) Regulations 2006 (SI 2006/206)

Made 1st February 2006

Laid before the House of Commons 2nd February 2006

Coming into force 6th April 2006

I   Citation, commencement and interpretation

(1) These Regulations may be cited as the Pension Schemes (Categories of Country and Requirements for Overseas Pension Schemes and Recognised Overseas Pension Schemes) Regulations 2006 and shall come into force on 6th April 2006.

(2) In these Regulations a reference, without more, to a numbered section or Schedule is a reference to the section of, or Schedule to, the Finance Act 2004 which is so numbered.

2   Requirements of an overseas pension scheme

(1) For the purposes of section 150(7) (meaning of overseas pension scheme) an overseas pension scheme must—

(a)   satisfy the requirements in paragraphs (2) and (3); or

(b)   be established (outside the United Kingdom) by an international organisation for the purpose of providing benefits for, or in respect of, past service as an employee of the organisation and satisfy the requirements in paragraph (4).

(2) This paragraph is satisfied if—

(a)   the scheme is an occupational pension scheme and there is, in the country or territory in which it is established, a body—

    (i)   which regulates occupational pension schemes; and

    (ii)   which regulates the scheme in question; and

(b)   the scheme is not an occupational pension scheme and there is in the country or territory in which it is established, a body—

    (i)   which regulates pension schemes other than occupational pension schemes; and

    (ii)   which regulates the scheme in question; or

(c)   neither sub-paragraph (a) or (b) is satisfied by reason only that no such regulatory body exists in the country or territory and—

    (i)   the scheme is established in another member State, Norway, Iceland or Liechtenstein; or

    (ii)   the scheme's rules provide that at least 70% of a member's UK tax-relieved scheme funds will be designated by the scheme manager for the purpose of providing that individual with an income for life, and the pension benefits payable to the member under the scheme (and any lump sum associated with those benefits) are payable no earlier than they would be if pension rule 1 in section 165 applied.

(3) This paragraph is satisfied if the scheme is recognised for tax purposes.

A scheme is "recognised for tax purposes" under the tax legislation of a country or territory in which it is established if it meets the primary conditions and also meets one of Conditions A and B.

Primary condition 1

The scheme is open to persons resident in the country or territory in which it is established.

Primary condition 2

The scheme is established in a country or territory where there is a system of taxation of personal income under which tax relief is available in respect of pensions and—

(a)   tax relief is not available to the member on contributions made to the scheme by the individual or, if the individual is an employee, by their employer, in respect of earnings to which benefits under the scheme relate; or

(b)   all or most of the benefits paid by the scheme to members who are not in serious ill-health are subject to taxation.

For the purposes of this condition "tax relief" includes the grant of an exemption from tax.

Condition A

The scheme is approved or recognised by, or registered with, the relevant tax authorities as a pension scheme in the country or territory in which it is established.

Condition B

If no system exists for the approval or recognition by, or registration with, relevant tax authorities of pension schemes in the country or territory in which it is established—

(a)   it must be resident there; and

(b)   its rules must provide that—

      (i)   at least 70% of a member's UK tax-relieved scheme funds will be designated by the scheme manager for the purpose of providing the member with an income for life, and

      (ii)   the pension benefits payable to the member under the scheme (and any lump sum associated with those benefits) must be payable no earlier than they would be if pension rule 1 in section 165 applied.

(4) In the case of an overseas pension scheme falling within paragraph (1)(b) the requirements are that—

(a)   the scheme rules must provide that at least 70% of a member's UK tax-relieved scheme funds will be designated by the scheme manager for the purpose of providing the member with an income for life, and

(b)   the pension benefits payable to the member under the scheme (and any lump sum associated with those benefits) under the scheme must be payable no earlier than they would be if pension rule 1 in section 165 applied.

(5) In this regulation—

"international organisation" means an organisation to which section 1 of the International Organisations Act 1968 applies by virtue of an Order in Council under subsection (1) of that section;

occupational pension scheme" has the meaning given by section 150(5); and

"UK tax-relieved scheme funds" means, in relation to a member, the sum of the member's UK tax-relieved fund and his relevant transfer fund, as defined respectively by regulations 2 and 3 of the Pension Schemes (Application of UK Provisions to Relevant Non-UK Schemes) Regulations 2006.

3 Recognised overseas pension schemes: prescribed countries or territories and prescribed conditions

(1) For the purposes of section 150(8) (recognised overseas pension schemes), in addition to satisfying the requirements set out in regulation 2 above, the pension scheme must—

(a)   be established in a country or territory mentioned in paragraph (2); or

(b)   satisfy the requirement in paragraph (4).

(2) The countries and territories referred to in paragraph (1)(a) are—

(a)   the member States of the European Communities, other than the United Kingdom;

(b)   Iceland, Liechtenstein and Norway; and

(c)   any country or territory in respect of which there is in force an Order in Council under section 788 of the Income and Corporation Taxes Act 1988 giving effect in the United Kingdom to an agreement which contains provision about—

      (i)   the exchange of information between the parties, and

      (ii)   non-discrimination.

(3) For the purposes of paragraph (2)(c)(ii) an agreement "contains provision about non-discrimination" if it provides that the nationals of a Contracting State shall not be subjected in the territory of the other Contracting State to any taxation, or any requirement connected to such taxation, which is other than, or more burdensome than, the taxation and connected requirements to which the nationals of the other State are or may be subjected in the same circumstances.

(4) The requirement is that, at the time of a transfer of sums or assets which would, subject to these Regulations, constitute a recognised transfer, the rules of the scheme must provide that—

(a)   at least 70% of the sums transferred will be designated by the scheme manager for the purpose of providing the member with an income for life;

(b)   the pension benefits (and any lump sum associated with those benefits) payable to the member under the scheme, to the extent that they relate to the transfer, are payable no earlier than they would be if pension rule 1 in section 165 applied; and

(c)   the scheme is open to persons resident in the country or territory in which it is established.

Pensions Schemes (Application of UK Provisions to Relevant Non-UK Schemes) Regulations 2006 (SI 2006/207)

Made 1st February 2006

Laid before the House of Commons 2nd February 2006

Coming into force 6th April 2006

PART 1
INTRODUCTION

1 Citation, commencement and interpretation

(1) These Regulations may be cited as the Pensions Schemes (Application of UK Provisions to Relevant Non-UK Schemes) Regulations 2006 and shall come into force on 6th April 2006.

(2) In these Regulations—

"the Act" means the Finance Act 2004 any reference (without more) to a numbered section or Schedule is a reference, as the case requires, to the section of, or Schedule to, the Act which bears that number;

"benefit crystallisation event 8" means the event which constitutes benefit crystallisation event 8 in section 216;

"recognised overseas pension scheme" has the meaning given by section 150(8); and

"relevant non-UK scheme" has the same meaning given by paragraph 1(5) of Schedule 34.

PART 2
APPLICATION AND COMPUTATION OF UK TAX CHARGES

2 Computation of a member's UK tax-relieved fund under a relevant non-UK scheme

The amount of a member's UK tax-relieved fund under a relevant non-UK scheme is the aggregate of—

(a) the amounts which, for each tax year before that in which the computation falls to be made, would have been arrived at in relation to arrangements under the relevant non-UK scheme relating to the individual as pension input amounts under sections 230 to 238 of the Act (annual allowance) as they apply by virtue of paragraph 8 of Schedule 34 to the Act, and

(b) the amount which would be so arrived at if the period beginning with 6th April of the tax year in which the computation falls to be made; and ending immediately before the making of the computation, were a tax year,

assuming that section 229(3) did not apply.

3 Computation of a member's relevant transfer fund

The amount of a member's relevant transfer fund under a relevant non-UK scheme (that scheme being referred to here as "the RNUKS") is the sum of—

(a) the amount crystallised by virtue of benefit crystallisation event 8 on the transfer from a UK registered scheme to the RNUKS; and

(b) so much of the member's UK tax-relieved fund under any other relevant non-UK scheme as has been transferred to the RNUKS but has not been subject to the unauthorised payments charge; and

(c) so much of the member's relevant transfer fund under any other relevant non-UK scheme as has been transferred to the RNUKS—

    (i) without being subject to the unauthorised payments charge; and

    (ii) at a time when the other relevant non-UK scheme is a recognised overseas pension scheme.

4 Attributing payments to particular funds under a relevant non-UK scheme

(1) This regulation applies to determine to which part of a relevant non-UK scheme a payment to, or in respect of, a member is referable.

(2) It shall be assumed that—

(a)   payments made by the scheme to or in respect of the member are made out of the member's UK tax-relieved fund in priority to any other fund under that scheme; and

(b)   the amount of the member's UK tax-relieved fund is reduced by the amount paid out of the scheme.

(3) If the member's UK tax-relieved fund is nil, or has been reduced to nil, it shall be assumed that—

(a)   payments made by the scheme to or in respect of the member are made out of the relevant transfer fund in priority to any other fund under that scheme; and

(b)   the amount of the relevant transfer fund is reduced by the amount paid out of the scheme.

PART 3

5   Modifications to Part 4 of the Finance Act 2004 in respect of relevant non-UK schemes

Part 4 of the Finance Act 2004 shall be modified in respect of relevant non-UK schemes, within the meaning of paragraph 1(5) of Schedule 34, in accordance with the following provisions of these Regulations.

6   Modification of pension rules

In section 165, in pension rules 4 and 6 omit from "but a scheme pension" to the end.

7   Modification of pension death benefit rules

In section 167 in pension death benefit rules 3 and 5 omit from "but a dependants' scheme pension" to the end.

8   Modification of section 227

In section 227(3)(b) for "scheme administrator" substitute "scheme manager".

9   Modification of section 231

In section 231—

(a)   in subsection (3)—

(i)   in paragraph (b) for "the retail prices index" substitute "a relevant index";

(ii)   omit paragraph (c); and

(b)   at the end add—

"(4) In this section "relevant index" means—

(a)   an index of the movement of retail prices maintained, or officially recognised, by the government of the country or territory in which the recognised overseas scheme is established; or

(b)   if there is no such index as is mentioned in paragraph (a) of this definition, the retail prices index.".

10   Modification of section 235

In section 235—

(a)   in subsection (3)—

(i)   in paragraph (b) for "the retail prices index" substitute "a relevant index";

(ii)   omit paragraph (c); and

(b)   at the end of the section add—

"(4) In this section "relevant index" means—

(a)   an index of the movement of retail prices maintained, or officially recognised, by the government of the country or territory in which the recognised overseas scheme is established; or

(b)   if there is no such index as is mentioned in paragraph (a) of this definition, the retail prices index.".

11   Modification of section 275

(1) In the heading of section 275 at the end add "and Non-EEA annuity provider".

(2) At the end of the section add—

"(3) In this Part "non-EEA annuity provider" means a person resident in a country or territory outside the European Economic Area—

(a)   whose normal business includes the provision of annuities; and

(b)   who is regulated in the conduct of that business—

  (i)   by the government of that country or territory; or

  (ii)   a body established under the law of that country or territory for the purpose of regulating such business.".

12   Modification of section 276

In section 276(2) for "scheme administrator" substitute "scheme manager".

13   Modification of section 279

(1) Section 279(1) shall be modified as follows.

(2) At the appropriate points in the alphabetical list insert—

""applicable pension scheme", in relation to a pension sharing order in respect of a member's spouse or ex-spouse, means a scheme which is—

  (a)   a recognised overseas pension scheme within the meaning of this Part; or

  (b)   a scheme which is recognised for tax purposes under the law of either the country or territory in which it is situate or that of the country or territory in which the pension sharing order is made;"; and

""ex-spouse", in relation to a member, means the other party to a marriage with the member that has been dissolved or annulled;";

(3) For the definitions of "pension credit" and "pension debit" substitute—

""pension credit" and "pension debit" mean respectively the amount by which—

  (a)   the entitlement of a member's spouse or ex-spouse under an applicable pension scheme, is increased; and

  (b)   the entitlement of a member under a qualifying recognised overseas pension scheme is decreased,

  pursuant to a pension sharing order;".

(4) For the definition of "pension sharing order or provision" substitute—

""pension sharing order" means an order of a court, by virtue of which amounts are transferred from a recognised overseas pension scheme of a member to an applicable pension scheme of that member's spouse or ex-spouse, in or in connection with proceedings relating to the dissolution or annulment of the marriage of the parties;".

14   Modification of Schedule 28

(1) Schedule 28 is modified as follows.

(2) In paragraph 1—

(a)   in sub-paragraph (a) after "registered medical practitioner" insert "or a recognised medical practitioner";

(b)   at the end of the paragraph add—

"In this paragraph "recognised medical practitioner" means a medical practitioner practising outside the United Kingdom who is authorised, licensed or registered to practise medicine in the country or territory, outside the United Kingdom, in which either the scheme or the member is resident.".

(3) In the following provisions for "scheme administrator" substitute "scheme manager".

The provisions are—

(a)   paragraph 1(a);

(b) paragraph 2 (in each place where the expression occurs);

(c) paragraph 10(3)(b);

(d) paragraph 13(3);

(e) paragraph 16(1) and (2);

(f) paragraph 24(3)(b); and

(g) paragraph 27(3).

(4) Omit paragraphs 3(1)(b), 6(1)(c), 17(1)(b) and 20(1)(c).

(5) In paragraph 15(2)(b) and (3) omit ", in the opinion of the scheme administrator".

(6) At the end of the Schedule add—

"PART 3
RELEVANT NON-UK SCHEMES—INTERPRETATION
Construction of references to insurance companies

28 (1) In this Schedule, in its application to a scheme established in a country or territory outside the European Economic Area, any reference to an insurance company includes a non-EEA annuity provider.

(2) Section 275(3) defines "non-EEA annuity provider".".

15 Modification of Schedule 29

(1) Schedule 29 is modified as follows.

(2) In paragraph 1 after sub-paragraph (4) insert—

"(4A) In determining whether all or part of the member's lifetime allowance is available—

(a) an amount treated as crystallising by virtue of benefit crystallisation event 8 shall be disregarded; and

(b) the amount of the allowance available shall be reduced by the aggregate of—

(i) the amount of any previous pension commencement lump sum paid to or in respect of the member by a recognised overseas pension scheme, to the extent that the lump sum is referable to the member's relevant transfer fund, and

(ii) the amount which would have crystallised by virtue of the member becoming entitled to a pension, had the scheme paying it been a registered pension scheme, to the extent that it is so referable.

(4B) For the purposes of sub-paragraph (4A) "the member's relevant transfer fund" has the meaning given in paragraph 4(2) of Schedule 34.".

(3) In paragraph 2—

(a) in sub-paragraph (6) for the definition of AAC substitute—

"AAC is the aggregate of—

(a) the amounts crystallised by each benefit crystallisation event (other than benefit crystallisation event 8) which has occurred in relation to the member before the member becomes entitled to the lump sum (or treated as crystallised) on each occasion on which entitlement to a pension arises; and

(b) the amount which would have crystallised, had the scheme paying it been a registered pension scheme—

(i) on entitlement arising to any pension commencement lump sum, to the extent that the lump sum is referable to the member's relevant transfer fund, or

(ii) on entitlement arising to a pension, to the extent that it is so referable.";

(b) after sub-paragraph (6) insert—

"(6A) The member's becoming entitled to a pension commencement lump sum, or to a pension, as mentioned in paragraph (b) of the definition of AAC in paragraph (6) shall be treated as a benefit crystallisation event for the purposes of sub-paragraph (7).".

(4) In paragraph 4—

(a) in sub-paragraph (1)(a) after "registered medical practitioner" insert "or a recognised medical practitioner";

(b)   at the end of the paragraph add—

"(3) In sub-paragraph (1) "recognised medical practitioner" means a medical practitioner practising outside the United Kingdom who is authorised, licensed or registered to practise medicine in the country or territory, outside the United Kingdom, in which either the scheme or the member is resident.

(4) In determining whether all or part of the member's lifetime allowance is available—

(a)   an amount crystallising by virtue of benefit crystallisation event 8 shall be disregarded; and

(b)   the amount of the allowance available shall be reduced by the aggregate of—

  (i)   the amount of any previous pension commencement lump sum which has been paid to or in respect of the member by a recognised overseas pension scheme, to the extent that it is referable to the member's relevant transfer fund and

  (ii)   the amount which would have crystallised on the member becoming entitled to a pension, had the scheme paying it been a registered pension scheme, to the extent that it is so referable.".

(5) In paragraph 5(1)(c) after "benefit crystallisation event" insert—

", other than an event which constitutes benefit crystallisation event 8".

(6) At the end of paragraph 7 add—

"(6) In determining whether all or part of the member's lifetime allowance is available—

(a)   an amount crystallising by virtue of benefit crystallisation event 8 shall be disregarded; and

(b)   the amount of the allowance available shall be reduced by the aggregate of—

  (i)   the amount of any previous pension commencement lump sum which has been paid to or in respect of the member by a recognised overseas pension scheme, to the extent that it is referable to the member's relevant transfer fund and

  (ii)   the amount which would have crystallised on the member becoming entitled to a pension, had the scheme paying it been a registered pension scheme, to the extent that it is so referable.".

(7) At the end of paragraph 10 add—

"(4) In determining whether all or part of the member's lifetime allowance is available—

(a)   an amount crystallising by virtue of benefit crystallisation event 8 shall be disregarded; and

(b)   the amount of the allowance available shall be reduced by the aggregate of—

  (i)   the amount of any previous pension commencement lump sum which has been paid to or in respect of the member by a recognised overseas pension scheme, to the extent that the lump sum is referable to the member's relevant transfer fund, and

  (ii)   the amount which would have crystallised on the member becoming entitled to a pension, had the scheme paying it been a registered pension scheme, to the extent that it is so referable.".

(8) In paragraph 11 after sub-paragraph (b) insert—

"(bb)   it is not paid from the relevant transfer fund of a qualifying recognised overseas pension scheme,".

(9) In paragraph 4(1)(a), and paragraph 19(1)(d) and (2)(e) for "scheme administrator" substitute "scheme manager".

16   Modification of Schedule 32

In paragraph 11(6) of Schedule 32—

(a)   for "the retail prices index" (in both places) substitute "a relevant index"; and

(b)   at the end add—

"Here "relevant index" means—

  (a)   an index of the movement of retail prices maintained, or officially recognised, by the government of the country or territory in which the recognised overseas scheme is established; or

  (b)   if there is no such index as is mentioned in paragraph (a) of this definition, the retail prices index.".

17   Modification of Schedule 34

In Schedule 34 after paragraph 19 add—

"Revenue and Customs discretion

19A (1) Sub-paragraph (2) applies to—

(a) the member payment provisions to a payment made (or treated by this Part as made) to or in respect of—

  (i) a relieved member of a relevant non-UK scheme, or

  (ii) a transfer member of such a scheme;

(b) the annual allowance provisions in relation to an individual who is a currently-relieved member of a currently-relieved non-UK scheme; and

(c) the lifetime allowance provision charge in relation to an individual who is a relieved member of a relieved non-UK pension scheme.

(2) If it appears to an officer of Revenue and Customs that, by reason of some non-compliance with the requirements set out in this Part, which in the officer's view does not materially affect the nature of a payment, the payment, or the member in respect of whom it is payable, would be treated less favourably by the strict application of the provisions mentioned in paragraph (1) than in the officer's view is appropriate, sub-paragraph (3) applies.

(3) If this sub-paragraph applies, an officer of Revenue and Customs—

(a) may decide, and

(b) if requested to do so by a member falling within any of the descriptions in paragraphs (a) to (c) of sub-paragraph (1), shall decide,

whether, notwithstanding the non-compliance referred to in sub-paragraph (2), the treatment which, but for that non-compliance, would have applied under this Part should apply to the payment or the member (as the case may be).

This is subject to the qualification in sub-paragraph (4).

(4) An officer of Revenue and Customs shall not make a decision under sub-paragraph (3) that, notwithstanding the difference referred to in sub-paragraph (2), the provisions of this Part shall apply to the payment or the member unless—

(a) it appears to the officer that the effect of the decision would be to reduce the total cumulative tax liability in respect of the charges mentioned in subparagraph (1) of the member whose tax liability would be affected by it, taking one year with another;

(b) the officer has first given at least 28 days' notice of his intention to make the decision to the member whose tax liability would by affected by it; and

(c) the member has—

  (i) consented to the making of the decision; or

  (ii) failed to respond to the notice within the period specified in paragraph (b).

(5) If an officer of Revenue and Customs decides under sub-paragraph (3) that—

(a) the conditions for the exercise of his discretion under that paragraph are not met; or

(b) the conditions for its exercise are met, but that it is otherwise inappropriate for him to exercise it in favour of the member,

the member may appeal against the decision.

(6) Subsections (3) to (5) of section 170 apply for the purposes of a decision by an officer of Revenue and Customs under sub-paragraph (3) as they apply to a decision under section 169(5).

(7) The Commissioners before whom an appeal under paragraph (5) is brought must consider—

(a) whether the conditions for the exercise of the discretion of an officer of Revenue and Customs have been met; and

(b) if they are satisfied that those conditions have been met, whether the discretion ought to have been exercised in favour of the member.

(8) If they decide that the conditions for the exercise of that discretion have not been met, they must dismiss the appeal.

(9) If they decide that the conditions for the exercise of that discretion have been met, they must decide whether the discretion ought to have been exercised in favour of the member.

(10) If they decide that although the conditions are met, the discretion ought not to have been exercised in favour of the member, they must dismiss the appeal.

(11) If they decide that the discretion ought to have been exercised in favour of the member they may so decide and the provisions of this Part shall apply accordingly to the member or the payment in question (as the case may be).

(12) A decision under sub-paragraph (8) or (10) is final but subject to any further appeal or any determination on, or in consequence of, a case stated.".

Pension Schemes (Information Requirements—Qualifying Overseas Pension Schemes, Qualifying Recognised Overseas Pensions Schemes and Corresponding Relief) Regulations 2006 (SI 2006/208)

Made 1st February 2006

Laid before the House of Commons 2nd February 2006

Coming into force 6th April 2006

1   Citation, commencement and interpretation

(1) These Regulations may be cited as the Pension Schemes (Information Requirements for Qualifying Overseas Pension Schemes, Qualifying Recognised Overseas Pension Schemes and Corresponding Relief) Regulations 2006 and shall come into force on 6th April 2006.

(2) In these Regulations—

"the Act" means the Finance Act 2004 and a reference to a numbered section or Schedule, without more, is a reference to the section of; or Schedule to, the Act bearing that number; and

"tax year" means a period beginning on 6th April of one year and ending on 5th April of the immediately following year.

2   Information—benefit crystallisation events in relation to relevant migrant members and individuals entitled to corresponding relief

(1) For the purposes of paragraph 5(2) of Schedule 33 and paragraph 51(4) of Schedule 36 (information about benefit crystallisation events in cases of relevant migrant members and individuals entitled to corresponding relief) the prescribed benefit crystallisation information is—

(a)   the name and address of the relevant migrant member or individual (as the case may be) in respect of whom there has been a benefit crystallisation event in the tax year; and

(b)   the date, amount and nature of the benefit crystallisation event.

(2) The information must be provided by 31st January next following the end of the tax year in which the benefit crystallisation event occurs.

3   Information—qualifying recognised overseas pension schemes

(1) For the purposes of section 169(4) (meaning of qualifying recognised overseas pension scheme), a qualifying recognised overseas pension scheme must provide to an officer of Revenue and Customs—

(a)   the name of the country or territory in which it is established;

(b)   in the case of a scheme falling within regulation 3(4) of the Pension Schemes (Categories of Country and Requirements for Overseas Pension Schemes and Recognised Overseas Pension Schemes) Regulations 2006, evidence demonstrating that it fulfils the requirement set out in that paragraph; and

(c)   any other evidence required in writing by the officer.

(2) When a qualifying recognised overseas pension scheme makes, or is treated under the relevant provisions as making, a payment in respect of a relevant member, it must provide to an officer of Revenue and Customs—

(a)   the name and address of the relevant member; and

(b)   the date, amount and nature of that payment.

Here "the relevant provisions" means sections 172 to 174 and paragraph 2A of Schedule 28.

This paragraph is subject to the qualifications in paragraphs (3) and (4).

(3) No obligation arises under paragraph (2) if the relevant member to whom the payment is made or treated as made is a person to whom the member payment provisions do not apply (see paragraph 2 of Schedule 34).

(4) In the case of a payment by way of a pension the obligation under paragraph (2) applies only to the first such payment.

(5) The information required by paragraph (2) must be provided by 31st January next following the tax year in which the payment is made or is treated as made.

This paragraph is subject to regulation 4.

(6) For the purposes of this regulation—

"payment" has the meaning given in section 161(2); and

"relevant member" means a member of a scheme in respect of whom there is a relevant transfer fund within the meaning of the Pension Schemes (Application of UK Provisions to Relevant Non-UK Schemes) Regulations 2006.

4 Notice in cases of serious prejudice to proper assessment or collection of tax

(1) If an officer of Revenue and Customs has reasonable grounds for believing that the pension scheme in question—

(a)   has failed or may fail to comply with any of the requirements imposed upon it under or by virtue of these Regulations, and

(b)   such failure is likely to have led or to lead to serious prejudice to the proper assessment or collection of tax,

paragraph (2) applies.

(2) If this paragraph applies, the officer may notify the pension scheme that he requires such information to be provided within 30 days of the issue of that notice, notwithstanding the provisions set out in regulations 2 and 3.

Pension Schemes (Relevant Migrant Members) Regulations 2006 (SI 2006/212)

Made 1st February 2006

Laid before the House of Commons 2nd February 2006

Coming into force 6th April 2006

I Citation and commencement

These Regulations may be cited as the Pension Schemes (Relevant Migrant Members) Regulations 2006 and shall come into force on 6th April 2006.

2 Alternative condition for relevant migrant member relief

(1) For the purposes of paragraph 4(c) of Schedule 33 to the Finance Act 2004 (meaning of "relevant migrant member"), the prescribed condition, in relation to the individual is set out in paragraph (2).

(2) The individual was at any time in the 10 years before the beginning of that period of residence, whether before or after the coming into force of these Regulations, entitled to tax relief in respect of contributions paid under the pension scheme under the law of the country or territory in which the individual was then resident.

The latest forms

Background

HMRC's Pensions Tax Simplification Newsletter No. 6, dated 11 November 2005, stated that the requirement for registered pension schemes to submit reports and returns of information online to HMRC would be postponed by at least six months following the start of the new tax regime. The following is an extract from that Newsletter:

> '2. Pension Schemes online – timing and content of releases
>
> Following a review of the progress being made on the development of Pension Schemes Online and an exercise with representatives of the Pensions Industry Working Group and our IT supplier to prioritise delivery of the online service we have decided to reduce the scope of the first release in April 2006 and to add a number of additional releases over the course of the first year. This will involve a "just in time" delivery of online functions, so that they generally become available when they are first needed. This will ensure that scheme administrators and practitioners will still be able to meet the majority of their statutory filing and reporting requirements online.
>
> In the first release at the beginning of April 2006 we will provide for online registration of a pension scheme for tax relief purposes and also for scheme administrators and practitioners to carry out pre-registration, registration, authorisation and maintenance of scheme administrator and practitioner details.
>
> Later releases will provide the facility for online filing of accounting for tax returns, event reports and other returns of information.
>
> Further details of these releases will be provided in due course.
>
> By April 2007 the remainder of the functionality for Pensions Schemes Online will be available and will include the online submission of the pension scheme return.
>
> 3. Postponement of mandatory online filing
>
> Whilst scheme administrators will still be able to carry out nearly all of their legislative requirements online from April 2006, the exception

will be for the small number of schemes that wind up after A Day, where there is a requirement to send in an event report within 3 months. We will now be offering flexibility over an interim period to enable the filing of this report and all other returns and reports of information, including registration of new pension schemes, by paper for a period of at least 6 months from 6 April 2006. This deferral of the introduction of mandatory online filing has been made in order to help scheme administrators given that the full range of facilities will not be available at A Day. Where the online functionality is available this will provide a quicker and more efficient service than one that is based on paper processes.

4. Test service for third party software

The first release of the test service in February 2006 will enable software developers to test their systems against what will be available from Pension Schemes Online from April 2006. Whilst this will not initially encompass the full functionality of the new online service, there will be further releases of the test service that will support the remaining releases of Pension Schemes Online.'

The forms

The HMRC website (http://www.hmrc.gov.uk/pensionschemes/tax-simp-draft-forms.htm) provides links to the latest versions of the draft forms that were first published in April 2005. HMRC does not anticipate there being any major changes to these forms. Any amendments to these forms will appear on the 'What's New' page of the HMRC website.

The forms available are as follows (with page ranges indicated):

- Registration for tax relief and exemptions (308–317)
- Registration for relief at source (318–324)
- Contracting out (Industry wide schemes) (325–334)
- Contracting out (other schemes) (335–350)
- Event report (351–395)
- Accounting for tax return (396–412)
- Registered pension scheme return (413–435)
- Protection of existing rights (436–447)
- Enhanced lifetime allowance (pension credit rights) (448–453)
- Enhanced lifetime allowance (international) (454–466)
- Declare as a scheme administrator of a deferred annuity contract (467)

In addition to the above, HMRC has also published some of the maintenance forms:

- Cessation of scheme administrator (468)
- Pre-register as a scheme administrator (469)
- Notify scheme administrator details (470)
- Change of scheme administrator/practitioner details (471–472)
- Authorising a practitioner (473–475)
- Add scheme administrator (476–477)
- Amend scheme details (478–481)

HMRC's Pension Tax Simplification Newsletter No. 10, dated 28 February 2006, included an Annex A entitled 'What can be done at A-Day'. This is a useful checklist, and is reproduced here.

Annex A

What can be done at A-Day

The following provides a brief summary of the options you will have at 6 April 2006 (A-Day) for submitting information to HMRC and amending information held by HMRC. Newsletter No 8, set out what will be available online from A-Day and this is reproduced in the table below. The final versions of all the forms noted below will be available on the HMRC Website at A-Day.

Please note you should not submit any forms before A-Day on the draft versions that are currently on the Internet. Any forms completed before A-Day will be returned as they will not be valid.

Action	Online Form Name	Online form available at A-Day	Who can submit the form online?	Paper Form Name and Number	Paper form available at A-Day	Who can sign the paper form?	Anything else?
1. Use Pension Schemes Online							
Register to use Pension Schemes Online: a) Pre-register to obtain an Activation Token and Scheme Administrator/Practitioner ID.	Register new user	Yes	Only the Scheme Administrator or Practitioner can pre-register themselves	Pre-register as a Scheme Administrator/ Practitioner APSS 161	Yes	Only the Scheme Administrator or Practitioner pre-registering	
b) Complete registration for the online service	Register new user	Yes	Only the Scheme Administrator or Practitioner can complete registration	Not applicable	No	Not applicable	This can only be done online as it requires the user registering to create their password
2. Scheme Registration							
Register a new scheme for tax relief and exemptions	Register a new pension scheme	Yes	Scheme Administrator	Pension Scheme Tax Registration APSS 100	Yes	Scheme Administrator	
Elect to contract out of state second pension.	Elect to contract out	No Proposed release Autumn 06	Scheme Administrator or Practitioner	Registered Pension Schemes -Election to Contract-out APSS 101	Yes	Employer, trustee or person responsible for the day to day management of the scheme	
Elect to contract out of state second pension by industry wide scheme	Elect to contract out	No Proposed release Autumn 06	Scheme Administrator or Practitioner	Registered Pension Schemes -Election to Contract-out for industry wide schemes APSS 102	Yes	Employer, trustee or person responsible for the day to day management of the scheme	
Register to operate relief at source or amend relief at source details	Register for Relief at Source or Amend Relief at Source	No Proposed release Autumn 06	Scheme Administrator or Practitioner	Relief at Source Details APSS 103	Yes	Scheme Administrator or Practitioner	
Send specimen signature(s) authorised to sign repayment claims	Not applicable	No	Not applicable	Relief at Source specimen signatures APSS 103A	Yes	Those authorised to sign repayments of tax relief at source on	This form is optional for providing samples of authorised signatures.

							contributions to registered pension schemes
Complete single registration form, to register for tax relief and exemptions, elect to contract-out and register to operate at tax relief at source	Register a new scheme	No Proposed release Autumn 06	Scheme Administrator	Pension Scheme Registration APSS 100A	Yes	Scheme Administrator	
Make your declaration as required under Section 270 Finance Act 2004 as the Scheme Administrator of a deferred annuity contract made on or after A-day	Declare as Scheme Administrator for a deferred annuity contract	Yes	Scheme Administrator	Declaration as a Scheme Administrator of a Deferred Annuity Contract scheme APSS 108	Yes	Scheme Administrator	This is only used for deferred annuity contracts made on or after A-day

3. Scheme Administrator/Practitioner Maintenance

Amend your details provided at pre-registration for Pension Schemes Online (see 1 above)	View or amend your details	Yes	The Scheme Administrator or Practitioner whose details are being amended	Change of Scheme Administrator or Practitioner user details APSS 153	Yes	The Scheme Administrator or Practitioner whose details are being amended	

4. Scheme Maintenance

Amend the scheme name or the establisher/sponsor details or client reference	Amend Scheme Details	No Proposed release Summer 06	Scheme Administrator or Practitioner	Amend Scheme details APSS 152	Yes	Scheme Administrator or Practitioner	
Amend contracting-out details	Not applicable	No	Not applicable	Contracting-out Maintenance APSS 155	Yes	Employer, trustee or person responsible for the day to day management of the scheme	
Scheme Administrator of a pension scheme wishes to authorise HM Revenue & Customs(HMRC) to deal with a Practitioner acting on their behalf.	Practitioner Management	Yes	Scheme Administrator	Authorising a Practitioner APSS 150	Yes	Scheme Administrator	
(a) A Scheme Administrator who was the Administrator of a scheme on 5 April 2006 wishes to have their details recorded on the pension scheme record, or (b) A Scheme Administrator who is appointed on or after A-day (other than the Scheme Administrator of a new deferred annuity contract made on or after A-day) should make their declaration as required under Section 270 Finance Act 2004	Add yourself as Scheme Administrator	Yes	Scheme Administrator	Add Scheme Administrator to a scheme APSS 151	Yes	Scheme Administrator	If the scheme record held by HMRC already shows a Scheme Administrator the known Scheme Administrator will need to associate the new/additional Scheme Administrator before this form can be processed (see below)
The Scheme Administrator recorded against the HMRC record for the pension scheme needs to advise HMRC there is a new/additional Scheme Administrator for the scheme.	Scheme Administrator Management	Yes	Scheme Administrator recorded on the HMRC record for the scheme	Associate Scheme Administrator to scheme APSS 154	Yes	Scheme Administrator recorded on the HMRC record for the scheme	

Description				Form	Online	Signatory	Notes
This is to allow the new/additional Scheme Administrator to add their details to the pension scheme record (this allows them to view pension scheme information) and make their declaration as required under Section 270 Finance Act 2004							
The appointment of a Scheme Administrator of a scheme is terminated they need to report the cessation to HMRC	Scheme Administrator Management	No Proposed release Summer 06	Scheme Administrator that has ceased	Cessation of Scheme Administrator APSS 160	Yes	Scheme Administrator that has ceased	
5. Reporting and returns							
The scheme has wound up this has to be reported to HMRC or The scheme has wound up and there are other events to report to HMRC as well	Event Report	No Proposed release April 07	Scheme Administrator or Practitioner	Event Report APSS 300	Yes	Scheme Administrator	
Claim in-year repayment of tax relief deducted at source from contributions	Not applicable	No	Not applicable	Relief at Source – interim claim APSS 105	Yes	Authorised signatory	Formerly the PP10
Make annual claim for repayment of tax relief deducted at source from contributions	Not applicable	No	Not applicable	Relief at Source – annual claim APSS 106 (Not available until October 2006)	Yes	Authorised signatory	Formerly the PP14
Make annual statistical return	Not applicable	No	Not applicable	Relief at Source – annual statistical return APSS 107 (Not available until October 2006)	Yes and magnetic media	Authorised signatory	Formerly the PP14 (Stats)
6. Enhanced LTA							
Protection of existing rights – Notifications for Primary Protection & Enhanced Protection	To be advised	No Release date to be agreed	Individual or agent	Protection of existing Rights APSS 200	Yes	Individual	Forms can be submitted from 6th April 06 to 5th April 09
Enhanced LTA (Pension credit rights)	To be advised	No Release date to be agreed	Individual or agent	Enhanced Lifetime Allowance (Pension Credit Rights) APSS 201	Yes	Individual	
Enhanced LTA (International)	To be advised	No Release date to be agreed Spring 07	Individual or agent	Enhanced Lifetime Allowance (International) APSS 202	Yes	Individual	
Authorise Scheme Administrator to view LTA Certificate	To be advised	No Release date to be agreed	Individual or agent	Authorise Scheme Administrator to view LTA Certificate APSS 203	Yes	Individual	

	To be advised	No	Scheme Administrator		Yes	Scheme Administrator
Request by Scheme Administrator to view LTA Certificate	To be advised	No Release date to be agreed	Scheme Administrator	Request by Scheme Administrator to view LTA Certificate APSS 209	Yes	Scheme Administrator
7. International						
Qualifying Overseas Pension Scheme (QOPS) Notification	Not applicable	No	Not applicable	Qualifying Overseas Pension Schemes (QOPS) APSS 250	Yes	Scheme manager
Qualifying Recognised Overseas Pension Scheme (QROPS) Notification	Not applicable	No	Not applicable	Qualifying Recognised Overseas Pension Scheme (QROPS) APSS 251	Yes	Scheme manager
Report of benefit crystallisation events	Not applicable	No	Not applicable	Report of benefit crystallisation events APSS 252	Yes	Scheme manager
Report of payments in respect of relevant members	Not applicable	No	Not applicable	Payments in respect of relevant members APSS 253	Yes	Scheme manager
Individual's election for a deemed benefit crystallisation event	Not applicable	No	Not applicable	Election for a deemed benefit crystallisation event APSS 254	Yes	Individual

Scheme Administrator / Practitioner ID

In addition to being required to complete registration for Pension Schemes Online these ID's are used to ensure as far as is possible that information is recorded against the correct record. For this reason many of the forms ask for the Scheme Administrator/Practitioner ID to make the link to the record. It is therefore recommended that if you did not take part in the recent pre-registration exercise you pre-register for Pension Schemes Online (see 1a) in the table above) and obtain a Scheme Administrator/Practitioner ID. For online submissions your user ID and password are linked to your ID (but knowing the ID is not enough to view the record or make submissions. The user ID and password are needed).

Registration for tax relief and exemptions

Notes on how to complete the information required to be registered : to obtain tax relief and exemptions, to operate relief at source, with the Pensions Regulator, as a stakeholder pension scheme and elect to contract out or to make a declaration that you are the Scheme Administrator of a deferred annuity contract made on or after 6 April 2006

General

These notes provide guidance to help you complete the information required on the registration screens. The notes are numbered to match the questions on the screens. They also include links to supplementary guidance, which you may need to read in order to understand more fully what information you have to provide. In particular the links give you access to advice about the meaning of the legislative terms that are referred to on the screen. However these links will not be available until the full guidance is published on the Internet later this year.

How to register with HMRC (HM Revenue & Customs) for tax relief and exemptions or make a declaration to HMRC that you are the Scheme Administrator of a deferred annuity contract made on or after 6 April 2006.

You must register your pension scheme on-line for tax relief and exemptions. Note that tax relief and exemptions will only apply from the date of registration and that date will not be earlier than the date on which the application is accepted by HMRC.

Completing the questions

You must complete all of the relevant boxes. You will not be allowed to move on and complete the registration unless all the information ~~~~~~~~~~~~~ the correct format.

First Page

DRAFT

"Do you want to" -please select as appropriate.
If you want to do any of the transactions listed then you should select the boxes appropriate to the transactions you want to carry out. You will then be presented with the relevant screens for completion.

If you select 'make a declaration to HMRC (HM Revenue & Customs) that you are the Scheme Administrator of a deferred annuity contract made on or after 6 April 2006', you will only need to provide the scheme name, the contract or policy number and complete box 4 & 5 of the declaration.

If you select to register as a Stakeholder Pension Scheme [Link]

You must also complete the following transactions.

- Register to operate relief at source [Link]
- Register with the Pensions Regulator [Link]
- Elect to contract out [Link]

1

If you select to register as a Stakeholder Pension Scheme but do not complete all these transactions your registration as a stakeholder pension scheme [Link] will not be accepted.

However the other transactions will be considered in their own right. For example, if you want to register as a Stakeholder Pension Scheme but only carry out the transactions to register for tax relief and exemptions and elect to contract out, the following will happen. We will deal with your application to register for tax relief and exemptions and providing it passes validation we will register the scheme and send you an acknowledgement of registration. Your election to contract out will also be dealt with and providing it passes validation you will receive a certificate in the post.

Pension Scheme Registration for tax relief and exemptions

Part 1 – About the Scheme

Q1.1   This is the name by which the scheme is known or in the case of a contract the member's name.

You <u>must</u> complete these details or you will not be allowed to proceed to the next question.

Q2   Select the type of legal structure of the scheme. You <u>must</u> select <u>one</u> but no more than one or you will not be allowed to proceed to the next question.

2.1   Single Trust under which all of the assets are held for the benefit of all members

This is where a pension scheme is set up under trust and that trust covers all members. And the terms of the trust do not specifically allocate assets to a particular member.

2.2   An annuity contract

This is a two party contract between an establisher of a scheme under section 154 Finance Act 2004 [Link] and a member.

If you select this box you <u>must</u> provide a policy or contract number or you will not be allowed to proceed to the next question.

Policy or Contract Number

This is the number you use to identify this scheme from any other scheme(s) of this type the member might have. It will also help to distinguish it from other policies/contracts which have already been registered by you relating to the same member. If this number is not provided it will appear the same scheme has been registered several times. You will not be allowed to proceed to the next question unless you provide this information.

2.3   An overall trust within which there are individual trusts applying for the benefit of each member

2

This is where a pension scheme is set up under trust and the arrangements [Link to the meaning of "arrangements"] within it are made under separate sub trusts. The scheme trustees have legal ownership of the assets but beneficial ownership is with the trustees of the sub trust.

2.4   An overall trust within which specific assets are held as, or within sub funds for each member.

This is where a pension scheme is set up under trust and some or all of the arrangements [link] include the allocating or earmarking of assets to the arrangement or arrangements.

2.5   A body Corporate [Link]

2.6   Other

DRAFT

If the legal structure is not one of the above then you must select this option and provide a brief description of how the scheme is constituted at 2.7 or you will not be allowed to proceed to the next question unless you provide this information.

2.7   Brief description

This must be completed only if 'other' at 2.6 is selected.

For example, if the scheme is established by deed poll, state

        Deed Poll

Q3   How many members of the scheme are there likely to be in the year ending 5 April xxxx?

You <u>must</u> select <u>one</u> but no more than one or you will not be allowed to proceed to the next question.

The number of members includes all members, active members, pensioner members, deferred members and pension credit members [link]

Q4   Does the scheme have at least one member with the ability to control the way in which scheme assets are used? [link]

You must answer 'yes' or 'no' you will not be allowed to proceed to the next question.

Control by a member will exist for the purposes of this question if:

a)   The asset is owned by a person who is connected to the member. Connected is as defined in Section 839 of Income and Corporation Taxes Act 1988 [Link]

b)   The member is a trustee of the scheme

3

310

c)   The member is connected to a trustee of the scheme. Connected is as defined in Section 839 of Income and Corporation Taxes Act 1988 [Link]

d)   The asset is one which is allocated or earmarked to a particular arrangement and the member whose arrangement it is can exercise day to day control over its use.

Q5   Who has established the scheme for the purpose of section 154 Finance Act 2004 [Link]?

You must provide details for each person who established the scheme. You will not be allowed to proceed to the next question until you have provided the details for at least one person.

5.1   Are you an individual or an organisation?

The purpose of this question is to provide you with the correct fields in which to enter the establisher's name. Title and surname are not applicable to organisations or trusts.

You must only select one box.

5.2   You must only complete this if you selected individual or you will not be allowed to proceed to the next question. If you selected individual in error you may go back and deselect it and select organisation.

Title by which known, for example Mr, Mrs, Miss, Ms

Surname

First name

You will not be allowed to proceed to the next question until you have provided these details.

5.3   You <u>must</u> only complete this if you selected organisation or you will not be allowed to proceed to the next question. If you selected individual in error you may go back and deselect it and select individual.

You will not be allowed to proceed to the next question until you have provided these details.

5.4   Address

You will not be allowed to proceed to the next question until you have provided these details.

5.5   If you selected yes you must provide the details at Q5.2 or Q5.3 and Q5.4 for each person who established the scheme or you will not be allowed to proceed to the next question.

4

Part 2   **Declaration**

You must read carefully each of the declarations below. If you are satisfied they are correct, you must select all five/two for the scheme to be registered for tax relief and exemptions

Your application will not proceed if you have not made the declarations required.

I declare

First box [Link to guidance on requirements to register a pension scheme]

You will not be presented with this declaration or the declarations at the second and third boxes if you are making a declaration you are a scheme administrator of a deferred annuity contract made after 5 April 2006

Box 3 [Link to guidance on Section 270 Finance Act 2004]

Name of Scheme Administrator

DRAFT

This will be pre-populated with your details. You should check they are correct. If they are not then you need to use the ' 'amend scheme administrator details' option to update your details following completion of registration.

Would you like a copy of the acknowledgement for this registration to go to a practitioner?

If you selected yes you <u>must</u> provide both the practitioners name and ID number otherwise a copy of the acknowledgement of registration cannot be sent to them.

If you have completed all the information required and it is provided in the correct format you will receive a message telling you your submission has been received.

If you have registered a pension scheme for tax relief and exemptions you will receive, very shortly after registration is complete, another message telling you to look in your secure mailbox. This is where your acknowledgement of tax registration will be placed. This acknowledgement will include the date of registration and the pension scheme tax reference. You should use the reference number provided the next time you access the service for this scheme or in all communication with HMRC. If you have opted out of electronic communications then you will also receive an acknowledgement of registration containing the same details in the post.

If you have made a declaration you are a Scheme Administrator of a deferred annuity contract made after 5 April 2006 you will receive a message, very shortly after making your declaration, telling you the pension scheme tax reference number. If you have opted out of electronic communication then you will receive a letter advising you of the pension scheme tax reference number. You should use the reference number provided the next time you access the service for this scheme or in all communication with HMRC.

5

Data Protection

HMRC is a Data Controller under the Data Protection Act. We hold information for the purposes specified in our notification made to the Data Protection Commissioner, and may use this information for any of them.

We may get information about you from others, or we may give information to them. If we do, it will only be as the law permits to

- Check accuracy of information

- Prevent or detect crime

- Protect public funds

We may check information we receive about you with what is already in our records. This can include information provided by you as well as others such as other government departments. We will not give information about you to anyone outside HMRC unless the law permits us to do so.

6

313

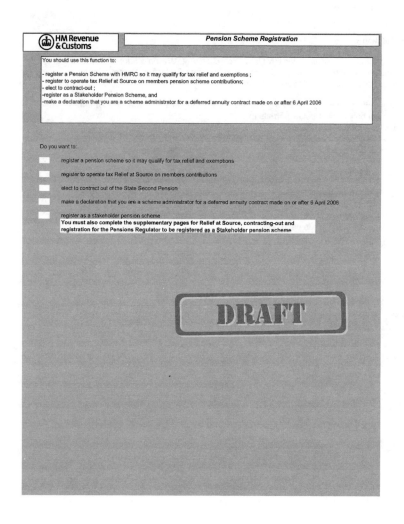

HM Revenue & Customs

Pension Scheme Registration

You should use this function to:

- register a Pension Scheme with HMRC so it may qualify for tax relief and exemptions ;
- register to operate tax Relief at Source on members pension scheme contributions;
- elect to contract-out ;
- register as a Stakeholder Pension Scheme, and
- make a declaration that you are a scheme administrator for a deferred annuity contract made on or after 6 April 2006

Do you want to:

☐ register a pension scheme so it may qualify for tax relief and exemptions

☐ register to operate tax Relief at Source on members contributions

☐ elect to contract out of the State Second Pension

☐ make a declaration that you are a scheme administrator for a deferred annuity contract made on or after 6 April 2006

☐ register as a stakeholder pension scheme
You must also complete the supplementary pages for Relief at Source, contracting-out and registration for the Pensions Regulator to be registered as a Stakeholder pension scheme

DRAFT

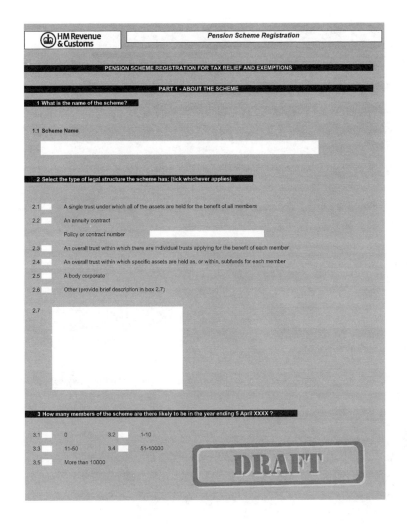

HM Revenue & Customs

Pension Scheme Registration

PENSION SCHEME REGISTRATION FOR TAX RELIEF AND EXEMPTIONS

PART 1 - ABOUT THE SCHEME

1 What is the name of the scheme?

1.1 Scheme Name

2 Select the type of legal structure the scheme has: (tick whichever applies)

2.1   A single trust under which all of the assets are held for the benefit of all members

2.2   An annuity contract

       Policy or contract number

2.3   An overall trust within which there are individual trusts applying for the benefit of each member

2.4   An overall trust within which specific assets are held as, or within, subfunds for each member

2.5   A body corporate

2.6   Other (provide brief description in box 2.7)

2.7

3 How many members of the scheme are there likely to be in the year ending 5 April XXXX ?

3.1   0   3.2   1-10

3.3   11-50   3.4   51-10000

3.5   More than 10000

DRAFT

4 Does the scheme have at least one member with the ability to control the way in which the scheme assets are used?

☐ Yes

☐ No

5 Who has established the scheme for the purposes of section 154 Finance Act 2004?

5.1 Is this person

☐ an individual?

☐ an organisation?

5.2 Individual name

Title
Surname
First name

5.3 Organisation name

5.4 Address

Postcode
Country

5.5 Was the scheme established by more than one person?

☐ Yes

How many?

DRAFT

PART 2 - DECLARATION

You **must** read carefully each of the declarations below. If you are satisfied they are correct, you **must** select all five for the scheme to be registered for tax relief and exemptions.

I declare that

☐ I confirm this scheme meets all the criteria to be registered as a pension scheme under Finance Act 2004

☐ to the best of my knowledge and belief, the information given in this application to register the pension scheme for the purposes of tax relief is correct and complete;

☐ the instrument or agreements by which this pension scheme is constituted do not entitle any person to unauthorised payments.

☐ I understand that as Scheme Administrator I am responsible for discharging the functions conferred or imposed on the scheme Administrator of the pension scheme by Finance Act 2004, and I intend to discharge those functions at all times, whether resident in the United Kingdom or another EU member state or a non-EU member EEA state.

☐ I understand that I may be liable to a penalty if a false statement is made on this declaration, and that false statements may also lead to prosecution.

Name of Scheme Administrator as defined in section 270 Finance Act 2004

Is the Scheme Administrator an individual ☐ or an organisation ☐ (tick as appropriate)

Individual Name

Title
Surname
First name

Organisation name

Scheme Administrator's address　　　　　　e-mail

Postcode　　　　　　Telephone number
Country

Scheme Administrator ID

Would you like a copy of the acknowledgement for this registration to go to a practitioner?

☐ Yes

Practitioner ID

DRAFT

Registration for relief at source

HM Revenue & Customs	*Relief at Source Details*

This form should be used to either register your scheme to operate tax relief at source or to notify any changes to a scheme that currently oprates tax relief at source. You can do this online by going to our website at www.hmrc.gov.uk and select 'Pension Schemes' under 'do it online'.

If you are using this form:

- for a new aplication to register to operate relief at source you must send us a paying in slip for the account shown below together with the Boards Resolution and original specimen signatures for the authorised signatories.

- to notify us of a change of bank account details - you must send us a paying in slip for the account shown below and the Boards Resolution.

- to notify us of a change in authorised signatories for repayment claims - you must send us the Boards Resolution and original specimen signatures for the authorised signatories.

Send these documents, together with this form, to HM Revenue & Customs, Audit & Pension Scheme Services, Castle Meadow Road, Nottingham, NG2 1LB.

We will not be able to process any repayment claims until we have the documetation shown above.

1 What is the name and reference number of the scheme?

1.1 Pension scheme name

1.2 Pension scheme tax reference

2 Do you wish to:-

2.1 Register the scheme to operate tax relief at source ☐ (go to 4.1)

2.2 Notify any changes to tax relief at source information for this scheme ☐ (go to Q3)

3 Which of the following do you wish to update

3.1 Change of Bank details ☐ (go to Q4)

3.2 Change of the signatories ☐ (go to Q5)

3.3 Change of the contacts ☐ (go to Q6)

4 Current bank or building society details

If you only have an overseas bank account with an account number containing more than 8 digits you will need to contact your bank to obtain an abridged 8 digit number

4.1 Name of bank or building society

Account name

Address of bank or building society

Account Number

Bank Sort Code

Postcode
Country

DRAFT

If this is a new registration, go to Q5.1

4.2 name of new bank or building society

New account name

Address of new bank or building society

New account number

New Sort Code

Postcode
Country

5 Current authorised signatories who can sign the tax repayment claims

5.1 Current authorised signatories

If you are amending details of a signatory, please enter details below of the person(s) who is/are being replaced.

	Title	First Name(s)	Surname
1			
2			
3			
4			
5			

DRAFT

If this is a new registration, go to Q6.1

5.2 New authorised signatories who can sign the tax repayment claims

Details of the signatory who is replacing a signatory in the corresponding box number at Q5.1 above.

	Title	First Name(s)	Surname
1			
2			
3			
4			
5			

6 Contact details

6.1 Current contact details

	Title	First Name(s)	Surname
1			
2			

	Telephone number	e-mail address
1		
2		

If this is a new registration, go to Q7

DRAFT

6.2 New contact details

	Title	First Name(s)	Surname
1			
2			

	Telephone number	e-mail address
1		
2		

7 Details of submitter

7.1 I attach the Boards Resolution showing the person(s) named at Question 5 as authorised signatories

I attach a bank paying in slip

7.2 **I am submitting this registration/amendment in my capacity as**

7.3 **Scheme Administrator**   Scheme Administrator ID

(also complete Q7.5 - 7.8)

or

7.4 **Practitioner**   Practitioner ID

7.5 Signature

7.6 Name

7.7 Organisation

7.8 Address

Postcode

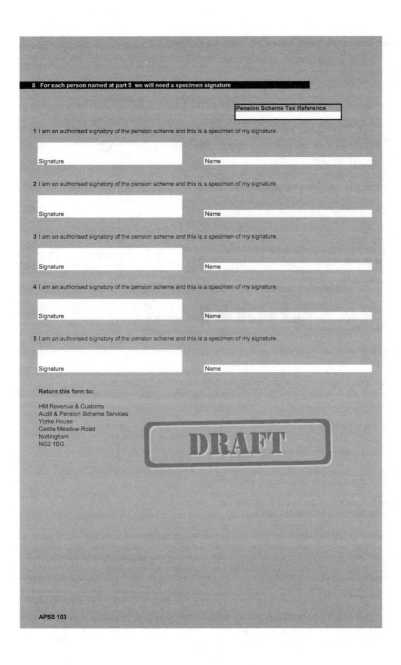

8 For each person named at part 5 we will need a specimen signature

Pension Scheme Tax Reference

1 I am an authorised signatory of the pension scheme and this is a specimen of my signature.

Signature   Name

2 I am an authorised signatory of the pension scheme and this is a specimen of my signature.

Signature   Name

3 I am an authorised signatory of the pension scheme and this is a specimen of my signature.

Signature   Name

4 I am an authorised signatory of the pension scheme and this is a specimen of my signature.

Signature   Name

5 I am an authorised signatory of the pension scheme and this is a specimen of my signature.

Signature   Name

Return this form to:

HM Revenue & Customs
Audit & Pension Scheme Services
Yorke House
Castle Meadow Road
Nottingham
NG2 1BG

DRAFT

APSS 103

Application to Operate Relief at Source - Completion Notes

General

These notes provide guidance on how to register your scheme to operate relief at source or to notify any changes to a scheme that currently operates relief at source.

The notes are intended to help you complete the form and each note is numbered to reflect the question number on the form. Supplementary guidance on relief at source can be found in the Registered Pension Schemes Manual (RPSM) which is available on our website at www.hmrc.gov.uk.

This information is required so that HMRC (HM Revenue & Customs) Audit & Pension Scheme Services can process tax relief claims.

Completing the Form

You must complete all of the boxes in the relevant Part(s) of the form that apply to your scheme. Please note that if the form is incomplete, or if you do not sign it and/or you do not send the required documentation, your registration will not be processed and the form will be returned to you. Use ticks (✓) where indicated.

1.1 Pension Scheme name.

This is the name by which the scheme is known.

1.2 Pension Scheme Tax Reference

The Pension Scheme Tax Reference (PSTR) is the unique reference allocated to your scheme by HMRC.

If the scheme was registered for tax relief and exemptions on or after 6 April 2006, or you made a declaration that you were the Scheme Administrator of a deferred annuity contract made on or after 6 April 2006

This is the reference notified to you by HMRC in an online message on successfully registering the pension scheme or making a declaration you were the Scheme Administrator of a deferred annuity contract made on or after 6 April 2006. If you opted out of receiving pension scheme notifications over the Internet you will have been sent a letter including the PSTR, acknowledging the scheme was registered for tax purposes or that your declaration has been received.

If the scheme was set up before 6 April 2006 and the application for approval was processed before 31 March 2006

You will have been sent an approval letter containing the Superannuation Fund (SF) reference number. The Pension Schemes Online service allows you to use this to access the scheme record for the first time. The PSTR will be given to the Scheme Administrator and/or authorised Practitioner the first time they access Pension Schemes Online on or after 6 April 2006.

If the scheme was set up before 6 April 2006 but the application for approval was processed on or after 31 March 2006

You will be sent an approval letter including the PSTR.

If the scheme was set up before 6 April 2006 and participated in the HMRC pre-registration exercise

The Scheme Administrator will be pre-registered to use Pension Schemes Online. They will be sent a letter containing an Activation Token to activate the new service, together with a separate letter containing the PSTR.

3. Which of the following do you wish to update

Please tick one or all of the boxes shown and complete the relevant supplementary questions as directed.

4. Current bank or building society details

4.1 If you are submitting a new registration for relief at source, you should provide the name, address and account details of the bank or building society into which you would like repayments to be made. If you are amending any details about the bank or building society to which you would like repayments to be made, you must supply name, address and account details of the account to which HMRC are currently making repayments.

4.2 If you are changing your bank or building society account, please provide the details of the new account.

5A Current authorised signatories who can sign the tax repayment claims

If you are submitting a new registration for relief at source you must provide the full names of up to 5 individuals appointed by a resolution of the Scheme Administrator's Board or equivalent managing body to sign claims on behalf of the Scheme Administrator.

If you are completing this form to amend the details of a current signatories, for example a signatory is being replaced by a new signatory, please enter the details of the person(s) who are being replaced.

5B New authorised signatories who can sign the tax repayment claim

If you have entered details at 5A relating to a person who is no longer an authorised signatory and they are being replaced, please enter the details of the new signatory.

6 Contact details

If this is a new registration for relief at source, you must provide the full name, telephone number and e-mail address of at least one individual within your organisation that we should contact if we have any enquiries about this form, or about claims under relief at source. This individual may also be an authorised signatory.

7 Signature

The form must be signed by the Scheme Administrator or practitioner acting on behalf of the scheme. The Scheme Administrator ID and the Practitioner ID should be included on the form and the name and address entered below.

What happens next?

The completed form, together with:

- The Board's Resolution,
- A bank/building society paying in slip for the account into which repayments are to be made, and
- Original specimen signatures of those authorised to sign repayment claims,

should be sent to:-

HM Revenue & Customs
Audit & Pension Scheme Services
Yorke House
Castle Meadow Road
Nottingham
NG2 1BG

Please note - any registation recei**ed** withou**t** the **supp**orting docu**m**ents will **be returned without bei**ng process**ed.**

Data Protection

HMRC is a Data Controller under the Data Protection Act. We hold information for the purposes specified in our notification made to the Data Protection Commissioner, and may use this information for any of them.

We may get information about you from others, or we may give information to them. If we do, it will only be as the law permits to

- Check accuracy of information
- Prevent or detect crime
- Protect public funds

We may check information we receive about you with what is already in our records. This can include information provided by you as well as others such as other government departments. We will not give information about you to anyone outside HMRC unless the law permits us to do so.

Contracting out (industry wide schemes)

DRAFT

Election to contract-out for an industry-wide money purchase and industry-wide money purchase stakeholder scheme

Notes to help you complete the form and submit it to HMRC

General

These notes provide guidance on how to elect to contract-out of the State Second Pension [Link] via an industry-wide money purchase[Link] and industry-wide money purchase stakeholder [Link] scheme.

Industry-wide money purchase schemes are centrally administered schemes [Link] in which only employers in a specified industry are eligible to participate.

An existing registered industry-wide money purchase scheme may apply to convert to an industry-wide money purchase stakeholder scheme. Whether such a scheme was already contracted-out prior to conversion or not, a new election to contract-out must be made to HMRC.

A scheme wishing to become a stakeholder pension scheme must register with HMRC to operate Relief at Source and also apply to the Pensions Regulator for stakeholder registration.

Industry-wide money purchase schemes may contract-out using a simplified election process :

- The person with the day to day management of the scheme acts as agent for each employer participating in the scheme.

- Consultation with independent trade unions may be carried out centrally providing the unions agree [Link].

- The notice of intention [Link] may be issued by the person responsible for the day to day management of the scheme but they must make it clear that it is being issued on behalf of the employer

- A single election to contract out may be made by the person responsible for the day to day management of the scheme on behalf of any number of participating employers [Link]. Details of each employer must be shown on the form and if necessary on a supplementary page.

The provisions for holding company elections [Link] do not apply to industry wide schemes using the simplified procedure. Each participating employer, whether a holding company [Link] or subsidiary [Link], must be listed on the on the form or the supplementary page and have their own contracting-out certificate.

To take advantage of this simplified procedure certain conditions must be met [Link].

1

How to notify HMRC

You must make an election to contract-out by either completing the form online, go to **www.hmrc.gov.uk** and select "Pension Schemes" under "do it online", or by printing the form, completing it and sending it to HMRC, Audit & Pension Scheme Services, Yorke House, Castle Meadow Road, Nottingham, NG2 1BG

Completing the form
These notes are intended to help you complete the boxes on the election form.

You must complete all the boxes in the relevant Part(s) of the form that apply to your scheme. An election to contract-out will not be complete unless all of the information requested is completed. Use ticks (√) where indicated.

Q1 Please state the

1.1 Please enter the ame by wh

1.2 Please enter the

> The Pension Scheme Tax Reference (PSTR) is the unique reference allocated to your scheme by HMRC

If the scheme was registered for tax relief on or after 6 April 2006 - this is the number notified to the Scheme Administratorby HMRC in an online message on successfully registering the pension scheme.. If the Scheme Administrator opted out of receiving the pension scheme notifications over the internet they will have been sent a letter including the PSTR, acknowledging the scheme was registered for tax purposes.

If the election to contract-out is submitted electronically to HMRC at the same time as the Registration application the scheme registration number will automatically be entered here.

If the scheme was set up before 6 April 2006 and the application for approval was processed before 31 March 2006 – the Scheme Administrator will have been sent an approval letter containing the Superannuation Fund (SF) reference number. The Pension Schemes Online service will allow the Scheme Administrator to use this to access the scheme record for the first time. The PSTR will be given to the Scheme Administrator and/or authorised Practitioner the first time they access Pension Schemes Online on or after 6 April 2006.

If the scheme was set up before 6 April 2006 but the application for approval was processed on or after 31 March 2006 the Scheme Administrator will be sent an approval letter including the PSTR.

If the scheme was set up before 6 April 2006 and participated in the HMRC data cleanse exercise the Scheme Administrator will be pre-registered to use Pension Schemes Online. They will have been sent a letter containing the PSTR.

2

1.3 SF Tax Reference

If the scheme was set up before 6 April 2006 and the application for approval was processed before 31 March 2006 the Scheme Administrator or Practitioner will have been sent an approval letter containing the Superannuation Fund (SF) reference number. The Pension Schemes Online service allows you to use this to elect to contract-out. The PSTR will be given to the Scheme Administrator and/or authorised Practitioner for the first time they access Pension Schemes Online on or after 6 April 2006.

1.4 What is the Scheme Contracted-out number (SCON)

If the scheme already has a SCON please enter it here.

Q2 What type of contracting-out certificate you are applying for

Please indicate the type of scheme for which you require a contracting-out certificate.

Industry-wide Money purchase scheme (COMP) [Link]
A scheme in which only employers in a specified industry are eligible to participate where the employer pays minimum payments which, along with other contributions from the employer or member, provide the member with a pension based on the value of his or her fund at retirement.

Industry –wide Money purchase Stakeholder Pension Scheme (COMPSHP) [Link]
A scheme in which only employers in a specified industry are eligible to participate which operates on the same basis as a COMP scheme but with stakeholder status.

Converting an existing industry-wide Money Purchase Scheme (COMP) to an industry-wide Money Purchase Stakeholder Pension Scheme (COMPSHP) [Link].
An existing money purchase scheme set up for employers in a specified industry which wants to convert to stakeholder status.

Q3 Effective date of contracting-out

Enter the date from which you want contracting-out to start [Link]. Where the election is from an existing industry-wide money purchase scheme applying to convert to an industry-wide money purchase stakeholder scheme, this date will be the date of the conversion, not the original contracting-out start date.

Q4 Who is the person responsible for the day to day management of the scheme

Please enter the name, address, telephone number and e-mail address of the person or persons resident in the UK having responsibility for the day to day management of the scheme, for example the Scheme Administrator. For an overseas scheme [Link], the person resident in the UK .

Please enter the reference number that you wish us to quote when contacting you.

.

3

Q5 Who is the main trustee for the scheme?

Please enter the name and address of the main trustee of the trust(s) [Link] if applicable, under which benefits will be paid.

Please enter the reference number, if any, that you wish us to quote when contacting you.

Q6 Which type of Notice has been issued?

Where possible, you should make an election to contract-out before the date from which the contracting-out certificate is to have effect [Link]. This may avoid retrospective adjustment of NIC's and claims for a refund [Link].

Before making the election you must give either:

- A notice of intention to contract-out [Link]
  or
- A notice of explanation [Link]

Notice of Intention

Where a notice of intention is applicable you cannot make an election before the date on which the notice of intention expires but you must make it within three months of that date [Link]

6.2 How was the notice issued?

The notice to employees must be given in writing [Link]. Please tick the appropriate box to confirm how the notice was issued.

6.3 Who have the copies of the notice been sent to?

Please tick the appropriate box(s) to confirm to whom the copies of the notice have been sent to [Link].

Q7 Employer details

Please enter details for all employments to be covered by the contracting –out certificate

Please enter the Employer's name and address

Please enter the Employers Company Registration Number [Link] if applicable. This is the 9 digit number obtained from Companies House.

If the employer has or has ever previously had an ECON [Link] please enter it here, if known.

Please enter the date the contracting-out for the employment is to start [Link].

If you need to make more entries please continue on a supplementary page.

4

Part 2 – Rebate of NI Contributions

Please enter the following details to allow rebates of National Insurance contributions to be paid to the scheme

8.1 Name of bank/building society

8.2 Address of bank/building society

DRAFT

8.3 Account details

Enter bank/building Society account name

Enter bank/building Society account number for payments of minimum contributions

Enter bank/building Society sort code number for payments of minimum contributions

8.4 Enter the magnetic tape number [Link] if you have one, otherwise leave blank. A magnetic tape number is a number allocated to a Scheme Administrator or Pension Provider by HMRC (NICO). This enables them to receive payment/acknowledgement information on magnetic tape, disk or cartridge.

8.5 Enter the name and address where payments information [Link] is to be sent.

Part 3

The form must be completed by the person responsible for the day to day management of the scheme, the employer or the main trustee.

Please put a (√) in the box to confirm that the scheme meets all the conditions in Regulation 6 of the Contracting-out Regulations (SI 1996/1172) that are applicable to the scheme.

Where the form is not submitted by the employer, each of the boxes should be ticked to confirm that the contents of the form have been approved by the Employer and that they have authorised the submission of the form on their behalf.

What happens next

On receipt of an election, which contains all of the required information, HMRC will issue contracting-out certificates. A separate contracting-out certificate will be issued to the person with the day to day management of the scheme in respect of each employer. It will be up to the person with the day to day management of the scheme to decide whether the certificates will be held centrally or given to each participating employer.

All employers participating in the scheme will be issued with a common ECON [Link] unless a participating employer already has an ECON in their own right. In this case that particular employer will retain their original ECON.

5

Amending the election

You can amend the election at any time before HMRC issues the contracting-out certificate if the amendment does not alter the categories or descriptions of the earners to which the election relates. This might include amendments to any details given on the election, which are subject to notice and consultation, provided that the correct information was shown on the notice or any minor amendment to details not subject to consultation and notice requirements.

If however an amendment would alter the categories or descriptions of earners, or incorrect information was shown on the original notice, the employer must issue fresh notices to all concerned, with the notice period running from when the new notice was issued.

Data Protection

HMRC is a Data Controller under the Data Protection Act. We hold information for the purposes specified in our notification made to the Data Protection Commissioner, and may use this information for any of them.

We may get information about you from others, or we may give information to them. If we do, it will only be as the law permits to

- Check accuracy of information

- Prevent or detect crime

- Protect public funds

We may check information we receive about you with what is already in our records. This can include information provided by you as well as others such as other government departments. We will not give information about you to anyone outside HMRC unless the law permits us to do so.

6

HM Revenue & Customs

Registered Pension Schemes - Election to Contract-Out for an Industry-wide money purchase and money purchase stakeholder scheme

Please use this form to elect for a contracting-out certificate for an Industry-wide scheme

Part 1 - General

1 What is the name and registration number of the scheme?

1.1 Pension scheme name

1.2 Pension Scheme Tax Reference

1.3 SF Reference

1.4 Scheme Contracted-out Number (SCON)

S

2 What type of certificate are you applying for?

☐ Industry-wide Money Purchase Scheme (COMP)

☐ Industry-wide money purchase Stakeholder Pension Scheme (COMP)

☐ Converting an existing Industry-wide Money Purchase Scheme to an Industry-wide Money Purchase Stakeholder Pension Scheme (COMPSHP)

3 Effective date of contracting-out?

4 Who is responsible for the day to day management of the scheme?

Name

Address

Postcode
Country

Telephone number

e-mail

reference number (if known)

5 Who is the main trustee for the scheme?

Name

Address

Postcode
Country

Telephone number

E-Mail

Trustee Reference number (if applicable)

6 Which type of notice has been issued?

6.1 Tick ✓ the appropriate box and fill in the necessary details

☐ A notice of intention which expired on _ _ / _ _ / _ _ _ _ has been given to the earners in in respect of whose employment the election is intended to be made.

☐ A notice of explanation has been given to the earners to whose employment the election relates:

6.2 How was the notice issued?

☐ by sending or delivering it in writing to each of them

☐ by exhibiting it conspicuously at the place of work and drawing each employee's attention to it in writing.

6.3 Copies of the notice have been sent to:

☐ the trustees

☐ the person responsible for the day to day management of the scheme

☐ the insurers/Friendly Society

☐ the Trade Union(s) recognised in relation to the earners concerned

DRAFT

20051013 - Contracting-out (Industry wide)(V1.1).xls

331

7 Information relating to the Employers

7.1 Please give details of all employments to be covered by the Contracting-out certificate

Employer's name

Employer's address

Postcode
Country

Company Registration Number if applicable

ECON if known
E

Required effective date
/ /

Employer's name

Employer's address

Postcode
Country

Company Registration Number if applicable

ECON if known
E

Required effective date
/ /

Employer's name

Employer's address

Postcode
Country

Company Registration Number if applicable

ECON if known
E

Required effective date
/ /

Employer's name

Employer's address

Postcode
Country

Company Registration Number if applicable

ECON if known
E

Required effective date
/ /

Employer's name

Employer's address

Postcode
Country

Company Registration Number if applicable

ECON if known
E

Required effective date
/ /

Employer's name

Employer's address

Postcode
Country

Company Registration Number if applicable

ECON if known
E

Required effective date
/ /

DRAFT

20051013 - Contracting-out (Industry wide)(V1.1).xls

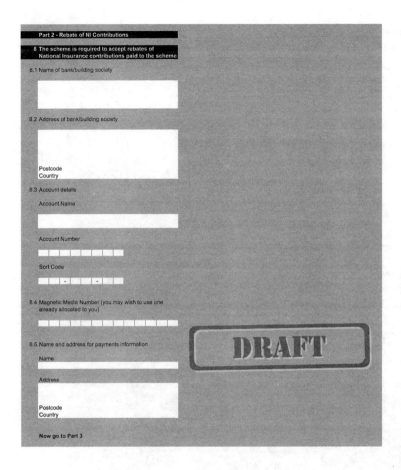

Part 2 - Rebate of NI Contributions

8 The scheme is required to accept rebates of National Insurance contributions paid to the scheme

8.1 Name of bank/building society

8.2 Address of bank/building society

Postcode
Country

8.3 Account details

Account Name

Account Number

Sort Code

8.4 Magnetic Media Number (you may wish to use one already allocated to you)

8.5 Name and address for payments information

Name

Address

Postcode
Country

Now go to Part 3

20051013 - Contracting-out (Industry wide)(V1.1).xls

Part 3

If the information supplied is incorrect or you do not meet the requirements to contract out, your certificate
may be withdrawn and recovery of the difference between the standard rate and reduced rate of National Insurance
contributions, as well as any age related rebates paid direct to the pension scheme may be sought.

☐ I confirm that the scheme meets the conditions set out in regulation 6 of the
Contracting-out Regulations (SI 1996/1172), so far as they apply to the scheme.

Signature

Date

☐ ☐ / ☐ ☐ / ☐ ☐ ☐ ☐

Capacity in which signed

☐ The person responsible for the day to day management of the scheme

☐ Employer

☐ Trustee

Where this form is not submitted by the employer

I declare

☐ The content of this form has been approved by the employers making this election

☐ The employers making this election have authorised me to submit this form.

DRAFT

20051013 - Contracting-out (Industry wide)(V1.1).xls

Contracting out (other schemes)

DRAFT

Election to contract-out

Notes to help you complete the form and submit it to HMRC

General

These notes provide guidance on how to elect to contract-out of the State Second Pension [Link] via a contracted-out pension scheme [Link].

An employer may elect that some or all of its employees are contracted out of the State Second Pension [Link] via a contracted-out occupational pension scheme [Link]. The scheme will then provide its members with an additional pension, which replaces the State Second Pension Scheme element of the state pension scheme [Link].

A scheme which is a personal pension scheme as defined in section 1 of the Pension Schemes Act 1993 [Link] may apply to be an Appropriate Personal Pension (APP) Scheme [Link]. An APP scheme can provide those of its members who wish to contract out of the State Second Pension with an additional pension replacing the State Second Pension for that employment in the state scheme.

You may also contract-out of the State Second Pension [Link] via the two types of Stakeholder pension schemes, Contracted-out Money Purchase Stakeholder pension scheme (COMPSHP) [Link] and Appropriate Personal Pension Stakeholder pension scheme (APPSHP) [Link].

An existing Money Purchase scheme or Personal Pension scheme may apply to convert to a stakeholder scheme. Whether such a scheme was already contracted-out prior to conversion or not, a new election to contract-out must be made to HMRC.

A scheme wishing to become a stakeholder pension scheme must register with HMRC to operate Relief at Source and also apply to the Pensions Regulator for stakeholder registration.

How to notify HMRC

You must make an election to contract-out by either completing the form online, go to www. hmrc.gov.uk and select "Pension Schemes" under "do it online", or by printing the form, completing it and sending it to HMRC, Audit & Pension Scheme Services, Yorke House, Castle Meadow Road, Nottingham, NG2 1BG..

Completing the form

These notes are intended to help you complete the boxes on the election form.

Please complete all the boxes in the relevant Part(s) of the form that apply to your scheme. An election to contract-out will not be complete unless all of the information requested is submitted. Use ticks (√) where indicated.

Q1 What is the name and registration number of the scheme?

1.1 Please enter the name by which the scheme is known

1.2 Please enter the Pension Scheme Tax Reference

1

The Pension Scheme Tax Reference (PSTR) is the unique reference allocated to your scheme by HMRC.

If the scheme was registered for tax relief on or after 6 April 2006 - this is the reference notified to the Scheme Administrator by HMRC in an online message on successfully registering the pension scheme.. If the Scheme Administrator opted out of receiving pension scheme notifications over the Internet they will have been sent a letter including the PSTR, acknowledging the scheme was registered for tax purposes.

If the Election to contract-out is submitted electronically to HMRC at the same time as the Registration application the scheme registration number will automatically be entered here.

If the scheme was set up before 6 April 2006 and the application for approval was processed before 31 March 2006 – the Scheme Administrator will have been sent an approval letter containing the Superannuation Fund (SF) reference number. The Pension Schemes Online service will allow the Scheme Administrator to use this to access the scheme record for the first time they login to the Scheme Administrator and/or authorised Practitioner the first time they access Pension Schemes Online on or after 6 April 2006.

If the scheme was set up before 6 April 2006 – but the application for approval was processed on or after 31 March 2006 your Scheme Administrator will be sent an approval letter including the PSTR.

If the scheme was set up before 6 April 2006 and participated in the HMRC data cleanse exercise the Scheme Administrator will be pre-registered to use the Pension Schemes Online. They will have been sent a letter containing the PSTR.

1.3 Please enter the SF Reference

If the scheme was set up before 6 April 2006 and the application for approval was processed before 31 March 2006 the Scheme Administrator or practitioner will have been sent an approval letter containing the Superannuation Fund (SF) reference number. The Pension Schemes Online service allows you to use this to elect to contract-out. The PSTR will be given to the Scheme Administrator and/or authorised Practitioner for the first time they access Pension Schemes Online on or after 6 April 2006.

1.4 Existing Scheme Contracted-out number (SCON) or Appropriate Scheme Number (ASCN)
If the scheme already has a SCON or an ASCN please enter it here.

Q2 What type of contracting-out certificate are you applying for?

Please indicate the type of scheme for which you require a contracting-out certificate.

Occupational Pension scheme – Money purchase Scheme (COMP)
A scheme which provides the member with a pension based on the value of his or her fund at retirement [Link].

2

Occupational Pension Scheme – Salary Related Scheme (COSR)
A scheme which provides members with a pension related to their earnings [Link].

Occupational Pension Scheme – Mixed Benefit Scheme (COMB)
A scheme which provides the member with a pension based on the value of his or her Contracted-out Money Purchase (COMP) fund on retirement. and Contracted-out Salary Related (COSR) benefits [Link].

This form should be used where the employer is contracting-out by reference to a COMB scheme for the first time. An Election to vary an existing COSR or COMP scheme to become a COMB scheme should be made on the Maintain Election to Contract-out form.

Occupational Pension Scheme - Industry-wide Salary Related (COSR)
A scheme which provides members with a pension related to their earnings in which only employers in a specified industry are eligible to participate [Link].

Contracted-out Money Purchase Stakeholder Pension Scheme (COMPSHP)
A scheme which operates on the same basis as a COMP scheme but with stakeholder status.

Converting an existing Contracted-out Money Purchase scheme to a Contracted-out Money Purchase Stakeholder Pension Scheme (COMPSHP).

Appropriate Personal Pension Scheme (APP)
A personal pension scheme which an individual may join as a means of contracting-out of the State Second Pension [Link].

Appropriate Personal Pension Stakeholder Scheme (APPSHP)
A scheme which operates on the same basis as an APP scheme but with Stakeholder status [Link]

Please note – Self-invested Personal Pensions (SIPPS) are prohibited from being Appropriate schemes for contracting-out purposes under Regulation 2 of The Personal pension Schemes (Appropriate Schemes) Regulations 1997.

Conversion of an existing Appropriate Personal Pension scheme to an Appropriate Personal Pension Stakeholder Pension Scheme (APPSHP).

Q3 Effective date of contracting-out

 Enter the date from which you want contracting-out to start [Link]. Where the election is from an existing money purchase or Personal Pension scheme applying to convert to a stakeholder scheme this date will be the conversion, not the original contracting-out start date.

Q4 Who is the person responsible for the day to day management of the scheme

Please enter the name, address, telephone number and e-mail address of the person or persons resident in the UK having responsibility for the day to day management of the scheme, for example the Scheme Administrator. For an overseas scheme, the person resident in the UK appointed .

3

Please enter the reference number that you wish us to quote when contacting you.

Q5 Who is the main trustee for the scheme?

Please enter the name and address of main trustee [Link] of the trust(s) if applicable, under which benefits will be paid.

Please enter the reference number, if applicable, that you wish us to quote when contacting you.

Q6 Is the scheme an occupational pension scheme?

If the scheme is an occupational pension scheme [Link] go to part 2 of the form. If the scheme is an Appropriate Personal Pension [Link] go to part 3 of the form.

Part 2 - Occupational Pension Schemes

Q7 Which type of Notice has been issued?

Where possible, you should make an election to contract-out before the date from which the contracting-out certificate is to have effect [Link]. This may avoid retrospective adjustment of NIC's and claims for a refund. [Link].

Before making the election you must give either:

- A notice of intention to contract-out [Link]
  or
- A notice of explanation [Link]

Notice of Intention [Link]

Where a notice of intention is applicable you cannot make an election before the date on which the notice of intention expires but you must make it within three months of that date [Link].

How was the notice issued?

The Notice to employees must be given in writing [Link]. Please tick the appropriate box to confirm how the notice was issued.

Who have the copies of the notice been sent to?

Please tick the appropriate box(s) to confirm to whom the copies of the notice have been sent to [Link].

4

Q8 What is the nature of the scheme?

Please put a √ in the relevant box(s) to indicate the type of scheme.

Public service
An occupational pension scheme established by or under Enactment, Royal Prerogative or Royal Charter as defined in section 1 of the Pension Schemes Act 1993 [Link].

Centralised
Put a √ if the scheme is one which has a common fund through which all the members' benefits are paid and as such there is an element of cross-subsidy between employers [Link]

Overseas
Put a √ if the scheme is an overseas scheme [Link]. An overseas scheme is a scheme, which is established under irrevocable trust, or by such other means as HMRC may approve [Link], and is administered wholly or primarily outside the United Kingdom. If you tick this box please complete question 9.

Industry-wide
Put a √ if the scheme is an industry-wide scheme [Link] scheme to which only employers in a specified industry centrally administered [Link] are eligible to participate.

DRAFT

Wholly insured
Put a √ if the scheme is a trust scheme which has no investments other than policies of insurance, the effecting of which constitutes the carrying out of long term business falling within Class 1 or 3 of Schedule 1 to the Insurance Companies Act 1982 [Link].

Centrally administered
Put a √ if the scheme is one which consists of a number of individual schemes which are administered on a central basis. There is no common fund and no element of cross subsidy [Link].

Individual Arrangement
Put a √ if the scheme applies specifically to one person, normally public service schemes [Link]

None of the above
Put a √ if one or more employers holds, or is to hold a Contracting-out certificate by reference to the scheme.

Q9 UK Contact Details (Overseas Scheme's only)

9.1 Please enter the name and address of the Scheme Auditor [Link]

9.2 Please enter the name and address of the person in the United Kingdom who has day to day responsibility for the scheme [Link].

5

Q10 What is the Revaluation Rate?

To be completed by COSR and COSR part of COMB schemes only
Put a √ in the appropriate box to confirm which method of revaluation [Link] the
scheme intends to use for any Guaranteed Minimum Pension (GMP) rights [Link]
held in the scheme.

Q11 Employer details

11.1 Please enter the Employer's name and address

11.2 Please enter the Employer's Tax Office Number and PAYE reference number

11.3 Please enter the Employers Company Registration Number [Link] if applicable.
This is the 9 digit number obtained from Companies House.

11.4 Put a √ in the appropriate box to indicate whether the employer currently has or
has ever had an Employer's Contracting-out Number (ECON) [Link]. If yes please
enter the ECON (if known).

115 Put a √ in the appropriate box to indicate whether the employer ever been
included on another employers contracting-out certificate.
If yes please enter the name address and ECON [Link] (if known) of the employer
that held the contracting-out certificate and the SCON [Link].
 If No go to question 11.6

11.6 Put a √ in the appropriate box to indicate whether the employer is a subsidiary
[Link] of a company that has ever been contracted out.
If yes please enter the name, address and ECON [Link] (if known) of that company
If no please go to question 11.7

11.7 Put a √ in the appropriate box to indicate whether the employer named in
question 11.1 is the Principal Employer [Link] for the scheme.

The Principal Employer is the company named in the trust deed which established
the scheme, or in any amended trust deed which replaces it whether or not they are
the holding company in the scheme or are contracted-out by reference to the
scheme.

If yes please go to question11.8
If no please enter the name, address, Company Registration Number (if applicable)
and the ECON [Link] (if known) for the Principal Employer.

11.8 Put a √ in the appropriate box to indicate the employments to be covered by the
Contracting-out certificate [Link] including where appropriate any exclusions.

11.9 Put a √ in the appropriate box to indicate whether any subsidiaries [Link] are to
be included in and covered by the contracting-out certificate.
If yes please enter the name, company registration number (if applicable) and their
ECON [Link] (if known). If you need to make more entries please continue on a
supplementary page.

6

Q12 Is the scheme entirely a Salary Related Scheme (COSR) [Link]

Put a √ in the appropriate box.
If the scheme is wholly a Salary Related Scheme (COSR) go straight to Part 5 of the form. A Mixed Benefit Scheme (COMB) is not considered to be a wholly Salary Related scheme.

If no please complete part 4 of the form

Part 3 Appropriate Personal Pension Schemes / Appropriate Personal Pension Stakeholder Schemes

Q 13 Who established the Scheme?

DRAFT

Please enter the name and address of the establisher [Link] of the scheme as shown in the governing documentation of the scheme.

Q14 What type of institution is making the application?

Please put a √ in the appropriate box to confirm the type of institution [Link] that is making the application.

Q15 What is the nature of the Scheme

Please put a √ in the appropriate box to confirm the investment basis [Link] on which the scheme is established.

Part 4 – Rebate of NI Contributions

To be completed by APP schemes, COMP schemes, COMP part of COMB schemes and Stakeholder pension schemes only

Please enter the following details to allow rebates of National Insurance contributions to be paid to the scheme.

16.1 Name of bank/building society

16.2 Address of bank/building society

16.3 Account details

Enter bank/building Society account name

Enter bank/building Society account number for payments of minimum contributions/age related rebates.

Enter bank/building Society sort code number for payments of minimum contributions/age related rebates.

7

341

Enter the magnetic tape number [Link] if you have one, otherwise leave blank. A magnetic tape number is a number allocated to the person responsible for the day to day management of the scheme or Pension Provider by HMRC (NICO). This enables them to receive payment/acknowledgement information on magnetic tape, disk or cartridge.

Enter the name and address where payments information [Link] is to be sent.

Part 5

Please put a √ in the box to confirm that the scheme meets all the conditions in Regulation 6 of the Contracting-out Regulations (SI 1996/1172) that are applicable to the scheme.

The form must be completed by the employer, the person responsible for the day to day management of the scheme, or the main trustee.

Where the scheme is an occupational pension scheme and this form is not being submitted by the employer electing to contract-out, each of the tick boxes should be ticked to confirm that the content of the form has been approved by the Employer and that they have authorised the submission of the form on their behalf. .

Supporting documents

For a contracted-out salary related scheme (COSR) [Link] or a COSR part of a newly contracted-out COMB scheme the following must be submitted in addition to the Election form;

- a reference scheme test certificate [Link] signed by the scheme actuary (or where appropriate an actuary appointed under regulation 24 of the Contracting-out Regulations), that the scheme-based contracting-out test is satisfied
- a statement from the actuary confirming that an interim schedule of contributions is in place [Link].

What happens next

DRAFT

Occupational Schemes

On receipt of an election form which contains all of the required information HMRC will issue contracting-out certificates in respect of each employer. This will show an ECON [Link], either the one that the employer already uses or a new one, and a SCON [Link]. These numbers are used to record and track National Insurance contributions and pension liabilities and should be quoted on all correspondence concerning contracting-out.

Amending the Election

You can amend your election at any time before HMRC issues the contracting-out certificate if the amendment does not alter the categories or descriptions of the earners [Link] to which the election relates. This might include amendment to any details given on the election which are subject to notice and consultation [Link],

8

provided that the correct information was shown on the notice or any minor amendment to details not subject to consultation and notice requirements.

If however an amendment would alter the categories or descriptions of earners [Link], or incorrect information was shown on the original notice, the employer must issue fresh notices to all concerned, with the notice period running from when the new notice was issued.

APP Schemes

DRAFT

On receipt of an election whi~~ch contains all of the required information~~ HMRC will issue an appropriate scheme certificate. This will allow individuals to Contract-out via the scheme. The certificate will show the ASCN [Link], which should be quoted on all future correspondence.

HMRC will also send a copy of the contracting-out certificate to the person responsible for the day to day management of the scheme.

Data Protection

HMRC is a Data Controller under the Data Protection Act. We hold information for the purposes specified in our notification made to the Data Protection Commissioner, and may use this information for any of them.

We may get information about you from others, or we may give information to them. If we do, it will only be as the law permits to

- Check accuracy of information

- Prevent or detect crime

- Protect public funds

We may check information we receive about you with what is already in our records. This can include information provided by you as well as others such as other government departments. We will not give information about you to anyone outside HMRC unless the law permits us to do so.

9

HM Revenue & Customs

Registered Pension Schemes - Election to Contract-Out

Please use this form to elect for a contracting-out certificate

Part 1 - General

1 What is the name and registration number of the scheme?

1.1 Pension scheme name

1.2 Pension Scheme Tax Reference

1.3 SF reference

1.4 Existing Scheme Contracted-out Number (SCON) or Appropriate Scheme Number (ASCN)

2 What type of contracting-out certificate are you applying for?

☐ Occupational Pension Scheme Money Purchase Scheme (COMP)

☐ Occupational Pension Scheme Salary Related Scheme (COSR)

☐ Occupational Pension Scheme Mixed Benefit Scheme (COMB)

☐ Industry-wide Salary Related Scheme(COSR)

☐ Contracted-out Money Purchase Stakeholder Pension Scheme (COMPSHP)

☐ Converting an existing Contracted-out Money Purchase scheme to a Contracted-out Money Purchase Stakeholder Pension Scheme (COMPSHP)

☐ Appropriate Personal Pension Scheme (APP)

☐ Appropriate Personal Pension Stakeholder Pension Scheme (APPSHP)

☐ Converting an existing Appropriate Personal Pension scheme to an Appropriate Personal Pension Stakeholder Pension Scheme (APPSHP)

Note - Self-Invested Personal Pensions (SIPPS) are prohibited from being Appropriate schemes for contracting-out purposes.

3 Effective date of contracting-out?

☐☐ / ☐☐ / ☐☐☐☐

4 Who is responsible for the day to day management of the scheme?

Name

Address

Postcode
Country

Telephone number

E-mail

Reference number (if applicable)

5 Who is the main trustee for the scheme?

Name

Address

Postcode
Country

Telephone number

E-mail

Trustee reference number (if applicable)

6 Is the scheme an occupational pension scheme?

☐ Yes - Go to section 2

☐ No - Go to section 3

DRAFT

20051013 - Contracting-out (V1.1).xls

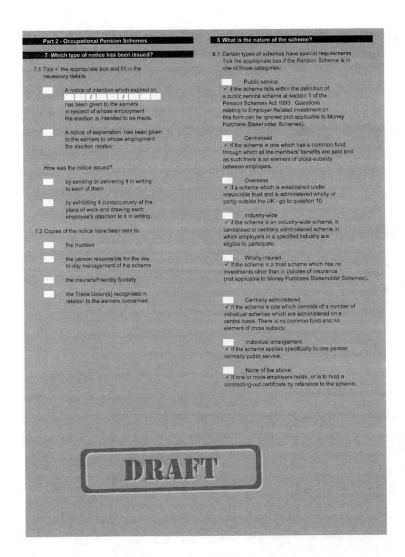

Part 2 - Occupational Pension Schemes

7 Which type of notice has been issued?

7.1 Tick ✓ the appropriate box and fill in the necessary details

☐ A notice of intention which expired on ☐☐/☐☐/☐☐☐☐ has been given to the earners in respect of whose employment the election is intended to be made.

☐ A notice of explanation has been given to the earners to whose employment the election relates:

How was the notice issued?

☐ by sending or delivering it in writing to each of them

☐ by exhibiting it conspicuously at the place of work and drawing each employee's attention to it in writing.

7.2 Copies of the notice have been sent to:

☐ the trustees

☐ the person responsible for the day to day management of the scheme

☐ the insurers/Friendly Society

☐ the Trade Union(s) recognised in relation to the earners concerned

8 What is the nature of the scheme?

8.1 Certain types of schemes have special requirements. Tick the appropriate box if the Pension Scheme is in one of those categories:

☐ Public service
✓ If the scheme falls within the definition of a public service scheme at section 1 of the Pension Schemes Act 1993. Questions relating to Employer Related investment on this form can be ignored (not applicable to Money Purchase Stakeholder Schemes).

☐ Centralised
✓ If the scheme is one which has a common fund through which all the members' benefits are paid and as such there is an element of cross-subsidy between employers.

☐ Overseas
✓ If a scheme which is established under irrevocable trust and is administered wholly or partly outside the UK - go to question 10

☐ Industry-wide
✓ If the scheme is an industry-wide scheme, a centralised or centrally administered scheme in which employers in a specified industry are eligible to participate.

☐ Wholly insured
✓ If the scheme is a trust scheme which has no investments other than in policies of insurance (not applicable to Money Purchase Stakeholder Schemes).

☐ Centrally administered
✓ If the scheme is one which consists of a number of individual schemes which are administered on a central basis. There is no common fund and no element of cross subsidy.

☐ Individual arrangement
✓ If the scheme applies specifically to one person, normally public service.

☐ None of the above
✓ If one or more employers holds, or is to hold a contracting-out certificate by reference to the scheme.

20051013 - Contracting-out (V1.1).xls

9 UK Contact Details (Overseas Schemes only)

9.1 Scheme Auditor Details

Name

Address

Postcode
Country

9.2 Details of the person responsible for the day to day running of the scheme in the UK

Name

Address

Postcode
Country

10 What is the Revaluation Rate? (COSR and COSR part of COMB schemes only)

10.1 Which method of revaluation does the scheme intend to use for any Guaranteed Minimum Pension (GMP) rights held in the scheme.

☐ Fixed Rate revaluation

☐ Section 148 revaluation

11 Employer Details

11.1 Name

Address

Postcode
Country

11.2 Tax Office Number & Employer's PAYE Reference

☐☐☐☐☐ / ☐☐☐☐☐☐☐☐☐☐

11.3 Employer's Company Registration Number (if appropriate)

☐☐☐☐☐☐☐☐☐☐☐☐☐☐☐

11.4 Have you ever been issued with an Employer's Contracted-out Number (ECON)?

☐ Yes   ☐ No

If Yes, please state the ECON (if known)

E ☐☐☐☐☐☐☐☐☐☐

11.5 Have you ever been included on another employer's contracting-out certificate - for example as a subsidiary on a holding company contracting-out certificate?

☐ Yes   ☐ No, go to 11.6

If Yes, state the name and address of the employer

Name

Address

Postcode
Country

ECON (if known)

E ☐☐☐☐☐☐☐☐☐☐

SCON (if known)

S ☐☐☐☐☐☐☐☐☐☐

11.6 Are you a subsidiary of a company which is ,or ever has been, contracted-out?

☐ Yes   ☐ No, go to 11.7

If Yes, state the full name and address of the holding company

Name

Address

Postcode
Country

Please state the ECON (if known)

E ☐☐☐☐☐☐☐☐☐☐

11.7 Principal Employer Details

Is the employer at 11.1 the Principal Employer for the scheme?

☐ Yes, go to 11.8

☐ No.
If No, state the full name and address of the Principle Employer.

Name

Address

Postcode
Country

Employer's Company Registration Number if appropriate

☐☐☐☐☐☐☐☐☐☐☐☐☐☐☐

Please state the ECON (if known)

E ☐☐☐☐☐☐☐☐☐☐

DRAFT

11.8 Which employments is the certificate to cover?

☐ All employments

☐ All employments except the following
   please list the exceptions:

11.9 Are there any subsidiaries to be included and covered
by the certificate?

☐ Yes   ☐ No

If Yes, provide the names, CRNs and ECONs (if known) of the subsidiaries to be included on the certificate

Name	CRN	ECON
		E
		E
		E
		E
		E
		E

12 Is the scheme entirely a Salary Related scheme (COSR)?

☐ Yes-Go to Part 5

☐ No-Go to Part 4

DRAFT

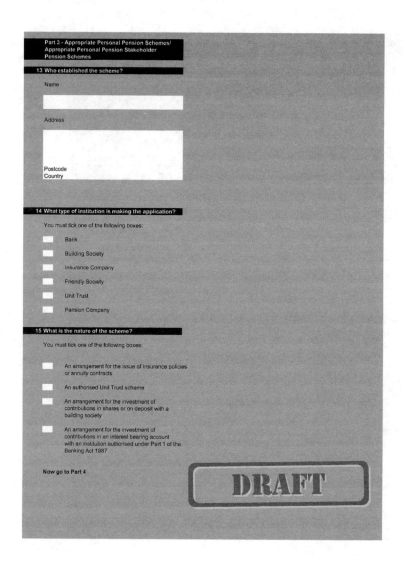

Part 3 - Appropriate Personal Pension Schemes/ Appropriate Personal Pension Stakeholder Pension Schemes

13 Who established the scheme?

Name

Address

Postcode
Country

14 What type of institution is making the application?

You must tick one of the following boxes:

- ☐ Bank
- ☐ Building Society
- ☐ Insurance Company
- ☐ Friendly Society
- ☐ Unit Trust
- ☐ Pension Company

15 What is the nature of the scheme?

You must tick one of the following boxes:

- ☐ An arrangement for the issue of insurance policies or annuity contracts
- ☐ An authorised Unit Trust scheme
- ☐ An arrangement for the investment of contributions in shares or on deposit with a building society
- ☐ An arrangement for the investment of contributions in an interest bearing account with an institution authorised under Part 1 of the Banking Act 1987

Now go to Part 4

DRAFT

20051013 - Contracting-out (V1.1).xls

Part 4 - Rebate of NI Contributions

16 The scheme is required to accept rebates of National Insurance contributions paid to the scheme (Appropriate Personal Pension Schemes, Contracted-out Money Purchase Schemes (COMPs), COMP part of COMB schemes and Stakeholder Pension Schemes only).

16.1 Name of bank/building society

16.2 Address of bank/building society

Postcode
Country

16.3 Account details

Account Name

Account Number

Sort Code

16.4 Magnetic Media Number (you may wish to use one already allocated to you)

16.5 Name and address for payments information

Name

Address

Postcode
Country

Now go to Part 5

DRAFT

Part 5

If the information supplied is incorrect or you do not meet the requirements to contract out, your certificate may be withdrawn and recovery of the difference between the standard rate and reduced rate of National Insurance contributions as well as any Age Related Rebates paid direct to the Pension Scheme, may be sought.

☐ I confirm that the scheme meets the conditions set out in regulation 6 of the Contracting-out Regulations (SI 1996/1172), so far as they apply to the scheme.

Signature

Date

Capacity in which signed

☐ The person responsible for the day to day management of the scheme

☐ Employer

☐ Trustee

Occupational pension scheme only

Where this form is not submitted by the employer electing to contract-out

I declare

☐ The content of this form has been approved by the employer making the election

☐ The employer making the election has authorised me to submit this form

DRAFT

20051013 - Contracting-out (V1.1).xls

Event report

Draft

Notes on Completion of an Event Report

General

These notes provide guidance on how to tell HM Revenue & Customs (HMRC) when certain events [Link] have occurred during the previous tax year.

The notes are intended to help you complete the questions on screen. They also include links to supplementary guidance, which you may need to read in order to understand more fully what information you have to provide. In particular, the links give you access to advice about the meaning of the legislative terms that are referred to in the form and the notes.

Multiple events of the same type

- If the same type of reportable event has occurred for more than one member of the pension scheme you will need to provide separately the details for each member in this Event Report.

- If the same type of reportable event has occurred **more than once for the same member** of the pension scheme you will need to provide separately the details for each occasion of this reportable event in this Event Report.

How to notify HMRC

You must complete and submit this form if certain events [Link] occur.

Please note there is a time limit [Link] for sending the form to HMRC.

Completing the form

You must complete all the required fields on the screens. You will not be able to submit the Event Report unless all required fields are completed and there is at least one event reported.

Page 1

Pension Scheme Tax Reference Number

The following types of pension schemes will have a Pension Scheme Tax Reference (PSTR)

1. Those registered for tax relief and exemptions on or after 6 April 2006, or you made a declaration you were the Scheme Administrator of a deferred annuity contract made on or after 6 April 2006.
2. Those established before 6 April 2006 and were approved for tax relief and exemptions and who took part in the pre-registration for Pension Schemes Online exercise

2

If the pension scheme is not one of the above leave this field blank and complete either the Superannuation Fund or Contract/policy number fields.

For those schemes in 1 above this is the number notified to you by HMRC in an electronic message on successfully registering the pension scheme or making a declaration you were the Scheme Administrator of a deferred annuity contract made on or after 6 April 2006. If you requested paper notices and reminders as well as electronic you will have been sent a letter including this number acknowledging the scheme was registered for tax purposes or that your declaration has been received.

For those schemes in 2 above this is the number provided in the letter sent by HMRC before 6 April 2006.

Superannuation Fund (SF) Reference

DRAFT

If you do not have a Pension Scheme Tax Reference (PSTR) and the pension scheme was established on or before 5 April 2006 and it **is not** a retirement annuity contract or a deferred annuity contract made on or before 5 April 2006.

This is the reference given to you on the letter notifying you the scheme was approved.

Contract or Policy number

If you do not have a Pension Scheme Tax Reference (PSTR) and the pension scheme was established on or before 5 April 2006 and it **is** a retirement annuity contract or a deferred annuity contract made on or before 5 April 2006.

You should enter the number you use to identify this scheme from any other scheme(s) of this type the member might have. It will also help to distinguish it from other contracts/policies.

Pension Scheme Name

This is the name by which the scheme is known or in the case of a two party contract between the member and the establisher, the member's name.

Part 1 Reportable Changes To The Scheme

Q1.1

You **must** select **yes**:

If the scheme has completed winding up [Link] and all the assets [Link] have been distributed and liabilities secured so nothing remains and there is a legal instrument formally winding up the scheme.

3

You do not need to make a report under this event heading if:

- the scheme is an annuity contract which was in existence at 6 April 2006 ["link" on Regulation 4(2)]
- the scheme is still in the process of distributing the schemes assets or securing liabilities as the scheme will still be subject to the normal reporting requirements.

Q1.2

You **must** select **yes**:

If the scheme now has at least one member who has the ability to control scheme assets and **it is not excluded from reporting by** [link to The Registered Pension Schemes Provision of Information Regulations Regulation 3 (4) (a) and (b)].

Control by a member will exist for the purposes of this question if:

a) The asset is owned by a person who is connected to the member. Connected is as defined in Section 839 of Income and Corporation Taxes Act 1988 [Link]

b) The member is a trustee of the scheme

c) The member is connected to a trustee of the scheme. Connected is as defined in Section 839 of Income and Corporation Taxes Act 1988

d) The asset is one that is allocated or earmarked to a particular arrangement and the member whose arrangement it is can exercise day to day control over its use.

For example:

The scheme is a Self Invested Personal Pension Scheme [Link] the assets of which are owned by the trustees of the scheme none of which are members or connected to the member. The scheme purchases agricultural land at the request of the member (who is a farmer) as part of his arrangement(s) within the scheme. The assets are owned by the scheme, not the member, but on a practical day to day basis he will be managing that asset and therefore controlling its use. It is possible because he has this type of control that he may be using it for purposes the trustees are unaware of because they are at a distance. For example he may be enjoying benefits such as fishing or shooting rights.

Q1.3

You **must** select **yes**:

If the scheme no longer has any member who has the ability to control scheme assets [Link] and **it is not excluded from reporting by** [link to The Registered Pension Schemes Provision of Information Regulations Regulation 3 (4) (a) and (b)].

4

Control by a member will no longer exist for the purposes of this question if none of the following apply:

a) The asset is owned by a person who is connected to the member. Connected is as defined in Section 839 of Income and Corporation Taxes Act 1988

b) The member is a trustee of the scheme and

c) The member is connected to the scheme. Connected is as defined in Section 839 of Income and Corporation Taxes Act 1988

d) The asset is one that is allocated or earmarked to a particular arrangement and the member whose arrangement it is can exercise day to day control over its use.

For example:

The scheme is a Self Invested Personal Pension Scheme [Link] the assets of which are owned by the trustees of the scheme none of which are members or connected to the member. The scheme purchases agricultural land at the request of the member (who is a farmer) as part of his arrangement(s) within the scheme. The assets are owned by the scheme not the member but on a practical day to day basis he will be managing that asset and therefore controlling its use. It is therefore possible because he has the type of control for him to be enjoying benefits such as fishing or shooting rights which the scheme trustees who are at a distance may be unaware of.

Q1.4

You **must** select **yes** if:

The scheme has changed its rules [Link] to permit the making of unauthorised member payments [link] or unauthorised employer payments [Link]

Q1.5

You **must** select **yes** if:

If the scheme has changed its rules to allow investment in assets other than or as well as policies of insurance.

5

Q1.6

You **must** select **yes** if:

If the scheme changed its rules **and** immediately before 6 April 2006 the scheme was treated as two or more schemes [Link]

Q1.7

You **must** select **yes**:

If the legal structure [Link] under which the scheme operates has changed during the year.

Q1.8

You **must** select **yes** if:

The number of members in (this includes active members, pensioner members, deferred members and pension credit members [link]) the scheme at the end of the tax year 5 April xx has changed bands since the end of the previous tax year.

Q1.1A

If you selected yes at Q1.1 you **must** complete the date the scheme was wound up [Link] or you will not be able to save or submit the report.

The date required is the date the scheme was legally recognised as wound up. For example in a trust based scheme this would be the date of the deed of winding up The date must be in the format dd/mm/yyyy. So for example 6 April 2006 would be 06/04/2006.

Q1.2A

If you selected yes to Q1.2 you **must** complete the date from which the scheme had at least one member who had the ability to control the way in which scheme assets are used or you will not be able to save or submit the report. The date should be in the format dd/mm/yyyy. So for example 6 April 2006 would be 06/04/2006.

When you have provided the date from which the scheme had a member able to exercise control over scheme assets you will be asked whether you wish to report details of any other events of this type during this reporting year. If so you will be presented with the screens to do so.

6

Q1.3A

If you selected yes to Q1.3 you **must** complete the date from which the scheme no longer had a member who had the ability to control the way in which scheme assets are used or you will not be able to save or submit the report. The date should be in the format dd/mm/yyyy. So for example 6 April 2006 would be 06/04/2006.

When you have provided the date the scheme no longer had a member able to exercise control over scheme assets you will be asked whether you wish to report details of any other events of this type during this reporting year. If so you will be presented with the screens to do so.

Q1.4A

DRAFT

If you selected yes to Q1.4 you **must** complete the date the change to the scheme rules to allow unauthorised is takes effect [Link] or you will not be able to save or submit the report. The date should be in the format dd/mm/yyyy. So for example 6 April 2006 would be 06/04/2006.

You **do not** need to make a report if the rules have been changed because:

a) The scheme was in existence at 5/4/06, and
b) Its rules at 5/4/06 permitted payments that were not considered to be authorised payments from 6/4/06 onwards, and
c) The change is to modify them to comply with the legislation effective from 6/4/06.

When you have provided the date the scheme changed rules you will be asked whether you wish to report any details of any other changes to its rules during this reporting year. If so you will be presented with the screens to do so.

Q1.5A

If you selected yes to Q1.5 you **must** complete the date the change to scheme rules to allow investment in assets other than policies of insurance takes effect or you will not be able to save or submit the report. The date should be in the format dd/mm/yyyy. So for example 6 April 2006 would be 06/04/2006.

When you have provided the date the scheme changed its rules or agreements you will be asked whether you wish to report any details of any other changes to its rules during this reporting year. If so you will be presented with the screens to do so.

Q1.6A

If you selected yes to Q1.6 you **must** complete the date the change to the scheme rules [Link] takes effect or you will not be able to save or submit the report. The date should be in the format dd/mm/yy. So for example 6 April 2006 would be 06/4/2006.

7

When you have provided the date the scheme changed its rules you will be asked whether you wish to report any details of any other changes to its rules during this reporting year. If so you will be presented with the screens to do so.

Q1.7A

If you selected yes to Q1.7 you **must** complete the date the legal structure [Link] changed or you will not be able to save or submit the report. The date should be in the format dd/mm/yy. So for example 6 April 2006 would be 06/4/2006.

When you have provided the date the scheme changed its legal structure you will be asked whether you wish to report any details of any other changes to legal structure during this reporting year. If so you will be presented with the screens to do so.

Q1.7B

DRAFT

If you selected yes a̶ ̶a̶ ̶r̶o̶ ̶y̶o̶u̶ ̶m̶u̶s̶t̶ ̶s̶e̶l̶e̶c̶t̶ ̶o̶n̶e̶ ̶o̶f̶ ̶t̶h̶e̶s̶e̶ boxes to indicate the new type of legal structure [Link]. You **must** select **one only**.

Single Trust under which all of the assets are held for the benefit of all members of the scheme

This is where a pension scheme is set up under trust and that trust covers all members. And the terms of the trust do not specifically allocate assets to a particular member.

An annuity contract

This is a two party contract between an establisher [Link] of a scheme and a member.

If you select this box you it would be helpful if you provide a policy or contract number

Policy or Contract Number

This is the number you use to identify this scheme from any other scheme(s) of this type the member might have. It will also help to distinguish it from other policies/contracts you have registered relating to the same member. You will not be allowed to save or submit the report if you do not provide this information.

An overall trust within which there are individual trusts applying for the benefit of each member

This is where a pension scheme is set up under trust and the arrangements [Link] within it are made under separate sub trusts. The scheme trustees have legal ownership of the assets but beneficial ownership is with the trustees of the sub trust.

8

An overall trust within which specific assets are held as, or within sub funds for each member.

This is where a pension scheme is set up under trust and some or all of the arrangements include the allocating or earmarking of assets to the arrangement or arrangements.

A Body corporate [Lir

DRAFT

Other

If the legal structure is not one of the above then you must select this and provide a brief description of how the scheme is now constituted or you will not be allowed to save or submit the report.

Brief description

This must be completed only if 'other' is selected.

For example, if the scheme is established by deed poll, state:

"Deed Poll"

Q1.8A

If you **select**ed yes at Q1.8 you **must** select one but no more than one of these boxes. Or you will not be able to save or submit the report.

You **must** tick the band that applies at the end of the tax year to which the report relates 5 April 20xx.

Reportable Movement of Scheme Funds

Q2.1

You **must** select **yes** if:

Any payment was made to or in respect of a member or to or in respect of an employer which is not an authorised payment [Link] or the payment is defined as an unauthorised payment.[Link]

Q2.2

You **must** select **yes** if:

As a result of the death of a member the scheme paid a lump sum death benefit [Link] which either on its own or when added to other lump sum death benefit payments from the scheme exceeds 50% of the standard lifetime allowance [Link] applicable when the member died.

Q2.3

You **must** select **yes** if:

A member who was in receipt of an ill-health pension paid under pension rule 1 in section 165(1) of Finance Act 2004 before the normal minimum pension age [Link] has given notice that the ill health condition [Link] that allowed his/her benefits to be paid 'early' is no longer met and his/her pension has ceased as a result.

Q2.4

You **must** select **yes** if:

If there was a benefit crystallisation event [Link] and the member has relied on an enhanced lifetime allowance [Link] or enhanced protection [Link] which has either reduced or eliminated a lifetime allowance charge[link].

Q2.5

You **must** select **yes** if:

A recognised transfer was made to a qualifying recognised overseas pension scheme [Link]

Q2.6

You **must** select **yes** if:

The sums or assets in respect of at least one member of the pension scheme meet Condition A or Condition B in paragraph 11 Schedule 28 Finance Act 2004 for the first time during the reporting year [link to guidance]

Q2.7

You **must** select **yes** if:

The scheme has paid any transfer lump sum death benefits [Link to guidance].

Q2.8

You **must** select **yes** if:

The scheme made a lump sum payment in respect of a member after the member died after reaching age 75 and it has not been reported as an unauthorised payment at Q2.1

Q2.1A

When you have provided details of an unauthorised payment you will be asked if you want to provide details of any further unauthorised payments for this member or

10

employer. After either providing the details of the additional payments or selecting no you will be asked whether you wish to report any other unauthorised payments for other members or employers. If you do you will be presented with the screens to do so.

If you selected yes to Q2.1 you **must** select **one** box. You **should not** select both or you will not be allowed to save or submit the report.

If the payment is in respect of a member or in respect of a sponsoring employer but was made to a person other than the member or the sponsoring employer then you should enter details of the member or the sponsoring employer who the payment was in respect of.

If a benefit in kind [Link] arises because an asset has been made available to a person connected [Link] to a member then the benefit is chargeable on the member. You should enter the member's details **not** the recipient's details.

DRAFT

Q2.1B

If you selected yes at Q2.1 and member payment at Q2.1A is selected you **must** enter the member's name in the correct format or you will not be able to save or submit the report.

If the unauthorised payment is a benefit in kind [link] arising as a result of an asset [link] made available to a person connected [link] to a member it is the member name required here.

Title by which known (Mr, Mrs, Miss, Ms)

Q2.1C

If you selected yes at Q2.1 and member payment at Q2.1A is selected you **must** complete the address of the person named at Q2.1B in the correct format or you will not be allowed to save or submit the report.

Q2.1D

If you selected member payment at Q2.1A you **must** complete the member's date of birth in the correct format or you will not be allowed to save or submit the report. The date should be in the format dd/mm/yyyy. So for example 6 April 2006 would be 06/04/2006.

Q2.1E

NINO is the member's National Insurance number (if known)

Q2.1F

The purpose of this question is to provide you with the correct fields in which to enter the payee's name and address. Title and surname are not applicable to organisations and trusts.

11

If you selected employer payment at Q2.1A you **must** complete **either** 2.1.3F or 2.1.4F but not both.

Q2.1G

If you selected employer payment at Q2.1A you **must** provide the address, in the correct format, of the employer or you will not be allowed to save or submit the report.

Q2.1H

If the employer is a company you **must** provide the company registration number.

Q2.1I

You **must** select **one** box. You should only select one box otherwise you will not be allowed to save or submit the report.

If more than one unauthorised payment [Link] has been made to a member or an employer in either

- The same category, o̶
- In different categories

You **must** provide separately the details for each payment.

Benefit in kind

If you **select** benefit in kind you **must** also select **one** box to indicate the type of benefit in kind[Link] provided or you will not be allowed to save or submit the report.

If there is more than one benefit provided you will need to complete separately the details of each benefit.

When you have provided details of a benefit in kind you will be asked if you want to provide details of any further benefits in kind for this member. After either providing the details of the additional benefits in kind or selecting no you will be asked whether you wish to report any benefits in kind for other members. If you do you will be presented with the screens to do so.

Transfer to an employer-financed retirement benefit scheme [link]

When you have provided details of a transfer to an employer-financed retirement benefit scheme you will be asked if you want to provide details of any further transfers to employer-financed retirement benefit schemes for this member. After either providing the details of the transfers or selecting no you will be asked whether you wish to report any transfers to an employer-financed retirement benefit schemes for other members. If you do you will be presented with the screens to do so.

12

Transfer to a non-recognised pension scheme which is not a qualifying recognised overseas pension scheme [Link]

When you have provided details of a transfer to a non-recognised pension scheme which is not a qualifying recognised overseas pension scheme you will be asked if you want to provide details of any further transfers to non-recognised pension schemes which are not qualifying recognised overseas pension schemes for this member. After either providing the details of the transfers or selecting no you will be asked whether you wish to report any transfers to non-recognised pension schemes which are not qualifying recognised overseas pension schemes for other members. If you do you will be presented with the screens to do so.

Error in calculating benefits

DRAFT

If you pay out excessive tax-free sums and this has resulted in a tax loss.

For example, a tax-free Pension Commencement Lump Sum miscalculated because of simple error or facts later came to light which show the tax free amount paid out was excessive. The difference between what should have been paid and what has been paid is an unauthorised payment.

When you have provided details of errors in calculating benefits you will be asked if you want to provide details of any further errors in calculating benefits for this member. After either providing the details of the errors in calculating benefits or selecting no you will be asked whether you wish to report errors in calculating benefits for other members. If you do you will be presented with the screens to do so.

Loans to the employer exceeding 50% of the value of the fund [Link]

When you have provided details of loans to the employer exceeding 50% of the value of the fund you will be asked if you want to provide details of any further loans to the employer exceeding 50% of the value of the fund for this employer. After either providing the details of the further loans to the employer exceeding 50% of the value of the fund or selecting no you will be asked whether you wish to further loans to the employer exceeding 50% of the value of the fund for other employers. If you do you will be presented with the screens to do so.

Benefits paid early [Link]

If the benefits were paid earlier than the normal minimum pension age [link] and they weren't for reasons (a) or (b) below then the amount of the benefits provided is an unauthorised payment reportable here. Normal minimum pension age before 6 April 2010 is age 50. On or after 6 April 2010 it is age 55.

The only valid reasons for benefits being paid early are:

13

a)   Ill health, [Link]

b)   Because the member was entitled to retain rights held at 5 April 06 to a normal
       retirement age below age 50 [link]

When you have provided details of benefits provided before the normal minimum
pension age you will be asked if you want to provide details of any further benefits
provided before the normal minimum pension age for this member. After either providing
the details of the further benefits provided before the normal minimum pension age or
selecting no you will be asked whether you wish to provide details of benefits provided
before the normal minimum pension age to other members. If you do you will be
presented with the screens to do so.

A scheme pension was paid using a non—relevant valuation factor [Link]

If you have used a valuation factor lower than the relevant valuation factor [Link] but you
did not seek HMRC agreement to use this factor. Then the difference between the value
of the scheme pension paid to the member and that using the relevant valuation
factor is an unauthorised payment.

When you have provided details that a scheme pension was paid using a non-relevant
valuation factor you will be asked if you want to provide details of any further pensions
paid using non-relevant valuation factors for this member. After either providing the
details of the further pensions paid using non-relevant valuation factors or selecting no
you will be asked whether you wish to provide details of any pensions paid using non-
relevant valuation factors to other members. If you do you will be presented with the
screens to do so.

Other

The list of unauthorised payments [link] above is not an exhaustive list but examples of
the most common unauthorised payments. If a payment has been made and it is not an
authorised payment [Link] and it is not in one of the categories above it should be
reported here. A short description is all that is needed similar to those provided above.

If you selected 'other' you **must** complete the brief description otherwise you will not be
allowed to save or submit the report.

Q2.1J

You must complete the amount or value otherwise you will not be allowed to save or
submit the report.

Q2.1K

You must complete the date that the payment was made or benefit made available or
you will not be allowed to save or submit the report . The date should be in the format
dd/mm/yyyy. So for example 6 April 2006 would be 06/4/2006.

14

Q2.2A

When you have provided details of a payment you will be asked if you want to provide details of any further payments made for this member. If you do you will be presented with the screens to do so. After either providing the details of the further payments to this member or selecting "no", you will be asked if you wish to report any other payments for other members. If you do you will be presented with the screens to do so.

If you selected yes at Q2.2 you must provide the name of the member, in the correct format, or you will not be allowed to save or submit the report.

Title by which known (Mr, Mrs, Miss, Ms)

Q2.2B

You must complete the address, in the correct format, of the person named in 2.2A or you will not be allowed to save or submit the report

Q2.2C

You must enter the member's date of birth, in the correct format, or you will not be able to save or submit the report. The date should be in the format dd/mm/yyyy. So for example 6 April 2006 would be 06/04/2006.

Q2.2D

NINO is the member's National Insurance number (if known)

Q2.2E

When you have provided details of a payment you will be asked if you want to provide details of any further payments made for this member to another person. If so you will be presented with the screens to do so.

Q2.2F

The purpose of this question is to provide you with the correct fields in which to enter the payee's name and address . Title and surname are not applicable to organisations or trusts.

You must complete one and only one or you will not be allowed to save or submit the report.

Q 2.2.G

You must provide the address, in the correct format, of the individual or organisation named or you will not be allowed to save or submit the report.

15

Q2.2H

You must provide here the amount paid to the individual or organisation whose details you have provided or you will not be allowed to save or submit the report.

Q2.2I

You must provide the date, in the correct format, when the payment was made or you will not be allowed to save or submit the report.
The date should be in the format dd/mm/yyyy. So for example 6 April 2006 would be 06/04/2006.

Q2.3A

When you have provided details of a pension that has ceased you will be asked whether you wish to report any other pensions that have ceased for this member. If you do you will be presented with the screens to do so. After either providing the details of the further pensions ceasing for this member or selecting "no" you will be asked if you wish to report any pensions ceasing for other members. If you do you will be presented with the screens to do so.

If you selected yes at Q2.3 you must provide the member's name and in the correct format or you will not be allowed to save or submit the report.

Title by which known (Mr, Mrs, Miss, Ms)

DRAFT

Q2.3B

You must enter the address, in the correct format, of the member named in Q2.3A or you will not be allowed to save or submit the report.

Q2.3C

You must enter the member's date of birth, in the correct format, or you will not be allowed to save or submit the report. The date should be in the format dd/mm/yyyy. So for example 6 April 2006 would be 06/04/2006

Q2.3D

NINO is the member's National Insurance number.

Q2.3E

You must enter the date non-payment commenced in the correct format
or you will not be allowed to save or submit the report. The date should be in the format dd/mm/yy. So for example 6 April 2006 would be 06/04/2006.

16

Q2.3F

You must enter the annual rate of the member's pension the member was entitled to at the date payment of the pension ceased or you will not be allowed to save or submit the report.

Q2.4A

When you have provide[...] details of a benefit crystallisation [...] the member relied on an enhanced protection or lifetime allowance to reduce or eliminate a lifetime allowance charge you will be asked whether you wish to report any further benefit crystallisation events where the member relied on an enhanced protection or lifetime allowance to reduce or eliminate a lifetime allowance charge of for this member. If you do you will be presented with the screens to do so. After either providing the additional details for this member or selecting "no" you will be asked if you wish to report any pensions benefit crystallisation events where the member relied on an enhanced protection or lifetime allowance to reduce or eliminate a lifetime allowance charge for other members. If you do you will be presented with the screens to do so.

If you selected yes at Q2.4 you must enter the member's name, in the correct format, or you will not be allowed to save or submit the report.

Title by which known (Mr, Mrs, Miss, Ms)

Q2.4B

You must provide the address, in the correct format, of the person named at Q2.4A or you will not be allowed to save or submit the report.

Q2.4C

You must provide the member's date of birth, in the correct format, or you will not be allowed to save or submit the report. The date should be in the format dd/mm/yyyy. So for example 6 April 2006 would be 06/04/2006

Q2.4D

NINO is the member's National Insurance number.(if known)

Q2.4E

You must provide the date, in the correct format, of the benefit crystallisation event [Link] or you will not be allowed to save or submit the report. The date should be in the format dd/mm/yyyy. So for example 6 April 2006 would be 06/04/2006

Q2.4F

You must enter the amount crystallised by the event [Link] or you will not be allowed to save or submit the report.

17

Q2.4G

You must enter the reference number given to you by the member which they received from HMRC or you will not be allowed to save or submit the report.

Q2.5A

DRAFT

When you have provided details of a member who has made a recognised transfer to a qualifying recognised overseas pension scheme you will be asked whether you wish to report details of any other recognised transfers to qualifying recognised overseas pension schemes for this member. If you do you will be presented with the screens to do so. When you have provided the additional details or selected 'no' you will be asked if there were any recognised transfers to qualifying recognised overseas pension schemes for other members. If so you will be presented with the screens to do so.

If you selected yes at Q2.5 you must enter the member's name and in the correct format or you will not be allowed to save or submit the report.

Title by which known (Mr, Mrs, Miss, Ms)

Q2.5B

You must enter the address, in the correct format, of the person named at Q2.5B or you will not be allowed to save or submit the report.

Q2.5C

You must enter the member's date of birth, in the correct format, or you will not be allowed to save or submit the report. The date should be in the format dd/mm/yyyy. So for example 6 April 2006 would be 06/04/2006

Q2.5D

NINO this is the members national insurance number.(If known)

Q2.5E

You must enter the date, in the correct format, of the transfer or you will not be allowed to save or submit the report. The date should be in the format dd/mm/yyyy. So for example 6 April 2006 would be 06/04/2006

Q2.5F

You must enter the amount if it was a cash transfer or the total market value of assets and cash if not wholly cash transfer or you will be able to save or submit the report.

Q2.5G

You must enter the name of the receiving scheme or you will not be allowed to save or submit the report

18

Q2.5H

You must enter the country or territory in which the receiving scheme is established and regulated or you will not be allowed to save or submit the report.

Q2.6A

If you selected yes at Q2.6 you **must** enter a number in each of the fields below otherwise you will not be allowed to save or submit the report.

For example there are three members of the scheme where the sums or assets in respect of these members of the pension scheme meet Condition A or Condition B in paragraph 11 Schedule 28 Finance Act 2004 for the first time during the reporting year **[link to guidance]**. The value of the funds or assets held for each member are as follows;

Member 1 -£75,00
Member 2 -£260,000
Member 3 -£425,000

In the field £1-£50,000 you would enter 0
In the field £50,001-£100,000 you would enter 1
In the field £100,001 - £250,000 you would enter 0
In the field £250,001- £500,000 you would enter 2
In the field more than £500,000 you would enter 0

Numbers should be rounded up or down to the nearest £.

Q2.7A

If you selected yes at Q2.7 you **must** enter a number in each of the fields below otherwise you will not be allowed to save or submit the report.

For example there are three members of the scheme for whom transfer lump sum death benefits were paid **[link to guidance]**. The value of the funds or assets held for each member are as follows;

Member 1 -£80,00
Member 2 -£300,000
Member 3 -£450,000

In the field £1-£50,000 you would enter 0
In the field £50,001-£100,000 you would enter 1
In the field £100,001 - £250,000 you would enter 0
In the field £250,001- £500,000 you would enter 2
In the field more than £500,000 you would enter 0

Numbers should be rounded up or down to the nearest £.

19

Q2.8A

When you have provided details of a lump sum payment you will be asked if you want to provide details of any further lump sum payments made for this member. If you do you will be presented with the screens to do so. After either providing the details of the further payments to this member or selecting "no", you will be asked if you wish to report any lump sum payments for other members. If you do you will be presented with the screens to do so.

If you selected yes at Q2.8 you **must** provide the name of the member, in the correct format, or you will not be allowed to save or submit the report.

Title by which known (Mr, Mrs, Miss, Ms

DRAFT

Q2.8B

You must complete the address, in the correct format, of the person named in 2.8A or you will not be allowed to save or submit the report

Q2.8C

You must enter the member's date of birth, in the correct format, or you will not be able to save or submit the report. The date should be in the format dd/mm/yyyy. So for example 6 April 2006 would be 06/04/2006.

Q2.8D

NINO is the member's National Insurance number (if known)

Q2.8E

The purpose of this question is to provide you with the correct fields in which to enter the payee's name and address . Title and surname are not applicable to organisations or trusts.

You must complete one and only one or you will not be allowed to save or submit the report.

Q 2.8F

You must provide the address, in the correct format, of the individual or organisation named or you will not be allowed to save or submit the report.

Q2.2G

You must provide here the amount paid to the individual or organisation whose details you have provided or you will not be allowed to save or submit the report.

20

Q2.2H

You must provide the date, in the correct format, when the payment was made or you will not be allowed to save or submit the report.
The date should be in the format dd/mm/yyyy. So for example 6 April 2006 would be 06/04/2006.

Q2.8I

DRAFT

You must provide details of the nature of the payment by selecting one box only below or you will not be allowed to save or submit the report. If you select other you must provide a brief description in the box provided or you will not be allowed to save or submit the report

Charity lump sum death benefit –[Link to guidance]
Transfer lump sum death benefit –[Link to guidance]
Commutation of a guaranteed lump sum death benefit –[Link to guidance]

Early Payment of Benefits

Q3.1

You **must** select **yes** if:

Benefits were paid before the normal minimum pension age [Link] to a member. (Normal minimum pension age before 6 April 2010 is age 50. On or after 6 April 2010 it is age 55) and in either the year to which this report relates or the preceding 6 years the member is/was

a)   A director of a company which is the sponsoring employer[link] or a company associated with the sponsoring employer. Sponsoring employer is the employer who established the scheme. or

A person connected[Link] to a director of a company which is the sponsoring employer or a company associated with the sponsoring employer. or

b)   A sole trader or a partner in a partnership that is/was the sponsoring employer or

c)   Connected to a person who is/was the sole owner or a partner in the sponsoring employer.

Q3.2

You **must** select **yes** if:

A serious ill health [link] lump sum has been paid to a member and in either the year to which this report relates or the preceding 6 years the member is/was

21

(a) A director of a company which is the sponsoring employer[link] or a company associated with the sponsoring employer. Sponsoring employer is the employer who established the scheme.   or

(b) A person connected[Link] to a director of a company which is the sponsoring employer or a company associated with the sponsoring employer.   or

(c) A sole trader [link] or a partner in a partnership that is/was the sponsoring employer or

(d) Connected to a person who is/was the sole owner or a partner in the sponsoring employer.

If the only benefits taken early have been reported under Q2.1 (as an unauthorised payment) or under Q3.2 you do not need to report them again here.

Q3.1A

DRAFT

When you have provided details of a member who has taken benefits before the normal minimum pension age you will be asked whether you wish to report details of any benefits taken before the normal minimum pension age by this member. If you do you will be presented with the screens to do so. After providing the additional details or selecting 'no' you will be asked whether you wish to report details of any other members who have taken benefits before the normal minimum pension age. You will be presented with further screens if you do.

If you selected yes at Q3.1 you **must** select at least one but no more than one box otherwise you will not be allowed to save or submit the report

Incapacity [Link]

Protected pension age [Link]

Other

If you select this you **must** provide a brief description in the box below or you will not be allowed to save or submit the report

Q3.1B

You must enter the member's name, in the correct format, or you will not be allowed to save or submit the report.

Title by which known (Mr, Mrs, Miss, Ms)

22

Q3.1C

You must enter the address, in the correct format, of the person named at Q3.1B or you will not be allowed to save or submit the report.

Q3.1D

You must enter the member's date of birth, in the correct format, or you will not be allowed to save and submit the report. The date should be in the format dd/mm/yyyy. So for example 6 April 2006 w̶̶̶̶ ̶̶̶̶̶̶̶̶̶̶̶

DRAFT

Q3.1E

NINO is the member's Nati̶̶̶̶̶̶̶̶̶̶̶̶̶ ̶̶̶̶̶̶̶̶̶̶̶̶̶̶̶̶ ̶̶̶̶̶ (̶i̶f̶ ̶k̶n̶o̶w̶n̶)

Q3.1F

You must enter the date, in the correct format, the benefits were taken or you will not be allowed to save or submit the report. The date should be in the format dd/mm/yyyy. So for example 6 April 2006 would be 06/04/2006

Q3.1G

You must enter the amount of the benefits provided or you will not be allowed to save or submit the report.

Q3.2A

When you have provided details of a member who has been paid a serious ill-health lump sum you will be asked whether you wish to report details of any further serious ill-health lump sum paid to this member. If you do you will be presented with the screens to do so. After providing the additional details or selecting 'no' you will be asked whether you wish to report details of any other members who have been paid a serious ill-health lump sum. You will be presented with further screens if you do.

If you selected yes at Q3.2 you must enter the member's name, in the correct format, or you will not be allowed to save or submit the report.

Title by which known (Mr, Mrs, Miss, Ms)

Q3.2B

You must enter the address of the person named Q3.2A or you will not be allowed to save or submit the report.

23

Q3.2C

You must enter the member's date of birth, in the correct format, or you will not be allowed to save or submit the report. The date should be in the format dd/mm/yyyy. So for example 6 April 2006 would be 06/04/2006

Q3.2D

NINO is the member's nation

DRAFT

Q3.2E

You must enter the date ,in the correct format, that the lump sum was paid or you will not be allowed to save or submit the report. The date should be in the format dd/mm/yyyy. So for example 6 April 2006 would be 06/04/2006

Q3.2F

You must enter the amount of the lump sum paid or you will not be allowed to save or submit the report.

Pension Commencement Lump Sums

Q4.1

You **must** select **yes** if:

A pension commencement lump sum [Link] has been paid to a member, and the amount paid is more than 7.5% but less than 25% of the standard lifetime allowance for the tax year in which the sum was paid [Link] and more than 25% of the members pension rights[Link],

Q4.2

You **must** select **yes** if:

A pension commencement lump sum [Link] has been paid to a member and an enhanced lifetime allowance or enhanced protection[Link] was claimed

Q4.1A

When you have provided details of a member who has been paid a pension commencement lump sum and the amount paid is:
- more than 7.5% of the standard lifetime allowance for the year in which it was paid, and
- it is less than 25% of the standard lifetime allowance for the in which it was paid, but
- more than 25% of the member's pension rights

24

You will be asked whether you wish to report details of any other such lump sums for this member. If you do you will be presented with the screens to do so. When you have either provided the additional details or selected 'no' you will be asked if there were any such lump sums paid to other members' and then presented with further screens if you do.

If you selected Yes at Q4.1 you must provide the member's name, in the correct format, or you will not be allowed to save or submit the report.

Title by which known (Mr, Mrs, ss, Ms)

DRAFT

Q4.1B

You must provide the address, in the correct format, or the person named at Q4.1B or you will not be allowed to save or submit the report.

Q4.1C

You must provide the member's date of birth, in the correct format, or you will not be allowed to save or submit the report. The date should be in the format dd/mm/yyyy. So for example 6 April 2006 would be 06/04/2006

Q4.1D

NINO is the member's national insurance number.(if known)

Q4.1E

You must enter the date, in the correct format, of payment or you will not be allowed to save or submit the report. The date should be in the format dd/mm/yyyy. So for example 6 April 2006 would be 06/04/2006

Q4.1F

You must enter the amount crystallised by the event [Link] or you will not be allowed to save or submit the report.Q4.1H

Q4.1G

You must enter the amount of the lump sum or you will not be allowed to save or submit the report.

Q4.2A

When you have provided details of a member who has been paid a pension commencement lump sum, and relied on an enhanced lifetime allowance or enhanced protection, you will be asked whether you wish to report details of any other pension commencement lump sum paid where this member relied on an enhanced lifetime allowance or enhanced protection. If you do you will be presented with the screens to do so. After you have provided the additional details or selected 'no' you will be asked if you want to provide details of any other members' have been paid a pension commencement lump sum and relied on an enhanced lifetime allowance or enhanced protection. If you do you will then be presented with further screens to do so.

If you selected yes at Q4.2 you must enter the member's name, in the correct format, or you will not be allowed to save or submit the report.

Title by which known (Mr, Mrs, Miss, Ms)

DRAFT

Q4.2B

You must enter the address, in the correct format, of the person named at Q4.2A or you will not be allowed to save or submit the report.

Q4.2C

You must enter the member's date of birth, in the correct format, or you will not be allowed to save or submit the report. that is required here. The date should be in the format dd/mm/yyyy. So for example 6 April 2006 would be 06/04/2006

Q4.2D

NINO is the member's National Insurance number (If known).

Q4.2E

You must enter the date, in the correct format, that the pension commencement lump sum was paid or you will not be allowed to save or submit the report. The date should be in the format dd/mm/yy. So for example 6 April 2006 would be 06/04/2006

Q4.2F

You must enter the amount of the pension commencement lump sum or you will not be allowed to save or submit the report.

Q4.2G

You must enter the reference number given to you by the member which they received from HMRC or you will not be allowed to save or submit the report.

Declaration

If you are a Scheme Administrator you will only be presented with the Scheme Administrator declaration which you must complete or you will not be allowed to submit the report.

If you are a Practitioner you will only be presented with the Practitioner's declaration which must be completed or you will not be allowed to submit the report.

26

Scheme Administrator Name

If you are **the Scheme Administrator** then the details will be pre-populated. You **need to ensure** they are still correct. If they are incorrect then when you have submitted this report you should use 'amend user details' to update your details

If you are the **Practitioner** you must enter the details of the Scheme Administrator who has approved the content of this report and authorised its submission to you

Data Protection

DRAFT

HMRC is a Data Controller under the Data Protection Act. We hold information for the purposes specified in our notification made to the Data Protection Commissioner, and may use this information for any of them.

We may get information about you from others, or we may give information to them. If we do it will only be as the law permits to

- check accuracy of information
- prevent or detect crime
- protect public funds

We may check information we receive about you with what is already in our records. This can include information provided by you as well as others such as other government departments. We will not give information about you to anyone outside HMRC unless the law permits us to do so.

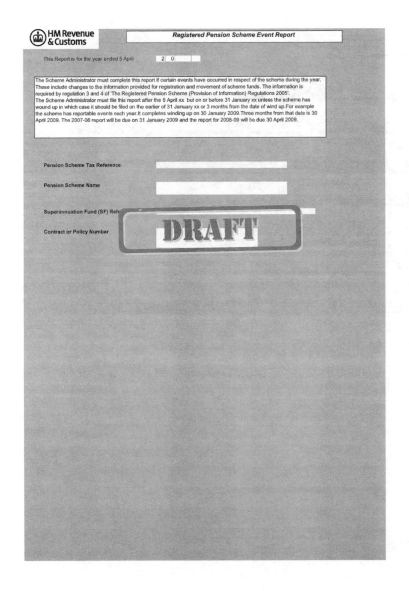

HM Revenue & Customs

Registered Pension Scheme Event Report

This Report is for the year ended 5 April 2 0 [ ] [ ]

The Scheme Administrator must complete this report if certain events have occurred in respect of the scheme during the year. These include changes to the information provided for registration and movement of scheme funds. The information is required by regulation 3 and 4 of 'The Registered Pension Scheme (Provision of Information) Regulations 2005'. The Scheme Administrator must file this report after the 5 April xx but on or before 31 January xx unless the scheme has wound up in which case it should be filed on the earlier of 31 January xx or 3 months from the date of wind up. For example the scheme has reportable events each year. It completes winding up on 30 January 2009. Three months from that date is 30 April 2009. The 2007-08 report will be due on 31 January 2009 and the report for 2008-09 will be due 30 April 2009.

Pension Scheme Tax Reference

Pension Scheme Name

Superannuation Fund (SF) Refe

Contract or Policy Number

DRAFT

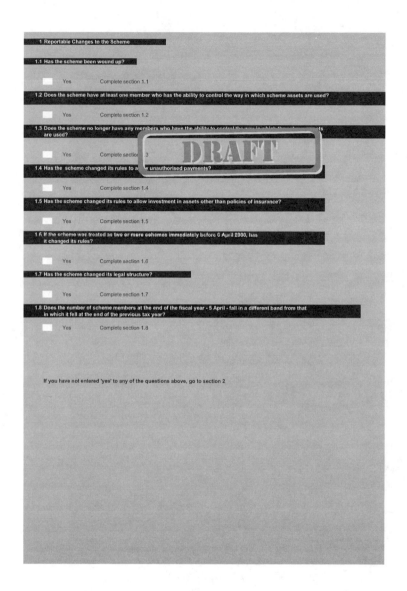

1 Reportable Changes to the Scheme

1.1 Has the scheme been wound up?

☐ Yes Complete section 1.1

1.2 Does the scheme have at least one member who has the ability to control the way in which scheme assets are used?

☐ Yes Complete section 1.2

1.3 Does the scheme no longer have any members who have the ability to control the way in which the scheme assets are used?

☐ Yes Complete section 1.3

1.4 Has the scheme changed its rules to allow unauthorised payments?

☐ Yes Complete section 1.4

1.5 Has the scheme changed its rules to allow investment in assets other than policies of insurance?

☐ Yes Complete section 1.5

1.6 If the scheme was treated as two or more schemes immediately before 6 April 2006, has it changed its rules?

☐ Yes Complete section 1.6

1.7 Has the scheme changed its legal structure?

☐ Yes Complete section 1.7

1.8 Does the number of scheme members at the end of the fiscal year - 5 April - fall in a different band from that in which it fell at the end of the previous tax year?

☐ Yes Complete section 1.8

If you have not entered 'yes' to any of the questions above, go to section 2

DRAFT

1 Reportable Changes to the Scheme

You need only answer the questions below where you have ticked Yes to that question on previous page

1.1 Has the scheme wound up?

1.1A Date wound up

☐☐ / ☐☐ / ☐☐☐☐

1.2 Does the scheme now have at least one member who has the ability to control the way in which scheme assets are used?

1.2A Date from which the scheme has at least one member who has the ability to control the way in which scheme assets are used.

☐☐ / ☐☐ / ☐☐☐☐

1.3 Does the scheme no longer have any members who have the ability to control the way in which scheme assets are used?

Date from which the scheme no longer has a member who has the ability to control the way in which scheme assets are used.

1.3A ☐☐ / ☐☐ / ☐☐☐☐

1.4 Has the scheme changed its rules to allow unauthorised payments?

1.4A Date change takes effect

☐☐ / ☐☐ / ☐☐☐☐

1.5 Has the scheme changed its rules to allow investments in assets other than policies of insurance?

1.5 Date change takes effect

☐☐ / ☐☐ / ☐☐☐☐

1.6 If the scheme was treated as two or more schemes immediately before 6 April 2006, has it changed its rules?

1.6A Date change takes effect

☐☐ / ☐☐ / ☐☐☐☐

1.7 Has the scheme changed its legal structure?

1.7A Date of change

☐☐ / ☐☐ / ☐☐☐☐

1.7B Select the type of legal structure the scheme now has

☐ A single trust under which all of the assets are held for the benefit of all members

☐ An annuity contract

Policy or contract Number _____

☐ An overall trust within which there are individual trusts applying for the benefit of each member

☐ An overall trust within which specific assets are held as, or within, sub-funds for each member

☐ A Body corporate

☐ Other (provide brief description)

_____

1.8 Does the number of scheme members at the end of the fiscal year - 5 April - fall in a different band from that in which it fell at the end of the previous tax year?

1.8A Select membership band applicable as at the end of the fiscal year - 5 April

☐ 0   ☐ 1-10   ☐ 11-50   ☐ 51-10000   ☐ 10001+

2 Reportable Movements of Scheme Funds

2.1 Have there been any unauthorised payments?

☐ Yes Complete section 2.1

2.2 Has there been any lump sum death benefit payments which either alone or when aggregated with other such payments from the scheme amounts to more than 50% of Standard Lifetime Allowance applicable when the member died?

☐ Yes Complete section 2.2

2.3 Has any ill-health pension ceased to ⬛⬛⬛ and because the ill-health condition is no longer met?

☐ Yes Complete section 3

DRAFT

2.4 Has any benefit crystallisation event occurred in relation to a member and the amount crystallised exceeds the Standard Lifetime Allowance or together with other amounts crystallised exceeds the Standard Lifetime Allowance and the member relied on either an enhanced lifetime allowance or enhanced protection to reduce or eliminate liability to the lifetime allowance charge?

☐ Yes Complete section 2.4

2.5 Has there been any recognised transfers to a qualifying recognised overseas scheme which is not a registered pension scheme?

☐ Yes Complete section 2.5

2.6 Did sums or assets in respect of at least one member of the pension scheme meet Condition A or Condition B in paragraph 11 of Schedule 28 Finance Act 2004 for the first time during the reporting year?

☐ Yes Complete section 2.6

2.7 Has the scheme paid any transfer lump sum death benefits?

☐ Yes Complete section 2.7

2.8 Did the scheme make any lump sum payment in respect of a member after the member died after reaching age 75 and has not been reported as an unauthorised payment at Q2.1

☐ Yes Complete section 2.8

If you have not entered 'yes' to any of the questions above, go to Section 3

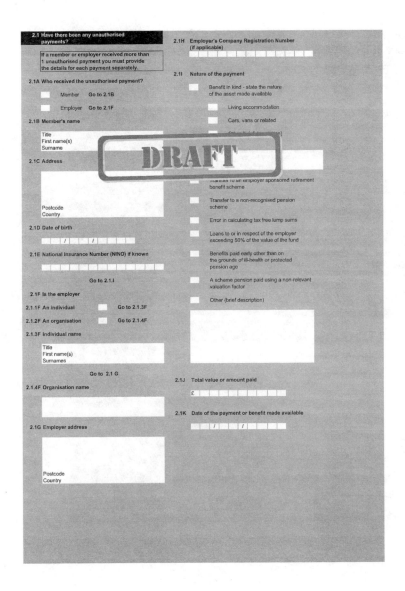

2.1 Have there been any unauthorised payments?

If a member or employer received more than 1 unauthorised payment you must provide the details for each payment separately.

2.1A Who received the unauthorised payment?

☐ Member   Go to 2.1B

☐ Employer   Go to 2.1F

2.1B Member's name

Title
First name(s)
Surname

2.1C Address

Postcode
Country

2.1D Date of birth

☐ ☐ / ☐ ☐ / ☐ ☐ ☐ ☐

2.1E National Insurance Number (NINO) if known

Go to 2.1.I

2.1F Is the employer

2.1.1F An individual   ☐   Go to 2.1.3F

2.1.2F An organisation   ☐   Go to 2.1.4F

2.1.3F Individual name

Title
First name(s)
Surnames

Go to 2.1 G

2.1.4F Organisation name

2.1G Employer address

Postcode
Country

2.1H Employer's Company Registration Number (if applicable)

2.1I Nature of the payment

☐ Benefit in kind - state the nature of the asset made available

☐ Living accommodation

☐ Cars, vans or related

☐ Other (brief description)

☐ Transfer to an employer sponsored retirement benefit scheme

☐ Transfer to a non-recognised pension scheme

☐ Error in calculating tax free lump sums

☐ Loans to or in respect of the employer exceeding 50% of the value of the fund

☐ Benefits paid early other than on the grounds of ill-health or protected pension age

☐ A scheme pension paid using a non-relevant valuation factor

☐ Other (brief description)

2.1J Total value or amount paid

£

2.1K Date of the payment or benefit made available

☐ ☐ / ☐ ☐ / ☐ ☐ ☐ ☐

DRAFT

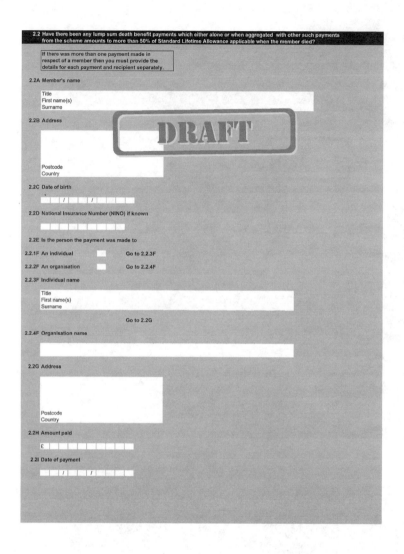

2.2 Have there been any lump sum death benefit payments which either alone or when aggregated with other such payments from the scheme amounts to more than 50% of Standard Lifetime Allowance applicable when the member died?

If there was more than one payment made in respect of a member then you must provide the details for each payment and recipient separately.

2.2A Member's name

Title
First name(s)
Surname

2.2B Address

Postcode
Country

2.2C Date of birth

2.2D National Insurance Number (NINO) if known

2.2E Is the person the payment was made to

2.2.1F An individual   Go to 2.2.3F

2.2.2F An organisation   Go to 2.2.4F

2.2.3F Individual name

Title
First name(s)
Surname

                 Go to 2.2G

2.2.4F Organisation name

2.2G Address

Postcode
Country

2.2H Amount paid

£

2.2I Date of payment

2.3 Has any ill-health pension ceased to be paid because the ill-health condition is no longer met?

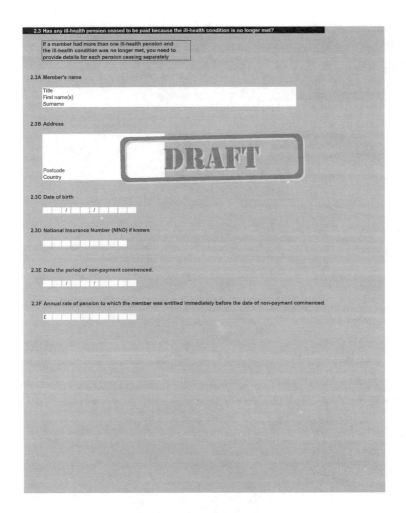

If a member had more than one ill-health pension and
the ill-health condition was no longer met, you need to
provide details for each pension ceasing separately

2.3A Member's name

Title
First name(s)
Surname

2.3B Address

Postcode
Country

2.3C Date of birth

2.3D National Insurance Number (NINO) if known

2.3E Date the period of non-payment commenced.

2.3F Annual rate of pension to which the member was entitled immediately before the date of non-payment commenced.

£

2.4 Has any benefit crystallisation event occurred in relation to a member and the amount crystallised exceeds the Standard Lifetime Allowance or together with other amounts crystallised exceeds the Standard Lifetime Allowance and the member relied on either an enhanced lifetime allowance or enhanced protection to reduce or eliminate liability to the lifetime allowance charge?

If the member had more than one benefit crystallisation event which exceeded the Standard Lifetime Allowance or when added to other amounts crystallised exceed the Lifetime Allowance and the member relied on an enhanced lifetime allowance or enhanced protection to reduce or eliminate liability to the lifetime allowance charge then details of each event must be provided separately.

2.4A Member's name

Title
First name(s)
Surname

2.4B Address

Postcode
Country

2.4C Date of birth

2.4D National Insurance Number (NINO) known

DRAFT

2.4E Date of benefit crystallisation event

2.4F Amount crystallised by the event

£

2.4G Reference number issued by HMRC to the member

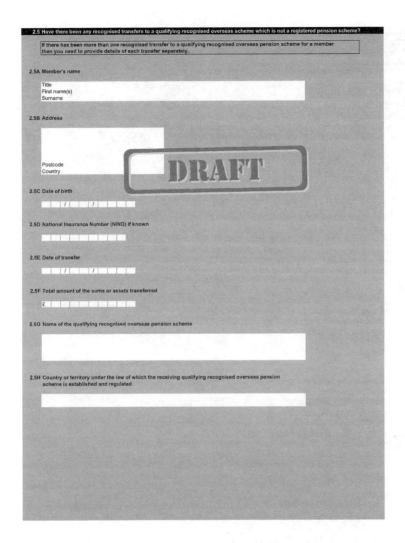

2.5 Have there been any recognised transfers to a qualifying recognised overseas scheme which is not a registered pension scheme?

If there has been more than one recognised transfer to a qualifying recognised overseas pension scheme for a member then you need to provide details of each transfer separately.

2.5A Member's name

Title
First name(s)
Surname

2.5B Address

Postcode
Country

2.5C Date of birth

2.5D National Insurance Number (NINO) if known

2.5E Date of transfer

2.5F Total amount of the sums or assets transferred

£

2.5G Name of the qualifying recognised overseas pension scheme

2.5H Country or territory under the law of which the receiving qualifying recognised overseas pension scheme is established and regulated

385

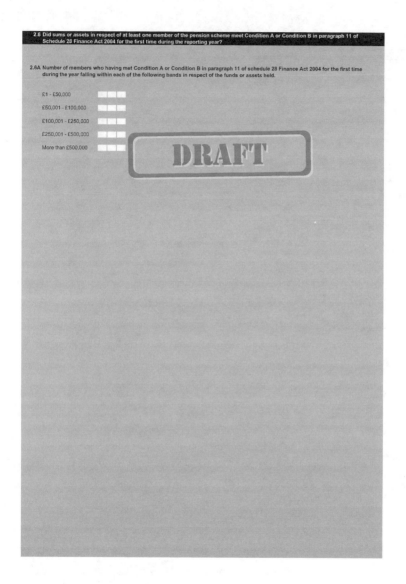

2.6 Did sums or assets in respect of at least one member of the pension scheme meet Condition A or Condition B in paragraph 11 of Schedule 28 Finance Act 2004 for the first time during the reporting year?

2.6A Number of members who having met Condition A or Condition B in paragraph 11 of schedule 28 Finance Act 2004 for the first time during the year falling within each of the following bands in respect of the funds or assets held.

£1 - £50,000

£50,001 - £100,000

£100,001 - £250,000

£250,001 - £500,000

More than £500,000

DRAFT

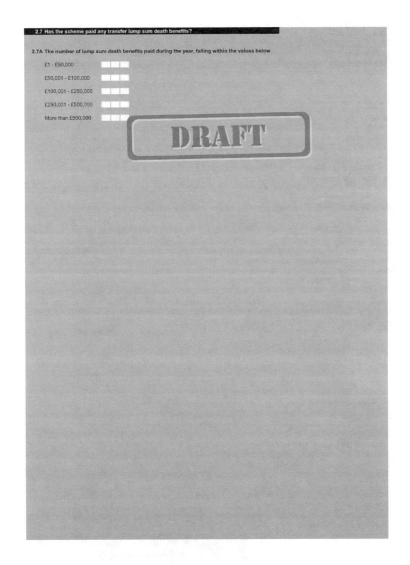

2.7 Has the scheme paid any transfer lump sum death benefits?

2.7A The number of lump sum death benefits paid during the year, falling within the values below

£1 - £50,000

£50,001 - £100,000

£100,001 - £250,000

£250,001 - £500,000

More than £500,000

DRAFT

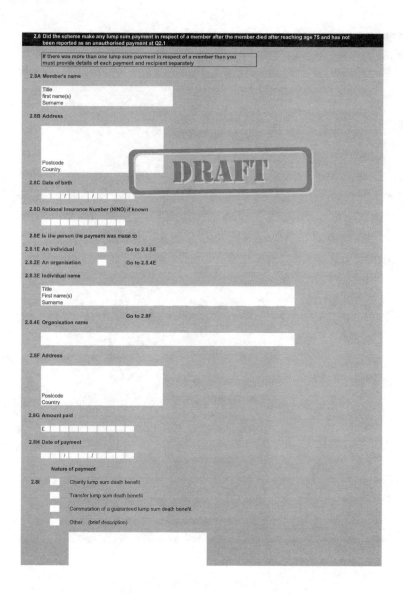

2.8 Did the scheme make any lump sum payment in respect of a member after the member died after reaching age 75 and has not been reported as an unauthorised payment at Q2.1

If there was more than one lump sum payment in respect of a member then you must provide details of each payment and recipient separately

2.8A Member's name

Title
first name(s)
Surname

2.8B Address

Postcode
Country

2.8C Date of birth

2.8D National Insurance Number (NINO) if known

2.8E Is the person the payment was made to

2.8.1E An individual   Go to 2.8.3E

2.8.2E An organisation   Go to 2.8.4E

2.8.3E Individual name

Title
First name(s)
Surname

Go to 2.8F

2.8.4E Organisation name

2.8F Address

Postcode
Country

2.8G Amount paid

£

2.8H Date of payment

Nature of payment

2.8I   Charity lump sum death benefit

          Transfer lump sum death benefit

          Commutation of a guaranteed lump sum death benefit

          Other   (brief description)

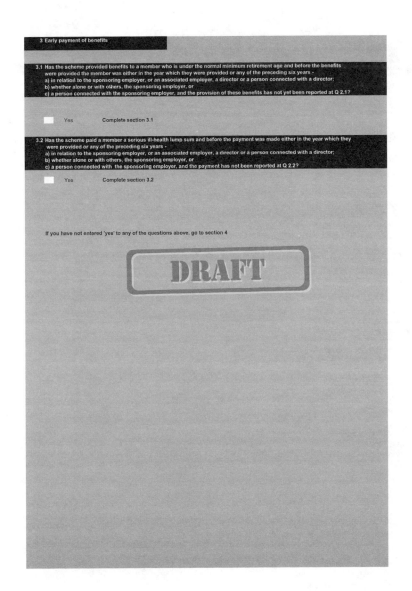

3 Early payment of benefits

3.1 Has the scheme provided benefits to a member who is under the normal minimum retirement age and before the benefits
were provided the member was either in the year which they were provided or any of the preceding six years -
a) in relation to the sponsoring employer, or an associated employer, a director or a person connected with a director;
b) whether alone or with others, the sponsoring employer, or
c) a person connected with the sponsoring employer, and the provision of these benefits has not yet been reported at Q 2.1?

☐   Yes   Complete section 3.1

3.2 Has the scheme paid a member a serious ill-health lump sum and before the payment was made either in the year which they
were provided or any of the preceding six years -
a) in relation to the sponsoring employer, or an associated employer, a director or a person connected with a director;
b) whether alone or with others, the sponsoring employer, or
c) a person connected with the sponsoring employer, and the payment has not been reported at Q 2.2?

☐   Yes   Complete section 3.2

If you have not entered 'yes' to any of the questions above, go to section 4

DRAFT

3.1 Has the scheme provided benefits to a member who is under the normal minimum retirement age and before the benefits were provided the member was either in the year which they were provided or any of the preceding six years -
a) in relation to the sponsoring employer, or an associated employer, a director or a person connected with a director;
b) whether alone or with others, the sponsoring employer, or
c) a person connected with the sponsoring employer, and the provision of these benefits has not yet been reported at Q 2.1?

If benefits were provided before the minimum retirement age more than once to a member you need to provide details for each of the benefit separately.

3.1A Reason the benefits were taken

☐ ill-health

☐ protected pension age

☐ Other (brief description)

DRAFT

3.1B Member's name

Title
First name(s)
Surname

3.1C Address

Postcode
Country

3.1D Date of birth

☐☐ / ☐☐ / ☐☐☐☐

3.1E National Insurance Number (NINO) if known

☐☐☐☐☐☐☐☐☐

3.1F Date when the benefits were taken

☐☐ / ☐☐ / ☐☐☐☐

3.1G Amount of the benefits

£ ☐☐☐☐☐☐☐☐☐

3.2 Has the scheme paid a member a serious ill-health lump sum and before the payment was made either in the year which they were provided or any of the preceding six years -
a) in relation to the sponsoring employer, or an associated employer, a director or a person connected with a director;
b) whether alone or with others, the sponsoring employer, or
c) a person connected with the sponsoring employer, and the payment has not been reported at Q 3.2?

If more than one serious ill-health lump sum was paid to a member you need to provide details of each payment separately

3.2A Member's name

Title
First name(s)
Surname

3.2B Address

Postcode
Country

DRAFT

3.2C Date of Birth

3.2D National Insurance Number (NINO) if known

3.2E Date of Payment

3.2F Amount

£

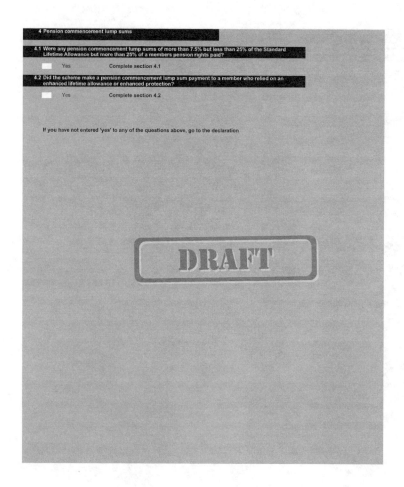

4 Pension commencement lump sums

4.1 Were any pension commencement lump sums of more than 7.5% but less than 25% of the Standard Lifetime Allowance but more than 25% of a members pension rights paid?

☐ Yes   Complete section 4.1

4.2 Did the scheme make a pension commencement lump sum payment to a member who relied on an enhanced lifetime allowance or enhanced protection?

☐ Yes   Complete section 4.2

If you have not entered 'yes' to any of the questions above, go to the declaration

DRAFT

4.1 Were any pension commencement lump sums of more than 7.5% but less than 25% of the Standard Lifetime Allowance but more than 25% of a members pension rights paid?

If more than one pension commencement lump sum was paid to a member of more than 7.5% but less than 25% of the Standard Lifetime Allowance but more than 25% of the member's pension rights then you need to provide details of each commencement lump sum separately.

4.1A Member's name

Title
First name(s)
Surname

4.1B Address

Postcode
Country

4.1C Date of birth

4.1D National Insurance Number (NINO) if known

4.1E Date of payment

4.1F The amount crystallised

£

4.1G Amount of lump sum

£

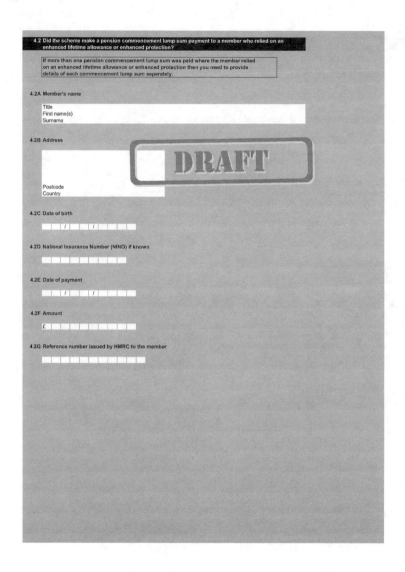

4.2 Did the scheme make a pension commencement lump sum payment to a member who relied on an enhanced lifetime allowance or enhanced protection?

If more than one pension commencement lump sum was paid where the member relied on an enhanced lifetime allowance or enhanced protection then you need to provide details of each commencement lump sum seperately.

4.2A Member's name

Title
First name(s)
Surname

4.2B Address

Postcode
Country

4.2C Date of birth

4.2D National Insurance Number (NINO) if known

4.2E Date of payment

4.2F Amount

£

4.2G Reference number issued by HMRC to the member

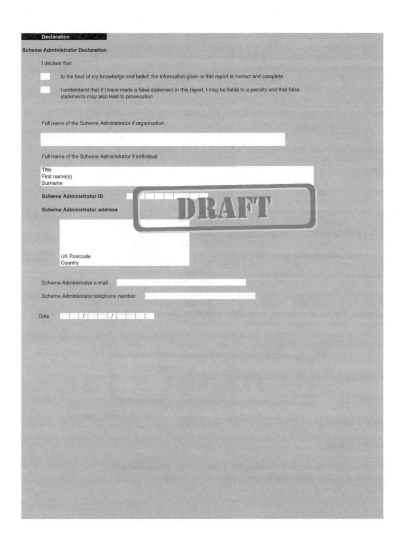

Declaration

Scheme Administrator Declaration

I declare that

☐ to the best of my knowledge and belief, the information given in this report is correct and complete

☐ I understand that if I have made a false statement in this report, I may be liable to a penalty and that false statements may also lead to prosecution

Full name of the Scheme Administrator if organisation

Full name of the Scheme Administrator if individual

Title
First name(s)
Surname

Scheme Administrator ID

Scheme Administrator address

DRAFT

UK Postcode
Country

Scheme Administrator e-mail

Scheme Administrator telephone number

Date ☐☐ / ☐☐ / ☐☐☐☐

Accounting for tax return

DRAFT

Accounting For Tax by Scheme Administrator (AFT): Return guidance notes

You should use this form to make a return of income tax to which the scheme administrator (link) of a registered pension scheme is liable under Part 4 of Finance Act 2004[Link]. You must submit the return by an authorised electronic method.

You may complete the return if you are yourself the scheme administrator or you are a practitioner who has been authorised to submit the return on behalf of the scheme administrator.

You must complete a separate return for each registered pension scheme for which you are a scheme administrator or a practitioner.

In some cases, funds from a registered pension scheme may have been used to purchase, from an insurance company, an annuity or other insurance type contract from which benefits are paid. If you are an insurance company and you make a payment from such a policy or contract on which a special lump sum death benefits charge arises, then you are the person liable to that charge and responsible for making a return of the liability.

You must make a return for each quarter in which a chargeable payment has been made. A quarter is the 3 month period ending on 31 March, 30 June, 30 September and 31 December in each year.

The filing date for the return is 45 days after the end of the quarterly return period.

1. Return Information

1.1 Quarter and Year

Select the year and quarter for which a return is being made

1.2 Amendments (link)

Select yes if you need to amend information on a return that has already been submitted. Select no if this is the first return submitted for a quarter.

2. Scheme Information

2.1 Insurance companies

Select yes if you are an insurance company that has made a payment in the quarter on which a special lump sum death benefits charge arises. Select no if you are a scheme administrator.

2.2 Pension Scheme Tax Reference

DRAFT

Pension scheme tax reference

- **If the scheme was registered for tax relief and exemptions on or after 6 April 2006, or you made a declaration you were the scheme administrator of a deferred annuity contract made on or after 6 April 2006**

This is the reference notified to you by HMRC in an electronic message on successfully registering the pension scheme or making a declaration you were the scheme administrator of a deferred annuity contract made on or after 6 April 2006. If you opted out of electronic communications you will have been sent a letter including this number acknowledging the scheme was registered for tax purposes or that your declaration has been received.

- **If the scheme was set up before 6 April 2006 and the application for approval was processed before 31 March 2006**

You will have been sent an approval letter containing the SF reference number. You can use this to access the scheme record for the first time on the new online service. The Pension Scheme tax reference will be given to the scheme administrator and/or authorised practitioner the first time they access Pension Schemes Online on or after 6 April 2006.

- **If the scheme was set up before 6 April 2006 but the application for approval was processed on or after 31 March 2006**

You will be sent an approval letter including the Pension Scheme tax reference.

- **If the scheme was set up before 6 April 2006 and participated in the HMRC data cleanse exercise**

The Scheme administrator will be pre-registered to use the new Pension Schemes Online service. They will be sent a letter containing a Data Access Token to access the new system, together with a separate letter containing the new pension scheme tax reference.

2.3 Pension Scheme name

Enter the full name of the registered pension scheme.

3. Summary of Information

3.1 Type of charge

Select yes for each charge that you are reporting in this return and for which you have accounted for the tax due. If this is the first return for a quarter, at least one charge must be selected. Nil returns are not required.

4. Short Service Refund Lump Sum Charge [link]

You should complete Section 4 if the registered pension scheme has made any short service refund lump sum payments in the quarter

4.1 Number of members

Enter the number of members that have received a short service refund lump sum the quarter.

DRAFT

4.2 Tax at 20%

Enter the total amount of tax due at the rate of 20%. Tax is charged at 20% on amounts paid to each individual member that do not exceed £10,800.

4.3 Tax at 40%

Enter the total amount of tax due at the rate of 40%. Tax is charged at 40% on amounts of more than £10,800 that have been paid to an individual member.

5. Special lump sum death benefits charge (link)

You should complete Section 5 if the registered pension scheme has made any payments on which a special lump sum death benefits charge arose in the quarter.

5.1 Number of deceased members

Enter the number of deceased members in respect of whom payments, giving rise to a special lump sum death benefits charge, were made in the quarter.

5.2 Tax at 35%

Enter the total amount of tax due at the rate of 35%.

6. Authorised surplus payments charge (link)

You should complete Section 6 if the registered pension scheme has made any authorised surplus payments to a sponsoring employer in the quarter. Boxes 6.3 to 6.7 should be completed for each sponsoring employer that has received a payment.

6.1 Number of sponsoring employers

Enter the numbers of sponsoring employers that have received an authorised surplus payment in the quarter.

6.2 Tax at 35%

Enter the total amount of tax due at the rate of 35%.

6.3 Name of sponsoring employer

Enter the full name of the sponsoring employer.

6.4 Address

Enter the full postal address of the sponsoring employer in the correct format

6.5 Company registration number

If the sponsoring employer receiving the payment is a company or another person registered with Companies House, enter the company registration number. Otherwise, leave it blank.

6.6 Date of payment

Enter the date on which the payment to the sponsoring employer was made in the format dd/mm/yyyy.

6.7 Tax at 35%

Enter the amount of tax due at the rate of 35% in relation to this sponsoring employer.

6.8 Further payments

Enter yes if you have still to report details of sponsoring employers to whom authorised surplus payments have been made. Enter no if you have now completed details for all authorised surplus payments to sponsoring employers.

7. Lifetime allowance charge (link)

You should complete Section 7 if a lifetime allowance charge arose in the quarter in relation to a member of the registered pension scheme. Boxes 7.3 to 7.9 must be completed for each member who was subject to the lifetime allowance charge. Boxes 7.7 to 7.9 must be completed for each benefit crystallisation event, in relation to the scheme, for a single member that fell within the quarter.

7.1 Number of members

Enter the number of members in respect of whom a lifetime allowance charge arose in the quarter.

7.2 Total Tax

Enter the total amount of tax due.

7.3 Name of member

Enter the full name of the member subject to the lifetime allowance charge.

7.4 Address

Enter the full postal address of the member in the correct format.

7.5 National Insurance Number

Enter the member's National Insurance Number if known

7.6 Date of birth

Enter the member's date of birth in the format dd/mm/yyyy.

7.7 Date of benefit crystallisation event [link?]

Enter the date of the benefit crystallisation event in the format dd/mm/yyyy.

7.8 Tax at 25%

Enter the amount of tax due in respect of this member at the rate of 25%. Tax is due at 25% in respect of so much (if any) of the chargeable amount as constitutes the retained amount [link]

7.9 Tax at 55%

Enter the amount of tax due in respect of this member at the rate of 55%. Tax is due at 55% in respect of so much (if any) of the chargeable amount as constitutes the lump sum amount [link].

7.10 Further benefit crystallisation events

Enter yes if the member had more than one benefit crystallisation event, in relation to the scheme, in the quarter where a lifetime allowance charge arose and you have still to report details of an event. Enter no if you have completed all the details for this member for this quarter.

7.11 Further members

Enter yes if you have still to report details in respect of a member. Enter no if you have now provided details for all members.

8. De-registration charge

You should complete Section 8 if HMRC has withdrawn the registration of the pension scheme.

8.1 Total tax

Enter the tax due at the rate of 40% on the value of the funds held for the purpose of the scheme immediately before the date of de-registration.

8.2 Enter the date on which registration was withdrawn in the format dd/mm/yyyy.

9. Total tax due

If the total tax due shown by the system is correct, press the confirm button. If you wish to amend any of the details at this stage, use the edit button to return to the relevant section.

10. Insurance companies

Complete section 10 if you are an insurance company liable as a scheme administrator to a special lump sum death benefits charge.

10.1 Contract or policy name

Enter the name of the contract or policy.

10.2 Contract or policy number

This should be a unique number that distinguishes this contract or policy from any other contract or policy held by the same person or any other person.

10.3 Tax at 35%

Enter the total amount of tax due at the rate of 35%.

Declaration

Complete the declaration and enter the full name of the scheme administrator or insurance company who has authorised submission of this return.

Payment Reference Number

When the return has been successfully submitted, the system will provide you with a payment reference number. You should send your payment of the tax due to HMRC by an approved electronic method (link to "How to pay") quoting this reference number.

Tax is payable without assessment and is due 45 days after the end of the quarterly return period.

Supplementary Information

a. Scheme Administrator

A Scheme Administrator is the person who is, or persons who are, appointed in accordance with the rules of the pension scheme to be responsible for the discharge of the functions conferred or imposed on the scheme administrator of the pension scheme by and under Part 4 of Finance Act 2004.

A person can only be a scheme administrator if he has made the required declaration set out at section 270(3) of Finance Act 2004.

A scheme administrator cannot include a person who is not resident in either the UK or another state which is a member of the EU or a non-member EEA State (currently these are Iceland, Liechtenstein ~~and N~~ ~~~~

b. Amendments

If you become aware of an error ~~in a return you should~~ ~~~~ amended return to HMRC for the quarter concerned. Do not try to correct it by way of an adjustment in a return for a later quarter.

Error includes:

* something which ought to have been included in the return for that quarter has not been so included,
* something which ought not to have been included in the return for that quarter has been so included
* some other error has occurred in the return for that quarter.

c. Short Service Refund Lump Sum Charge

A short service refund lump sum is a refund of contributions paid following an election by the member made under Section 101AB(1)(b) Pensions Act 1993.

d. **Lump sum death benefits**

The special lump sum death benefits charge arises where

* a pension protection lump sum death benefit
* an annuity protection lump sum death benefit
* an unsecured pension fund lump sum death benefit

is paid by a registered pension scheme.

The tax charge becomes due and payable for the quarter in which the lump sum death benefit is paid rather than at the date of the deceased member's death.

Under the transitional provisions in Schedule 36, the tax charge does not apply to any pension protection lump sum death benefit, annuity protection lump sum death benefit or unsecured pension fund lump sum death benefit paid by virtue of sub-paragraphs (3) to (8), or in the circumstances set out in sub-paragraph 10(a), of paragraph 36 of that Schedule.

e. **Authorised surplus payments charge**

Certain schemes are exempt from the tax charge by virtue of the sponsoring and/or participating employer's tax status – see section 207(6) of Finance Act 2004. Examples include charities and other entities that are exempt from income and/or corporation tax such as Local Authorities. Where an authorised surplus payment is made to an employer that is exempt by virtue of section 207(6) the authorised surplus payments charge does not apply. These payments should therefore **not** be included in this return.

If the scheme commenced winding up before 19th March 1986 the authorised surplus payments charge does not apply irrespective of the employer's tax status

f. **Lifetime allowance charge**

Where any of the tax due under the lifetime allowance charge is to be met by the scheme rather than by the individual then the amount liable to the charge will include the scheme-funded tax payment

Data Protection

HMRC is a Data Controller under the Data Protection Act. We hold information for the purposes specified in our notification made to the Data Protection Commissioner, and may use this information for any of them.

We may get information about you from others, or we may give information to them. If we do, it will only be as the law permits to

- check accuracy of information
- prevent or detect crime
- protect public funds

We may check information we receive about you with what is already in our records. This can include information provided by you as well as others such as other government departments. We will not give information about you to anyone outside HMRC unless the law permits us to do so.

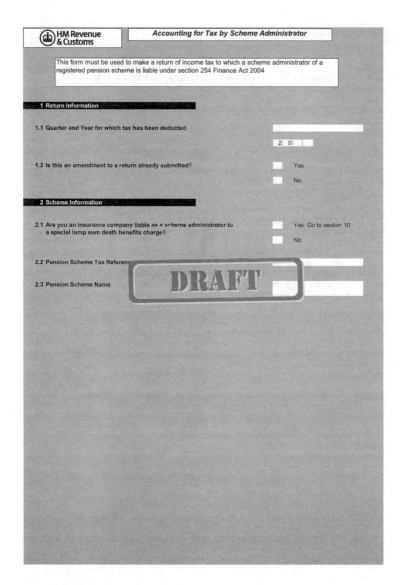

HM Revenue & Customs

Accounting for Tax by Scheme Administrator

This form must be used to make a return of income tax to which a scheme administrator of a registered pension scheme is liable under section 254 Finance Act 2004

1 Return Information

1.1 Quarter and Year for which tax has been deducted

2 0

1.2 Is this an amendment to a return already submitted?

☐ Yes

☐ No

2 Scheme Information

2.1 Are you an insurance company liable as a scheme administrator to a special lump sum death benefits charge?

☐ Yes. Go to section 10

☐ No

2.2 Pension Scheme Tax Reference

2.3 Pension Scheme Name

DRAFT

20051018 - AFT(v3.3).xls

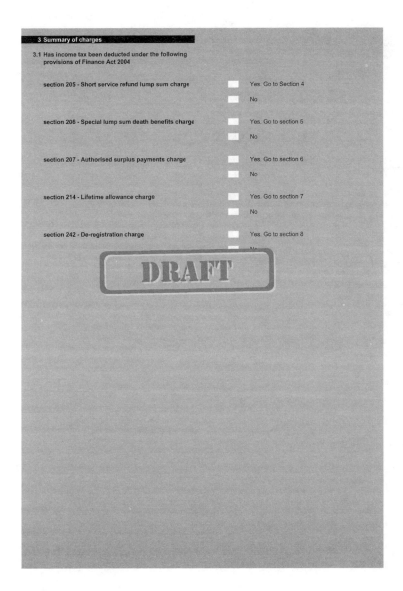

3 Summary of charges

3.1 Has income tax been deducted under the following
provisions of Finance Act 2004

section 205 - Short service refund lump sum charge   ☐ Yes. Go to Section 4
                                                           ☐ No

section 206 - Special lump sum death benefits charge   ☐ Yes. Go to section 5
                                                           ☐ No

section 207 - Authorised surplus payments charge   ☐ Yes. Go to section 6
                                                           ☐ No

section 214 - Lifetime allowance charge   ☐ Yes. Go to section 7
                                                           ☐ No

section 242 - De-registration charge   ☐ Yes. Go to section 8
                                                           ☐ No

20051018 - AFT(v3.3).xls

4 Short Service Refund Lump Sum Charge

4.1 Number of members who
received a short service refund lump sum in this quarter

4.2 Total amount of tax at the
rate of 20% due and payable

£

DRAFT

4.3 Total amount of tax at the
rate of 40% due and payable

£

20051018 - AFT(v3.3).xls

5 Special Lump Sum Death Benefits Charge

5.1 Number of deceased members
in respect of whom special lump sum death
benefits charges arose in this quarter

5.2 Total amount of tax at the rate
of 35% due and payable

£

DRAFT

20051018 - AFT(v3.3).xls

6 Authorised Surplus Payments Charge

6.1 Number of employers who received
an authorised surplus payment in the quarter

6.2 Amount of tax at the rate of 35%
due and payable

£

DRAFT

6.3 Employer name

6.4 Full registered address

Postcode
Country

6.5 Employer's Companies Registration
Number if appropriate

6.6 Date of the payment

/   /

6.7 Amount of tax at the rate of 35%
due and payable

£

6.8 Do you have further payments to report?

Yes.Go to 6.3

No

20051018 - AFT(v3.3).xls

7 Lifetime Allowance Charge

7.1 Number of members in the quarter who have been subject to a lifetime allowance charge(s)

7.2 Total amount of tax due and payable

£

7.3 Name

Title
Surname
First name

7.4 Address

DRAFT

Postcode
Country

7.5 National Insurance Number (NINO), if known

7.6 Date of birth

/ /

7.7 Date of the benefit crystallisation event

/ /

7.8 Amount of lifetime allowance charge at the rate of 25% due and payable

£

7.9 Amount of lifetime allowance charge at the rate of 55% due and payable

£

7.10 Does this member have another benefit crystallisation event to report?

Yes. Go to 7.7

No

7.11 Are there further members subject to the lifetime allowance charge?

Yes. Go to 7.3

No

20051018 - AFT(v3.3).xls

The latest forms

9 Total Tax Due

9.1 The total tax due on this return is

section 205 - Short service refund lump sum charge £ [ ] Edit

section 206 - Special lump sum death benefits charge £ [ ] Edit

section 207 - Authorised surplus payments charge £ [ ] Edit

section 214 - Lifetime allowance charge £ [ ] Edit

section 242-De-registration charge £ [ ] Edit

Total £ [ ]

9.2 Click to confirm the details are correct

[ ] Confirm. Go to declaration

DRAFT

10 Insurance companies

10.1 Contract or policy name

10.2 Contract or policy number

10.3 Amount of tax at the rate of 35% due and payable £ [ ]

Go to declaration

20051018 - AFT(v3.3).xls

411

11 Declaration

Scheme Administrator Declaration

I declare that

11.1 to the best of my knowledge and belief, the information given in this tax return is correct and complete

11.2 I understand that if I have made a false statement on this tax return, I may be liable to a penalty, and that false statements may also lead to prosecution.

Practitioner Declaration

I declare that

11.3 the content of this tax return has been approved by the scheme administrator named below

11.4 The Scheme Administrator named below has authorised me to submit this tax return

11.5 Full name of the scheme administrator if organisation

11.5.1 Full name of the scheme administrator if individual

Title
Surname
First name

DRAFT

11.6 Scheme administrator ID

11.7 Scheme administrator address

Postcode
Country

11.8 Scheme administrator email

11.9 Scheme administrator telephone number

20051018 - AFT(v3.3).xls

Registered pension scheme return

DRAFT

Registered Pension Scheme Return

Notes to help you complete this Return

General

These notes provide guidance on how to complete the Registered Pension Scheme Return. The notes are intended to help you complete the boxes on the form. They also include links to supplementary guidance, which you may need to read in order to understand more fully what information you have to provide. In particular, the links give you access to advice about the meaning of the legislative terms that are referred to in the form and the notes. However these links will not be available until the full guidance has been written and is placed on the Internet later this year.

How to complete this Return

If you are the Scheme Administrator [Link] of a tax registered pension scheme, and have been sent a notice under section 250 Finance Act 2004[Link] requiring you to make a return, you must do so by 31 January next following the end of the tax year for which a return is required. Otherwise you will be liable to a penalty of £100, and you could be liable to further penalties.

This guide has step by step instructions to help you as Scheme Administrator to fill in your return. You may arrange for a practitioner who has been authorised by you to complete and submit the return on your behalf if you wish

The notes are numbered to match the boxes in your return.

This return is issued by The Pension Scheme Service. Further technical guidance is available at our website at Link. Other offices of HMRC will not be able to advise you about this return.

Completing the Return

This return can only be submitted online. When you complete the form online you will only be presented with the questions you need to answer, which will be determined by the answers to earlier questions. For example, if you answer No to a question you will not be shown the options you would have seen if you had answered Yes.

Q1 Has this return been completed for a period other than the year ending 5 April?

If audited accounts have been prepared for the scheme that cover accounting periods ending in the tax year to which the return notice relates, the period for which you should make the return is all of the accounting periods ending in the tax year shown on the notice which you were sent requiring you to make a return.

If audited accounts have not been prepared, or if none cover accounting periods ending in the tax year to which the return notice relates, you should make a return for the tax year ended 5 April shown on the notice which you were sent requiring you to make a return.

1

DRAFT

Audited accounts for this purpose means accounts of the scheme audited by a
suitably qualified independent person or firm recognised as such under the
Companies Act. But accounts audited by any of the following people will not count
as audited accounts for the purpose of establishing the period of the pension scheme
return-
- a member of the scheme
- an employee of the Scheme Administrator
- a sponsoring employer of the scheme

1.1   If the return is to be made for accounting periods enter here the number of
       periods covered.
1.2   Enter here the start date of the first period covered and the end date of the
       last period covered.

Q2 Is this an Occupational Pension Scheme ?

An occupational pension scheme is a pension scheme established by an employer or
employers and capable of providing pension benefits for or in respect of employees.

**Q3 Was the aggregate of payments to and from the scheme greater than
£100,000 for the period covered by this return?**

If the aggregate amount is less than £100,000 enter the amount in the box only. If
the aggregate is greater then complete the individual boxes.
The aggregate of payments to and from the scheme is the total of-
3.1   Pension contributions received from all sources.
3.2   Transfer payments received from other pension schemes on behalf of any
scheme member.
3.3   Transfer payments made to other schemes on behalf any scheme member.
3.4   Lump sum benefit payments and lump sum death benefit payments.
3.5   Payments to purchase annuities, or for a contract from an insurance company
to provide a scheme pension.
3.6   Capital sums borrowed.
3.7   Other payments to or from the pension scheme, excluding payments of
       pension.

**Q4 At the end date of the period of the return did the scheme own net assets
with a value before pension liabilities greater than £400,000 ?**

If you are completing the return for accounting periods, enter the total based on the
asset values adopted in the accounts.
Otherwise, use the asset values adopted in the latest actuarial valuation of scheme
assets prior to the end of the tax year of the return.

If audited accounts were not prepared, and no actuarial valuation was obtained, enter
the market value of scheme assets at the end of the tax year of the return.

2

414

DRAFT

Q5 At any time from xx/xx/xxxx to xx/xx/xxxx, did the scheme own assets that it had acquired from or subsequently sold to-

You must answer yes if your scheme owned assets at any time during the return period, which it had acquired at any time within or prior to the return period from any of the persons specified in a, b, c or d.
And you must answer yes if your scheme sold any assets to the persons specified during the period of the return.

5 a   a sponsoring employer or any person connected with that employer.

Where the scheme is an occupational pension scheme, a sponsoring employer is the employer or employers who established the scheme for the purpose of providing benefits for some or all of their employees in respect to their employment with the employer or employers. It also includes any other employer whose employees are having benefits provided under the scheme in respect of their employment with that employer.

A scheme will not have a sponsoring employer if the scheme is not an occupational pension scheme

If the sponsoring employer is a company, a person is connected to that employer if that person has control of the company or if that person, together with another person or persons connected to him or her, has control of the company.
If the sponsoring employer is an individual or a partnership, a person is connected to the employer if they are connected to that individual or any one or more partner(s).

For the purpose of al of questions 5 a, b, c and d, person includes an individual, a company, a partnership, and a trustee of a settlement, and "connected with" has the same meaning as in Section 839 Income and Corporation Taxes Act 1988.

5 b   a person who is a director of or a person who is connected to a director of a close company that is also a sponsoring employer?

The meaning of "director" is defined at Section 417(5) Taxes Act 1988 [Link]. A close company is defined at Section 414, Income & Corporation Taxes Act 1988[Link], and is broadly a company whose assets are controlled by five or fewer participators..

5 c   a person who is either a sole owner or partner or a person connected with the sole owner or partner of a business which is a sponsoring employer.

5 d   a member or person connected with a member.

A member includes active members [Link], deferred members[Link], pensioner members[Link] or pension credit members[Link]of your scheme.

5.1   Connected party transaction means any of the transactions referred to in question 5.

A member's arrangement is those assets of a scheme, or any apportionment of assets, allocated to or designated to or earmarked for the provision of benefits for that member. See separate notes section on supplementary questions.

3

DRAFT

Q6 At any time from xx/xx/xxxx, did the scheme own any shares in the sponsoring employer if it is a company?

Where the scheme is an occupational pension scheme, a sponsoring employer is the employer or employers who established the scheme for the purpose of providing benefits for some or all of their employees in respect to their employment with the employer or employers. It also includes any other employer whose employees are having benefits provided under the scheme in respect of their employment with that employer.

A scheme will not have a sponsor~~ing~~ employer in relation to it if the scheme is not an occupational pension scheme.

6.2 If you are completing the return for accounting periods, enter the cost or market value of the shares adopted in the accounts.

Otherwise, use the cost or market value of the shares adopted in the latest actuarial valuation of scheme assets prior to the end of the tax year of the return.

If audited accounts were not prepared, and no actuarial valuation was obtained, enter the market value of the shares at the end of the tax year of the return or at the date of disposal if earlier.

Q7 Did the scheme own any land or interest in land , from xx/xx/xxxx to xx/xx/xxxx , that it had acquired from or subsequently sold to a connected party?

A connected party means any person or company as specified at Question 5 a, b, c and d.

Land includes houses and buildings of any kind.

7.1 If you are completing the return for accounting periods, enter the cost or market value of the land or interest in land adopted in the accounts.

Otherwise, use the cost or market value of the land or interest in land adopted in the latest actuarial valuation of scheme assets prior to the end of the tax year of the return.

If audited accounts were not prepared, and no actuarial valuation was obtained, enter the market value of the land or interest in land at the end of the tax year of the return.

7.2 A premium is a lump sum paid in connection with the granting of a lease or tenancy.

Q 8 At any time from xxxx to xxxxx were any amounts outstanding from loans made to connected parties.

A connected party means any person or company as specified at Question 5 a, b, c and d.

Amounts outstanding means capital sums owing under the terms of the loan, together with any interest or other charges due but remaining unpaid.

4

416

DRAFT

Q9 At any time from xx/xx/xxxx, did the scheme own any assets acquired from a connected party, other than shares, land, interest in land or loans ?

Party means any person or other body.
A party is connected to the scheme if it is within any of the categories defined in question 5.

You do not need to include here details of any assets used for normal administrative purposes of the pension scheme, such as office premises and equipment or motor vehicles used by administrative staff employed by the scheme.

9.1 If you are completing the return for accounting periods, enter the cost or market value of the assets adopted in the accounts.

Otherwise, use the cost or market value of the assets adopted in the latest actuarial valuation of scheme assets prior to the end of the tax year of the return.

If audited accounts were not prepared, and no actuarial valuation was obtained, enter the market value of the assets at the end of the tax year of the return.

9.3 Motor vehicles includes all road vehicles and tractors, but not construction plant such as mechanical excavators. Other forms of transport includes all rail rolling stock, air and water craft.
Plant and machinery includes all industrial machinery and construction plant, and agricultural machinery except tractors.
Works of art includes paintings, sculptures, ceramics, ancient artefacts and antique furniture.
Fixtures and fittings includes other internal fittings which are not plant and are not works of art.
Other- include here any other relevant assets not mentioned above.

9.6 Motor vehicles includes all road vehicles and tractors, but not construction plant such as mechanical excavators. Other forms of transport includes all rail rolling stock, air and water craft.
Plant and machinery includes all industrial machinery and construction plant, and agricultural machinery except tractors.
Works of art includes paintings, sculptures, ceramics, ancient artefacts and antique furniture.
Fixtures and fittings includes other internal fittings which are not plant and are not works of art.
Other- include here any other relevant assets not mentioned above.

Q10 At any time from xx/xx/xxxx to xx/xx/xxxx, was there any cash, cash on deposit or current account balances held by the scheme?

If you are completing the return for accounting periods you can show adjusted opening and closing balances per the scheme accounts.

Q 11. At any time from xx/xx/xxxx to xx/xx/xxxx, did the scheme own any assets acquired at arms length?

Assets acquired at arm's length means assets which were not acquired from any of the persons or companies specified at Question 5 a, b, c and d.

5

DRAFT

You do not need to include here details of any assets used for normal administrative purposes of the pension scheme, such as office premises and equipment or motor vehicles used by administrative staff employed by the scheme.

11.1 If you are completing the return for accounting periods, enter the cost or market value of the land or interest in land adopted in the accounts.

Otherwise, use the cost or market value of the land or interest in land adopted in the latest actuarial valuation of scheme assets prior to the end of the tax year of the return.

If audited accounts were not prepared, and no actuarial valuation was obtained, enter the market value of the land or interest in land at the end of the tax year of the return.

11.3 Motor vehicles includes all road vehicles and tractors, but not construction plant such as mechanical excavators. Other forms of transport includes all rail rolling stock, air and water craft.
Plant and machinery includes all industrial machinery and construction plant, and agricultural machinery except tractors.
Works of art includes paintings, sculptures, ceramics, ancient artefacts and antique furniture.
Fixtures and fittings includes other internal fittings which are not plant and are not works of art.
Other- include here any other relevant assets not mentioned above.

11.6 Motor vehicles includes all road vehicles and tractors, but not construction plant such as mechanical excavators. Other forms of transport includes all rail rolling stock, air and water craft.
Plant and machinery includes all industrial machinery and construction plant, and agricultural machinery except tractors.
Works of art includes paintings, sculptures, ceramics, ancient artefacts and antique furniture.
Fixtures and fittings includes other internal fittings which are not plant and are not works of art.
Other- include here any other relevant assets not mentioned above.

Declaration

You must tick both administrator declaration boxes to complete the declaration.
Or if the practitioner has completed the return then the practitioner must tick both practitioner declaration boxes to complete the declaration.

Supplementary Questions

Complete a set of supplementary pages for each arrangement with "connected party transactions- see 5.1.
Where a member has more than one arrangement within your scheme, complete one set of supplementary pages only for that member, answering the questions in respect of all of that member's arrangements.

Question B

See question 6 guidance.

6

DRAFT

A person is connected to an individual if that person is the husband or wife or relative of that individual.
A person is connected to an individual if that person is the wife or husband of a relative of that individual.
A person is connected to an individual if that person is the wife or husband of a relative of that individual's husband or wife.
A relative means brother, sister, ancestor or lineal descendant.

Question C

See question 7 guidance.

Question D

See question 9 guidance.

Data Protection

HMRC (HM Revenue & Customs) is a Data Controller under the Data Protection Act. We hold information for the purposes specified in our notification made to the Data Protection Commissioner, and may use this information for any of them.

We may get information about you from others, or we may give information to them. If we do, it will only be as the law permits to

- Check accuracy of information
- Prevent or detect crime
- Protect public funds

We may check information we receive about you with what is already in our records. This can include information provided by you as well as others such as other government departments. We will not give information about you to anyone outside HMRC unless the law permits us to do so.

7

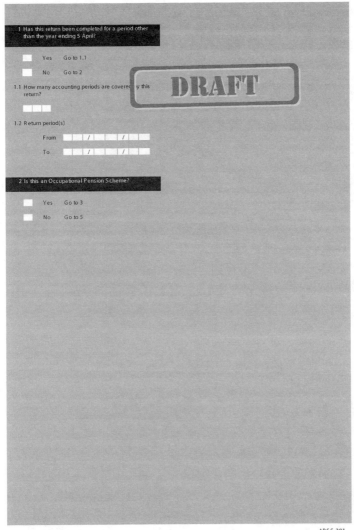

1 Has this return been completed for a period other than the year ending 5 April?

☐ Yes Go to 1.1

☐ No Go to 2

1.1 How many accounting periods are covered by this return?

☐☐☐

1.2 Return period(s)

From ☐☐☐/☐☐/☐☐☐

To ☐☐☐/☐☐/☐☐☐

2 Is this an Occupational Pension Scheme?

☐ Yes Go to 3

☐ No Go to 5

DRAFT

APSS 301

421

3 From xx/xx/xxxx, was the aggregate of payments to and from the scheme greater than £100,000?

☐   Yes   Go to 3.1

☐   No

Amount   £ [   ]

          Go to 4

3.1 Total amount of the pension contributions received from xx/xx/xxxx to xx/xx/xxxx

£ [   ]

DRAFT

3.2 Total amount of transfer-in payments from xx/xx/xxxx to xx/xx/xxxx

£ [   ]

3.3 Total amount of transfer-out payments from xx/xx/xxxx to xx/xx/xxxx

£ [   ]

3.4 Total amount paid out in lump sums and lump sum death benefits from xx/xx/xxxx to xx/xx/xxxx

£ [   ]

3.5 Total amount paid out to purchase life time annuities and scheme pensions from an insurance company from xx/xx/xxxx to xx/xx/xxxx

£ [   ]

3.6 Total amount borrowed from xx/xx/xxxx to xx/xx/xxxx

£ [   ]

3.7 Other (brief description and amount)

[   ]

£ [   ]

4 At the end date of the period of the return did the scheme own net assets with a value before pension liabilities greater than £400,000 ?

☐   Yes   Go to 5

☐   No

Amount   £ ☐☐☐☐☐☐☐☐☐☐☐☐

      Go to 5

DRAFT

5 At any time from xx/xx/xxxx to xx/xx/xxxx, did the scheme own assets that it had acquired from or subsequently sold to

a.   a sponsoring employer or any person connected with that employer?

   or

b.   a person who is a director of or a person who is connected to a director of a close company that is also a sponsoring employer?

   or

c.   a person who is either a sole owner or partner or a person connected with the sole owner or partner of a business which is a sponsoring employer?

   or

d.   a member or person connected with a member?

☐   Yes   If yes answered at 2, go to 6. If no answered at 2 go to 5.1

☐   No   If yes answered at 2 and no   at 3 and 4, go to declaration
                If yes answered at 2 and yes at 3 and 4, go to 10
                If no answered at 2, go to declaration

5.1 How many members' arrangements included connected party transactions?

☐☐☐☐☐   (only asked for non OPSs)

go to supplementary page

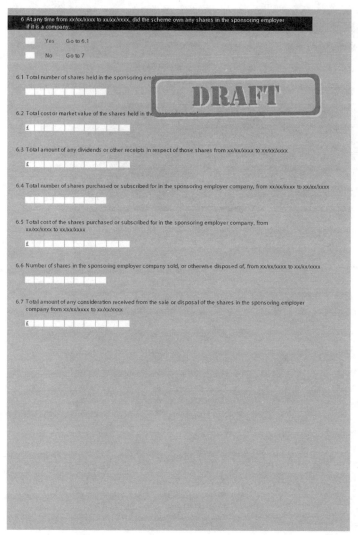

6 At any time from xx/xx/xxxx to xx/xx/xxxx, did the scheme own any shares in the sponsoring employer if it is a company:

☐ Yes Go to 6.1

☐ No Go to 7

6.1 Total number of shares held in the sponsoring employer

6.2 Total cost or market value of the shares held in the sponsoring employer

£

6.3 Total amount of any dividends or other receipts in respect of those shares from xx/xx/xxxx to xx/xx/xxxx

£

6.4 Total number of shares purchased or subscribed for in the sponsoring employer company, from xx/xx/xxxx to xx/xx/xxxx

6.5 Total cost of the shares purchased or subscribed for in the sponsoring employer company, from xx/xx/xxxx to xx/xx/xxxx

£

6.6 Number of shares in the sponsoring employer company sold, or otherwise disposed of, from xx/xx/xxxx to xx/xx/xxxx

6.7 Total amount of any consideration received from the sale or disposal of the shares in the sponsoring employer company from xx/xx/xxxx to xx/xx/xxxx

£

APSS 301

424

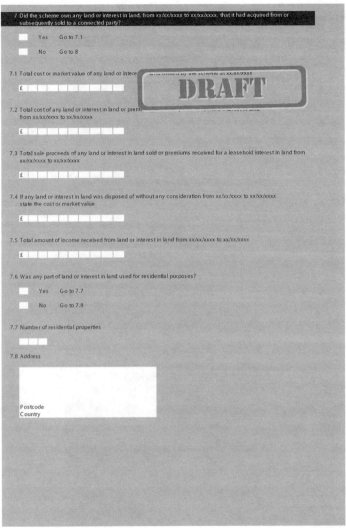

7 Did the scheme own any land or interest in land, from xx/xx/xxxx to xx/xx/xxxx, that it had acquired from or subsequently sold to a connected party?

- [ ] Yes   Go to 7.1
- [ ] No   Go to 8

7.1 Total cost or market value of any land or interest ~~and owned by the scheme at xx/xx/xxxx~~

£ [ ][ ][ ][ ][ ][ ][ ][ ][ ][ ][ ]

7.2 Total cost of any land or interest in land or prem~~...~~ from xx/xx/xxxx to xx/xx/xxxx

£ [ ][ ][ ][ ][ ][ ][ ][ ][ ][ ][ ]

7.3 Total sale proceeds of any land or interest in land sold or premiums received for a leasehold interest in land from xx/xx/xxxx to xx/xx/xxxx

£ [ ][ ][ ][ ][ ][ ][ ][ ][ ][ ][ ]

7.4 If any land or interest in land was disposed of without any consideration from xx/xx/xxxx to xx/xx/xxxx state the cost or market value

£ [ ][ ][ ][ ][ ][ ][ ][ ][ ][ ][ ]

7.5 Total amount of income received from land or interest in land from xx/xx/xxxx to xx/xx/xxxx

£ [ ][ ][ ][ ][ ][ ][ ][ ][ ][ ][ ]

7.6 Was any part of land or interest in land used for residential purposes?

- [ ] Yes   Go to 7.7
- [ ] No   Go to 7.8

7.7 Number of residential properties

[ ][ ][ ]

7.8 Address

```



Postcode
Country
```

APSS 301

8 At any time from xx/xx/xxxx to xx/xx/xxxx, were any amounts outstanding from loans made to connected parties?

☐ Yes Go to 8.1

☐ No Go to 9

DRAFT

8.1 Total amount outstanding at xx/xx/xxxx

£ ☐☐☐☐☐☐☐☐☐☐☐

8.2 Total additional amount of any loans made from xx/xx/xxxx to xx/xx/xxxx

£ ☐☐☐☐☐☐☐☐☐☐☐

8.3 Total amount of any loans repaid from xx/xx/xxxx to xx/xx/xxxx

£ ☐☐☐☐☐☐☐☐☐☐☐

8.4 Total amount of interest received from xx/xx/xxxx to xx/xx/xxxx

£ ☐☐☐☐☐☐☐☐☐☐☐

APSS 301

9 At any time from xx/xx/xxxx to xx/xx/xxxx, did the scheme own any assets acquired from a connected party, other than shares, land, interest in land or loans?

☐ Yes Go to 9.1

☐ No Go to 10

9.1 Total cost or market value of any such assets at xx/xx/xxxx

£ ☐☐☐☐☐☐☐☐☐☐☐

9.2 Did the scheme acquire any such assets from a connected party from xx/xx/xxxx to xx/xxxx?

☐ Yes Go to 9.3

☐ No Go to 9.5

9.3 Nature of any such assets acquired from xx/xx/xxxx to xx/xx/xxxx

☐ Motor Vehicles

☐ Other forms of transport

☐ Plant & machinery

☐ Works of art

☐ Fixtures and fittings

☐ Other (brief description)

9.4 Total cost of any such assets acquired from a connected party from xx/xx/xxxx to xx/xx/xxxx

£ ☐☐☐☐☐☐☐☐☐☐☐

9.5 Did you dispose of any such assets from xx/xx/xxxx to xx/xx/xxxx acquired from a connected party

☐ Yes Go to 9.6

☐ No Go to 9.8

9.6 Nature of any such assets disposed of from xx/xx/xxxx to xx/xx/xxxx

☐ Motor Vehicles

☐ Other forms of transport

☐ Plant & machinery

☐ Works of art

☐ Fixtures and fittings

☐ Other (brief description)

DRAFT

9.7 Total sale proceeds from the disposal of any such assets from xx/xx/xxxx to xx/xx/xxxx

£ ☐☐☐☐☐☐☐☐☐☐☐

9.8 Total amount of any income received from such assets from xx/xx/xxxx to xx/xx/xxxx
If this was none, state "£0"

£ ☐☐☐☐☐☐☐☐☐☐☐

APSS 301

427

10 At any time from xx/xx/xxxx to xx/xx/xxxx, was there any cash, cash on deposit or current account balances held by the scheme?

☐ Yes Go to 10.1

☐ No Go to 11

10.1 Total amount of all cash and bank balances at xx/xx

£ ☐☐☐☐☐☐☐☐☐☐☐

DRAFT

10.2 Total amount of all cash and bank balances at xx/xx/x

£ ☐☐☐☐☐☐☐☐☐☐☐

10.3 Total amount of interest credited to these accounts from xx/xx/xxxx to xx/xx/xxxx

£ ☐☐☐☐☐☐☐☐☐☐☐

APSS 301

428

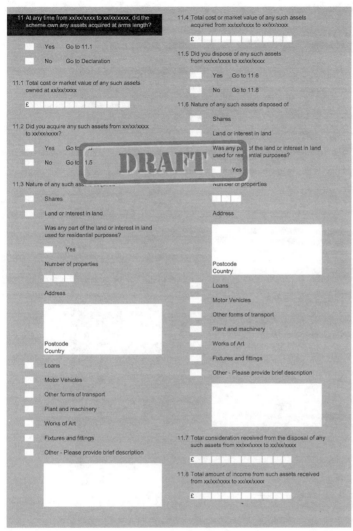

11 At any time from xx/xx/xxxx to xx/xx/xxxx, did the scheme own any assets acquired at arms length?

☐ Yes Go to 11.1

☐ No Go to Declaration

11.1 Total cost or market value of any such assets owned at xx/xx/xxxx

£ ☐☐☐☐☐☐☐☐☐☐

11.2 Did you acquire any such assets from xx/xx/xxxx to xx/xx/xxxx?

☐ Yes Go to 11.3

☐ No Go to 11.5

11.3 Nature of any such assets acquired

☐ Shares

☐ Land or interest in land

Was any part of the land or interest in land used for residential purposes?

☐ Yes

Number of properties

☐☐☐☐

Address

☐

Postcode
Country

☐ Loans

☐ Motor Vehicles

☐ Other forms of transport

☐ Plant and machinery

☐ Works of Art

☐ Fixtures and fittings

☐ Other - Please provide brief description

☐

11.4 Total cost or market value of any such assets acquired from xx/xx/xxxx to xx/xx/xxxx

£ ☐☐☐☐☐☐☐☐☐☐

11.5 Did you dispose of any such assets from xx/xx/xxxx to xx/xx/xxxx

☐ Yes Go to 11.6

☐ No Go to 11.8

11.6 Nature of any such assets disposed of

☐ Shares

☐ Land or interest in land

Was any part of the land or interest in land used for residential purposes?

☐ Yes

Number of properties

☐☐☐☐

Address

☐

Postcode
Country

☐ Loans

☐ Motor Vehicles

☐ Other forms of transport

☐ Plant and machinery

☐ Works of Art

☐ Fixtures and fittings

☐ Other - Please provide brief description

☐

11.7 Total consideration received from the disposal of any such assets from xx/xx/xxxx to xx/xx/xxxx

£ ☐☐☐☐☐☐☐☐☐☐

11.8 Total amount of income from such assets received from xx/xx/xxxx to xx/xx/xxxx

£ ☐☐☐☐☐☐☐☐☐☐

DRAFT

APSS 301

429

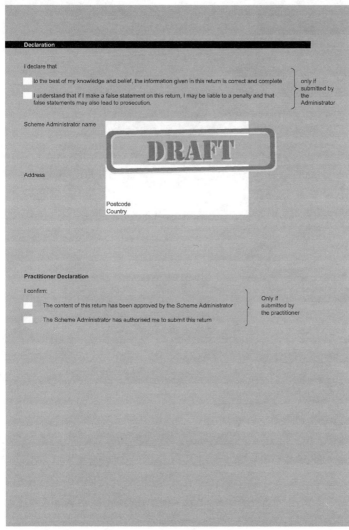

Declaration

I declare that

☐ to the best of my knowledge and belief, the information given in this return is correct and complete

☐ I understand that if I make a false statement on this return, I may be liable to a penalty and that false statements may also lead to prosecution.

⎫
⎬ only if
⎭ submitted by
the
Administrator

Scheme Administrator name

DRAFT

Address

Postcode
Country

Practitioner Declaration

I confirm:

☐ The content of this return has been approved by the Scheme Administrator

☐ The Scheme Administrator has authorised me to submit this return

⎫
⎬ Only if
⎭ submitted by
the practitioner

APSS 301

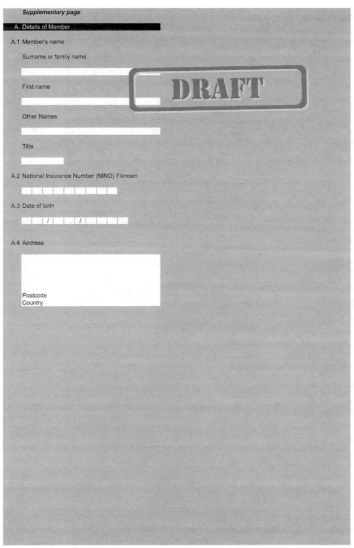

Supplementary page

A. Details of Member

A.1 Member's name

Surname or family name

First name

DRAFT

Other Names

Title

A.2 National Insurance Number (NINO) if known

A.3 Date of birth

A.4 Address

Postcode
Country

APSS 301a

431

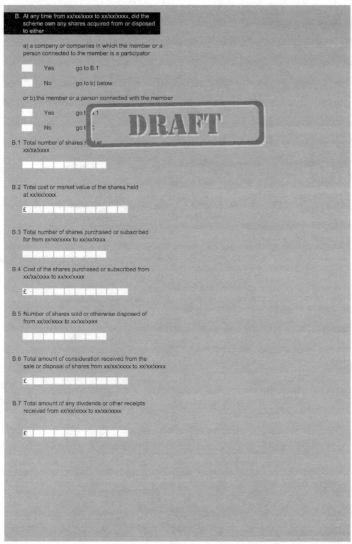

B. At any time from xx/xx/xxxx to xx/xx/xxxx, did the scheme own any shares acquired from or disposed to either

a) a company or companies in which the member or a person connected to the member is a participator

☐ Yes   go to B.1

☐ No   go to b) below

or b) the member or a person connected with the member

☐ Yes   go to B.1

☐ No   go to C

B.1 Total number of shares held at xx/xx/xxxx

B.2 Total cost or market value of the shares held at xx/xx/xxxx

£

B.3 Total number of shares purchased or subscribed for from xx/xx/xxxx to xx/xx/xxxx

B.4 Cost of the shares purchased or subscribed from xx/xx/xxxx to xx/xx/xxxx

£

B.5 Number of shares sold or otherwise disposed of from xx/xx/xxxx to xx/xx/xxxx

B.6 Total amount of consideration received from the sale or disposal of shares from xx/xx/xxxx to xx/xx/xxxx

£

B.7 Total amount of any dividends or other receipts received from xx/xx/xxxx to xx/xx/xxxx

£

APSS 301a

432

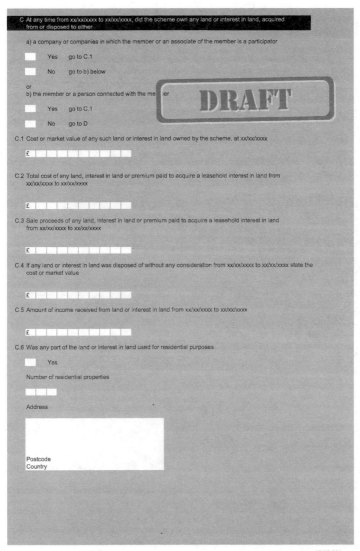

C At any time from xx/xx/xxxx to xx/xx/xxxx, did the scheme own any land or interest in land, acquired from or disposed to either

a) a company or companies in which the member or an associate of the member is a participator

☐ Yes go to C.1

☐ No go to b) below

or
b) the member or a person connected with the member

☐ Yes go to C.1

☐ No go to D

C.1 Cost or market value of any such land or interest in land owned by the scheme, at xx/xx/xxxx

£ ☐☐☐☐☐☐☐☐☐☐☐

C.2 Total cost of any land, interest in land or premium paid to acquire a leasehold interest in land from xx/xx/xxxx to xx/xx/xxxx

£ ☐☐☐☐☐☐☐☐☐☐☐

C.3 Sale proceeds of any land, interest in land or premium paid to acquire a leasehold interest in land from xx/xx/xxxx to xx/xx/xxxx

£ ☐☐☐☐☐☐☐☐☐☐☐

C.4 If any land or interest in land was disposed of without any consideration from xx/xx/xxxx to xx/xx/xxxx state the cost or market value

£ ☐☐☐☐☐☐☐☐☐☐☐

C.5 Amount of income received from land or interest in land from xx/xx/xxxx to xx/xx/xxxx

£ ☐☐☐☐☐☐☐☐☐☐☐

C.6 Was any part of the land or interest in land used for residential purposes

☐ Yes

Number of residential properties

☐☐☐

Address

Postcode
Country

APSS 301a

433

D At any time from xx/xx/xxxx to xx/xx/xxxx, did the scheme own any assets other than shares, land, interest in land or loans acquired from or sold to

a) a company or companies in which the member or a person connected with a member is a participator

☐   Yes   go to D.1

☐   No   go to b) below

b) the member or a person connected with the member

☐   Yes   go to D.1

☐   No   go to declaration

D.1 Total cost or market value of any such assets at the xx/xx/xxxx

£ ☐☐☐☐☐☐☐☐☐☐☐

D.2 Did you acquire any such assets from xx/xx/xxxx to xx/xx/xxxx

☐   Yes   go to D.3

☐   No   go to D.5

D.3 Nature of any such assets acquired from xx/xx/xxxx to xx/xx/xxxx

☐   Motor Vehicles

☐   Other forms of transport

☐   Plant & machinery

☐   Works of art

☐   Fixtures and fittings

☐   Other (brief description)

D.4 Total cost of any such assets acquired from xx/xx/xxxx to xx/xx/xxxx

£ ☐☐☐☐☐☐☐☐☐☐☐

D.5 Did you dispose of any such assets from xx/xx/xxxx to xx/xx/xxxx

☐   Yes   go to D.6

☐   No   go to declaration

D.6 Nature of any such assets purchased from xx/xx/xxxx to xx/xx/xxxx

☐   Motor Vehicles

☐   Other forms of transport

☐   Plant & machinery

☐   Works of art

☐   Fixtures and fittings

☐   Other (brief description)

D.7 Total sale, or other disposal, proceeds of any assets such assets from xx/xx/xxxx to xx/xx/xxxx

£ ☐☐☐☐☐☐☐☐☐☐☐

D.8 Total amount of any income received from xx/xx/xxxx to xx/xx/xxxx
If this was none please state "£0"

£ ☐☐☐☐☐☐☐☐☐☐☐

DRAFT

APSS 301a

434

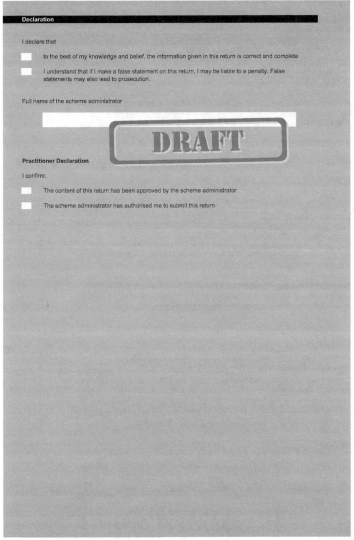

Declaration

I declare that

☐ to the best of my knowledge and belief, the information given in this return is correct and complete

☐ I understand that if I make a false statement on this return, I may be liable to a penalty. False statements may also lead to prosecution.

Full name of the scheme administrator

Practitioner Declaration

I confirm:

☐ The content of this return has been approved by the scheme administrator

☐ The scheme administrator has authorised me to submit this return

APSS 301a

Protection of existing rights

Protection of Existing Rights

Notes to help you complete the notification to HMRC

General

These notes provide guidance on how to notify us of an enhancement to your lifetime allowance. Transitional protection allows the pension rights you built up before 6 April 2006 to come into payment from 6 April 2006 where the amount of the payment would otherwise trigger an additional tax charge under the rules of the new pension system.

Transitional protection covers pension rights held in tax approved occupational pension schemes, personal pension schemes, retirement annuity contracts and deferred annuity contracts.

If you have pension rights accrued before 6 April 2006 you will be able to notify protection from the lifetime allowance charge when those rights come into payment after 6 April 2006. You will also be able to protect your lump sum rights where those rights exceed £375,000 on 5 April 2006.

Transitional protection is available in two forms, enhanced protection and primary protection.

These notes are intended to help you complete the boxes on the notification form. Supplementary guidance can be found in the Registered Pension Schemes Manual (RPSM) which is available on our website at www.hmrc.gov.uk.

How to notify HMRC

You must notify HMRC of your intention to rely on transitional protection by completing this form and sending it to HMRC, Audit & Pension Scheme Services, Yorke House, Castle Meadow Road, Nottingham, NG2 1BG. We must receive this form on or before the 5 April 2009.

You must retain all documents relating to the information given in the notification for a period of six years from the date you send your notification to HMRC.

Completing the Form

You must complete all of the boxes in the relevant Part(s) of the form that apply to you. Please note that if you do not do that or if you do not sign the form it will be returned to you as incomplete. Use ticks (√) where indicated.

1

Part 1 - Your Details

Please complete your details

1.1 Surname or family name

First name

All other names in full

Title by which known, for example, Mr, Mrs, Miss, Ms,

1.2 National Insurance Number (if known)

1.3 Unique Taxpayer Reference (UTR)

This is Self Assessment (SA) reference number (also called the Unique Taxpayer Reference (UTR)) allocated to the individual for use for Self Assessment.

1.4 Date of birth

1.5 Address

This should be your personal address. This will be the address to which HMRC will send the certificate regarding your transitional protection.

1.6 Is this an amendment to an existing notification?

Please tick the "yes" box if you are amending information that you submitted in an earlier notification. You must fill in all of the form that applies to your type of notification, not just the part(s) that you wish to amend. If an earlier notification became incorrect as a consequence of a subsequent action or decision, for example, you lose or voluntarily give up enhanced protection, you should read the guidance on correcting earlier notifications within the Registered Pension Schemes Manual.

If you tick the "yes" box, you must enter the certificate number that was shown on the certificate issued to you in response to the earlier notification.

Please tick the "no" box if you have not sent HMRC an earlier notification.

Part 2 Type of protection being applied for

Indicate by ticking the appropriate box(s) the form of transitional protection you intend to rely on.

2.1 Enhanced Protection

If you have pension rights that have not come into payment (uncrystallised) at 5 April 2006, you can claim protection from the lifetime allowance charge when those rights come into payment (crystallise) after 5 April 2006.

Whilst you retain enhanced protection there will be no liability to the lifetime allowance charge.

2

To notify enhanced protection:

- You must not have been an 'active' member of a registered pension scheme at any time after 5 April 2006 (see note 3.1).

- The value of your uncrystallised pension rights on 5 April 2006 must not be excessive.

- Any such excess rights must be surrendered before you can notify enhanced protection.

Refer to RPSM03104000 for further guidance on Enhanced Protection.

2.2 Primary Protection

If you have pension rights valued at more than £1.5 million on 5 April 2006 you can notify protection from the lifetime allowance charge when those rights crystallise after 5 April 2006.

Under primary protection you will have a personal lifetime allowance which is greater than the standard lifetime allowance . This is achieved by giving you an enhancement factor that will be applied to the current standard lifetime allowance at the date your benefits are taken. The lifetime allowance charge will apply only to benefits paid after your personal lifetime allowance has been used up.

Refer to RPSM03102000 for further guidance on Primary Protection.

Applying for both forms of transitional protection

If the value of your pension rights at 5 April 2006 exceeds £1.5million you may notify both forms of transitional protection. This can be done on the one form or on separate occasions. However all notifications must be made to HMRC by 5 April 2009. Where both forms of protection are notified at the same time, enhanced protection will take precedence and your protection will operate on that basis until enhanced protection is lost or you voluntarily give it up.. When your enhanced protection ceases your transitional protection will revert to primary protection.

Part 3 Enhanced Protection

DRAFT

Answer all questions in this part if you are applying for enhanced protection.

3.1. Indicate by ticking the appropriate box whether you have been an "active" member of a pension scheme at any time after 5 April 2006.

You are considered to be an 'active' member of a registered pension scheme when:-

- Relevant benefit accrual occurs under any of your arrangements in a registered pension scheme. Relevant benefit accrual occurs in different ways depending on whether the arrangement under which your benefits are being provided is a money purchase arrangement or a defined benefit or cash balance arrangement.

- A transfer is made from any of your arrangements in a registered pension scheme and that transfer is not a "permitted transfer".

3

- You set up a new arrangement under a registered pension scheme otherwise than to receive a "permitted transfer".

If you have been an "active" member of a registered pension scheme after 5 April 2006 you are not eligible to notify enhanced protection. Do not complete this form unless you are notifying HMRC of an intention to rely on primary protection.

Refer to the Registered Pension Schemes Manual at www.hmrc.go.uk for further guidance on 'relevant benefit accrual' (see RPSM03104080), 'money purchase arrangements' (see RPSM03104510), 'defined benefit or cash balance arrangements' (see RPSM03104520) and 'permitted transfers' (see RPSM03104090).

3.2. Indicate by ticking the appropriate box whether on 5 April 2006 you had pension rights that have not yet come into payment in a scheme wholly or partly funded by an employer.

A pension right that has not yet come into payment (uncrystallised) is where on 5 April 2006 you had not become entitled to the present payment of benefits in respect of those rights. Where income withdrawal/drawdown under a personal pension scheme or an occupational pension scheme or deferred annuity contract has begun the rights have crystallised. Refer

Pension schemes funded or partly funded by

  i.   retirement benefit schemes approved under Chapter 1 Part IV ICTA 1988.
  ii. schemes formerly approved under section 208 ICTA 1970.
  iii. relevant statutory schemes (as defined in section 611 ICTA 1988).
  iv. deferred annuity contracts entered into in relation to i. to iii. inclusive.

  For the purposes of this question pension rights held in a group personal pension schemes are not to be included as schemes funded or partly funded by an employer.

3.3. Indicate whether the value of your pension rights that had not come into payment was within the maximum permitted in pension schemes funded wholly or partly by an employer.

Where you have uncrystallised pension rights in a scheme that is funded or partly funded by an employer (see note 3.2), the value of those pension rights must be tested against the maximum permitted pension (MPP).

Before 6 April 2006 there were limits on the benefits that could be provided by an approved occupational pension scheme. This limit is defined in paragraph 9 Schedule 36 FA 2004 as the MPP . Where the value of your pension rights that have not come into payment, as calculated under paragraph 8 Schedule 36 FA 2004, are more than the value of the MPP you cannot take rights above the MPP into enhanced protection. Rights above the MPP are known as excess rights.

Refer to RPSM03101510 for further guidance on the maximum permitted pension.

4

3.4. If you advised at question 3.3 that the value of your pension rights were not within the maximum permitted please indicate whether these "excess rights" have been surrendered.

Under paragraph 12(5) schedule 36 FA 2004 you cannot give notice of an intention to rely on enhanced protection where your uncrystallised pension rights on 5 April 2006 are excessive. Excess rights will arise whenever the value of your pension rights for an employment are greater than the value of the MPP for that employment. Such excess rights must be surrendered in accordance with the Regulations before you can notify enhanced protection.

You cannot apply for enhanced protection until you surrender your excess rights in accordance with the Regulations. Do not complete this form unless you are notifying HMRC of your intention to rely on primary protection.

Refer to RPSM03104030 for further guidance on surrendering your excess rights.

3.5. Indicate if you have lump sum rights exceeding £375,000 at 5 April 2006.

When you notify your intention to rely on enhanced protection for your pension rights, transitional protection will also be available where you have lump sum rights of more than £375,000 on 5 April 2006.

The amount of your lump sum rights on 5 April 2006 is the aggregate of your crystallised lump sum rights in relevant existing pensions and your lump sum rights that have not yet come into payment (uncrystallised) in relevant pension arrangements. Refer to RPSM03105040 for further guidance.

If you notify HMRC of your intention to rely on enhanced protection you will be able to take your lump sum rights as a percentage of the total value of the lump sum plus residual pension that come into payment on or after 6 April 2006 . The percentage will be derived from the value of your uncrystallised lump sum rights on 5 April 2006 and the value of your uncrystallised pension rights. This percentage will be shown on the HMRC certificate. Refer to RPSM03101050 for further guidance.

3.6. If you have lump sum rights exceeding £375,00 please give the value of your lump sum rights that had not come into payment on 5 April 2006.

Lump sum rights are considered to have come into payment on 5 April 2006 if they were due and payable on or before that date even though they are actually paid after 5 April 2006. Such lump sum rights are crystallised lump sum rights and should not be included in the amount in Box 3.6.

How your lump sum rights from relevant pension arrangements are valued on 5 April 2006 depends on whether the arrangements are occupational pension schemes, personal pension schemes or schemes funded or partly funded by an employer and deferred annuity contracts.

Where you have uncrystallised lump sum rights in a scheme that is funded or partly funded by an employer, those pension rights must be tested against the limits on the benefits that such schemes could provide before 6 April 2006. This limit is defined in paragraph 26 Schedule 36 FA 2004 as the maximum permitted lump sum. Where the value of your uncrystallised lump sum rights exceeds the value of the maximum permitted lump sum, the maximum permitted lump sum

5

440

value becomes the value of the lump sum rights that may be protected. Refer to RPSM03105080 for further guidance.

3.7. Please give the value of your pension rights that had not come into payment on 5 April 2006.

See note 3.2 regarding rights that have not come into payment.

The value of your pension rights that had not come into payment (uncrystallised) is the aggregate value of your pension rights on 5 April 2006 under each relevant pension arrangement.

Where you have uncrystallised pension rights in a scheme that is funded or partly funded by an employer (see note 3.2), those pension rights must be tested against the MPP.

Part 4 Primary Protection

Answer all questions in this part if you are notifying HMRC of an intention to rely on primary protection.

4.1. Give the value of your pension rights that had not come into payment on 5 April 2006 for:

a) **rights that are held under schemes funded wholly or partly by an employer**

See the notes at 3.2 for how to value your pension rights that have not come into payment on 5 April 2006 in schemes that are wholly funded or partly funded by an employer.

For the purposes of this question please include the value for rights held under group personal pensions in the Personal Pension and Retirement Annuity Contracts category below.

Indicate whether the pension rights for the employment were within the maximum value permitted

See note 3.3 for how to calculate whether your pension rights that have not come into payment are within the maximum permitted pension (MPP). If the value of your rights are more than the maximum permitted pension (MPP) the MPP becomes the value of your rights which may be protected and this should be the amount entered here.

b) **for schemes held under personal pension schemes and Retirement Annuity Contracts.**

For the purposes of this question please include the value for rights held under group personal pensions in this category.

4.2. Please give a value for your pension rights that were in payment on 5 April 2006.

6

The value of your pension rights that are in payment (crystallised) on 5 April 2006 must be taken into account in arriving at the figure for transitional protection purposes. Crystallised pension rights are relevant existing pensions being paid to you. Refer to RPSM03101020 for further guidance.

4.3 Indicate if you have lump sum rights exceeding £375,000 at 5 April 2006.

When you notify HMRC of your intention to rely on primary protection for your pension rights, transitional protection will also be available where you have lump sum rights of more than £375,000.

See note 3.5 on valuing your lump sum rights.

The protection of lump sum rights under primary protection is achieved by valuing your uncrystallised lump sum rights at 5 April 2006 and using this figure as the base amount for your protection. You will then be able to take your lump sum from benefits coming into payment as you choose, providing you have not used up 100% of your personal lifetime allowance. The value of the lump sum rights on 5 April 2006 will be increased in the same way as the standard lifetime allowance.

4.4 If you have lump sum rights exceeding £375,00 please give the value of your lump sum rights that had not come into payment on 5 April 2006.

See the notes at 3.6 for how to value your lump sum rights that have not come into payment on 5 April 2006.

4.5 Valuation of Assets

Please indicate whether any of your pension rights that had not come into payment on 5 April 2006 were held in a money purchase arrangement, where the investments held to provide benefits for the member comprised of assets other than insurance contracts or policies, units in unit trust schemes or shares in open-ended investment companies.

4.6 If you have answered yes to question 4.6 please indicate the nature of those assets and the value of the assets under each category.

Property or interest in land - Land includes houses and buildings of any kind

Unquoted shares - These are shares that are not quoted on a recognised stock exchange

Chose in Action – A "chose in action" is something which is not corporeal, tangible, movable or visible and of which a person has not the present enjoyment but merely a right to recover it (if withheld) by action.

Cash - includes cash on deposit or in a current account.

Loans

Works of art - Includes paintings, sculptures, ceramics, ancient artefacts and antique furniture.

Other - any other relevant assets not falling within the categories above.

7

Do not include copies of any valuations you have obtained with this form. HMRC may ask to see them at a later date

Now go to section 5.

Declaration

If someone else, acting on your behalf, filled in this form you must still sign the form yourself to confirm to HMRC that, to the best of your knowledge, it is correct and complete.

This form must be completed by the person claiming transitional protection except in exceptional circumstances.

These are:-

- If someone dies, their person~~al~~ ~~may complete the notification.~~
- For persons who are mentally incapable of dealing with the notification, it may be completed by the following authorised persons:
  - In England and Wales or Northern Ireland, by the person's attorney or receiver, or the person managing or administering their property and affairs
  - In Scotland, by the person's guardian within the meaning of the Adults with Incapacity (Scotland) Act 2000.
  - In a country or territory outside the UK, by a person legally authorised to act on their behalf in that country or territory.

For a person who is not physically capable of dealing with the notification, it may be completed on their behalf by a person having a power of attorney or non-UK equivalent in relation to the affairs of that person.

If you are signing for someone else please enter the capacity in which you are signing and also enter your name and address in the relevant boxes.

The form should be sent by post to HMRC, Audit & Pension Scheme Services, Yorke House, Castle meadow Road, Nottingham, NG2 1BG.

What happens next?

Once HMRC has processed this information it will send you a certificate with a unique reference number giving details of your enhanced lifetime allowance.

HMRC may make enquiries about the information you have provided in your notification and ask you to provide the records from which it was taken. When your pension rights come into payment after 6 April 2006 you must show your certificate to the scheme administrator when you need transitional protection to eliminate or reduce a lifetime allowance charge or receive a transitionally protected lump sum.

Data Protection

HMRC is a Data Controller under the Data Protection Act. We hold information for the purposes specified in our notification made to the Data Protection Commissioner, and may use this information for any of them.

8

443

We may get information about you from others, or we may give information to them. If we do, it will only be as the law permits to

- Check accuracy of information
- Prevent or detect crime
- Protect public funds

We may check information we receive about you with what is already in our records. This can include information provided by you as well as others such as other government departments. We will not give information about you to anyone outside HMRC unless the law permits us to do so.

9

HM Revenue & Customs

Protection Of Existing Rights

You should use this form to to notify an intention to rely on Paragraph 7 Schedule 36 Finance Act 2004 (Primary Protection) or Paragraph 12 Schedule 36 Finance Act 2004 (Enhanced Protection). It must be received by HMRC on or before 5 April 2009.

Please write in CAPITALS, using blue or black ink

1 Your details

1.1 Name

Surname

First name

Other names

Title

1.2 National Insurance Number (NINO) (if known)

1.3 Unique Taxpayer Reference (UTR)

1.4 Date of birth

1.5 Address

Postcode

Country

1.6 Is this an amendment to an existing notification?

Yes.   Enter the certificate reference number

No

2 Which type of protection are you notifying?

Tick one or both boxes

2.1   Enhanced protection   Complete Section 3
(see note at 2.1)

2.2   Primary protection   Complete Section 4

3 Enhanced Protection

3.1 Have you been an "active" member of a registered scheme at any time after 5 April 2006 (see note 3.1)

Yes   You have no basis for enhanced protection. Do not complete this form unless you are notifying primary protection, in which case go to Section 4

No   Go to Question 3.2

3.2 Did you have pension rights that had not yet come into payment in a pension scheme funded or partly funded by an employer on 5 April 2006? (See note 3.2)

Yes   Go to Question 3.3

No   Go to Question 3.5

3.3 Were the pension rights for the employment (or for each employment if more than one employment), within the maximum value permitted? (see note 3.3)

Yes   Go to Question 3.5

No   Go to Question 3.4

3.4 Have you surrendered your "excess rights"? (see note 3.4)

Yes   Go to Question 3.5

No   You have no basis for enhanced protection. Do not complete this form unless you are notifying primary protection, in which case go to Section 4

3.5 Did you have lump sum rights exceeding £375,000 on 5 April 2006? (see note 3.5)

Yes   Go to Question 3.6

No   Go to Section 4 if you are also notifying Primary Protection, otherwise go to Section 5

3.6 Value of your lump sum rights on 5 April 2006 that had not come into payment

£

3.7 Value of your pension rights on 5 April 2006 that had not come into payment

£

Complete Section 4 if you are also notifying Primary Protection, otherwise go to Section 5

20050922 - Transitional Protection (v1.1).xls

4 Primary Protection

4.1 Value of your pension rights on 5 April 2006 that had not come into payment (see note 4.1)

(a) Schemes funded or partly funded by an employer

£ ⬚⬚⬚⬚⬚⬚⬚⬚⬚⬚

Were the pension rights for the employment (or for each employment if more than one employment), within the maximum value permitted?

⬚ Yes

⬚ No

(b) Personal Pension and Retirement Annuity Contracts

£ ⬚⬚⬚⬚⬚⬚⬚⬚⬚⬚

4.2 Value of your pension rights in payment on 5 April 2006

£ ⬚⬚⬚⬚⬚⬚⬚⬚⬚⬚

4.3 Did you have lump sum rights exceeding £375,000 on 5 April 2006? (see note 4.3)

⬚ Yes   Go to Question 4.4

⬚ No   Go to Question 4.5

4.4 Value of your lump sum rights on 5 April 2006 that had not come into payment

£ ⬚⬚⬚⬚⬚⬚⬚⬚⬚⬚

4.5 Are the pension rights that have not yet come into payment on 5 April 2006 money purchase rights, valued by underpinning assets? (see note 4.5)

⬚ Yes   Go to Question 4.6

⬚ No   Go to Section 5

4.6 Value of the asset(s) at 5 April 2006

Property or interest in land (land includes property)

£ ⬚⬚⬚⬚⬚⬚⬚⬚⬚⬚

Unquoted shares

£ ⬚⬚⬚⬚⬚⬚⬚⬚⬚⬚

Choses in action (see note 4.6)

£ ⬚⬚⬚⬚⬚⬚⬚⬚⬚⬚

Cash (includes cash on deposit or in a current account)

£ ⬚⬚⬚⬚⬚⬚⬚⬚⬚⬚

Loans

£ ⬚⬚⬚⬚⬚⬚⬚⬚⬚⬚

Works of Art

£ ⬚⬚⬚⬚⬚⬚⬚⬚⬚⬚

Other

£ ⬚⬚⬚⬚⬚⬚⬚⬚⬚⬚

Go to Section 5

DRAFT

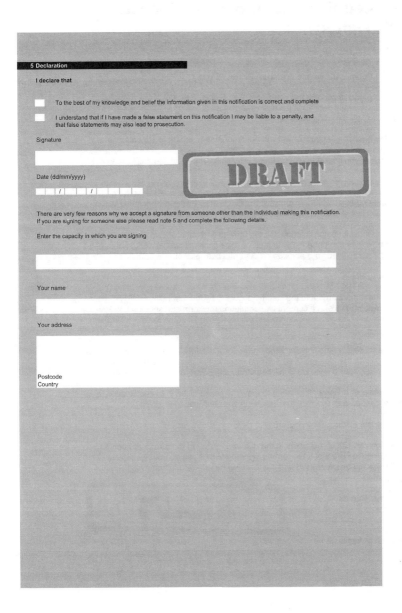

5 Declaration

I declare that

☐ To the best of my knowledge and belief the information given in this notification is correct and complete

☐ I understand that if I have made a false statement on this notification I may be liable to a penalty, and that false statements may also lead to prosecution.

Signature

Date (dd/mm/yyyy)

DRAFT

There are very few reasons why we accept a signature from someone other than the individual making this notification. If you are signing for someone else please read note 5 and complete the following details.

Enter the capacity in which you are signing

Your name

Your address

Postcode
Country

Enhanced lifetime allowance (pension credit rights)

Enhanced Lifetime Allowance (Pension Credit Rights)

Notes to help you complete the notification to HMRC (HM Revenue & Customs)

General

These notes provide guidance on how to notify an enhancement to your lifetime allowance if conditions in paragraph 18 Schedule 36 and section 220 of the Finance Act 2004 are met. If you intend to rely on these provisions you must use this form to notify HMRC

The notes are intended to help you complete the boxes on the notification form. Supplementary guidance can be found in the Registered Pension Schemes Manual (RPSM) which is available on our website at www.hmrc.gov.uk.

You may find it useful before completing the form to find out more about pension credit rights and how they can enhance your lifetime allowance . How this works will depend on whether you received your pension credit rights before or after 6 April 2006.

How to notify HMRC

To receive the enhancement to the lifetime allowance you must notify HMRC of your intention to rely on this enhancement by completing this form and sending it to HMRC, Audit & Pension Scheme Services, Yorke House, Castle Meadow Road, Nottingham, NG2 1BG.

Please note there is a time limit for sending the form to HMRC. The time limit is different depending on whether you received pension credit rights before or after 6 April 2006. Refer to the Registered Pension Schemes Manual (RPSM) for further guidance.

You must retain all documents relating to the information given in the notification for a period of six years from the date that you send your notification to HMRC.

Completing the Form

You must complete all of the boxes in the relevant Part(s) of the form that apply to you and sign it. Please note that if the form is incomplete or if you do not sign it, your notification will not be processed and the form will be returned to you. Use ticks (✓) where indicated.

Part 1 – Your Details

Please complete your details

1.1 Surname or family name

    First name

    All other names in full

Title by which known for example, Mr, Mrs, Miss, Ms,

1.2 National Insurance Number (if known)

1.3 Unique Taxpayer Reference (UTR)

This is the Self Assessment (SA) reference number (also called the Unique Taxpayer Reference (UTR)) allocated to the individual for use for Self Assessment.

1.4 Date of birth

1.5 Address

This should be your personal address. It will be the address to which HMRC certificate regarding your enhancement will be sent.

1.6 Is this an amendment to an existing notification?

Please tick the "yes" box if you are amending information that you submitted in an earlier notification. You should fill in all of the relevant parts of the new form as if you were submitting a new notification. Exceptionally, if an earlier notification became incorrect as a consequence of a subsequent action you should refer to the Registered Pension Schemes Manual for further guidance on correcting earlier notifications.

If you tick the "yes" box also enter the certificate reference number that was shown on the certificate issued to you in response to the earlier notification.

Please tick the "no" box if you have not sent HMRC an earlier notification

Part 2 – Information about the Pension Credit Rights

2.1 Amount of the Pension Credit Rights and the date you became legally entitled to that credit. Please enter the value of the pension credit rights you acquired. If the pension credit rights were acquired on or after 6 April 2006 they must have come from a pension or annuity already in payment . If the pension credit rights did not come from a pension or annuity already in payment you are not entitled to an enhancement to your lifetime allowance and you do not need to complete this form. The date you became legally entitled to the credit is the effective date of the pension sharing order.

2.2 If any of the dates in 2.1 are on or after 6 April 2006 did the pension credit rights come from a pension or annuity already in payment?

You should fill in this box only if you acquired pension credit rights on or after 6 April 2006.

Declaration

You must sign and date the form. The form should be sent to HMRC, Audit & Pension Scheme Services, Yorke House, Castle meadow Road, Nottingham, NG2 1BG.

If someone else, acting on your behalf, filled in this form you must still sign the form to confirm to HMRC, that, to the best of your knowledge, it is correct and complete.

There are only a few exceptions to that requirement.

These are:-

- If someone dies, their personal representative may complete the notification.
- For persons who are mentally incapable of dealing with the notification, it may be completed by the following authorised persons:
- In England and Wales or Northern Ireland, by the person's attorney or receiver, or the person managing or administering their property and affairs
- In Scotland, by the person's guardian within the meaning of the Adults with Incapacity (Scotland) Act 2000.
- In a country or territory outside the UK, by a person legally authorised to act on their behalf in that country or territory.

For a person who is not physically capable of dealing with the notification, it may be completed on their behalf by a person having a power of attorney or non-UK equivalent in relation to the affairs of that person.

If you are signing for someone else please enter the capacity in which you are signing and also enter your name and address in the relevant boxes.

What happens next?

Once HMRC has processed your form we will send you a certificate with a unique reference number giving you details of your enhanced lifetime allowance. HMRC may then make enquiries about the information you have provided and ask you to provide the records from which it was taken.

When your pension rights come into payment on or after 6 April 2006 you must provide your certificate details to the scheme administrator when you need enhancement from pension credit rights to eliminate or reduce a lifetime allowance charge.

Data Protection

HMRC is a Data Controller under the Data Protection Act. We hold information for the purposes specified in our notification made to the Data Protection Commissioner, and may use this information for any of them.

We may get information about you from others, or we may give information to them. If we do, it will only be as the law permits to

- Check accuracy of information
- Prevent or detect crime
- Protect public funds

We may check information we receive about you with what is already in our records. This can include information provided by you as well as others such as other government departments. We will not give information about you to anyone outside HMRC unless the law permits us to do so.

(crown) HM Revenue & Customs	**Enhanced Lifetime Allowance (Pension Credit Rights)**

You should use this form to notify your intention to rely on paragraph 18 Schedule 36 Finance Act 2004 (pre-commencement pension credits) or Section 220 Finance Act 2004 (Pension credits from previously crystallised rights). If you are notifying your intention to rely on paragraph 18 Schedule 36 Finance Act 2004 the form must be received by the Inland Revenue on or before 5 April 2009. Where you are notifying your intention to rely on Schedule 220 Finance Act 2004 the time limit for the notification is 31 January following the end of the tax year five years after the end of the tax year in which you legally became entitled to the pension credit.

Write in CAPITALS, using blue or black ink.

1 Your details

1.1 Name

Surname

First name

Oth[er] names

Title

1.2 National Insurance Number (NINO) (if known)

1.3 Unique Taxpayer Reference (UTR)

1.4 Date of birth

1.5 Address

Postcode
Country

1.6 Is this an amendment to an existing notification?

☐ Yes.   Enter the certificate reference number

☐ No

2 Information about the Pension Credit Rights

2.1 Enter the amount of the Pension Credit Rights received and the date you became legally entitled to that credit

£

/   /

[En]ter the amount of the Pension Credit Rights [rec]eived and the date you became legally entitled [to t]hat credit

/   /

Enter the amount of the Pension Credit Rights received and the date you became legally entitled to that credit

£

/   /

Enter the amount of the Pension Credit Rights received and the date you became legally entitled to that credit

£

/   /

2.2 If any of the dates in 2.1 are on or after 6 April 2006 did the pension credit rights come from a pension or annuity already in payment (see note 2.2)?

☐ Yes

☐ No

DRAFT

20050922 - Additional PLA (v1.1).xls

452

3 Declaration

I declare that

☐ to the best of my knowledge and belief the information given in this notification is correct and complete

☐ I understand that if I have made a false statement in this report, I may be liable to a penalty, and that false statements may also lead to prosecution.

Signature

DRAFT

There are very few reasons why we accept a signature from someone other than the individual making this notification. If you are signing for someone else please read the attached notes and complete the following details

Enter the capacity in which you are signing

Your name and address

Postcode
Country

20050922 - Additional PLA (v1.1).xls

453

Enhanced lifetime allowance (international)

Enhanced Lifetime Allowance (International)

Notes to help you complete the notification to HMRC (HM Revenue & Customs)

General

These notes provide guidance on how to make a notification for an "international enhancement" of your lifetime allowance if the conditions in sections 221-223 or in sections 224-226 of the Finance Act 2004 (FA 2004) are met. If you intend to rely on these provisions you must use this form to notify HMRC.

The notes are intended to help you complete the boxes on the notification form. Supplementary guidance can be found in the Registered Pension Schemes Manual (RPSM) which is available on our website at www.hmrc.gov.uk.

You may find it useful before completing the notification form to find out more about what international enhancement is and about who is eligible to make a notification. Refer to RPSM13200010 for further guidance.

DRAFT

How to notify HMRC

You must notify HMRC of your intention to rely on either section 221 FA 2004 for a "non-resident factor", or on section 224 FA 2004 for a "recognised overseas scheme transfer factor". You may do this by completing this form and sending it to HMRC, Audit & Pension Scheme Services, Yorke House, Castle Meadow Road, Nottingham, NG2 1BG.

If you require further guidance refer to RPSM13200050 for guidance on the "non-resident factor" and RPSM13200120 for guidance on the "recognised overseas scheme transfer factor"

Please note that there is a time limit for sending HMRC the form. This is no later than five years after the 31st January following the end of the tax year in which either the accrual period ends (for non-residence factor) or the transfer took place (for recognised overseas scheme transfer factor).

You must retain all documents relating to the information given in the notification for a period of six years from the date you send your notification to HMRC.

Completing the Form

You must complete all of the boxes in the relevant Part(s) of the form that apply to you and sign it. Please note that if the form is incomplete or if you do not sign it, your notification will not be processed and the form will be returned to you. Use ticks (✓) where indicated.

Part 1 - Your Details

Please complete your details

1.1   Surname or family name

        First name

        All other names in full

        Title by which known for example Mr, Mrs, Miss, Ms,

1.2   National Insurance Number (if known)

1.3   Date of birth

1.4   Address

        This should be your personal address. It will be the address to which the
        HMRC certificate will be sent.

1.5   Is this an amendment to an existing notification?

        Please tick the "yes" box if you are amending an earlier notification that was
        incorrect by submitting a new form providing the correct information. You
        should fill in all of the relevant parts of the new form as if you were submitting
        a new notification. Exceptionally, if an earlier notification became incorrect as
        a consequence of a subsequent action you should refer to the Registered
        Pension Schemes Manual for further guidance on correcting earlier
        notifications.

        If you tick the "yes" box also enter the certificate reference number that was
        shown on the certificate issued to you in response to the earlier notification.

        Please tick the "no" box if you have not sent HMRC an earlier notification

Part 2 Summary of Information

Please indicate whether you are notifying HMRC of an intention to rely on section
221 Finance Act 2004 or on section 224 Finance Act 2004 by ticking either box 2.1 or
2.2. If you want to notify HMRC of an intention to rely on both of those sections you
should complete separate forms for each. Please note that if you want to notify non-
residence factors under section 221 FA 2004 in respect of separate registered
pension schemes you should fill in a form for each one.

2.1 Notification of intention to rely on S221 FA04

        You should tick box 2.1 if you are notifying an enhancement factor in respect of
        part of an active membership period relating to an arrangement under a
        registered pension scheme during which you were a relevant overseas
        individual. Refer to RPSM13200060 for further guidance on what is a relevant
        overseas individual.

If you tick box 2.1 please also tick one of the following five boxes either to state the type of arrangement of which you are a member or to show that you have different types of arrangement within the same scheme.

2.1.1 Money Purchase Cash Balance Arrangement

If you are a member of such an arrangement under a registered pension scheme you can notify a cash balance arrangement non-residence factor by completing Parts 3 and 4 of the form.

2.1.2 Other Money Purchase Arrangement

If you are a member of such an arrangement under a registered pension scheme you can notify an "other money purchase arrangement" non-residence factor by completing Parts 3 and 5 of the form.

2.1.3 Defined Benefit Arrangement

If you are a member of such an arrangement under a registered pension scheme you can notify a defined benefits arrangement non-residence factor by completing Parts 3 and 6 of the form.

2.1.4 Scheme with Multiple Arrangements

If you are a member of such a scheme and you can notify a non-residence factor in respect of all of the above three types of arrangement under the scheme please complete Parts 3, 4, 5 and 6 of the form. If you are making a notification in respect of two types of arrangement please complete Part 3 and whichever two of Parts 4, 5 and 6 that are relevant.

If you are a member of such a scheme and you are notifying a non-residence factor in respect of a hybrid arrangement under the scheme you should calculate your hybrid arrangement factor on the basis explained in the note below on box 2.1.5. You will need to include the resulting amount(s) in whichever of Parts 4, 5 or 6 applies. You should need the guidance below to do that.

2.1.5 Hybrid Arrangement

DRAFT

Your hybrid arrangement enhancement factor will be the greater or greatest of:-

- the cash balance arrangement non-residence factor ,
- the other money purchase arrangement non-residence factor, or
- the defined benefits arrangement non-residence factor .

If you are a member of a hybrid arrangement you should complete Part 3 and only that one of Parts 4, 5 and 6 of the form which would give you the highest amount. To work out which of those Parts is the one to complete you will need to compare the relevant amounts referred to in Parts 4, 5 and 6.

2.2 Notification of intention to rely on S224 FA04

You should tick box 2.2 if you are notifying an enhancement factor in respect of a transfer from an arrangement under a recognised overseas pension scheme to an arrangement under an UK registered pension scheme that was made after 5 April 2006.

If you tick box 2.2 please go straight to Part 7.

Part 3 Period of Overseas Membership of a UK Registered Pension Scheme

Please complete all of the boxes in this Part if you are notifying HMRC of an intention to rely on Section 221 Finance Act 2004.

3.1   Scheme name.

3.2   Scheme address. This should be the address of the Scheme Administrator. If you do not know that you should enter the address that you usually use to write to your scheme.

3.3   Period for which you were a relevant overseas individual during an active membership period .

Please insert the appropriate dates for that part of an active membership period relating to your arrangement throughout which you were a relevant overseas individual . The dates should be in dd/mm/yyyy format (so 6 April 2006 would be 06/04/2006).

If you want to make a notification in respect of two or more such parts of an active membership period you should submit a separate form for each part.

You should also submit separate forms if a "benefit crystallisation event" occurred whilst you were a relevant overseas individual and were still accruing benefits under an arrangement. One form should relate to the active membership period up to the date of that "benefit crystallisation event" and the other form should relate to the following active membership period.

The date in the "From" box must be the latest of the following dates:

- the date when you became a "relevant overseas individual" ,
- the date when benefits first began to accrue to you or in respect of you under the arrangement, or
- 6 April 2006.

The date in the "To" box must be the earliest of the following dates:

- the date of the "benefit crystallisation event" ,
- the date when you ceased to be a "relevant overseas individual" , or
- the date when benefits ceased to accrue to you or in respect of you under the arrangement.

Part 4 Money Purchase Cash Balance Arrangements

You should complete this part if your arrangement is a Money Purchase Cash Balance Arrangement .

4.1   Closing value of the rights under the arrangement.

Please insert the value of your Money Purchase Cash Balance rights under your arrangement as at the date that you have inserted in the "To" box in 3.3. This is the amount that would have been available to provide benefits to you or in respect of you if you had become entitled to the immediate payment of the benefits at that date. When valuing those rights you must apply certain valuation assumptions .

4.2   Opening value of the rights under the arrangement.

Please insert here the value of your Money Purchase Cash Balance rights under your arrangement as at the date that you have inserted in the "From" box In 3.3. This is the amount that would have been available to provide benefits to you or in respect of you if you had become entitled to the immediate payment of the benefits at that date. When valuing those rights you must apply certain valuation assumptions .

HMRC will calculate your cash balance arrangement non-residence factor on the basis of the information that you have provided.

Part 5 Other Money Purchase Arrangements

You should complete this part if your arrangement is an other money purchase arrangement .

5.1   Contributions made during the period.

Please state the total of the contributions that you have made to your arrangement and of the contributions made on your behalf (for example, by your employer) during the period between the dates shown at 3.3 on the form.

HMRC will calculate your other money purchase arrangement non-residence factor on the basis of the information that you have provided.

Part 6 Defined Benefits Arrangements

You should complete this part if your arrangement is a defined benefits arrangement .

6.1   Pension entitlement at the end of the period.

Please insert here your pension entitlement under your arrangement as at the date that you have inserted in the "To" box in 3.3. That is the annual rate of pension which would have been payable to you if you had become entitled to payment of it as at that date. When calculating your entitlement you must apply certain valuation assumptions .

6.2   Pension entitlement at the start of the period.

Please insert here your pension entitlement under your arrangement as at the date that you have inserted in the "From" box in 3.3. The second and third sentences of 6.1 above apply here as well.

6.3   Are you entitled to a separate lump sum?

You should only tick this box if you are entitled to a separate lump sum under your arrangement. A separate lump sum is a lump sum cash benefit that you are automatically entitled to. Do **not** tick the "yes" box if you are only entitled to a lump sum if you give up some of your prospective pension entitlement. Ask your Scheme Administrator if you are not sure.

6.4   Amount of lump sum at the end of the period.

You should fill in this box only if you ticked "yes" in box 6.3. This is your separate lump sum entitlement under your arrangement as at the date that you have inserted in the "To" box in 3.3. When calculating your entitlement you must apply certain valuation assumptions.

6.5   Amount of lump sum at the start of the period.

You should fill in this box only if you ticked "yes" in box 6.3. This is your separate lump sum entitlement under your arrangement as at the date that you have inserted in the "From" box in 3.3. When calculating your entitlement you must apply certain valuation assumptions .

HMRC will calculate your defined benefits arrangement non-residence factor on the basis of the information provided.

Part 7 Transfer from Recognised Overseas Pension Scheme.

You should complete all of the boxes in this Part if you are notifying HMRC of an intention to rely on Section 224 FA 2004 for a recognised overseas scheme transfer factor .

Please note that if you want to make a notification of more than one enhancement factor - in respect of transfers from different recognised overseas schemes, transfers to different UK registered schemes, or transfers made on different dates you must submit a separate form for each transfer.

However, if you have made transfers from more than one arrangement under a recognised overseas scheme to the same UK registered scheme at the same time you can complete one form for the combined transfers. If you do that you should show the total figure for the transfers from those different arrangements in each of the boxes at 7.2 and 7.3.

7.1   Date of the current transfer

Enter the date on which the transfer from your arrangement under a recognised overseas pension scheme to your registered pension scheme in respect of which you are notifying an enhancement factor took place in dd/mm/yyyy format (6 April 2006 would be 06/04/2006).

7.2   Total value transferred on that date.

This is the total value transferred from your arrangement under a recognised overseas pension scheme on the date that you have inserted at section 7.1. It is the aggregate of the amount of any sums transferred and of the market value of any assets transferred.

7.3 Value of any non-cash assets included in the total transfer.

This is the total value of any non-cash assets (e.g. property or shares) transferred as part of the transfer from your arrangement under a recognised overseas pension scheme to your registered pension scheme as at the date that you have inserted at section 7.1. Do not include any monetary amounts transferred by cheque or by electronic transmission.

7.4 Relevant relievable amounts as at that date.

Complete this box if you have a relevant relievable amount . You will have a relevant relievable amount if you were **not** a relevant overseas individual for part of your overseas arrangement active membership period . If you have two or more such parts of your overseas arrangement active membership period you will need to add together the amounts relating to those separate parts and record the total amount.

Please state your relevant relievable amount as at the date you have inserted in box 7.1.

How to Calculate Your Relevant Relievable Amount

The relevant relievable amount is calculated in a number of different ways. The basis of calculation depends on the type of your arrangement (or arrangements) under a recognised overseas pension scheme.

Cash Balance Arrangement

If your overseas arrangement is a Cash Balance Arrangement you will need to read the guidance on how to calculate the 'cash balance relevant relievable amount' . Refer to RPSM13100190 for further guidance.

Other Money Purchase Arrangement

If your overseas arrangement is an Other Money Purchase Arrangement you will need to read the guidance on how to calculate the 'other money purchase relevant relievable amount' . Refer to RPSM13100200 for further guidance.

Defined Benefits Arrangement

If your overseas arrangement is a Defined Benefits Arrangement you will need to read the guidance on how to calculate the 'defined benefits relevant relievable amount' . Refer to RPSM13100210 for further guidance.

Scheme with multiple arrangements

This is a scheme that contains more than one of the types of arrangement referred to in this note on Part 7.4. There are separate entitlements to the different types of benefit from those arrangements. So a member could, for example, receive other money purchase benefits from one arrangement and defined benefits from another arrangement within the same scheme.

Please note that if your recognised overseas pension scheme is a scheme with multiple arrangements you should calculate the relevant relievable amount for the type of arrangement from which the transfer was made. You should then insert this figure in the box at 7.4. However, if you have transferred from two or more types of arrangement under the same recognised overseas scheme to the same UK registered scheme at the same time, and are completing only one form in respect of the combined transfers, you should insert in the box at 7.4 the total of the figures calculated for each of those different arrangements.

Hybrid Arrangement

If your recognised overseas pension scheme is a Hybrid Arrangement you will need to read the guidance on how to calculate the 'hybrid arrangement relevant relievable amount'. Refer to RPSM13100220 for further guidance.

7.5   Name of the transferring scheme.

7.6   Address of the transferring scheme. This should be the address of the scheme manager. If you do not know that you should enter the address that you usually use to correspond with your scheme.

7.7   Name of the receiving scheme.

7.8   Address of the receiving scheme. This should be the address of the Scheme Administrator. If you do not know that you should enter the address that you usually use to correspond with your scheme.

Declaration

You must sign and date the form and send it by post to HMRC, Audit & Pension Schemes Services, Yorke House, Castle Meadow Road, Nottingham, NG2 1BG.

If someone else, acting on your behalf, filled in this form you must still sign the form to confirm to HMRC that, to the best of your knowledge, it is correct and complete.

There are only a few exceptions to that requirement.

These are:-

- If someone dies, their personal representative may complete the notification.
- For persons who are mentally incapable of dealing with the notification, it may be completed by the following authorised persons:
- In England and Wales or Northern Ireland, by the person's attorney or receiver, or the person managing or administering their property and affairs
- In Scotland, by the person's guardian within the meaning of the Adults with Incapacity (Scotland) Act 2000.
- In a country or territory outside the UK, by a person legally authorised to act on their behalf in that country or territory.

For a person who is not physically capable of dealing with the notification, it may be completed on their behalf by a person having a power of attorney or non-UK equivalent in relation to the affairs of that person.

If you are signing for someone else please enter the capacity in which you are signing and also enter your name and address in the relevant boxes.

What happens next?

Once HMRC has processed this information we will send you a certificate with a unique reference number giving details of your enhanced lifetime allowance. HMRC may make enquiries about the information you have provided and ask you to provide the records from which it was taken.

When your pension rights come into payment on or after 6 April 2006 you must provide your certificate details to the Scheme Administrator when you need international protection to eliminate or reduce a lifetime allowance charge.

Data Protection

The Inland Revenue is a Data Controller under the Data Protection Act. We hold information for the purposes specified in our notification made to the Data Protection Commissioner, and may use this information for any of them.

We may get information about you from others, or we may give information to them. If we do, it will only be as the law permits to

- Check accuracy of informatio
- Prevent or detect crime
- Protect public funds

DRAFT

We may check information we receive about you with what is already in our records. This can include information provided by you as well as others such as other government departments. We will not give information about you to anyone outside the Inland Revenue unless the law permits us to do so.

HM Revenue & Customs	Enhanced Lifetime Allowance (International)

You should use this form to notify intention to rely on section 221 Finance Act 2004 (s221FA04) (individuals who are relevant overseas individuals) or section 224 Finance Act 2004(s224FA04) (transfer from a recognised overseas pension scheme).The time limit for this notification is 31 January following the end of the tax year five years after the end of the tax year in which the accrual period ends or in which the recognised overseas scheme transfer took place.

Write in CAPITALS, using blue or black ink.

1 Your details

1.1 Name

Surname

First name

Other names

Title

1.2 National Insurance Number (NINO) (if known)

1.3 Unique Taxpayer Reference (UTR)

1.4 Date of birth

1.5 Address

Postcode
Country

1.6 Is this an amendment to an existing notification?

☐ Yes   Enter the certificate reference number

☐ No

2 Summary of Information

Tick the appropriate box

2.1 ☐ **Notification of intention to rely on s221 FA04**

Individuals who are members of a UK Registered Scheme and who are relevant overseas individuals.

Select one of the following schemes

2.1.1 ☐ Money Purchase Cash Balance Arrangement.
Complete section 3 and Section 4

2.1.2 ☐ Other Money Purchase Arrangement
Complete section 3 and Section 5

2.1.3 ☐ Defined benefit arrangement:
Complete section 3 and Section 6

2.1.4 ☐ Scheme with multiple arrangements.
Complete section 3 and as appropriate sections 4 or 5 or 6

2.1.5 ☐ Hybrid arrangement:
Complete sections 3 and as appropriate either sections 4 or 5 or 6

2.2 ☐ **Notification of intention to rely on s224 FA04**

Transfer from a recognised overseas pension scheme
Complete section 7

DRAFT

20050922 - International (v1.1).xls

463

3 Period of Overseas Membership of a UK Registered Pension Scheme

3.1 Scheme name

3.2 Scheme address

Postcode
Country

3.3 Period for which you were a relevant overseas individual throughout an active membership period

From

To

4 Money Purchase cash balance arrangements

4.1 Closing value of the rights under the arrangement

£

4.2 Opening value of the rights under the arrangement

£

5 Other Money Purchase arrangements

5.1 Contributions made during the period

£

6 Defined Benefit arrangements

6.1 Pension entitlement at the end of the period

£

6.2 Pension entitlement at the start of the period

£

6.3 Are you entitled to a separate lump sum?

    Yes   Complete 6.4 and 6.5

    No   Go to next section

6.4 Amount of lump sum at the end of the period

£

6.5 Amount of lump sum at the start of the period

£

DRAFT

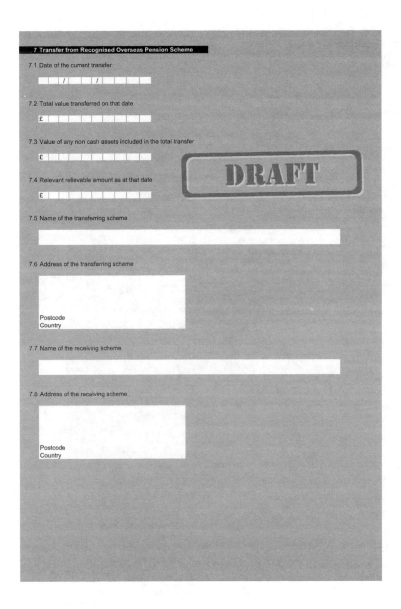

7 Transfer from Recognised Overseas Pension Scheme

7.1 Date of the current transfer

[ ][ ][ ] / [ ][ ] / [ ][ ][ ][ ]

7.2 Total value transferred on that date

£ [ ][ ][ ][ ][ ][ ][ ][ ][ ][ ]

7.3 Value of any non cash assets included in the total transfer

£ [ ][ ][ ][ ][ ][ ][ ][ ][ ][ ]

7.4 Relevant relievable amount as at that date

£ [ ][ ][ ][ ][ ][ ][ ][ ][ ][ ]

7.5 Name of the transferring scheme

7.6 Address of the transferring scheme

Postcode
Country

7.7 Name of the receiving scheme

7.8 Address of the receiving scheme

Postcode
Country

DRAFT

Declaration

I declare that

☐ to the best of my knowledge and belief the information given on this notification is correct and complete.

☐ I understand that if I have made a false statement in this report, I may be liable to a penalty, and that false statements may also lead to prosecution.

Signature

DRAFT

Date

☐☐ / ☐☐ / ☐☐☐☐

There are very few reasons why we accept a signature from someone other than the individual making this notification. If you are signing for someone else please read the attached notes and complete the following details.

Enter the capacity in which you are signing

Your name

Your address

Postcode
Country

Declare as a scheme administrator of a deferred annuity contract

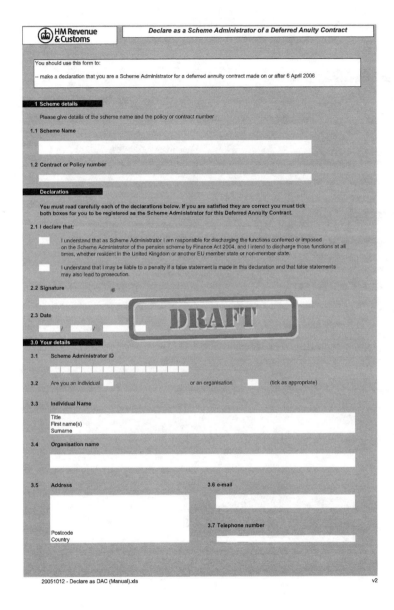

Cessation of scheme administrator

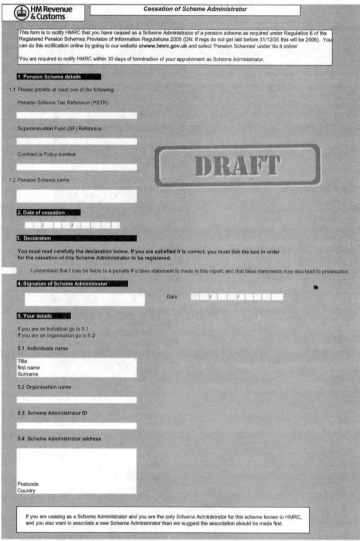

Pre-register as a scheme administrator

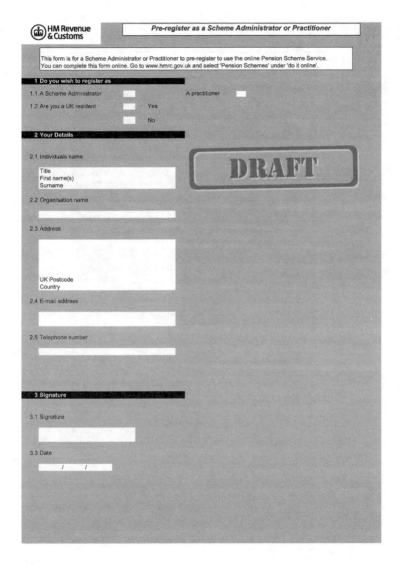

Notify scheme administrator details

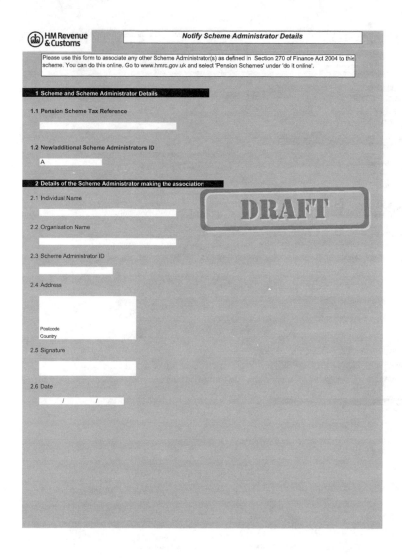

Change of scheme administrator/practitioner details

HM Revenue & Customs	**Change of Scheme Administrator / Practitioner Details**

Please use this form to notify HMRC of changes to your registration/contact details. You can complete this form online. Go to www.hmrc.gov.uk and select"Pension Schemes" under"do it online".

1 Scheme Administrator / Practitioner Details

Scheme Administrators ID   A

Practitioners ID

1.1.1 Is it change of

Name	☐	(go to 1.1.2)
Address	☐	(go to 1.1.3)
E-mail	☐	(go to 1.1.4)
Telephone No	☐	(go to 1.1.5)
Preferred communication channel	☐	(go to 1.1.6)

1.1.2 Change of name

DRAFT

Individual Scheme Administrator/Practitioner current name

Title   Forename

Surname

Scheme Administrator / Practitioners current organisation name

Individual Scheme Administrators / Practitioners new name

Title   Forename

Surname

Scheme Administrator / Practitioners new organisation name

1.1.3 Change of address

Scheme Administrator/Practitioner current address

Address Line 1
Address Line 2
Address Line 3
Address Line 4

Postcode

Country

Scheme Administrator/Practitioner new address

Address Line 1
Address Line 2
Address Line 3
Address Line 4

Postcode

Country

20050906 Change of Administrator or Practitioner Details v0.3.xls

1.1.4 E-mail address - add or change

Scheme Administrator/Practitioner current e-mail address

Scheme Administrator/Practitioner new e-mail address

1.1.5 Change of telephone number

Scheme Administrator/Practitioner current telephone number

Scheme Administrator/Practitioner new telephone number

1.1.6 Change from/to electronic communication as preferred channel

Do you wish HMRC to send communications to you electronically?

Do you wish HMRC to send communications to you through the post?

2 Details of the person submitting this form

2.1 Signature

2.2 Name (please print in capital letters)

2.3 Date

/   /

2.4 I am submitting this form in my capacity as

Scheme Administrator   Scheme Administrator ID

Practitioner   Practitioner ID

2.5 Address

Postcode
Country

DRAFT

Authorising a practitioner

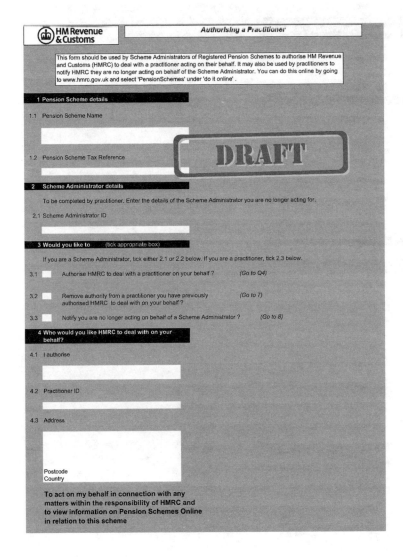

| HM Revenue & Customs | Authorising a Practitioner |

This form should be used by Scheme Administrators of Registered Pension Schemes to authorise HM Revenue and Customs (HMRC) to deal with a practitioner acting on their behalf. It may also be used by practitioners to notify HMRC they are no longer acting on behalf of the Scheme Administrator. You can do this online by going to www.hmrc.gov.uk and select 'PensionSchemes' under 'do it online' .

1 Pension Scheme details

1.1 Pension Scheme Name

1.2 Pension Scheme Tax Reference

DRAFT

2 Scheme Administrator details

To be completed by practitioner. Enter the details of the Scheme Administrator you are no longer acting for.

2.1 Scheme Administrator ID

3 Would you like to (tick appropriate box)

If you are a Scheme Administrator, tick either 2.1 or 2.2 below. If you are a practitioner, tick 2.3 below.

3.1 ☐ Authorise HMRC to deal with a practitioner on your behalf ? *(Go to Q4)*

3.2 ☐ Remove authority from a practitioner you have previously authorised HMRC to deal with on your behalf ? *(Go to 7)*

3.3 ☐ Notify you are no longer acting on behalf of a Scheme Administrator ? *(Go to 8)*

4 Who would you like HMRC to deal with on your behalf?

4.1 I authorise

4.2 Practitioner ID

4.3 Address

Postcode
Country

To act on my behalf in connection with any matters within the responsibility of HMRC and to view information on Pension Schemes Online in relation to this scheme

5 Client reference you have been given by your practitioner

5.1 Client reference

6 Do you want this authorisation to replace all previous authorisations given?

DRAFT

6.1 ☐ Yes *(Go to 8)*

6.2 ☐ No *(Go to 7)*

7 Give details of the practitioner(s) you no longer wish HMRC to deal with on your behalf

7.1 Practitioner Name   Practitioner ID

8 Your details

8.1 Individual name

Title
First Name(s)
Surname

(Go to 8.3)

8.2 Organisation name

8.3 Your Scheme Administrator or practitioner ID

8.4 Your address

postcode
country

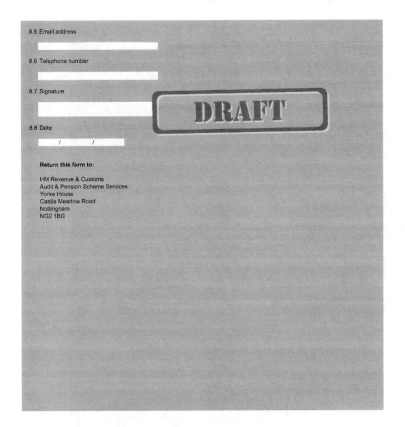

8.5 Email address

8.6 Telephone number

8.7 Signature

8.8 Date

     /   /

Return this form to:

HM Revenue & Customs
Audit & Pension Scheme Services
Yorke House
Castle Meadow Road
Nottingham
NG2 1BG

The latest forms

Add scheme administrator

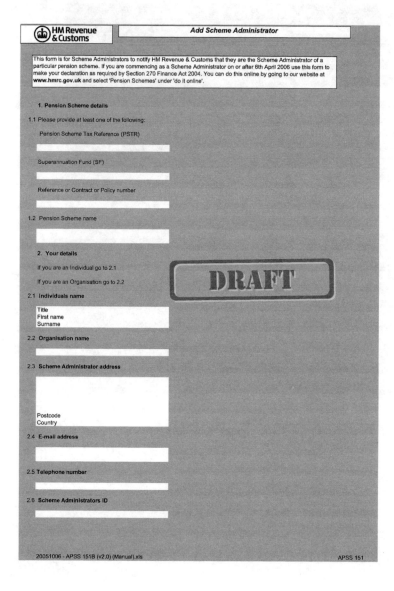

2.7 Were you the Scheme Administrator of the above named Pension Scheme before 6th April 2006

Yes ☐ Either go to 4 or complete your application online by going to our website at
www.hmrc.gov.uk and select 'Pension Schemes' under 'do it online'.
You do not need to complete the declaration

No ☐ Either go to 3 or complete your application online by going to our website at
www.hmrc.gov.uk and select ' 'Pension Schemes' under 'do it online'.

3. Declaration

You **must** read carefully each of the declarations below. If you are satisfied they are correct, you **must** tick
both boxes for you to be registered as a Scheme Administrator for the Pension Scheme.

☐ I understand that as Scheme Administrator I am responsible for discharging the functions
conferred or imposed on the Scheme Administrator of the Pension Scheme by Finance
Act 2004, and I intend to discharge those functions at all times, whether resident in the
United Kingdom or another EU memer state or non - member EEA state;

☐ I understand that I may be liable to a penalty if a false statement is made in this declaration,
and that false statements may also lead to prosecution.

4. Signature of the Scheme Administrator

Date ☐ ☐ / ☐ ☐ / ☐ ☐ ☐ ☐

DRAFT

Amend scheme details

HM Revenue & Customs

Amend Scheme Details

Please use this form to notify to the HMRC of changes of registration information for a registered pension scheme (other than those changes detailed at SI xxx) You can complete this form online. Go to www.hmrc.gov.uk and select 'Pension Schemes' under ' do it online'.

1 Pension Scheme Details

1.1	Please provide at least one of the following:
	Pension Scheme Tax Reference
	Superannuation Fund (SF) Reference
	Contract or policy number
1.2	Pension Scheme Name

2 Are changes in relation to (please tick relevant boxes)

| 2.1 | Pension scheme name | | (go to 2.1a) |
| 2.1a | New pension scheme name | | |

2.2	Establisher details		
2.2a	Do you wish to update a current Scheme Establisher/Sponsor Details?		(go to 2.3)
2.2b	Do you wish to notify a New Scheme Establisher/Sponsor?		(go to 2.8)
2.2c	Do you wish to notify an cessation of a Scheme Establisher/Sponsor?		(go to 2.11)
2.3	Is the current Establisher/Sponsor:		
	An individual?		(Go to 2)
	An Organisation		(Go to 2)

DRAFT

2.3a	Current Name of Scheme Establisher/Sponsor (Individual)
	Title
	First Name(s)
	Surname
	(Go to 2.4)
2.3b	Current Name of Scheme Establisher/Sponsor (Organisation)

2.4	Current Address of Scheme Establisher/Sponsor
	Address Line 1
	Address Line 2
	Address Line 3
	Address Line 4
	UK Postcode
	Country

2.5a	New Name of Scheme Establisher/Sponsor (Individual)
	Title
	First name(s)
	Surnames
	(Go to Q2.6)
2.5b	New Name of Scheme Establisher/Sponsor (Organisation)

2.6 New Address of Scheme Establisher/Sponsor

Address Line 1

Address Line 2

Address Line 3

Address Line 4

UK Postcode

Country

2.7 Date of change   /   /

If you did not tick either 2.2b or 2.2c, go to Q3

2.8 Is the New Scheme Establisher/Sponsor:

An individual?   (Go to 2.8a)

An Organisation   (Go to 2.8b)

2.8a New Scheme Establisher/Sponsor Name (Individual)

Title

First Name(s)

Surname

(Go to 2.9)

2.8b New Scheme Establisher/Sponsor Name (Organisation)

2.9 New Scheme Establisher Address

Address Line 1

Address Line 2

Address Line 3

Address Line 4

Postcode

Country

2.10 Start date of new Establisher/Sponsor

/   /

If you did not tick 2.2c, go to Q3

2.11 Is the ceasing Establisher/Sponsor:

An individual?   (Go to 2.11a)

An Organisation   (Go to 2.11b)

DRAFT

2.11a Cessation of Scheme Establisher/Sponsor

Scheme Establisher/Sponsor Name (Individual)

Title

First Name(s)

Surname

(Go to 2.12)

2.11b Scheme Establisher/Sponsor Name (Organisation)

2.12 Scheme Establisher/Sponsor Address

Address Line 1

Address Line 2

Address Line 3

Address Line 4

UK Postcode

Country

DRAFT

2.13 Date of Cessation

/ /

3 Do you wish to change your Client Reference for a Scheme Administrator

3.1 Scheme Administrator ID

3.2 Current Client Reference

3.3 New Client Reference

3.4 Date of change

/ /

4 Do you want to update any other records for this scheme?

If you want us to update any other records with the above changes, you must provide the relevant reference details below

4.1 Contracting out

SCON / ECON / ASCON Reference number

4.2 Pension Regulator

Pension Scheme Registration Number

4.3 Relief at Source

RAS Reference

4.4 VAT

VAT Registration number

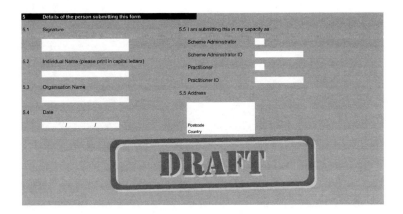

20051017 - Amend Scheme Details v0.8.xls

Table of statutes

Paragraph references printed in **bold** type in this Table indicate where an Act is set out in part or in full.

Table of statutory instruments

Paragraph references printed in **bold** type in this Table indicate where a Statutory Instrument is set out in part or in full.

Index